ACADEMIC INF(

COMPETENCE-BASED STRATEGIC MANAGEMENT

THE STRATEGIC MANAGEMENT SERIES

Series Editor
HOWARD THOMAS

STRATEGIC THINKING
Leadership and the Management of Change
Edited by
JOHN HENDRY AND GERRY JOHNSON
WITH JULIA NEWTON

COMPETENCE BASED COMPETITION
Edited by
GARY HAMEL AND AIMÉ HEENE

BUILDING THE STRATEGICALLY-RESPONSIVE ORGANIZATION
Edited by
HOWARD THOMAS, DON O'NEAL, ROD WHITE AND DAVID HURST

STRATEGIC RENAISSANCE AND
BUSINESS TRANSFORMATION
Edited by
HOWARD THOMAS, DON O'NEAL AND JAMES KELLY

STRATEGIC LEARNING AND
KNOWLEDGE MANAGEMENT
Edited by
RON SANCHEZ AND AIMÉ HEENE

COMPETENCE-BASED STRATEGIC
MANAGEMENT
Edited by
AIMÉ HEENE AND RON SANCHEZ

Further titles in preparation

THE STRATEGIC MANAGEMENT SERIES

COMPETENCE-BASED STRATEGIC MANAGEMENT

Edited by

Aimé Heene and Ron Sanchez

JOHN WILEY & SONS

Chichester · New York · Brisbane · Toronto · Singapore

Copyright © 1997 by John Wiley & Sons Ltd,
Baffins Lane, Chichester,
West Sussex PO19 1UD, England

National 01243 779777
International (+44) 1243 779777

e-mail (for orders and customer service enquiries):
cs. books @ wiley.co.uk.
Visit our home page on
http://www.wiley.co.uk
or
http://www.wiley.com

Other Wiley Editorial Offices

John Wiley & Sons, Inc., 605 Third Avenue,
New York, NY 10158-0012, USA

Jacaranda Wiley Ltd, 33 Park Road, Milton,
Queensland 4064, Australia

John Wiley & Sons (Canada) Ltd, 22 Worcester Road,
Rexdale, Ontario M9W IL1, Canada

John Wiley & Sons (Asia) Pte Ltd, 2 Clementi Loop #02-01,
Jin Xing Distripark, Singapore 129809

Library of Congress Cataloging-in-Publication Data

Competence-based strategic management / edited by Aimé Heene and Ron
Sanchez.
    p.   cm. — (The strategic management series)
    Includes bibliographical references and index.
    ISBN 0-471-96880-3 (cloth)
    1. Strategic planning.   2. Organizational effectiveness.
I. Heene, Aimé.   II. Sanchez, Ron.   III. Series.
HD30.28.C646   1996
658.4'012—dc20   96–24651
                                                                            CIP

British Library Cataloguing in Publication Data

A catalogue record for this book is available from the British Library

ISBN 0-471-96880-3

Typeset in 10.5/12pt Palatino by Acorn Bookwork, Salisbury, Wiltshire
Printed and bound in Great Britain by Biddles Ltd, Guildford and King's Lynn
This book is printed on acid-free paper responsibly manufactured from sustainable
forestation, for which at least two trees are planted for each one used for paper production.

Contents

Contributors   vii

Series Preface   xv

Preface   xix

SECTION I: COMPETENCE CONCEPTS FOR STRATEGIC MANAGEMENT

1   **Competence-based Strategic Management: Concepts and Issues for Theory, Research, and Practice**   3
R. Sanchez, A. Heene

2   **Competence Theory Building: Reconnecting Management Research and Management Practice**   43
J. T. Mahoney, R. Sanchez

3   **Predicting Rent Generation in Competence-based Competition**   65
E. Mosakowski, W. McKelvey

SECTION II: COMPETENCE DYNAMICS

4   **Strategic Renewal in Large Complex Organizations: A Competence-based View**   89
C. Baden-Fuller, H. W. Volberda

5   **Customers as the Originators of Change in Competence Building: A Case Study**   111
J. Wallin

6   **Strategizing for Innovation: Competence Analysis in Assessing Strategic Change**   127
T. Durand

7   **Assessing the Organizational Capacity to Change**   151
      J. A. Black, K. B. Boal

8   **Strategic Defense and Competence-based Competition**   169
      Z. Rotem, R. Amit

SECTION III: COMPETENCE SYSTEMICS

9   **Competence Levels within Firms: A Static and Dynamic
      Analysis**   195
      V. Chiesa, R. Manzini

10   **Integrating Corporate Strategy and Competence-building
      Processes: A Case Study**   215
      E. Cremer, P.-X. Meschi

SECTION IV: COGNITION IN MANAGING COMPETENCES

11   **The Blind Spots of Competence Identification:
      A System-theoretic Perspective**   245
      R. van der Vorst

12   **On Building and Leveraging Competences Across
      Organizational Borders: A Socio-cognitive Framework**   267
      J. Stein

SECTION V: HOLISM IN MANAGING COMPETENCES

13   **Dynamic Corporate Coherence and Competence-based
      Competition: Theoretical Foundations and Strategic
      Implications**   287
      J. F. Christensen, N. J. Foss

14   **Reflection as a Building Block for Strategic Thinking and
      the Development of an Organizational Philosophy**   313
      W. D'hanis, L. Perneel

Index   331

Contributors

RAPHAEL AMIT
Faculty of Commerce and Business Administration, The University of British Columbia, 2053 Main Mall, Vancouver, BC, Canada, V6T 1TZ.
Raphael Amit is the Peter Wall Distinguished Professor at the Faculty of Commerce and Business Administration, University of British Columbia (UBC). He is the founding director of the W. Maurice Young Entrepreneurship and Venture Capital Research Centre. Trained as a business economist, he received a PhD in Management from Northwestern University. Before joining UBC, he served on the faculty of the J.L. Kellogg Graduate School of Management, Northwestern University. Dr Amit is on the editorial boards of the *Strategic Management Journal* and *Organization Science* and has completed a three-year term as an associate editor of *Management Science*. His research and teaching interests center on entrepreneurship in independent and corporate settings and on strategic management.

CHARLES BADEN-FULLER
City University Business School, Frobisher Crescent, Barbican Centre, London EC2Y 8HB, UK.
Charles Baden-Fuller is currently Centenary Professor of Strategy, City University Business School, London, and Research Professor, University of Rotterdam, Erasmus, The Netherlands. Previously he held positions at University of Bath (1987–94) and The London Business School (1979–87). He has published extensively in the field of strategy in *The Strategic Management Journal, Journal of Management Studies, The Economic Journal, Long Range Planning* and in numerous other outlets. He also co-authored with John Stopford *Rejuvenating the Mature Business*, published by Harvard Business Press and Routledge (1994). Currently he is engaged in funded projects examining change in large complex European organizations as well as the development of strategic outsourcing and networked organizations.

JANICE BLACK
Eli Broad College of Business, Michigan State University N475 North Business Complex, East Lansing, MI 48824–1122, USA.
Janice A. Black received her doctorate in Business Administration with a focus on Strategic Management from Texas Tech University in August 1995. She has been teaching at the tertiary level since 1989 and has taught a broad range of courses. She is currently an assistant professor at Michigan State University. Her current research interests include strategic resources, organizational change, innovation-driven markets, and entrepreneurship. She is also investigating the resources involved in having a distance education competence and with creating a distance education course on Small Business Management. She has published in *The Strategic Management Journal, Entrepreneurship, Theory and Practice* and has presented papers at the regional, national and international levels.

KIMBERLY BOAL
Area of Management, College of Business Administration, Texas Tech University, 15th and Flint Avenue, Lubbock, TX 79409, USA.
Kimberly (Kim) Boal received his PhD from the University of Wisconsin-Madison in Organizational Behavior and Organization and Management Theory. He has been a full-time faculty member at Utah State University, the University of Nevada-Reno, and Texas Tech University, where he is currently an associate professor. In addition, he has been a visiting professor at the University of Minnesota. He has published on a variety of areas including intrinsic motivation, organizational commitment and job involvement; strategic leadership; corporate social responsibility; strategic planning; the resource-based view of the firm; and philosophy of science. His current research projects focus on strategic groups, strategic adaptation, and charismatic leadership.

VITTORIO CHIESA
CNR-ITIA and Politecnico di Milano, CNR-ITIA, Viale Lombardia 20/A, 20131 Milano, Italy.
Vittorio Chiesa is Senior Researcher at the National Research Council of Italy (Istituto di Tecnologie Industriali e Automazione), Milano. He is a lecturer in Business Economics and Organization at Politecnico di Milano and in International Management at Mip-Politecnico di Milano (MBA Program of Politecnico). He is also a lecturer in Technology Strategy at LIUC (Libero Istituto Universitario Carlo Cattaneo) at Castellanza. He obtained his master's degree in Electronic Engineering at Politecnico di Milano. He was previously with Ciba-Geigy and Pirelli. He has been visiting researcher at London Business School in

the Operations Management Department. His main research areas are R&D and technology strategy, R&D management, and innovation management in multinational corporations.

JENS FRØSLEV CHRISTENSEN
Institute of Industrial Economics and Strategy, Copenhagen Business School, Nansengade 19, 6, 1366 Copenhagen K, Denmark.
Jens Frøslev Christensen has been associate professor at the Department of Industrial Economics and Strategy, Copenhagen Business School, since 1982 and has been head of the department since 1994. His main research interests are management of innovation and technology, and business and corporate strategy. He has published several books and numerous articles in, among other journals, *Research Policy* and *Economics of Innovation and New Technology*. At present he is engaged on a research project concerning corporate coherence and management of technology in large Danish corporations.

ERIC CREMER
Programme Doctorne–IAE Aix-en-Provence, Université Aix-Marseille III, Clos Guiot, Boulevard des Camus, 13540 Puyricard, France.
Eric Cremer worked for four years as a consultant in strategy and management of technologies. He has been involved in large projects of European alliances in R&D and industrial plant development. In 1995 he joined a major company in the construction industry to carry out the marketing management of a computing networks and telecommunication division. He is doing a PhD in Business Administration at the Institut d'Administration de Entreprises (IAE) of Aix-en-Provence (Université Aix Marseille III). His current research deals with collective learning, competence building and competence-based formulation of strategy.

WANDA D'HANIS
Nikè Consul c.v.b.a., Bredabaan 928, 2930-Brasschaat, Belgium.
Wanda D'hanis (Dr.phil. 1947) studied ancient philology and philosophy in Antwerp, Louvain, and Frankfurt/Main. She holds the Chair of Philosophy at the Flemish College for Translators (Antwerp), runs the program on Management & Reflection at the College of Eindhoven (The Netherlands) and is reading in the management program of the University of Prague. She runs Nikè Consult-Management & Reflection c.v.b.a., which propagates critical reflection as a building block for strategic thinking and the development of œganizations. Among its activities are consulting and change programs. Recently she published

'Reflections on business process re-engineering', in *Business Process Re-engineering: Myth & Reality*, edited by Colin Coulson-Thomas (European COBRA project - EG T 1004) (London: Kogan Page, 1994).

THOMAS DURAND
Ecole Centrale Paris, F-92295 Châtenay Malabry, France.
Thomas Durand is Professor of Business Strategy at Ecole Centrale Paris where he heads the Strategy and Technology Research unit. He works in the field of strategic management, the management of technology and innovation, as well as on public policies for research, science technology transfer, and the promotion of innovation. He has published a number of articles in the field over the last ten years. Thomas Durand has worked extensively with companies and government bodies on these topics for both research projects and consulting assignments.

NICOLAI J. FOSS
Institute of Industrial Economics and Strategy, Copenhagen Business School, Nansengade 19, 6, 1366 Copenhagen K, Denmark.
Nicolai J. Foss obtained his PhD from Copenhagen Business School, where he is presently employed as assistant professor. His research and teaching center around the theory of economic organization and strategic management, particularly the competence-based competition perspective. Nicolai J. Foss's work on these matters has been published in journals such as *Journal of Management Studies*, *Organization Science* and *Journal of Evolutionary Economics*. With Christian Knudsen, he is the editor of *Towards a Competence Theory of the Firm* (London: Routledge, 1996).

AIMÉ HEENE
De Vlerick School voor Management, Bellevne 6, Ledeberg (Gent), B-9050, Belgium.
Professor dr Aimé Heene holds a PhD in Educational Sciences and an MBA from De Vlerick School voor Management. He is an associate professor at the University of Gent, the vice-president of the Dutch–Flemish Academy for Management, a founding member and secretary of the Flemish Strategy Society and a member of the advisory board of the European Foundation for Business Qualification. Professor Heene is an Associate Director of Coopers & Lybrand Management Consulting and a fellow of the China-Europe Management Center at Fudan University (Shanghai) during the summer of 1996. He has served as a co-editor of *Competence-Based Competition* (Wiley, 1995; with Gary Hamel) and *Dynamics of Competence-Based Competition* (Elsevier, 1996; with Ron Sanchez and Howard Thomas).

JOSEPH T. MAHONEY
Department of Business Administration, University of Illinois at Urbana-Champaign, 1206 South Sixth Street, Champaign, IL 61820, USA.
Joseph T. Mahoney is Associate Professor of Business Administration at the University of Illinois at Urbana-Champaign. He received a BA (1980), MA (1984), and PhD (1989) from the University of Pennsylvania. His doctorate from the Wharton School is in business economics. He has published in several management and strategy journals. His primary interests are corporate governance and organizational economics. He serves on the editorial board of *the Strategic Management Journal*.

RAFFAELLA MANZINI
Libero Istituto Universitario Carlo Cattane, Corso Matteotti 22, 21053 Castellanza (Varese), Italy.
Raffaella Manzini is research assistant at the Libero Istituto Universitario Carlo Cattaneo (LIUC), Castellanza (Varese). She teaches Economics and Business Organization at LIUC and Politecnico di Milano. She obtained her master's degree in Management Engineering at Politecnico di Milano. Her research interests are strategic management, especially green strategy, and technology-based strategy.

BILL MCKELVEY
UCLA, The Anderson School, Los Angeles, CA 90095, USA.
Bill McKelvey is Professor of Strategic Management at the Anderson School at UCLA. He is a leading authority on organizational taxonomy, evolution, and design. In addition to articles, he authored a book, *Organizational Systematics*. He is now working on a new book, entitled *Quasi-natural Organization Science*. This book synthesizes the semantic conception of theory from philosophy of science, instrumental conveniences used in analytical mechanics to foster mathematical and computational modeling, the analysis of stochastic micro-states, multi-level and co-evolutionary aspects of Darwinian selectionist theory, and complexity theory, particularly forces creating autocatalytic dissipative structures at the so-called "edge of chaos." A recent paper is entitled "Complexity vs. Selection Among Coevolutionary Firms: A Complexity Theory of Strategic Organizing".

PIERRE-XAVIER MESCHI
Laboratoire CRET-LOG, Faculté des Science Economiques, Université Aix-Marseille II, 14 Rue Puvis de Chavannes, 13001 Marseille, France.
Pierre-Xavier Meschi is lecturer (maître de conférences) in human resources management and organizational behaviour at the Faculté des

Sciences Economiques (Université Aix-Marseille II). He earned his doctorate in business administration at the Institut d'Administration des Entreprises of Aix-en-Provence (Université Aix-Marseille III). He is a research associate at the CRET-LOG center. His current research interests include strategic human resources management, social and cultural issues, international alliances, and networks.

ELAINE MOSAKOWSKI
UCLA, The Anderson School, Los Angeles, CA 90095, USA.
Elaine Mosakowski is an assistant professor in the area of Strategy and Organizations at UCLA's Anderson School of Management. Her research examines many issues related to the resource-based view of strategy and competence-based strategic management, such as the impact of uncertainty and causal ambiguity on strategic decisions, how expectations shape organizational choices, and the problem of studying idiosyncracy systematically. She has written both conceptual and empirical papers on these topics, including studies of entrepreneurial firms in the computer industry and a global population of foreign exchange trading rooms.

LUC PERNEEL
Niké Consult c.v.b.a., Bredabaan 928, 2930 Brasschaat, Belgium.
Luc Perneel (dr phil. 1949) studied philosophy in Louvain and Jerusalem. In 1980 he took his doctor's degree in Mathematical Logic. Successively he was system-engineer and project manager of the International Logistic Project of Philips, manager of logistic planning and control of Volvo Car Sint-Truiden (Belgium), senior organization consultant of Volvo Car Helmond (Netherlands) and interim director of strategy at the ZOL (Netherlands), a cluster of socio-economic companies. Inspired by his studies and his broad industrial experience, he founded the management consultancy bureau Niké Consult—Management & Reflection in 1990.

ZEEV ROTEM
Faculty of Management, The Leon Recannati Graduate School of Business, Tel Aviv University, Ramat Aviv, 69978, Tel Aviv, Israel.
Zeev Rotem is a lecturer in Strategic Management at the Faculty of Management, Tel Aviv University, Israel. He received his PhD in Strategic Management from Tel Aviv University. He has been a visiting research fellow at the Harvard Business School and has presented his work at several conferences of the Strategic Management Society. He is a retired Lt. Colonel of the Israeli Air Force and has served in senior managerial and business positions. He consults for

Israeli firms and his research interests include competence-based theory and competitiveness.

RON SANCHEZ
Graduate School of Management, University of Western Australia, Nedlands, WA 6907, Australia.
Ron Sanchez has degrees in psychology, comparative literature, architecture, engineering, and business administration. He received his PhD in Technology Strategy from MIT. He has taught strategic management, and technology management, strategy, and policy courses at the MIT, the University of Illinois, of Warwick Business School, and ESSEC. Prior to becoming a management researcher, he was a consultant in establishing international joint ventures for product and market development. He is now associate professor of management in the Graduate School of Management at the University of Western Australia.

JOHAN STEIN
The Economic Research Institute, Stockholm School of Economics, Box 6501, S-113 83 Stockholm, Sweden.
Johan Stein is an assistant professor at the Department of Organization and Management, Stockholm School of Economics. His research focuses on learning and structural change in organizational and interorganizational settings. The link between these two settings is emphasized in his research.

ROLAND VAN DER VORST
Nijmegen Business School, PO Box 9108, 6500 HK Nijmegen, The Netherlands.
Roland van der Vorst obtained a master's degree in both Business Administration and Communication Studies at the University of Nijmegen. He is finishing his PhD in Strategic Brand Management. Besides branding, his research interests are systems theory, second-order cybernetics and competence-based strategic management. He is especially interested in relating strategic brand management to competence-based strategic management.

HENK W. VOLBERDA
Rotterdam School of Management, Erasmus University, PO Box 1738, 3000 DR, The Netherlands.
Henk W. Volberda is Associate Professor of Strategic Management at the Rotterdam School of Management, Erasmus University, The Netherlands. In 1992 he received his PhD cum laude in Business Administration from the University of Groningen. For his dissertation

entitled *Organizational Flexibility: Change and Preservation* he received the ERASM Research Award and the Igor Ansoff Award 1993. He is a member of the Editorial Review Board of *Organization Science*, the Editorial Board of *M&O*, and the Advisory Board of *M&O Quarterly*. His research interests include strategic flexibility, core competences, new organizational forms, and strategic management of innovation. He is currently studying the process of strategic renewal within large European corporations.

JOHAN WALLIN
SMG Finland Oy, Mikokatu 18 A, FIN-00100 Helsinki, Finland.
Johan Wallin holds a MSc in industrial economics from the Helsinki University of Technology and an MA in economics from the Swedish School of Economics in Helsinki. After 15 years in different executive positions within the fur trade he joined SMG Finland Oy in 1991. He is now responsible for the Finnish operations of the international SIFO-SMG Group, as well as the chairman of its partnership.

Series Preface

Like the competitive environments with which it is concerned, the theory and practice of strategic management are changing rapidly. The field's early emphasis on industry structures and other concepts from industrial organization economics, were joined in the mid-1980s by attention to the characteristics of individual firms, as typified by the resource-based view of the firm. While each of these perspectives has brought useful insights to strategy theory and practice, neither offers a completely satisfactory framework for understanding and managing the dynamics of strategic change in firms or industries.

In the late 1980s, a shift to focus on the competences of firms and the role of competences in shaping competition brought a more dynamic and future-oriented focus to strategy. The concept of competence is, increasingly, providing a framework for renewed discussions between strategy academics and strategic managers interested in creating new theory for strategic management in dynamic environments.

Competence-Based Strategic Management brings together the central concepts in competence-based strategic management and highlights important new integration of theory and practice. Divided into five sections, the volume discusses fundamental concepts and current issues in the competence perspective and suggests new approaches to linking theory and practice; explores the dynamics of competence-based competition; investigates processes for managing competences systemically; focuses on processes for managing the cognitions of decision-makers who will lead changes in organizational competences, and concludes with holistic perspectives on competence.

This volume provides a major contribution to extending the emerging theory of competence-based competition. It elaborates some new approaches to integrating the theory and practice of strategic management. It adds to the industry structure and resource-based perspectives on strategy developed in the 1980s, and introduces competence as the central concept for understanding competition and strategic management. It also develops a new view of strategy that links dynamic, systemic, cognitive, and holistic perspectives on management. The book includes both theory chapters and case studies that show applications in management practice.

This volume represents a significant step forward in developing theory and practice for competence-based strategic management. It is a major extension of the work begun in the edited volumes *Competence-Based Competition* by Gary Hamel and Aimé Heene (Wiley 1994) and *Dynamics of Competence-Based Competition* by Ron Sanchez, Aimé Heene, and Howard Thomas (Elsevier Pergamon 1996). Readers interested in the competence perspective would no doubt find it useful also to consult the companion to this volume, *Strategic Learning and Knowledge Management* by Ron Sanchez and Aimé Heene (Wiley 1996), which investigates the key role of learning and knowledge in competence theory and practice.

Preface

Like the competitive environments with which they are concerned, the theory and practice of strategic management are changing rapidly. The field's early emphasis on industry structures and other concepts from industrial organization economics was joined in the mid-1980s by attention to the characteristics of individual firms, as typified by the now well-known resource-based view of the firm. While each of these perspectives has brought useful insights to strategy theory and practice, neither offers a completely satisfactory framework for understanding and managing the dynamics of strategic change in firms or industries.

In the late 1980s, a shift to a focus on the *competences* of firms and the role of competences in shaping competition brought a more dynamic and future-oriented focus to strategy. Introduced to the field through a series of well-known articles and books by C.K. Prahalad and Gary Hamel, the competence perspective has attracted growing attention from strategy researchers and practitioners alike. The concept of competence is increasingly providing a framework for renewed discussions between strategy academics and strategic managers interested in creating new theory for strategic management in dynamic environments.

The competence perspective is also attracting researchers from many disciplinary backgrounds. The diversity of perspectives now joining together in an effort to understand organizational competence and the dynamics of competence-based competition has reinvigorated research and practice in strategy by introducing new concepts for a more dynamic, systemic, cognitive, and holistic theory to guide strategic management. This volume explores some of the central ideas in the emerging theory of competence, and it elaborates some new approaches to integrating theory and practice in competence-based strategic management.

Section I discusses fundamental concepts and current issues in the competence perspective and suggests a new approach to linking theory and practice in developing this perspective.

Section II explores the dynamics of competence-based strategic management. Chapters in this section examine processes for strategic renewal in large organizations, the role of customers in stimulating organizational change, strategizing for innovation, the organizational capacity to change, and strategies for defending existing competences.

To change the competences of a firm and to leverage its existing competences more effectively requires managing the firm as an open system of stocks and flows of assets and capabilities. Accordingly, Section III investigates processes for managing competences systematically. A framework is presented for analyzing competence at various system levels within a firm. The integration of competence-building processes with corporate strategy is explored at several levels of the firm through a case study.

Strategic decisions set directions for changes in competences, and Section IV investigates key processes for managing the cognitions of decision makers who will lead changes in organizational competences. The chapters investigate likely forms of "blind spots" in managerial cognitions about competences and processes for stimulating building of new competences within networks of firms.

Section V concludes the volume with a holistic perspective on competence. The chapters suggest theoretical and practical approaches to achieving organizational coherence, as well as the need to develop a more reflective, philosophical vision of the firm as an organization.

A volume such as this comes about only through the combined efforts of many people, not least of whom are the authors. Though not a direct contributor to this volume, Howard Thomas has assisted the development of the competence perspective and this volume in many ways, both as series editor and as a colleague. In addition, we wish to express our appreciation to the Strategic Management Society for supporting the publication of this volume and to the European Institute for Advanced Studies in Management for administrative assistance in organizing international conferences on competence theory building in 1993 and 1995.

Aimé Heene wishes to thank the De Vlerick School voor Management for the continuing support of his research and teaching in competence-based competition, as well as his work on this volume. Ron Sanchez thanks the University of Illinois at Urbana-Champaign and Ecole Supérieure des Sciences Economiques et Commerciales (ESSEC) for their institutional support during preparation of this volume.

AIMÉ HEENE   RON SANCHEZ
Gent, Belgium   *Urbana, Illinois, and Cergy-Pontoise, France*

Section I

Competence Concepts for Strategic Management

1

Competence-based Strategic Management: Concepts and Issues for Theory, Research, and Practice

RON SANCHEZ, AIMÉ HEENE

INTRODUCTION

Initially stimulated by Hamel (1989) and Prahalad and Hamel (1990, 1993, 1995), the interest shown by both strategy academics and practitioners in competence and competence-based competition has continued to gather momentum in the 1990s. From the outset, the competence movement's emphasis on developing organizational vision and building new capabilities has found an unusually "broad resonance" (Rumelt, 1994) among strategy researchers and managers interested in finding new approaches to managing organizations competing in dynamic environments.

The challenge of building new theory for competence-based strategic management has been taken up by a growing circle of researchers and practitioners. Since 1992, a series of international workshops on competence-based competition has fueled new research investigating various

Competence-based Strategic Management.
Edited by Aimé Heene and Ron Sanchez.
Copyright © 1997 John Wiley & Sons Ltd.

aspects of competence and competence-based competition (Hamel and Heene, 1994; Sanchez, Heene, and Thomas, 1996a). The objective of this new literature is building new theory for strategic management based on a central concept of organizational competence. The motivation for this emerging research is a perception held by many strategy researchers and practitioners that current strategy theory is not adequately addressing the dynamic competitive environments in which many firms compete today, nor the challenges which managers face in creating and managing organizational capabilities.

Our recent book with Howard Thomas sought to pull together several perspectives on competence by putting forward a concept of competence that incorporates specific *dynamic, systemic, cognitive* and *holistic* properties (Sanchez, Heene, and Thomas, 1996b). We also proposed a derived vocabulary for discussing competence and key related concepts such as assets, resources, capabilities, skills, goals, and knowledge. This effort to define a vocabulary of competence-based competition has provided an important tool for our own theoretical explorations of the dynamic, systemic, cognitive, and holistic characteristics of competence (Sanchez and Heene, 1996a; Sanchez and Thomas, 1996; Gorman, Thomas, and Sanchez, 1996), as well as for further explorations by others (e.g. authors in this volume). It is notable that this movement has also attracted the interest and support of a number of practitioners, who are finding that the emerging theory of competence and its associated vocabulary have significant correspondence (or "resonance" in Rumelt's word) with the actual challenges they face as strategic managers.

The articulation of a foundational concept of competence and a derived vocabulary for analyzing competence-based competition has also enabled better communication and improved coherence within the theory-building process being carried out by a growing network of researchers and practitioners from many countries and perspectives. As this research progresses, not only are new insights into the nature of competence emerging, but because these insights are developed through a common conceptual framework and vocabulary, we are also beginning to see more clearly important interrelationships among the dynamic, systemic, cognitive, and holistic aspects of competence. In the discussion which follows, we undertake to give an updated explanation of the multidimensional concept of competence now being developed within the competence theory-building movement. We also discuss several directions for further research and application in practice.

Importantly, we also identify several fundamental issues for the field of strategy now coming to the surface in various areas of competence theory building. The effort to build new competence-based theory for strategic management has brought into sharp focus what we believe are central theoretical issues that need to be recognized and discussed within the field of strategy. In the most basic sense, we suggest that the competence perspective is making plain the need for *theory in strategy* that recognizes more fully the realities—above all, the *uncertainties*—faced by managers and organizations in the *practice of strategic management*. We therefore discuss several ways in which strategy theory and research have become disconnected from the actual decision making, resource deploying, capability building, knowledge creating and other strategic processes of firms. We also suggest ways in which competence theory is now attempting to reconnect strategy theory and the realities of strategic management in these areas.

Reconnecting strategy theory and practice will require renewed efforts to open the "black box" of the firm to investigate the processes within firms that identify, build, acquire, deploy, protect, and retire resources—in effect, to recognize theoretically and investigate empirically the close interrelationships between (indeed, perhaps even the inseparability of) "process" and "content" within organizations. We suggest with Mahoney and Sanchez (this volume) that reconnecting strategy research and strategy practice will necessitate integration of more research "from the inside" of firms with the positivist empirical mode of research "from the outside" (Evered and Louis, 1982) that is now so prominent in the field of strategy.

At an even more fundamental level, we suggest that current strategy theory based on industrial organization economics and the resource-based view of the firm may have arrived at a critical epistemological impasse. We argue that *in dynamic and uncertain environments,* the form of positivist theory building and research on which those perspectives are currently based may lead to *ex post* theoretical explanations of competitive environments and strategically important resources, but in their current forms, these theoretical perspectives have limited ability to make *ex ante* predictions of competitive outcomes. Industrial organization, for example, has yet to address the ways in which either managerial cognitions or cooperative interactions between firms shape the structural evolution of an industry (Gorman, Thomas, and Sanchez, 1996). In addition, the strategically important "structural" characteristics of dynamic markets increasingly have to do with intra- and interfirm processes for creating knowledge and information assets, rather than the control of production and distribution assets that is the focus of attention in much industrial organization theory (Sanchez, 1996a). Similarly, the resource-based view has not yet addressed theoretically the influence of managerial cognition on resource development processes at the firm or industry level, nor the fundamental impact on the strategic value of resources of firms' differing abilities in directing and coordinating the use of resources.

Because these theories have not yet incorporated important dynamic, cognitive, and systemic aspects of real competitive environments, in practice they thus far offer only limited insights into principles for the effective strategic management of firms in dynamic, uncertain environments. The insights available from these theoretical perspectives in strategy may become more useful to the practice of strategic management, however, by being linked to competence theory's explicitly dynamic, systemic, cognitive, and holistic approach to strategy theory. We propose, in effect, competence theory's attention to the *organizational* and *cognitive processes* of firms and industries constitutes a shift to "higher-order content variables" that provide the theoretical means to move beyond the current limitations of industrial organization and resource-base theories.

We also address a basic problem in using industrial organization and resource-based theory to study and ultimately to improve firm performance, which we take to be a central objective of theory and practice in the field of strategy. As we discuss below, an exclusive reliance on non-teleological positivist theory and empirical methods in industrial organization and resource-based perspectives would raise fundamental issues about both the concepts of managerial and firm performance in strategy theory and their operationalization in strategy research. We suggest that competence theory's effort to open the "black box" of the firm to investigate *organizational goals* and *managerial strategic logics* is a logically necessary next step in building strategy theory that is more capable of distinguishing good performance attributable to effective management from competitive success due to mere "luck" (Barney, 1986). We also propose that adopting an explicitly teleological approach is necessary in operationalizing a concept of performance that would enable strategy research to overcome the *tautology problem* in the resource-based approach to strategy theory.

Our discussion is developed in the following way. We first recapitulate the basic concepts for competence theory and practice suggested in recent work. Some key definitions in the vocabulary of competence are reviewed to clarify the features of the concept of competence being used in much current competence theory building. We then revisit several objectives for competence theory building and practice, and we review recent work on the dynamic, systemic, cognitive, and holistic aspects of competence for progress in meeting those objectives. We then consider some fundamental theoretical, empirical, and epistemological issues which we believe the work in competence theory is now raising for the field of strategy. We conclude with an appraisal of the ways in which current competence theory building has the potential to reconnect strategy research with strategy practice and thereby provide a useful framework for competence-based strategic management.

BASIC CONCEPTS FOR COMPETENCE THEORY AND PRACTICE

We have suggested previously that *competence* is proving to be an attractive and effective "conceptual linchpin" for theory building and practice in strategy, because

> analyzing competition as a dynamic contest between competences seems to strike a useful balance between a need to encompass the complexity and dynamism of real-world competition, on the one hand, and the need for sensemaking by humans with limited cognitive capabilities for understanding dynamic complexity, on the other. [T]aking competences as the unit of analysis in strategy research and theory-building appears to cast the right size conceptual net into the sea of competitive interactions between firms (Sanchez, Heene, and Thomas, 1996b: 6).

The concept of competence to which we refer tries to incorporate and integrate essential dynamic, systemic, cognitive, and holistic aspects of organizations. To accomplish this, competence theory invokes several key concepts that are expressed through a specific vocabulary, as we discuss below.

Firms are characterized as *open systems* which pursue *strategic goals* that comprise sets of objectives distinctive to each firm. In pursuit of these goals, each firm develops and follows a rationale or *strategic logic* for achieving some level of goal attainment. The strategic logic of an organization shapes the *management processes* that determine how a firm identifies, acquires, and uses *resources*. The resources a firm uses in pursuit of its goals inevitably reside both within the firm *(firm-specific resources)* and in other organizations *(firm-addressable resources)*. Firms are likely to differ significantly in their approaches to managing the *systemic interdependencies* within their own internal resources and processes and with other firms' resources and processes. Firms can therefore be fundamentally distinguished not only by their resource endowments at any point in time but also by their distinctive sets of strategic goals, by their strategic logics for achieving their distinctive goals, and by the different ways in which firms *coordinate deployments* of both firm-specific and firm-addressable resources in pursuit of their goals.

Competence, then, is the ability of an organization to sustain coordinated deployments of resources in ways that promise to help that organization achieve its goals. A firm engages in *competence leveraging* when it coordinates deployments of resources in ways that do not require *qualitative changes* in the assets, capabilities, or modes of coordination used by the firm. *Competence building* occurs when firms acquire and use new and qualitatively different assets, capabilities, and modes of coordination. Competences take time, effort, and resources to develop and to use, and firms will be distinguished by their characteristic mixes of competence building and competence-leveraging activities in pursuing their distinctive sets of long- and near-term goals (Sanchez and Thomas, 1996). Strategically important differences between firms therefore arise from each firm's distinctive mix of competence building and competence-leveraging activities, which in turn are determined by each firm's set of goals, by its strategic logic for achieving its goals, and by the way in which each firm coordinates its deployments of resources in pursuit of its goals.

The *competitive dynamics* of an industry are driven by changing managerial perceptions and organizational processes for goal setting that lead to distinctive patterns of competence building and competence-leveraging activities by the firms in a given industry. Firms' various patterns of competence building and leveraging may lead to both convergences and divergences of firm competences in an industry. In addition, to secure the use of firm-addressable resources under the control of other firms, firms may engage in market transactions or may enter into *competence alliances* that link one firm's competences or resources to those of other firms. Interactions between firms in competence building and leveraging may therefore be both competitive and collaborative, and firms may maintain simultaneous competitive and collaborative competence building or leveraging relationships with other firms.

This view of strategic competition as a contest between firms in competence building and leveraging provides a conceptual framework for elaborating Prahalad and Hamel's (1993) notion of "strategy as stretch and leverage". As firms try to build new competences and leverage existing competences into new markets, they create new technologies, new organizational forms, new kinds of products, and new kinds of product strategies that change the competitive environments of industries (Sanchez, 1995). Thus, competing in building and leveraging competences is fundamentally a contest between the cognitions of strategic managers in imagining the new competences that will be the basis for the "industries of the future" (Prahalad and Hamel, 1995), and between firms' distinctive organizational processes for creating those competences.

In dynamic environments, building and leveraging competences requires flexibility in acquiring and deploying new resources effectively in changing circumstances. Thus, in dynamic environments, creating "higher-order" capabilities like organizational learning that improve the *strategic flexibility* (Sanchez, 1993, 1995) of an organization becomes critical to building, leveraging, and maintaining competences. Competence-based competition in its most dynamic forms may therefore be likened to a state of perpetual corporate entrepreneurialism in which continuous learning about how to build and leverage new competences more effectively becomes a central activity of competence-based strategic management.

OBJECTIVES FOR COMPETENCE THEORY AND PRACTICE

The concept of competence and competence-based competition appears to offer a conceptual framework for theory building and management practice capable of yielding new insights into key processes of dynamic competitive environments. We have previously suggested some of the ways in which competence theory may bring new possibilities for understanding and managing firms and their competitive interactions (Sanchez, Heene, and Thomas, 1996b). In particular, the dynamic, systemic, cognitive, and holistic dimensions of competence theory suggest possibilities for *integrating* a number of aspects of strategy theory which thus far have largely been independent theoretical domains.

INTEGRATING "PROCESS" AND "CONTENT" PERSPECTIVES

The systems view in competence theory makes it clear that the strategic usefulness of a resource to a firm depends on the way it is combined, coordinated, and deployed with other firm-specific and firm-addressable resources. In economic terms, firms' differing abilities to extract value from the use of the same resources means that the *exchange value* of a resource in strategic factor markets (Barney, 1986) is not the same as the potential *value-in-use* of the resource, which depends on the relative ability of a specific firm to use a resource to greatest strategic effect. Because a firm's approaches to coordinating deployments of resources (a "process" variable) governs the strategic advantages which the firm can obtain from specific resources (a "content" variable), process and content can be seen as interdependent and not readily separable in either theory or practice. Thus, competence theory provides a framework for integrating strategy perspectives on organizational processes with perspectives on resource endowments.

INTEGRATING INDUSTRY STRUCTURES AND CHANGE DYNAMICS

Competence theory provides a vehicle for understanding how competence building and leveraging by firms drive industry evolution. The competence building of firms leads to asset, capability, and knowledge structures within industries that both support and constrain subsequent competence leveraging. Prior strategy theory has often regarded industry structures as exogenously determined (e.g. by technologies of production), while firm processes that have wrought changes in industry structures by "changing the rules of competition" have not received systematic attention. Competence theory, however, recognizes managerial cognition and organizational capacities for learning as engines of strategic change that largely determine both the resource endowments of individual firms and the collective resource endowments that define industry structures.

INTEGRATING COMPETITIVE AND COOPERATIVE PROCESSES

Competence theory recognizes that firms are open systems that depend on inputs of many kinds of resources from other firms, as well as on access to markets for their products. Recognizing that firms in an industry compete for critical resources as well as for product markets and at the same time cooperate in many ways to create new resources and markets (e.g. by collaborative development of new technologies or by setting product standards) allows competition and cooperation between firms to be seen as interdependent processes, not dichotomous strategic alternatives to be selected opportunistically.

Competence theory also provides a lens for understanding more clearly some *complex phenomena* within and between firms that have been difficult to represent adequately in other strategy perspectives.

THE NATURE AND CRITICAL ROLES OF COGNITION AND COORDINATION

Important differences in firms' relative abilities to target and coordinate deployments of resources imply that some firms may achieve distinctive competences by using resources that are similar to those available to or used by other firms. By the same token, firms with unique and valuable resource endowments (e.g. prime retail locations or superior technology) may fail to develop distinctive competences because they are not effective in coordinating or targeting those resources. Competence theory's emphasis on the role of managerial cognitions in targeting resources and on organizational capabilities in coordinating resource deployments provides a framework for elaborating important differences in firms' abilities to integrate skills (Hamel, 1994) and other resources that are key determinants of competitive outcomes.

The Systemic Interdependencies that make up a Firm's Competences

Many systemically interdependent assets, capabilities, and coordination processes are required to build and leverage competences successfully, and many may have to be obtained from other firms. Systemic interdependencies among resources and capabilities may often make it problematic to determine the relative importance to a firm of specific resources and capabilities, since many closely interrelated resources and capabilities may be essential to achieving competence and competing successfully in a market. Competence theory therefore suggests that a firm must manage its competence(s) *as a system* and avoid excessive focusing of managerial attention on developing and managing a "single competence" judged by some criteria to be "core".

The Growing Use of Networks and Alliances

Viewing firms as open systems that depend on resource flows from other firms to build and leverage competences helps explain the growing use of networks and alliances in dynamic markets. By linking existing competences or resources in networks, cooperating firms may increase their strategic flexibilities (Sanchez, 1993, 1995) by *jointly* realizing asset mass efficiencies, achieving the advantages of asset interconnectedness and overcoming time-compression diseconomies (Dierickx and Cool, 1989) that would not be available to the stand-alone firm. This perspective also suggests that in a dynamic market context, longevity of interfirm relationships may not be an essential characteristic of successful collaborations. Networks of firms may function like competence alliances (Sanchez, Heene, and Thomas, 1996b) in which firms may enter a succession of short-term arrangements for the explicit purpose of more quickly reconfiguring a temporary chain of resources to take advantage of short-lived market opportunities (Sanchez, 1995).

THE ROLE OF LEARNING AS A CRITICAL STRATEGIC VARIABLE

Competence theory suggests that a firm's ability to learn and acquire new capabilities may be more important determinants of its competitive success in dynamic markets than the firm's current endowment of unique resources or the industry structure it currently faces. Sustainable competitive advantage in the long run is seen to arise from a superior ability to identify, build, and leverage new competences (Sanchez and Heene, 1996a,b).

THE HOLISTIC NATURE OF STRATEGIC GOALS AND PERFORMANCE

Sanchez and Thomas (1996) have proposed that the concept of firm performance must recognize that firms have complex and distinctive sets of strategic goals which must be managed holistically in order to sustain competence building and leveraging processes. Adopting purely economic parameters of performance that are of primary importance to only a single group of resource providers—e.g. returns to providers of financial resources—is therefore taken to be conceptually inadequate as a basis for judging the viability and sustainability of a firm as a complex, dynamic, human system that requires many forms of inputs from many kinds of stakeholders.

We next consider ways in which recent work on the dynamic, systemic, cognitive, and holistic aspects of competence is making progress in meeting these objectives for theory building and practice.

COMPETENCE DYNAMICS

Environmental and organizational change and their coevolving dynamics are central themes in the emerging theory of competence and competence-based competition. These dynamics are now being investigated at several levels of analysis:

- Interactions of people and groups within firms (Baden-Fuller and Volberda, this volume; Boisot, Griffiths, and Moles, 1996; Chiesa and Manzini, this volume; Christensen and Foss, this volume; Cremer and Meschi, this volume; Løwendahl and Haanes, 1996; Post, 1996; Sanchez and Heene, 1996a; Volberda, 1996; Winterscheid and McNabb, 1996; Wright, 1996a,b)

- Interactions between firms and resource providers outside the firm (Klavans and Deeds, 1996; Roehl, 1996; Sanchez, 1996b; Stein, this volume)
- Interactions between firms and customers (Elfring and Baven, 1996; Lang 1996; Lewis and Gregory, 1996; Sivula, van den Bosch, and Elfring, 1996; Wallin, this volume)
- Interactions between competing and cooperating firms (Easton and Araujo, 1996; Gorman, Thomas, and Sanchez, 1996; Jensen, 1996; Quelin, 1996; Rispoli, 1996; Rotem and Amit, this volume; Sanchez, 1996c; Tallman and Atchison, 1996).

Competence dynamics at all levels of analysis are linked by the concepts of competence building and levaraging. *Competence building* is "any process by which a firm achieves qualitative changes to its existing stocks of assets and capabilities, including new abilities to coordinate and deploy new or existing assets and capabilities in ways that help the firm achieve its goals" (Sanchez, Heene, and Thomas, 1996b). Thus, competence building may include both acquisition of qualitatively different assets (for example, new kinds of production equipment) that can be used in conjunction with a firm's existing capabilities, as well as acquisition of new capabilities (i.e. new patterns of action in the use of new or existing assets). Acquiring new assets and capabilities requires interactions of many people and groups within firms and interactions between firms and other entities. Understanding the dynamics of competence building thus requires analysis of interrelated processes at several levels of interaction.

Competence leveraging occurs when a firm applies its "existing competences to current or new market opportunities in ways that do not require qualitative changes in the firm's assets or capabilities" (Sanchez, Heene, and Thomas, 1996b). A firm may leverage existing competences simply by using its current stocks of assets and capabilities, or it may leverage competences by making quantitative changes in the stocks of assets and capabilities the firm already uses (i.e. like-kind assets). Competence leveraging, of course, constitutes a large part of resource deployments by most firms, and the effectiveness of a firm's processes for leveraging competences directly impacts its ability to compete successfully in the near term. The resulting need to be effective in leveraging existing competences imposes substantial claims on a firm's management processes, often creating a significant tension between the need to allocate resources to competence leveraging to meet current competitive demands and the need to allocate resources to building new competences that can influence competitive outcomes in the future. In dynamic environments, a firm's ability to continuously build new competences will be essential to sustaining a competitively advantaged position in its markets, in many instances eclipsing in strategic significance the firm's current stocks of assets and capabilities (or current "accumulation of resources"). Indeed, firms that develop superior competence-building capabilities may try to accelerate their rate of competence building to create competitive dynamics that disadvantage firms with lesser competence-building abilities (Sanchez, 1995).

Managing competence building in the midst of the need to maintain effective processes for leveraging competences has been characterized by Baden-Fuller and Volberda (this volume) as a need to interrelate renewal processes and organizational stability. They suggest that this need can be managed through four processes of renewal: venturing, restructuring, reanimation, and rejuvenation. These processes are described using concepts drawn from population ecology, organizational economics, administrative theory, corporate entrepreneurship, and innovation theory. Baden-Fuller and Volberda also assess the likely effectiveness of these processes in conditions of urgency, risk, and technological change.

The processes of initiating and managing changes in competences have been studied by Wallin (this volume) and Durand (this volume). Wallin discusses the role of customers in identifying opportunities for change and influencing the goal-setting process within ABB Flakt Oy, the Finnish subsidiary of the multinational ABB. Viewing customers as "co-producers" of new products helps ABB Flakt Oy to identify useful new competences. These competences are characterized within ABB Flakt Oy through four capabilities: the capability of the firm to develop and maintain relationships with its customers (relationship capability), the capability of the firm to design products that deliver value to customers (transformative capability), the capability to create new kinds of product performance (generative capability), and the capability to deploy both firm-specific and firm-addressable resources (integrative capability). Recognizing these four dimensions of competence provides a framework for both goal setting in competence building and developing insights into key aspects of industry change dynamics.

Durand takes another view of change dynamics in considering ways in which exogenous industry-level changes in competences can impact firm-level competence building. Mapping the concepts and terminology of competence-based competition proposed by Sanchez, Heene, and Thomas (1996b) onto his own studies of innovation processes, Durand proposes that innovation as a change in competence at the firm level can be understood through a decomposition of competence building into required changes in "stand-alone assets" (assets which can be transferred and used without need for "major cognitive inputs"), cognitive capabilities at both individual and collective levels, and organizational processes and routines, organizational structures, and behavior and organizational culture. Sanchez and Heene (1996a) propose a hierarchical ordering of an organization's stocks of assets and capabilities that is characterized by increasing time requirements to effect change ("dynamic response times," as discussed in the next section). Durand's assessment of the likely difficulties of effecting changes in the five dimensions of competence building that he identifies leads him to propose a different ordering of assets and capabilities from that proposed by Sanchez and Heene, most notably in identifying changes in organizational culture as the most difficult dimension in competence building.

Bringing another perspective to the tension between processes for competence leveraging and competence building, Black and Boal (this volume) investigate the effects of discipline, stretch, trust, and support on the ability of a firm to maintain current performance and simultaneously build new competences. Characterizing the ability of a firm to engage in competence building as an organizational capacity to change, they identify important categories of combinations of discipline, stretch, trust, and support within an organization that lead to relationships or configurations among the internal resources of a firm (enhancing, compensating, suppressing, and substituting) that impact a firm's strategic flexibility to leverage competences effectively while building new competences. They also report tests in the context of US manufacturing firms that suggest that certain configurations are associated with greater organizational ability to both maintain high current performance and undergo changes in competences.

The dynamics of competence-based competition include important processes for maintaining and defending the current competences of firms, as well as building new competences. Rotem and Amit (this volume) conceptualize a process of "strategic defense" to preserve the rent-producing ability of a firm's competences from four kinds of identified threats: imitation, substitution, resource mobilization, and value reduction. To respond to these threats, strategic defense processes require gathering competitive intelligence and selecting strategies that seek either to preserve or alter existing competences. They identify tactical actions which may help to carry out both preservation and alteration strategies. Investigating a sample of 69 Israeli manufacturing firms in 13 industries, they find that when those firms are faced with intense competition, various categories of firms tend to rely on certain preservation strategies carried out through specific tactics. Notably, they find that low-performing firms tend to rely on strategies for preserving existing competences, while high-performing firms tend to pursue alteration strategies that lead to competence building in the form of improving the flexibilities of current resources.

COMPETENCE SYSTEMICS

Sanchez and Heene (1996a) have proposed a model of the firm as a goal-seeking open system (see Figure 1.1) in which interrelated tangible and intangible assets are organized under a firm's strategic logic for achieving its goals and coordinated by using various management processes for leveraging and building new competences. The firm functions as an open system in that it must constantly replenish its stocks of tangible and intangible assets (including capabilities) through its interfaces with other firms and markets. Strategic change is motivated by managers' perceptions of *strategic gaps* between the perceived and desired states of assets and processes within the firm (which Sanchez and Heene term "system elements"). Firms both compete and cooperate with other firms in efforts to obtain the resource flows and market responses needed to close the strategic gaps that motivate firm behavior.

The open-system view of the firm proposed by Sanchez and Heene seeks to extend the resource-based view of the firm as a collection of asset stocks and flows (Dierickx and Cool, 1989) by explicitly recognizing the critical effects of

- Managerial cognitions that influence what kinds of asset stocks and flows the firm will try to achieve
- Managerial coordination abilities in deploying resources and managing asset flows
- Managerial abilities to support organizational learning and to manage knowledge assets effectively in processes for qualitatively changing a firm's asset stocks and flows.

Changes in asset stocks and flows within the firm are managed through feedback loops called *control loops*. These control loops are subject to increasing *internal* causal ambiguities as managers try to monitor and change "higher-order" system elements in the firm, especially its strategic logic and management processes. Competence building in dynamic environments can therefore be seen as beginning with a search by managers for *implied* strategic gaps in the firm's

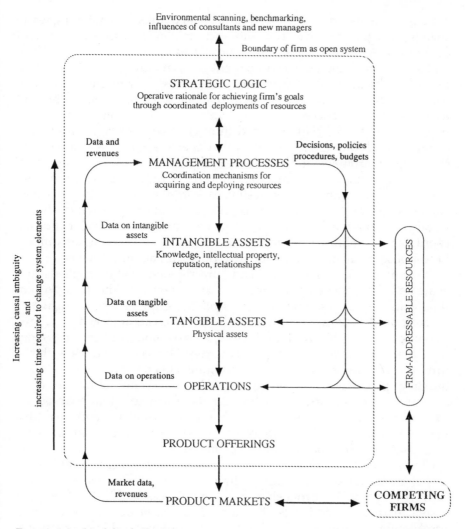

FIGURE 1.1 Model of the firm as an open system (adapted from Sanchez and Heene, 1996a: 41).

system elements. In this way the system model recognizes both different kinds and levels of uncertainties involved in strategic change and the cognitive processes of managers as they confront and try to manage the causal ambiguities resulting from those uncertainties.

In the Sanchez and Heene model, higher-order system elements also exhibit long *dynamic response times* as a firm tries to undergo strategic change. Sanchez and Heene propose that higher-order, cognition-based system elements are often more difficult and thus will take longer to change than lower system elements such as tangible assets and current operations. As a result, the time required to change a firm's stocks of higher system elements encounters critical dynamic system effects that limit the rate at which a firm can change in a dynamic environment. Sanchez and Heene suggest that managing causal ambiguity and dynamic system effects in a dynamic and uncertain environment requires *strategic flexibility* obtained through *flexible resources* and *flexible coordination abilities* (Sanchez, 1995) that enable a range of responses to changing environmental conditions. Flexible resources are more likely to be useful in a dynamic and uncertain future than specific-use resources; acquiring flexible resources can therefore help managers compensate for their limited cognitive abilities to predict future resource requirements precisely. Managers must also develop flexible coordination abilities to redeploy the firm's flexible resources quickly in response to changes in competitive opportunities and threats.

A number of researchers and practitioners have applied and evaluated the Sanchez and Heene system model of the firm. Wallin (this volume), for example, describes relationships between a firm and its customers in terms of interrelated "value-creation systems". Christensen and Foss (this volume) investigate asset interconnectedness and the synergistic, dynamic complementarities between activities within a firm to propose a concept of corporate coherence in competence-building processes. Løwendahl and Haanes (1996) adopt an open system view of the firm to analyze "units of activity" that span across firm boundaries in competence building processes. Black and Boal (this volume) investigate the relationships between resources within firms that enable flexible coordination capabilities.

Chiesa and Manzini (this volume) extend the Sanchez and Heene model's hierarchical ordering of processes and resources within the firm as a system by proposing that competences within the firm as a system exist at three levels. The most basic level of competence is a firm's ability to use its capabilities to provide marketable outputs—i.e. the operations level of the firm. The second level of competence involves the deployment of specific sets of knowledge and skills that enable the firm to create value for its customers in distinctive ways. The highest level of competence is characterized by a "firm's ability to envisage the evolution of the characteristics, boundaries, and actors of the competitive context and [to] promote and develop management principles" appropriate to its evolving context that support its actions and help it accomplish its goals. Thus, the first level of competence is critical in leveraging existing competences, the second in improving the market performance of a firm in competence leveraging, and the third in identifying and building new competences, including using existing capabilities in new ways.

Cremer and Meschi (this volume) investigate one company's approach to managing competence building and leveraging processes so as to "improve and harmonize the collective competences embedded in the diverse functions" of the firm as a system. They study the competence-building program of Merlin Gerin, a large 15 000-employee) French firm in the Groupe Schneider companies, with a view to understanding the "strategic architecture" (Hamel and Prahalad, 1994) of competence-building process. They describe Merlin Gerin's creation of a "network of functions" *(reseau des fonctions)* to establish "a formal link between the process of competence building and the objectives defined by corporate top management". Providing an unusually detailed look into one firm's competence-building process, they describe several phases in creating this network as the firm moves towards a well-defined organizational architecture for competence building.

COGNITION IN MANAGING COMPETENCES

A systems view of the firm highlights the cognitive challenges that managers face in the pursuit of "strategy as stretch and leverage" (Prahalad and Hamel, 1993). When firms compete to "stretch" beyond their current competences, competition takes on the character of a *contest between managerial cognitions* (Sanchez, Heene, and Thomas, 1996b) to identify the kinds of competences that will be important in the future and that will become the focus of firm goals for competence building. Sanchez and Thomas (1996) extend the Sanchez and Heene (1996a) systems view of the firm to investigate the goal-setting and goal-seeking behaviors of firms. They develop a basic *taxonomy of strategic goal-seeking behaviors* that firms are likely to pursue. A firm's managers' choices of specific goals and forms of goal-seeking behavior lead to a firm's distinctive pattern of competence building and leveraging activities. Managerial cognition therefore plays a major role in directing the competence-building dynamics that shape industry structures (Gorman, Thomas, and Sanchez, 1996).

Cognitive processes that are important in setting directions for competence building within firms are discussed in several recent papers. Boisot, Griffiths, and Moles (1996) draw on a firm's organizational, cultural, and technological processes to represent the way in which "socially relevant knowledge gets structured within and between firms." Durand (this volume) proposes ways in which a firm's processes and routines, organizational structure, and culture affect the ability of a firm to detect, interpret, and respond to technological change. Hall (1996) investigates the important role of positive feedback loops in organizations as learning systems, noting that command-and-control management systems are essentially negative feedback systems that may severely restrict processes that are essential to creating new intangible assets.

Klavans and Deeds (1996) investigate the role of managerial responses to value-creation opportunities as a key characteristic influencing firms' choices of different modes of competence building in the dynamic conditions of the biotechnology industry. Sanchez (1996b) suggests various impediments to the acquisition of new knowledge (and thus new competences) by firms, including difficulties of managers in recognizing the value of new knowledge and of firms in using new knowledge effectively.

Sivula, van den Bosch, and Elfring (1996) investigate the interactions between a firm and its clients in a knowledge-intensive business service (e.g. consulting engineering) as a source of learning and competence building. Wallin (this volume) provides a case study that suggests ways in which relationships with customers can lead to better understanding of evolving needs and thus of useful new competences. Quelin (1996) argues that the path-dependency that constrains a firm's competence building can be overcome to some extent by using strategic alliances to acquire new knowledge and capabilities. Wright (1996b) also argues that firms as learning organizations may be systemically biased towards "intellectual codification" or "tangible integration" in their knowledge development processes.

In the Sanchez and Heene (1996a) model of the firm as a system, managers establish data gathering and interpreting processes to guide the competence leveraging and building of the firm. Van der Vorst (this volume) extends this theme by arguing that the very act of conceptualizing a competence creates cognitive "blind spots" that bias a firm's subsequent competence building and leveraging activities. Blind spots result when managers' conceptualizations of a firm's competence lead to patterns in a firm's monitoring of its environment that narrow the range of new directions for competence building a firm is likely to discover. He draws on systems theory to propose a preliminary methodology for enhancing cognitive variety to avoid major blind spots in managerial cognition—and thereby to improve the strategic flexibility of the firm.

Stein (this volume) develops a socio-cognitive framework to investigate coordination mechanisms for competence building and leveraging. He studies ways in which tensions among the different managerial perceptions of strategic gaps in a network of firms can motivate changes in the beliefs shared by those firms and in their social representations (such as rules and routines). Stein argues that this tension is important in achieving the "'creative destruction' of established competences" within networks by promoting questioning of established management practices and strategic logics in networked firms. Three case studies of Swedish networks of firms suggest the usefulness of this framework for understanding competence-building processes involving interactions among several firms.

HOLISM IN MANAGING COMPETENCES

The need for concepts and measures of firm performance beyond financial returns and profitability has been widely discussed in the management literature (e.g. Burke and Litwin, 1992; Hitt and Ireland, 1986; Chakravarthy, 1986; Venkatraman and Ramanujian, 1986). The taxonomy of strategic goal-seeking behavior suggested by Sanchez and Thomas (1996) proposes a multidimensional perspective on firm performance that enables a more holistic conception of performance than the focus on profit maximization or rent generation often found in economic perspectives in strategy research.[1]

As firms engage in competence leveraging and competence building, each firm will generate distinctive patterns of resource flows based on its specific set of goals and its organizational processes for deploying resources. Thus, to understand competence building requires a view of firms as human–social–economic systems. Moreover, managing competence building calls for expanding management capabilities beyond those needed to manage flows of funds, materials, and goods.

---

[1]However, Sanchez and Thomas (1996) first analyze goal-seeking behavior in an economic context. They show that the concept of *firm value* in contemporary finance theory recognizes the economic value of both competence leveraging and competence building. They characterize a firm's competence-building activities as a process of investing current cash flows and new capital infusions in competences that create *real options* (Myers, 1977) to generate new cash flows in the future—which Sanchez (1993, 1995) identifies as *strategic options* to develop, produce, and market products in the future. A firm's competence-leveraging activities are then characterized as the exercise of at least some of a firm's existing strategic options created by prior competence building. Exercising strategic options produces new cash flows to fund new investments in creating new strategic options, which allows the firm to exercise new options in the future, etc. Sanchez and Thomas thus depict these interdependent processes of competence building and leveraging as a "virtuous circle" of increasing firm value driven by creating and exercising strategic options.

Successful competence building requires that managers be capable of improving flows of information, knowledge, and conjecture to and within the firm, as well as designing incentive structures that encourage desired forms of change within an organization.

Achieving coherence across the multiple processes of competence building and leveraging which a firm must perform well is the subject of Christensen and Foss's (this volume) discussion of corporate coherence. They develop a concept of dynamic corporate coherence that suggests ways in which a firm may improve its ability to explore and exploit forms of synergies across its various competences, capabilities, and assets. They propose several approaches to exploring and exploiting synergies that suggest new concepts for characterizing related diversification, the M-form corporation, and the concept of competence itself.

An exclusive focus on economic aspects of firms and exclusively quantitative representations of firm performance is described as a growing—but alienating and socially undesirable—trend by D'hanis and Perneel (this volume). To counteract this trend within firms, they propose a framework for holistic "reflection" by managers about "meaning and value" in four areas of firm activity: strategy, operations, policy, and execution. They suggest that reflection in each of these areas is characterized by different "thinking dynamics". They propose, therefore, that individuals with different "thinking profiles" may be needed in a top management team in order to achieve balanced leadership in creating well-integrated organizational processes.

SOME FUNDAMENTAL ISSUES IN STRATEGY THEORY

We now turn to some fundamental theoretical, empirical, and epistemological issues which current competence theory building is raising for the field of strategy. We suggest that several interrelated theoretical problems need to be recognized and discussed within the field, not only because these problems have significant implications for future theory building in strategy but also because they appear to be limiting the ability of current strategy theory to suggest useful principles for improving the strategic management of organizations in dynamic environments. We summarize below a number of issues surfacing in the dynamic, systemic, cognitive, and holistic perspectives of competence theory. Some of these issues are discussed in greater detail by Mahoney and Sanchez (this volume) and Mosakowski and McKelvey (this volume) and we freely incorporate into our discussion some of the issues raised and ideas put forward in their chapters.[2]

ISSUES RAISED BY A DYNAMIC PERSPECTIVE

Strategy studies organizations, their interactions, and their relative performance in competitive environments. We have suggested that the competence theory-building movement is currently much concerned with firms in *dynamic* environments, by which we refer to environments in which technologies and markets are undergoing significant change and in which this change is to some (potentially a large) extent unpredictable. It is important, therefore, to consider carefully the theoretical implications of studying firms in contexts of dynamic uncertainty. In essence, we must ask how "deeply" the uncertain change processes in dynamic environments extend into the phenomena we are studying and into their underlying structure of causal relationships. For theory building in strategy, the issue can be stated in this way: Are the organizational and competitive phenomena we are studying stable at a given level of analysis, or are new forms of phenomena (organizations and their interactions) appearing, while some familiar forms are disappearing? The answer to these questions greatly affect both the appropriateness of alternative research methodologies and the attention which should be given to uncertainty in strategy theory.

Choice of Research Methodology

Understanding the stability versus changeability of phenomena being studied is essential in selecting effective research methods for theory building. We consider the effectiveness of two methodological approaches—positivism and pragmatism[3] (Mahoney and Sanchez, this volume)—as polar examples in current strategy research.

---

[2]We also note that not all the views we express here are reflected in these chapters or shared by their authors.

[3]The "pure form" of positivist inquiry is non-teleological; it ignores any motives or goals which human or social units of analysis might have and relies strictly on what can be observed from the outside to describe, classify, and investigate phenomena of interest. The pragmatic method, on the other hand, would include investigation of phenomena (firms and industries) "from the inside" (Evered and Louis, 1982). This mode of inquiry (often used in various kinds of organization and human resources studies) views firms and industries as

Footnote continued overleaf

The positivist empirical method (used by the industrial organization strain of strategy theory, for example) describes firms and industries using currently observable characteristics of firms as seen "from the outside" (Evered and Louis, 1981). If the phenomena being addressed by strategy theory are stable over a time horizon of interest, then the positivist empirical model of theory building applied at the firm or industry level may be used to describe important categories of phenomena (e.g. types of firms and industry structures), to discover fundamental relationships among those phenomena (e.g. kinds of competitive interactions between one type of firm and others, leading to certain kinds of outcomes), and to make predictions (e.g. about outcomes of competitive interactions between different kinds of firms in the future). On the other hand, if the basic phenomena of interest are undergoing change and may even be catalysts for change, then the positivist empirical method that considers only what is currently observable "from the outside" may lead to theories that have limited ability to make predictions about future outcomes. A more pragmatic mode of inquiry that looks inside the "black box" of the firm to understand *processes* within firms—and indeed the motivations of decision makers and actors that make up firms—may be essential to recognizing evolving categories of phenomena and relationships.

Combining pragmatic inquiry from the inside and positivist inquiry from the outside may be necessary to develop theory that is more capable of predicting the appearance of new organizational forms and new kinds of interactions within and between organizations. The theory building approaches used by researchers in strategy cover the spectrum from pragmatic to positivist, but there is very little effort to connect—much less to integrate—diverse streams of research. If strategy theory is to have any ability to *anticipate* changes in firms and industries in dynamic environments, the institutions of our field will have to place more emphasis on integrating positivist and pragmatic research.

Competence theory building, which is inherently integrative in its approach, is usefully drawing on both modes of inquiry. Our sense at this time is that in dynamic environments (at the firm and industry

---

phenomena whose important characteristics for categorization may be contextually embedded and therefore may have to be discovered by researchers through close, often interactive observation within the unit of analysis. Similarly, discovering important relationships between phenomena may require inquiry into the motives and goals of people and organizations being studied. Thus, the pragmatic mode of research includes teleological inquiry into motivations and goal-seeking objectives to gain insights into important characteristics and relationships in evolving phenomena of interest.

level), positivist inquiry may be useful in understanding the *constraints* on change (i.e. the stable, difficult-to-change characteristics of firms and industries), while pragmatic inquiry may be useful in understanding the *incentives* for change (as expressed through the motives of people and the goals of organizations). Theoretical integration of these two kinds of insights may enable development of theory that illuminates change dynamics and the basic ways in which they may reshape firms and their interactions.

Role of Uncertainty in Strategy Theory

When phenomena being studied are complex and undergoing change, the discovery of evolving categories of phenomena and relationships among these phenomena may still not make possible prediction of specific future outcomes with confidence. Complexity and change in competitive environments will usually imply some residual level of uncertainty about future outcomes (Sanchez, 1993) which cannot be adequately resolved by applying available theory. In other words, the predictions of theory will be probabilistic, not deterministic (Mosakowski and McKelvey, this volume). The critical issue for strategy theory then becomes: Is available strategy theory capable of "seeing through" current manifestations of complexity and change to underlying evolutions of phenomena and relationships and of yielding insights that would suggest ways to improve the management of firms in complex, dynamic environments?

We suggest that strategy theory based on industrial organization economics and the resource-based view of the firm may be facing a critical theoretical impasse that limits their ability to offer useful principles for improving the management of firms in dynamic environments. Both strains of strategy theory are strongly influenced by the positivist[4] approach to theory and research, which we have argued are appropriate to studying stable phenomena. As a result of this positivist orientation, and perhaps because past competitive events (which are "stable" once they have happened) are amenable to positivist inquiry, these strains of strategy theory appear to be most capable of providing

---

[4]Mahoney and Sanchez (this volume) suggest that the variety of economic theory we refer to here is more properly referred to as *positivistic* rather than *positivist*, because "positivist" economic theory actually makes very strong teleological assumptions about human motives and goals—i.e. that all rational people are utility maximizers with ordered preferences for goods, thus implying both motives of continuous self-interest and clearly definable goals for consumption.

ex post explanations of industry structures and strategically important resources. In their current forms, these theoretical perspectives appear limited in their ability to make *ex ante* predictions of competitive outcomes in dynamic environments, and therefore as stand-alone theories they offer limited insights into principles for the effective strategic management of firms in dynamic environments.

We propose that three interrelated approaches in the current effort to build competence theory may lead to better insights into complex and dynamic competitive interactions, resulting in better ability to make *ex ante* predictions of competitive outcomes, and therefore in a greater potential for suggesting principles for effective strategic management in dynamic environments.

Mosakowski and McKelvey (this volume) propose an approach to overcoming the tautology problem in the resource-based approach to strategy. The tautology problem derives from a fundamental circularity in the reasoning of the resource-based view that is characterized by Porter (1991: 108) in the following way: "Successful firms are successful because they have unique resources. [Therefore] they should nurture these resources to be successful." In dynamic environments in which the resources that are strategically important may be changing as competitive environments change, it is difficult to appraise the useful-ness of theory that states that the resources that will eventually be strategically important will be rare and valuable, or of research that suggests what resources appear to have been valuable to firms in past competitive outcomes. In effect, unless *ex post* explanations are also accompanied by a rationale suggesting why events in the future will be similar in important respects to events in the past, they have no clear relevance for making *ex ante* predictions in changing competitive environments.[5] Thus, Mosakowski and McKelvey address the need to improve the ability of strategy theory to identify *ex ante competences that are likely to be valuable in the future.*

The approach of Mosakowski and McKelvey is to shift the temporal locus for assessing the strategic value of competences from the late-downstream stage of rent generation to an earlier stage which they term "intermediate outcomes". By assessing the ability of a firm's competences to create product attributes (Huang, 1993; Bogner and Thomas, 1996) that will be regarded favorably by product markets, it becomes more feasible to predict relationships between a firm's current competences and its potential for generating rents, at least in the near

---

[5]The result, in our view, is the irony of a strategy "content" theory that is incapable of *ex ante* identification of strategically important content.

future. Assessing the value of competences by reference to product market preferences also helps to identify significant differences in the current competences of different firms.

The approach used by Mosakowski and McKelvey does not, of course, wholly overcome the difficulty of making predictions in dynamic product markets. What they do show, however, is that in building strategy theory it may be important to trade a reduced time horizon for an improved ability to predict which competences will prove most valuable in the future. In effect, in dynamic environments, the chain of causality linking competences and market outcomes becomes more discernible as the temporal and causal "distance" between cause and effect is reduced. Although Mosakowski and McKelvey's approach does not solve the problem of *ex ante* identification of competences that will be most valuable in the long term, they show that analysis at the level of interactions between firm capabilities and product market preferences can lead to a rationale for making *ex ante* predictions and providing useful guidance to strategic managers over an intermediate time horizon.

The theoretical problem posed by residual uncertainty about which competences will be most valuable in the longer term is also being approached in competence theory building through the concept of strategic flexibility (Sanchez, 1993, 1995; Sanchez and Heene, 1996a). This approach recognizes that while it may be impossible to predict exactly what competences and resulting product attributes will be valued most by markets in the long term (or even in the short term when there is significant diversity among current market preferences), it may be more feasible to identify a *range* of future (or current) market preferences which are likely to be sources of value if served well by a firm's competences. Thus, this approach tries to overcome the difficulty of *ex ante* prediction in dynamic environments by proposing that a firm acquire *flexible resources* which can be used to serve a range of market preferences, as well as develop *coordination flexibility* in deploying those resources to serve a range of market preferences. In essence, this approach proposes that competences based on flexible resources and flexible coordination capabilities give firms *ex ante* a greater range of potentially advantageous responses in future competitive conditions that cannot be predicted with precision in dynamic environments (Sanchez, 1993, 1995). Thus, building strategy theory that helps to identify flexible resources and flexible coordination capabilities should lead to better *ex ante* insights into principles for improving strategic management in dynamic environments.

The third approach to addressing the uncertainty of dynamic markets in competence theory building is investigation into the processes that enable a firm both to quickly build new competences in response to environmental changes (or in response to opportunities to initiate change in the environment favorable to the firm) and at the same time to be effective in leveraging its existing competences. Because a firm's ability to change by building new competences requires a number of interrelated process capabilities that promote organizational learning, create new information flows, and design new incentive structures (Sanchez and Heene, 1996a), in dynamic environments an ability to change competences may be more important to the long-term success of a firm than its current resource endowments. Thus, competence theory's emphasis on managerial *practices* and organization *processes* constitutes, in effect, a shift to "higher-order *content* variables" that provide a direct theoretical link between a firm's current competence-building abilities and its potential to perform well in the future.

Issues Raised by a Systems Perspective

Research into the ways in which firms function as open systems (Sanchez and Heene, 1996a) is raising several theoretical and empirical issues about the direction of causal relationships, the strategic value of resources and coordination capabilities, boundary setting in theory and research, the adequacy of theory focused on variables that are necessary—but not sufficient—to explain competitive success, and the influence of inappropriate metaphors on strategic thinking.

Unidirectional versus Multidirectional Causality

Developing theory from a perspective on firms as open systems composed of interdependent elements leads to a perception that unidirectional causal relationships of the sort typically stipulated by reductionist theories may not represent the actual functioning of complex systems like firms or industries. As suggested in Figure 1.1, when the state of one system element both affects and is affected by the state of another system element, it is not possible to establish a unidirectional cause-and-effect relationship between the two variables. Consequently, in a system analysis of a firm it is unlikely that there will be elements in the firm that are clearly "means" and others which are "ends". Are assets and capabilities "means" that help achieve an "end" of cash flows, or are cash flows "means" that help achieve "ends" of building new assets and capabilities? In complex and simple systems alike,

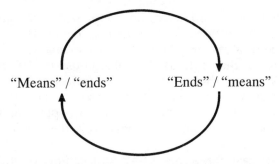

FIGURE 1.2 Multidirectional causalities and intermingling of "means" and "ends" in firms as systems

system elements are unlikely to fall neatly into unidirectional causal relationships of means and ends, as suggested in Figure 1.2.

Since all elements within a firm (and many elements outside the firm, as well) affect each other to at least some extent, the causal relationships in a firm will usually be "multidirectional", not unidirectional.[6] Thus, the use of theory and empirical methods premised on simple unidirectional, "independent variable-dependent variable", reductionist relationships may be incapable of achieving generalization, prediction, and falsification within complex systems in the usual manner of normal science. When multiple elements within a system are interdependent, developing understanding of the behavior of a given system may require dynamic modeling that explicitly recognizes the multidirectional causal relationships among elements in that system. This mode of research and its associated theory base (control theory) are not often applied in current strategy research, but may nevertheless prove to be an important avenue for building theory that more fully captures the complexities and interdependencies within firms and their competitive contexts.

Strategic Value of Resources and Coordination Capabilities

As we have mentioned earlier, a systems perspective on firms makes it clear that the potential strategic value of a resource depends on the

---

[6]Of course, the influence of one element on another may be more pronounced than vice versa under specific conditions. When system elements are linked through multiple feedback loops, however, the dynamic behavior of such a complex system may include reversals of the dominant influence relationship as conditions change.

way it is combined, coordinated, and deployed with other resources within a firm-as-a-system. The economic consequence is that the exchange value of a resource in strategic factor markets (Barney, 1986) is not likely to be the same as the value-in-use of that resource in a given firm. Whatever the exchange value (price) of a resource in the marketplace, the strategic value of that resource to a given firm will depend on the purposes to which the firm can apply the resource and the ability of the firm to coordinate effectively the use of that resource with other resources.

There are at least three interesting implications of the use-context dependency of the value of resources. First, specific forms of coordination capability are process variables which, by virtue of their differential impacts on the value which a firm can obtain from use of specific resources, are "higher-order content variables" of central importance to competence theory building. Second, the distinction between process and content variables that is often made in strategy research may be overlooking important systemic interdependencies between resources and their context and mode of use. Third, resources which can be exchanged in strategic factor markets should not be regarded as resources that cannot have strategic value. When a firm has a superior ability to identify valuable uses for and/or to more effectively coordinate resources that can be obtained in markets, the ready availability of those resources may create valuable *strategic options* for the firm that other firms do not have *and* that it would not otherwise have, given the inevitable costs of internalizing resources (Sanchez, 1993). The superior strategic options of firms that can access a wider range of market-sourced resources, moreover, can be a source of international competitive advantages for firms that can access well developed domestic markets for quality components and other inputs (Porter, 1990).

Boundary Setting

The view of the firm as an open system also makes evident many important interdependencies between firms and many other kinds of entities, such as markets, governments, associations, and communities. Awareness of the embeddedness of firms in a complex matrix of relationships suggests that setting conceptual boundaries simply at the legal boundaries of a firm may not always result in a useful unit of analysis in strategy theory and research. We suggest that as competence theory building continues, the legal construct of a "firm" as a unit of analysis in strategy research will be augmented by increasing use of more "micro" units of analysis (such as groups or processes within firms) and more "macro" units of analysis (such as networks of firms and industry-level dynamics).

Necessary but not Sufficient Conditions

The interdependencies of system elements within a firm and between firms raise questions about the adequacy of strategy theory that focuses on certain variables that appear necessary—but not *sufficient*—to explain competitive success. This tendency is reflected in the early strategy theory focus on industry structures (e.g. Porter, 1980), in the current resource-based view's preoccupation with the few unique or rare resources asserted to have the ability to generate rents (e.g. Barney, 1991), and in the desire to identify and focus management attention on "core" competences that are taken to be sources of competitive advantage (e.g. Prahalad and Hamel, 1990). Sanchez, Heene, and Thomas (1996b) have argued that one cannot really identify "core" competences before there is a well-articulated concept of competence *per se*. We add here not only that there remains a need for further development of the concept of competence before there can be a basis for identifying "core" competences, but also that the evident systemic nature of competence may make identification of "core" competences considerably more problematic than is currently recognized by much of the "core competence" literature. We expect that the notion of "core competence" may eventually yield to a recognition that achieving any form of competence requires a web of interrelated capabilities and resources, none of which, taken alone, is sufficient to explain—or, more importantly, to achieve—competitive success.

Influence of Inappropriate Metaphors on Strategic Thinking

The open-system perspective on organizations suggests that much thought in strategy may be motivated by inappropriate metaphors that inhibit understanding of the nature of competences and of the dynamics of competence-based competition. Perhaps the most common current metaphors in strategy—the characterization of the "firm" as an atomistic economic entity or as an accumulation of resources—are among the most inappropriate for understanding the embedded and dynamic nature of competences and the ways in which competences shape and are shaped by the dynamics of competition. We suggest that a more appropriate metaphor for strategic thought would suggest greater permeability, interconnectedness, and animation than suggested by the image of an atomistic firm or of a resource accumulation. Perhaps thinking of the firm as a force field (borrowed from electromagnetics), an adapting and mutating organism (borrowed from evolutionary theory), or a self-organizing system (borrowed from complexity theory) would provide more useful metaphors for strategic thought.

ISSUES RAISED BY A COGNITIVE PERSPECTIVE

We have already suggested above that dynamic and complex environments create important uncertainties which must be recognized by researchers building new strategy theory. Mahoney and Sanchez (this volume) propose that strategic managers must also try to understand competitive phenomena and their underlying relationships and therefore are, in effect, engaged in a process of strategy theory building in a specific competitive context. The uncertainties of the dynamic complexities of specific competitive contexts impose significant cognitive limits on managers which must also be recognized in strategy theory and addressed in the practice of strategic management. We also suggest that incorporating the cognitions of managers in the concept of competence is an essential step in improving our ability to distinguish superior firm performance from "luck" (Barney, 1986).

Distinguishing Performance from "Luck"

In an uncertain environment, only probabilistic explanation or prediction is possible. Since outcomes are not deterministic, there will always be some uncertainty as to the degree to which some performance outcome for a firm resulted from good (or bad) strategic management or from "luck"[7] or "stochastic factors" in the firm's environment (Mosakowski and McKelvey, this volume).

We suggest that there are two fundamentally unresolvable epistemological dilemmas when *firm* or *managerial performance* is investigated

---

[7]Barney (1986) has also argued that if a firm has relatively successful outcomes that are not due to luck, its superior performance must have resulted from possession of a resource endowment of "asymmetric information". The concept of an endowment of asymmetric information may be useful for explaining differential performance among firms from an *ex post* perspective, but it is clearly *ex ante* problematic in a dynamically uncertain environment. We suggest that this concept for explaining superior performance has limited ability to "pierce the veil of ignorance" (Rawls, 1971) which shrouds the future in uncertain environments and thus has limited (if any) ability to suggest principles for improving strategic management in such environments.

using strictly positivist theory and methodology that consider only variables that are observable "from the outside". The dilemmas arise from two essential variables that would remain unaddressed in this research approach: First, it is logically impossible for a researcher to judge the performance of a firm in achieving its goals unless the researcher first determines what *the goals of the firm* are—a process which requires at least some inquiry from the inside. (The invoking of an exogenous concept of firm performance—e.g. profitability or market share growth—is an epistemological issue we discuss further under the holistic perspective below.) Second, distinguishing good or bad management performance from good or bad luck in the firm's efforts to attain its goals is also impossible if a researcher fails to look inside the "black box" of the firm to determine the rationale or *strategic logic* followed by managers in the pursuit of those goals. If a researcher makes no effort to determine whether management had developed and was following a strategic logic for attaining firm goals, there is no logical basis for suggesting that any degree of goal attainment achieved by a firm may have resulted from management rather than from chance. Conversely, if a researcher does determine that managers did have a strategic logic for goal attainment, and if any subsequent actions that are consistent with the firm's strategic logic seem to contribute to some degree of goal attainment, then there is at least a plausible chain of causality to support an explanation of management's possible role in achieving firm goals.

This reasoning implies that in dynamically uncertain environments there is a *teleological imperative* to be addressed in any theory and research methodology that aspire to improve our ability to distinguish firm and management performance from luck. Only by looking inside the "black box" of the firm can we determine the goals of firms and establish possible (i.e. probabilistically indicated) impacts of strategic managers on goal attainment by firms.

Issues Raised by a Holistic Perspective

Sanchez and Thomas (1996) have argued for a holistic concept of firm performance that looks beyond the readily observable financial effects of a firm's current competence leveraging to recognize the multiple forms of competence-building activities that must be carried out by firms in dynamic environments. We add to their proposal some further ideas that arise from a holistic perspective on competence and competence-based competition—namely, that concepts of performance must recognize that goals are specific to each firm if the study of firm performance is to be a scientific undertaking, and that concepts of performance must also recognize the inevitable intermingling of means and ends in organizations.

Specificity of Firm Goals

Sanchez, Heene, and Thomas (1996b) have argued that firms are distinguished by their distinctive sets of goals, as well as by their individual approaches to attaining those goals. If that is so, and if science seeks to describe and understand the world as it is, and if the goal of strategy is to be *scientific* in its investigation of firm performance, then we suggest that research into firm performance that ignores the specificity and diversity of goals of firms risks departing from the methods of scientific research in investigating firm performance. For example, if a researcher frames a study of firm performance around an invoked exogenous concept of firm performance (perhaps incorporating financial or market share measures reported in a readily available "data set"), but neglects to develop parameters of performance that reflect the actual goals of the firms being investigated, there is no posited chain of causality to support development of hypotheses linking independent variables in the study to the actual goal-seeking behaviors of the firms studied. As a result, a study with such a design is incapable of explaining how different variables might be affecting the performance of firms in pursuing their distinctive sets of goals.[8]

There is thus a second basis for the teleological imperative in strategy research that we have suggested earlier. If the objective of strategy is to improve firm performance *defined as attainment of firm goals*, we propose that it is fundamental to a scientific undertaking to first determine the actual goals of firms in order to establish parameters that reflect performance in attaining firm goals. Non-teleological positivist inquiry, which stipulates both dependent and independent variables without looking inside the "black boxes" of the firms studied to ascertain firm goals, can only discover associations between variables derived from the concept of firm performance invoked by the researcher. A fundamental—but generally unaddressed—issue in

---

[8]Whatever the dependent variable(s) invoked in "performance research" framed in this mode, a rarely recognized or acknowledged source of variability in hypothesized relationships between dependent and independent variables in such studies is the extent to which the performance parameters (dependent variables) invoked by the researcher differ from the actual goals of the firms studied.

strategy research is the extent to which the performance goals based on observable financial and product market data that are commonly invoked in positivist research correspond to the actual goals of firms in different competitive contexts.

Intermingling of "Means" and "Ends"

When a firm is viewed both systemically and holistically, not only do causal effects flow in multiple directions among interdependent elements (as discussed under the systemic perspective) but distinctions between ends and means may be impossible to determine purely from analysis of variables observable "from the outside". Which system elements are regarded as ends (i.e. goals) within an organization may only be discovered through inquiry "from the inside"—hence, another reason for the teleological imperative in strategy research.

Whether a system element is regarded as a means or an end within an organization may vary with the different perspectives of the people and entities who make up the firm as a system. To a manager, research and development to develop better products may be viewed as a means to achieve an end of improved financial performance, while to a product development engineer, improved financial performance may be seen as a means to an end of developing interesting new technology to use in new products. Thus, in actual organizations means and ends are often intermingled, so that system elements can be seen simultaneously as means and ends by different actors within the system.

A fundamental challenge to strategy researchers and strategic managers alike in building competence theory is therefore increasing our understanding of how to achieve *organizational coherence* that brings all the elements of a firm as a system into alignment to create strategic goals and means that will be supported throughout the firm (cf. Christensen and Foss, this volume). We suggest that creating greater organizational coherence will require development of principles for integrating work designs and incentive structures such that the *means* by which a firm intends to accomplish overall strategic goals are perceived as attractive *ends* by each provider of resources required by the firm as a system. Thus, in both competence theory and practice, understanding how to align and enlarge transactions benefits (Zajac and Olsen, 1993) within and between firms will be as essential as recognizing and managing transactions risks (Williamson, 1991) in gaining greater insights into principles for effective organization design.

FURTHER ISSUES IN COMPETENCE RESEARCH AND PRACTICE

As we have noted earlier, competence theory building is making plain the need for *theory in strategy* that recognizes more fully the realities faced by managers and organizations in the *practice of strategic management*. Mahoney and Sanchez (this volume) suggest that strategy as an academic field appears to have accepted the institutionalization of dissociated theories of strategy—e.g. theories focused exclusively on economic, on cognitive, or on other single aspects of firms. They suggest that academic strategy's acceptance of (and we would add, its apparent enthusiasm for) dissociated strategy theory and research has caused strategy theory to become disconnected from the actual decision making, resource deploying, capability building, knowledge creating, and other critical processes of firms. They further suggest that the movement to build competence theory that will integrate previously dissociated theoretical perspectives amounts to an opportunity—and a necessity—to reconnect strategy theory to the realities of strategy practice.

Mahoney and Sanchez suggest that reconnecting strategy research and strategy practice will necessitate integration of more research "from the inside" of firms with the positivist empirical mode of research "from the outside" (Evered and Louis, 1981) that now dominates the field of strategy. They propose a new model of strategy research "from the inside" that joins researchers and managers in a process of double-loop learning: researchers interested in building generalizable theories of strategy interact with managers who must apply strategy theories in specific competitive contexts. The experiences of strategic managers in specific competitive contexts can help inform the intuitions and articulate the generalized theory of researchers, while researchers can help managers become aware of emerging strategy theory and assess the implications of new theory for specific competitive contexts. Mahoney and Sanchez propose that this double-loop learning approach to building strategy theory can help reconnect strategy theory with the realities faced by strategic managers in dynamic environments.

CONCLUSION: DIRECTIONS FOR FURTHER COMPETENCE RESEARCH

The current state of theory in competence-based competition suggests several directions for further theory development and refinement. We note below five directions which seem particularly important to advancing competence theory, research, and practice.

STRATEGIC LEARNING AND KNOWLEDGE MANAGEMENT

Effective creation and management of knowledge (Nonaka and Takeuchi, 1995; Sanchez and Heene, 1996c) is a foundation of competence building and leveraging. Improving our understanding of organizational learning and ways of managing knowledge is therefore essential to advancing our understanding of building and leveraging organizational competence. A well-defined vocabulary is the toolkit of conceptual analysis. Our available vocabulary for classifying and analyzing learning and knowledge is strikingly limited and as a result currently provides us very blunt instruments ill-suited to the subtleties of the task. Efforts to develop concepts and vocabulary for studying learning and knowledge and their roles in organizational competence are now beginning (e.g. Boisot, 1995; Boisot, Griffiths, and Moles, 1996; Sanchez, 1996b; Wright, 1996a,b), but these are only first steps along what is sure to become a major avenue of strategy research.

COORDINATION

We know relatively little about the workings of coordination mechanisms within and between firms. As a result, we have little basis for imagining what kinds of new coordination mechanisms may become available to firms as information and telecommunications technologies continue their rapid evolutions. We need both better defined concepts of *coordination* and a more developed vocabulary for describing kinds of coordination mechanisms. We need much better insights into how coordination processes work within and between organizations and how competitive environments are or could be affected by new kinds of coordination capabilities (Sanchez, 1995). Also, we need to understand if processes for coordinating competence building differ in some fundamental ways from processes for coordinating competence leveraging, and if so, how they can be reconciled within firms.

We suggest that while commitment to and control of specific assets may play central roles in theories of strategy appropriate for stable technological and market contexts, coordination capability will play a fundamental role in competence-based strategy theory for dynamic contexts (Sanchez, 1995, 1996a). As we have suggested earlier, organizational process capabilities appear to be the "higher-order content variables" needed to classify firms and build strategy theory in dynamic environments.

MANAGERIAL AND ORGANIZATIONAL COGNITION

We now have, at best, only a rudimentary understanding of the ways in which managerial cognitions are formed and modified over time. We need to investigate the potential contributions of research in cognition and in social representation to our efforts to understand how managers perceive both opportunities to build new competences and necessities for retiring existing competences.

GOVERNANCE MECHANISMS IN FIRMS AS OPEN SYSTEMS

As we have suggested earlier (Sanchez, Heene, and Thomas 1996b), we still need a much better understanding of the governance mechanisms that might provide structures for guiding the dynamics of open systems (or networks) of firms in competence-based competition. Given the uncertainties of dynamic environments, we must try to understand what norms govern exchanges of firm-addressable resources when the potential strategic value of exchanged resources cannot be assessed with a high level of confidence. How do firms go about evaluating and linking their respective assets and capabilities in efforts to build new competences in dynamic environments?

A SHARED VOCABULARY FOR CONTINUING THE CONVERSATION

If the work on competence being carried on by a growing number of people is to continue as a true conversation (Mahoney and Pandian, 1992) rather than deteriorating into a cacophony of idiosyncratic language and conceptual frameworks, we must continue the effort started in Sanchez, Heene, and Thomas (1996b) to develop a well-defined, conceptually grounded vocabulary of competence and competence-based competition. Careful attention to defining carefully what each writer means by *competence* and related terms is essential to continued development of concepts which will underpin a theory of competence. While many researchers will no doubt want to propose useful variations or modifications to the concepts and definitions suggested by Sanchez, Heene, and Thomas, relating proposals to a common set of concepts and definitions can provide a vehicle for realizing the ways in which new ideas about competence might differ from and eventually connect with each other. The need for an established vocabulary that can be shared by researchers will become increasingly acute as additional theoretical perspectives are brought into the effort to fashion a dynamic, systemic, cognitive, and holistic theory of competence for strategic management.

ACKNOWLEDGEMENTS

The authors would like to acknowledge their indebtedness to Joseph T. Mahoney, Bill McKelvey, and Elaine Mosakowski for extended discussions of several of the issues addressed in this chapter. While the views we present do not necessarily correspond to those of our colleagues on all points, our own thinking about the issues we raise here has greatly benefited from our discussions with them.

REFERENCES

Barney, J. (1986). Strategic factor markets: expectations, luck, and business strategy. *Management Science*, **32**, 1231–41.

Barney, J. (1991). Firm resources and sustained competitive advantage. *Journal of Management*, **17**, 99–120.

Bogner, W.C. and Thomas, H. (1996). From skills to competences: The "play-out" of resource bundles across firms. In Sanchez, R., Heene, A., and Thomas, H. (eds), *Dynamics of Competence-Based Competition: Theory and Practice in the New Strategic Management*. Oxford: Elsevier.

Boisot, M.H. (1995). *The Information Space* London: Routledge.

Boisot, M. Griffiths, D., and Moles, V. (1996). The dilemma of competence: differentiation *versus* integration in the pursuit of learning. In Sanchez, R. and Heene, A. (eds), *Strategic Learning and Knowledge Management*. Chichester: John Wiley.

Burke, W. W. and Litwin G.H. (1992). A causal model of organizational performance and change. *Journal of Management*, **18**(3), 523–45.

Chakravarthy, B.S. (1986). Measuring strategic performance. *Strategic Management Journal*, **7**, 437–58.

Dierickx, I. and Cool, K. (1989). Asset stock accumulation and sustainability of competitive advantage. *Management Science*, **35**, 1504–11.

Easton, G. and Araujo, L. (1996). Characterizing organizational competences: Combining resource base and industrial networks approaches. In Sanchez, R., Heene, A., and Thomas, H. (eds), *Dynamics of Competence-Based Competition: Theory and Practice in the New Strategic Management*. Oxford: Elsevier.

Elfring, T. and Baven, G. (1996). Spinning-off capabilities: Competence development in knowledge-intensive services. In Sanchez, R., Heene, A., and Thomas. H. (eds), *Dynamics of Competence-Based Competition: Theory and Practice in the New Strategic Management* Oxford: Elsevier.

Evered, R. and Louis, M.R. (1981). Alternative perspectives in the organizational sciences "Inquiry from the inside" and inquiry from the outside. *Academy of Management Review*, **6**(3), 385–95.

Gorman, P. Thomas, H., and Sanchez, R. (1996). Industry dynamics in competence-based competition. In Sanchez, R., Heene, A., and Thomas, H. (eds), *Dynamics of Competence-Based Competition: Theory and Practice in the New Strategic Management*. Oxford: Elsevier.

Hall, R. (1996). Complex systems, complex learning, and competence building. In Sanchez, R. and Heene, A. (eds), *Strategic Learning and Knowledge Management*, Chichester: John Wiley.

Hamel, G. (1989). Strategic intent. *Harvard Business Review*, **67**, 63–76.

Hamel, G. (1994). The concept of core competence. In Hamel, G. and Heene, A. (eds), *Competence-Based Competition*. Chichester: John Wiley.

Hamel, G. and Heene, A. (eds) (1994), *Competence-Based Competition*. New York: John Wiley.

Hitt, M.A., and Ireland, R.D. (1986), Relationships among corporate level distinctive competencies, diversification strategy, corporate structure, and performance. *Journal of Management Studies*, **23**(4).

Huang, K.S.H. (1993). *Integrating Vertical and Horizontal Dimensions in a Spatial Framework of Strategic Product Competition: An application to the U.S. photocopier industry*. PhD dissertation (Business Economics), Harvard University, Cambridge, MA 02138, USA.

Jensen, O. (1996). Competence development by small firms in a vertically-constrained industry structure. In Sanchez, R., Heene, A., and Thomas, H. (eds), *Dynamics of Competence-Based Competition: Theory and Practice in the New Strategic Management*. Oxford: Elsevier.

Klavans, R. and Deeds, D.L. (1996). Competence building in biotechnology start-ups: The role of scientific discovery, technical development, and absorptive capacity. In Sanchez, R. and Heene, A. (eds), *Strategic Learning and Knowledge Management*. Chichester: John Wiley.

Lang, J.W. (1996). Leveraging knowledge across firm boundaries: Achieving strategic flexibility through modularisation and alliances. In Sanchez, R. and Heene, A. (eds), *Strategic Learning and Knowledge Management*. Chichester: John Wiley.

Lewis, M.A. and Gregory, M.J. (1996). Developing and applying a process approach to competence analysis. In Sanchez, R., Heene, A., and Thomas, H. (eds), *Dynamics of Competence-Based Competition: Theory and Practice in the New Strategic Management*. Oxford: Elsevier.

Lowendahl, B. and Haanes, K. (1996). The unit of activity: A new way to understand competence building and leveraging. In Sanchez, R. and Heene, A. (eds), *Strategic Learning and Knowledge Management*. Chichester: John Wiley.

Mahoney, J.T. and Pandian, J.R. (1992). The resource-based view within the conversation of strategic management. *Strategic Management Journal*, **13**(5), 363–80.

Myers, S.C. (1977). Determinants of corporate borrowing. *Journal of Financial Economics*, **5**, 147–75.

Nonaka, I. and Takeuchi, H. (1995). *The Knowledge-Creating Company*. Oxford: Oxford University Press.

Porter, M. (1980). *Competitive Strategy*. New York: Free Press.

Porter, M. (1990). *The Competitive Advantage of Nations*. New York: Free Press.

Porter, M. (1991). Towards a dynamic theory of strategy. *Strategic Management Journal*, **12**, 95–117.

Post, H.A. (1996). Modularity in product design, development, and organization: A case study of the Baan Company. In Sanchez, R. and Heene, A. (eds) *Strategic Learning and Knowledge Management*. Chichester: John Wiley.

Prahalad, C.K. and Hamel G. (1990). The core competencies of the corporation. *Harvard Business Review*, **68** (3), 79–93.

Prahalad, C.K. and Hamel, G. (1993). Strategy as stretch and leverage. *Harvard Business Review*, March-April.

Prahalad, C.K. and Hamel, G. (1995). *Competing for the Future*. Boston, MA: Harvard Business School Press.

Quélin, B. (1996). Appropriability and the creation of new capabilities through strategic alliances. In Sanchez, R. and Heene, A. (eds,) *Strategic Learning and Knowledge Management*. Chichester: John Wiley.

Rawls, J. (1971). *A Theory of Justice*. Cambridge, MA: Harvard University Press.

Rispoli, M. (1996). Competitive analysis and competence-based strategies in the hotel industry. In Sanchez, R., Heene, A. and Thomas, H. (eds) *Dynamics of Competence-Based Competition: Theory and Practice in the New Strategic Management*. Oxford: Elsevier.

Roehl, T. (1996). The role of international R&D in the competence-building strategies of Japanese pharmaceutical firms. In Sanchez, R., Heene, A. and Thomas, H. (eds), *Dynamics of Competence-Based Competition: Theory and Practice in the New Strategic Management*. Oxford: Elsevier.

Rumelt, R.P. (1994). Foreword. In Hamel, G. and Heene, A. (eds), *Competence-Based Competition*. New York: John Wiley.

Sanchez, R. (1993). Strategic flexibility, firm organization, and managerial work in dynamic markets: A strategic options perspective. *Advances in Strategic Management*, **9**, 251–91.

Sanchez, R. (1995). Strategic flexibility in product competition, *Strategic Management Journal*, **16** (Summer), 135–59.

Sanchez, R. (1996a). Strategic product creation: Managing new interactions of technology, markets, and organizations. *European Management Journal*, **14** (2).

Sanchez, R. (1996b). Managing articulated knowledge in competence-based competition. In Sanchez, R. and Heene, A. (eds) *Strategic Learning and Knowledge Management*. Chichester: John Wiley.

Sanchez, R. (1996c). Quick-connect technologies for product creation: Implications for competence-based competition. In Sanchez, R., Heene, A., and Thomas, H. (eds), *Dynamics of Competence-Based Competition: Theory and Practice in the New Strategic Management*. Oxford: Elsevier.

Sanchez, R. and Heene, A. (1996a). A systems view of the firm in competence-based competition. In Sanchez, R., Heene, A. and Thomas, H. (eds), *Dynamics of Competence-Based Competition: Theory and Practice in the New Strategic Management*. Oxford: Elsevier.

Sanchez, R. and Heene, A. (1996b). A competence perspective on strategic learning and knowledge management. In Sanchez, R. and Heene, A. (eds) *Strategic Learning and Knowledge Management*. Chichester: John Wiley.

Sanchez, R. and Heene, A. (eds) (1996c). *Strategic Learning and Knowledge Management*. Chichester: John Wiley.

Sanchez, R. Heene, A., and Thomas H. (eds) (1996a) *Dynamics of Competence-Based Competition: Theory and Practice in the New Strategic Management*. Oxford: Elsevier.

Sanchez, R. Heene, A., and Thomas H. (1996b). Towards the theory and practice of competence-based competition. In Sanchez, R., Heene, A., and Thomas, H. (eds) *Dynamics of Competence-Based Competition: Theory and Practice in the New Strategic Management*. Oxford: Elsevier.

Sanchez, R. and Thomas, H. (1996). Strategic goals In Sanchez, R., Heene, A., and Thomas, H. (eds) *Dynamics of Competence-Based Competition: Theory and Practice in the New Strategic Management*. Oxford: Elsevier.

Sivula, P., van den Bosch, F.A.J. and Elfring, T. (1996). Competence building by incorporating clients into the development of a business service firm's knowledge base. In Sanchez, R. and Heene, A. (eds) *Strategic Learning and Knowledge Management*. Chichester: John Wiley.

Tallman, S. and Atchison, D.L. (1996). Competence-based competition and the evolution of strategic groups. In Sanchez, R., Heene, A., and Thomas, H. (eds) *Dynamics of Competence-Based Competition: Theory and Practice in the New Strategic Management*. Oxford: Elsevier.

Venkatraman, N. and Ramanujian, V. (1986). Measurement of business performance in strategy research: A comparison of approaches. *Academy of Management Review*, **11**(4), 801–14.

Volberda, H.W. (1996). Flexible configuration strategies within Philips Semiconductors: A strategic process of entrepreneurial revitalization. In Sanchez, R., Heene, A. and Thomas, H. (eds), *Dynamics of Competence-Based Competition: Theory and Practice in the New Strategic Management*. Oxford: Elsevier.

Williamson, O.E. (1991). Strategizing, economizing, and economic organization. *Strategic Management Journal*, **12** (winter special issue), 75–94.

Winterscheid, B. and McNabb, S. (1996). From national to global product development competence in the telecommunications industry: Structure and process in leveraging competences. In Sanchez, R., Heene, A., and Thomas, H. (eds) *Dynamics of Competence-Based Competition: Theory and Practice in the New Strategic Management*. Oxford: Elsevier.

Wright, R.W. (1996a). The role of imitable vs. inimitable competences in the evolution of the semiconductor industry. In Sanchez, R., Heene, A., and Thomas, H. (eds) *Dynamics of Competence-Based Competition: Theory and Practice in the New Strategic Management*. Oxford: Elsevier.

Wright, R.W. (1996b). Tangible integration versus intellectual codification skills: A comparison of learning processes in developing logic and memory semiconductors. In Sanchez, R. and Heene, A. (eds) *Strategic Learning and Knowledge Management*. Chichester: John Wiley.

Zajac, E.J. and Olsen, C.P. (1993). From transactions cost to transactional value analysis: Implications for the study of interorganizational strategies. *Journal of Management Studies*, **30**(1), 131–45.

2

Competence Theory Building: Reconnecting Management Research and Management Practice

JOSEPH T. MAHONEY, RON SANCHEZ

This chapter suggests that an essential task in building a competence-based theory of strategy is to integrate previously unconnected theories singularly focused on the *economic content* or the *cognitive processes* of strategy making. We discuss the integration of such *dissociative theories* at three levels: (1) the strategy making and testing processes of managers competing in specific contexts; (2) the theory building and testing processes of researchers looking for insights that are generalizable across competitive contexts; and (3) the interactions between managers and researchers in building a general theory of competence that also works in specific contexts. To accomplish these ends, we suggest that strategy researchers and managers should be engaged in an interactive, reciprocating process in building competence theory. We propose that researchers and managers embark on a new theory-building process in which the generalized theories of researchers and

Competence-based Strategic Management.
Edited by Aimé Heene and Ron Sanchez.
Copyright © 1997 John Wiley & Sons Ltd.

the contextual theories of managers may evolve in a dynamic of double-loop learning.

INTRODUCTION

Both managers as practitioners of strategy and academics as builders and testers of strategy theory have a mission of pragmatic inquiry—i.e. a shared objective to develop theory that "works"[1] to improve the performance of organizations. The ostensible differences in the theory-building missions of practitioners and researchers arise from differences in the emphasis which each group of strategists places on discovering theory of specific versus general applicability. Strategy practitioners' efforts to find ways of competing successfully in their competitive environments are, in essence, efforts to develop strategy theories that work in a specific competitive context. Strategy researchers, on the other hand, are typically interested in developing strategy theories that work in general categories of competitive contexts or generally in all observed contexts.

In pursuit of their respective objectives in building strategy theory that works, both groups of strategists now face a challenge of reconceptualizing the meaning of strategy in the dynamic context of competence-based competition. Competence theory proposes that achieving economic success in competitive markets requires imaginative direction and effective coordination of knowledge and capabilities, all of which ultimately arise from human cognitive processes (Sanchez, Heene, and Thomas, 1996). Accordingly, this chapter suggests that an essential task in building a competence-based theory of strategy is to integrate previously unconnected theories singularly focused on the *economic content* or the *cognitive processes* of strategy making. Borrowing the concept of *dissociation* from behavioral psychology,[2] we characterize theories that focus only on the economic or only on the cognitive aspects of strategy as *dissociative theories* which must be integrated to gain new insights into the nature and processes of competence in a dynamic context.

The process of building a competence theory should aim to integrate economic and cognitive concerns at three "levels": (1) the strategy

---

[1]We adopt here the view that a strategy theory that "works" is one that helps a firm achieve its goals, which are likely to include multiple interrelated objectives beyond that of simply maximizing current profits (Sanchez and Thomas, 1996).
[2]*Dissociation* is defined as "the separation of an idea or activity from the mainstream of consciousness or of behavior" (*Webster's New Collegiate Dictionary*, 1981: 328).

making and testing processes of managers competing in specific contexts; (2) the theory building and testing processes of researchers looking for insights that are generalizable across competitive contexts; and (3) the interactions between managers and researchers in building a general theory of competence that also works in specific contexts.

This chapter develops these ideas in the following way. The next section discusses dissociative patterns of thought. It suggests that certain kinds of insights may result from dissociative thinking about complex phenomena, but that realizing the benefits of those insights in the contexts of real organizations requires integration of the multiple insights arising from dissociative modes of inquiry. We also suggest that integration of dissociative ideas may require a shift in the focus of much current theory building in strategy.

The third section addresses the importance of overcoming dissociative thinking in strategy theory building at the firm level—i.e. strategy making by managers. Problems of organizational dysfunction that result when strategy practitioners engage in dissociative thinking suggest that integrating economic objectives and cognitive processes is also essential to devising effective strategies for a firm in a specific competitive context.

The fourth section suggests that strategy researchers interested in building a theory of competence-based competition face fundamentally the same problem of integrating economic and cognitive concerns faced by managers. As Huff (1981: 83) notes: ". . . the limitations of scientific inquiry as normally practiced are not different in kind from the limitations of everyone's normal attempts to make sense of the world." Just as managers must devise strategy theories that integrate strategy formulation and implementation in meeting the "market test for competence" in a specific context (Sanchez, Heene and Thomas, 1996), strategy researchers must develop an integrative competence theory that meets a "market test" of having at least some degree of applicability across competitive contexts.

The fifth section suggests that the goals of managers to develop integrative strategy theories in specific contexts and the goals of strategy researchers to develop integrative strategy theories that have general applicability should be pursued in a much more interactive manner than has typically been the case in the past. In the quest for broadly generalizable results, strategy researchers have often paid inadequate attention to concepts employed by managers to achieve integration of economic and cognitive concerns in specific competitive contexts. We suggest, therefore, that research to develop a theory of competence-based strategy should not emulate the prevailing model of strategy research, in which researchers typically propose "espoused theories" of management that are dissociated from the "theories-in-use" of managers.[3] Rather, researchers and managers should be engaged in an interactive, reciprocating process of theory building.

We propose that interactive processes linking researchers and managers in building an integrative theory of competence-based strategy may be carried out as a knowledge-creation process in which the generalized theories of researchers and the contextual theories of managers evolve in a dynamic of double-loop learning (Argyris and Schön, 1978). This interactive double-loop learning process can benefit competence theory researchers by providing them with a contextually rich set of managers' insights to support an inferential process of grounded theory building "from the inside out", while managers may benefit from researchers' generalized insights that can be adapted and applied "from the outside in" in existing or new competitive situations.[4] If competence theory building is approached in this interactive mode, competence theory may be able to achieve an integration of the product and process of thought (Simon 1982) that has thus far eluded dissociative strategy theories.

The final section provides conclusions and recommendations.

DISSOCIATIVE PATTERNS OF THOUGHT

As humans confronting the dynamic complexity of the "real world", the limited ability of researchers and managers alike to fully comprehend the world as it is becomes evident. Confronted with complex phenomena, the human mind resorts to a set of basic dissociative cognitive techniques[5] in an effort to "make sense" of what is being observed. Some fundamental sense-making techniques are

---

[3]Argyris and Schön (1978) use the terms "espoused theories" and "theories in use" in the context of a single firm. We apply their terms in the broader context of strategy researchers who propose general "espoused theories" that are dissociated from the specific "theories in use" of managers.

[4]The term *grounded theory building* was introduced by Glaser and Strauss (1967). The concepts of theory building "from the inside out" and "from the outside in" allude to Evered and Louis' (1981) concepts of "inquiry from the inside" and "inquiry from the outside" in organizational sciences.

[5]We are referring here to cognitive techniques or patterns of thought which are intentionally invoked by the thinker in a process of sense-making. When these techniques are used intendedly to begin analysis of complex situations, they differ from cognitive heuristics and biases (Hogarth, 1987; Kahneman, Slovic, and Tversky, 1982) that unconsciously and thus unintendedly influence cognitive processes.

1. Analyzing dynamically interrelated phenomena as if their inter-relationships are invariant over time (static or comparative statics analysis)
2. Reducing a continuum of possibilities to extreme polar cases or to a limited set of polar and intermediate cases
3. Analyzing phenomena ostensibly subject to multiple influences as if they were subject to a single influence or a limited set of influences.

These and related techniques may lead to important insights into—or *theories* about—the nature of phenomena of interest and their interrelationships under the relevant simplifying assumptions (static analysis, polar cases, single source of influence). Of course, insights into causal relationships derived from such dissociative theoretical analysis are not universally "true"; they only suggest *possible tendencies* in phenomena in a real-world setting that is actually dynamic, continuous, and subject to multiple influences. The ability of a dissociative theory to explain or predict actual behaviors in the "real world" has to be tested in various contexts in order to determine how reliable or powerful its derived insights really are in practice. Testing the explanations or predictions of dissociative theory may lead not only to refinement of the original insights suggested by purely theoretical analysis, but also to better understanding of how the influences predicted by multiple dissociative theories may actually be interacting in the observable world. Thus, the findings of various dissociative theories may provide a basis for developing a more integrated theoretical understanding that explains or predicts actual phenomena better than any single dissociative theory.

In trying to develop insights into the strategic management of organizations in competence-based competition, the gains to be had from developing an integrative strategy theory appear to be as great in magnitude as the strategic hazards which may result from relying on insights from a single dissociative theoretical perspective. In particular, this chapter focuses on the desirability—indeed, the *necessity* for competence theory—of integrating two patterns of dissociative thinking that have become endemic in strategy theorizing: an exclusive focus on (1) the *economic content* of strategy formulation *or* (2) the *cognitive processes*[6] of strategy implementation.

The dichotomization of thinking about strategy formulation and

---

[6]We use the expression *cognitive processes* broadly to include not just individual psychological processes but also organizational social processes that may affect both individual and organizational cognitive processes.

implementation is a problem that is not unfamiliar to strategic management researchers. At the 1979 Pittsburgh conference which marked the founding of the Strategic Management Society (Schendel and Hofer, 1979), for example, the lines were already being drawn between researchers in the "strategy (formulation) content" camp and those in the "strategy (implementation) process" camp. The separation between these dissociated perspectives became entrenched in strategy research and practice during the 1980s and into the 1990s.

One—though certainly not the only—motive for the separation of content and process in theory building in strategic management may have been the desire of many early strategy researchers to make a "science" of strategic management. Much early strategy research reflected (implicitly or explicitly) a key presumption of positivistic economics,[7] which had gained substantial institutional visibility and influence in the economics discipline and in US business schools in the 1960s and 1970s: that the psychological processes of decision makers and other people in a firm were irrelevant for the purposes of scientific investigation of economic activity. A mode of strategy theorizing about firms arose which emulated the strongly dissociative theorizing of positivistic economics. Deductive reasoning from the first principles of economic theory (in which the actual cognitive processes of humans were assumed to be irrelevant) was taken to be sufficient for the prediction of firm behaviors, thereby eliminating the need to gather from empirical observation any particulars about actual managerial decision making and other organizational processes inside firms.

Simon (1957, 1982) was perhaps the most vocal early critic of this positivistic viewpoint in economics. Through his research into organizational decision making (Simon, 1947) and human cognitive processes (Simon, 1989), he suggested an alternative approach to management science based on the principle of *bounded rationality*:

> The capacity of the human mind for formulating and solving complex problems is very small compared with the size of the problems whose solution is required for objectively rational behavior in the real world—or even for a reasonable approximation to such objective rationality (Simon, 1957: 198).

---

[7]We use the term *positivistic* here instead of *positivist* advisedly. A truly positivist science is non-teleological–that is, it makes no assumptions about or attention to the motives or goals of the subjects of study. The movement in economics which we refer to here as *positivistic* is not truly positivist because it actually makes very strong assumptions about human motives and goals: that all [rational] people are *utility maximizers*, where utility derives from an ordering of *preferences* for goods (Pearce, 1992: 445). In effect, positivistic economics assumes both a *motive* of constant attention to self-interest (utility maximization) and *goals* for consumption (expressed through preferences for goods).

Through the concept of bounded rationality, Simon (1957) sought to integrate the dissociative theory of economics, which was focused on predicting firm behaviors (the content of a formulated strategy) solely on the basis of variables observable outside a firm, and theories of organizational action grounded in the cognitive and decision-making limitations of people within firms (the actual processes of strategy formulation and implementation).

Simon's (1982) efforts to offer an alternative to the dissociative theorizing of positivistic economics is relevant to efforts to develop a theory of competence, which recognizes both that organizations must perform well to survive in a complex competitive environment and that managers and researchers alike have significant cognitive limitations in comprehending and responding to complexity. In this regard, it is useful to recall Simon's (1976) further distinction between *substantive rationality* and *procedural rationality*. Substantive rationality is the rationality of the economist; it identifies the economic *ends* that perfectly rational managers with perfect information[8] would pursue in a well-defined environmental context. Procedural rationality is the rationality of decision makers in actual organizations; it reflects the limited *means* or procedures which humans employ in an effort to make decisions in a complex, poorly defined, and changing environment where information is always imperfect and incomplete. The dilemma of strategic management to be addressed by competence theory, then, is that market pressures push managers to attain the economic ends (profitability, growth) demanded by a substantive rationality, while managers must try to attain those ends with the means of a procedural rationality that is always limited and imperfect relative to the challenges posed by a dynamic competitive environment.

In a fundamental sense, the emerging research agenda of competence theory building may be thought of as an opportunity to overcome dissociative thinking in strategy by integrating the economic ends of substantive rationality with the cognitive means of procedural rationality. To borrow once again from Simon (1982), the rationality required in strategic management must reflect both the *product* (economic content) and *process* (cognitive processes) of thought. The remainder of this chapter suggests how an integration of the product of substantive rationality and the processes of procedural rationality may be achieved in building a competence theory. Figure 2.1 compares some of the disso-

---

[8]In recent years the economic model of substantive rationality has been extended to include the case of asymmetric information in principal–agent models of the firm (e.g. Eisenhardt, 1989; Jensen and Meckling, 1976).

Dichotomies in current strategy theory	Desired integration in competence theory
Positivistic economics versus human cognition	Economic objectives and cognitive processes
Substantive rationality versus procedural rationality	Bounded rationality (substantive rationality constrained by procedural rationality)
Strategy content versus strategy process	Strategy content defined by processes (*i.e.* by capabilities in action)
Strategy formulation versus implementation	Formulation integrated with implementation

FIGURE 2.1   Dissociative patterns of thought to be integrated in competence theory

ciative patterns of thought characteristic of current strategy theories to the integrations of theory to be sought in building a theory of competence-based competition.

MANAGERS' NEED FOR STRATEGIC INTEGRATION

A firm may be viewed as an open system (Sanchez and Heene, 1996) that tries to attain a distinct set of goals (Sanchez and Thomas, 1996) in a complex, dynamic competitive environment. The efforts of the firm to attain its goals are guided by a strategic logic (Sanchez, Heene, and Thomas, 1996) which is a rationale (either explicit or implicit) as to how the development and deployment of specific assets and capabilities will help the firm attain its goals in a given competitive context. The current strategic logic of a firm may be thought of as the current theory of the firm's decision makers as to how they can best achieve the goals of the firm in its competitive context. The strategic logic of managers must meet the market test for competence by continuously bringing forth product offerings that satisfy customer needs better than the product offerings of competing firms. Thus, the strategy theories of managers about how to compete in a specific context must be constantly tested, refined, and in some cases redefined to remain or become competitive in the marketplace. This aspect of managers' strategy theory building and testing is suggested by the feedback loop shown in Figure 2.2.

For managers engaged in the continuous process of theory building and testing suggested in Figure 2.2, the problem of theoretical integration often manifests itself in the search for practical ways to devise and

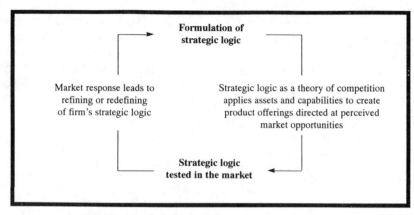

FIGURE 2.2   Contextual strategy theories of managers face the market test for competence

manage human processes that are cognitively limited and thus only procedurally rational, but that nonetheless appear capable of achieving strategic goals that have often been formulated in substantively rational economic terms such as profit growth and return on investment. Managers engaged in this search are, in effect, engaged in an ongoing process of trying to integrate dissociative theories of process and content in ways that will enable them to compete successfully in a specific competitive environment. Moreover, the integrative strategy theories of managers are then continuously tested in the marketplace.

In the same way that strategy researchers may lapse into dissociative thinking in their "ivory towers" in academia (Mintzberg, 1994), however, top managers of companies may become dissociated from the actual processes of their firms and product markets, especially when they perceive strong pressures from shareholders for continuous improvements in current financial returns. Top managers who become dissociated from their firms and markets may begin to treat strategic management as simply a job of defining the economic performance goals of a firm and of exercising "discipline" to make sure that lower level managers attain those goals. Top managers with this conception of strategic management typically give little or no attention to the challenge of developing and deploying the assets and capabilities needed to attain those goals.[9]

---

[9]"Managing by the numbers" is an expression that refers to a conception of strategic management in which top managers intentionally dissociate themselves from processes of the firms they are managing and focus exclusively on setting and enforcing goals for economic performance. For an exemplar of this conception of strategic management, see *Managing* by Harold Geneen (1984), former chairman of ITT.

Even when top management becomes involved in product market issues, a strategic management team with a "top-down" management style may develop its own "ivory tower" approach to strategy making that is unconnected to the competitive realities facing the firm at the business unit and functional levels of the organization. Hill and Jones (1995: 16) provide the following example:

> ... [W]hen demographic data indicated that houses and families were shrinking, planners at General Electric's appliance group concluded that smaller appliances were the wave of the future. Because the planners had little contact with home builders and retailers, they did not realize that kitchens and bathrooms were the two rooms that were not shrinking. Nor did they appreciate that working women wanted big refrigerators to cut down on trips to the supermarket. The result was that General Electric wasted a lot of time designing small appliances for which there was only limited demand.

GE's formulation of a strategy that was unconnected to observable market trends may have resulted from a simple lack of communication between marketing staff and strategic decision makers. Incidents of this kind, however, may also be symptomatic of strategic decision making by managers whose strategy theories have become dissociated from the market or internal processes of the firm. The dissociation of managers defining the strategic logic of the firm for competing in the future from understanding that is currently available within the firm about market trends and other matters can be recognized as simply one expression of a more fundamental problem facing any organization: the dissociation of processes for formulating strategic goals from the organizational processes for realizing those goals.

The conceptual and organizational dissociation of strategic ends and means within a firm is often reflected by top management's articulation of narrow economic goals (ends), the achievement of which will require development and deployment of assets and capabilities (means) under significant cognitive constraints that are not recognized or addressed by top management. The practice of strategy by top managers can therefore benefit from a theory of competence-based competition that specifically recognizes the tendency of organizations to dissociate strategic ends and means and suggests ways to overcome this fundamental form of strategic dysfunction within the firm as a learning system.

STRATEGY RESEARCH: INQUIRY FROM THE INSIDE AND INQUIRY FROM THE OUTSIDE

Evered and Louis (1981) note the existence of multiple dissociated research perspectives in the organizational sciences. They characterize these research approaches as falling into categories of "inquiry from the outside" or "inquiry from the inside". Inquiry from the outside is motivated by a positivist, deductive orientation to scientific research; it relies on "objective" external observations of firms to predict behaviors. Inquiry from the inside is motivated by a pragmatic, infer-ential orientation to scientific research; it gathers and interprets "subjective" data by studying organizations from the inside.

The positivist paradigm of "inquiry from the outside" assumes the perspective of a detached, neutral onlooker (e.g. an academic researcher) who uses *a priori* categories based on prior theoretical frameworks to test and refine theory, with the objective of developing universal and generalizable theory capable of making expla-nations and predictions that are not dependent on a given context. The pragmatic paradigm of "inquiry from the inside" is the perspective of someone who is immersed in the processes of an organization, who is actively participating in the experiences of the organization, and who is searching for situationally relevant knowledge. A researcher conducting inquiry from the inside creates categories for entities, relationships, and phenomena that seem useful in describing the specific context he or she is researching. This experiential know-ledge is what Polanyi (1962) calls "personal knowledge"; it is con-textually embedded and can be interpreted correctly, and acted upon appropriately, only in particular settings (Nonaka and Takeuchi, 1995).

The positivist and pragmatic modes of inquiry differ in their invoca-tion of theory. The positivist mode of inquiry invokes a "reconstructed logic"(Kaplan, 1964), a theoretical explanation that is presumed to be operative in the situation under study and that is used *a priori* to explain and predict observable behaviors. The pragmatic researcher, on the other hand, tries to discover the "logic-in-use" (Kaplan, 1964) in the situation under study, the rationale which actually appears to be motivating observable behaviors.

Argyris and Schön (1978) note an analogous tendency to dissociation in the theory building and testing carried out by managers in their competitive contexts. Top managers in a firm may articulate "espoused theories" that they believe explain outcomes in their firm's interactions with the competitive environment. Close observation within those firms, however, may reveal "theories-in-use" by others in the firm (and indeed sometimes by top managers with "espoused theories") that differ from the espoused theories of top managers. The dissociation of espoused theory from theory-in-use may result from the increasing dissociation of top managers from the actual processes within their firms, leading to significant differences between the perceptions of top managers and the actualities within their firms and their product markets.[10]

The next section suggests that a new model for strategy theory building that interactively links researchers and managers in a "double-loop" learning process may help to overcome the tendencies within both groups of strategists towards dissociative patterns of thought.

A New Model for Building a Theory of Competence-Based Strategy

The problems arising from dissociative thinking may occur at every stage in the strategic sense-making process. Just as the thinking of managers formulating strategy can become dissociated from the processes for implementing strategy, strategy researchers may ignore the need to link strategy content with strategy process, with the result that inquiry from the outside becomes intellectually dissociated from inquiry from the inside. We propose that in building a competence-based theory of strategy, these dissociations of thought constitute fundamental practical and intellectual problem that must be overcome both in the practice of strategy by managers and in the theory building and testing of strategy researchers. The challenge of building a theory of competence-based competition that recognizes the inseparability of strategy content and process (Sanchez, Heene and Thomas, 1996) requires reconnecting the generalized strategy theory of researchers with the contextually-rich strategy theories of practitioners. In building a new theory of strategy, it will be important to heed Weick's (1989: 521) suggestion that researchers should give equal attention to problems defined by theorists and those defined by practitioners.

A mission of reconnecting understanding from the outside and understanding from the inside requires processes of research and practice with much greater intensity of interaction between managers and researchers that is purposefully focused on the theory-building process. We propose that the effort to build a competence-based theory of strategy provides an opportunity to define an alternative

---

[10]Strategy researchers who interview top executives as a process of inquiry from the inside sometimes come to suspect that the pronounced dissociation of some top managers may make the "executive interview" mode of inquiry more like a form of inquiry from the outside than inquiry from the inside.

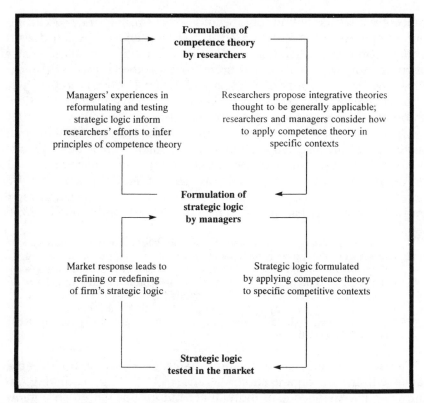

FIGURE 2.3   Double-loop learning by managers and researchers as a new model for competence theory building

model for strategy theory building based on purposeful double-loop learning (Argyris and Schön, 1978) between managers and researchers, as suggested by Figure 2.3. Double-loop learning may transform and improve the processes of theory building by both managers concerned with competing in specific competitive contexts and researchers concerned with discovering general principles of competence theory.

DOUBLE-LOOP LEARNING'S IMPACT ON THEORY BUILDING BY MANAGERS

Argyris and Schön (1978) characterized organizational learning as the detection and correction of error. Learning may occur at different conceptual levels within organizations.[11] Learning may occur at a purely operational level when error detection and correction does not lead to significant alteration of the firm's activities or goals. Strategic learning, however, is a "higher-order" organizational process (Sanchez, 1994) that in the words of Argyris and Schön (1978: 3), occurs "when error is detected and corrected in ways that involve the modification of an organization's underlying norms, policies, and objectives".

The detection and correction of errors at the strategic level of understanding within an organization is often made problematic precisely because the dissociation of espoused theory and theory-in-use is so prevalent in—and so often unknowingly or stoically accepted by—organizations and their managers. The problem of dissociation for the individual manager has been described by Argyris and Schön (1978: 11):

> When someone is asked how he would behave under certain circumstances, the answer he usually gives is his espoused theory of action for that situation. This is the theory of action to which he gives his allegiance and which, upon request, he communicates to others. However, the theory that actually governs his actions is his theory-in-use, which may or may not be compatible with his espoused theory; furthermore, the individual may or may not be aware of the incompatibility of the two theories.

The actual theories-in-use in an organization may be poorly articulated within an organization, because articulating, codifying, and diffusing the knowledge of individuals and groups within an organization may require significant effort, cost, and managerial attention.[12] When the knowledge-in-use within an organization is not well articulated, the collective of theories-in-use in the organization may not be apparent or accessible to anyone in the organization. When top managers are unaware of and thus dissociated from the actual theories-in-use in their firm, the dissociative theories which they espouse may well be at odds with the theories-in-use in many or all parts of the firm. In such cases, the authority and power of the position of top managers may exert an influence that discourages or even forbids discussion of theories-in-use that differ from the espoused theories of top management. When theories-in-use cannot be openly

---

[11]Nonaka and Takeuchi (1995) make a basic distinction between tacit knowledge and explicit knowledge. Boisot (1995) categorizes knowledge by its concreteness versus abstractness and by the degree to which knowledge has been "coded" or "uncoded". Sanchez (1996a,b) suggests that knowledge may be categorized by state, process and purpose levels of understanding, which correspond to an organization's "know-how' (practical understanding), "know-why" (theoretical understanding), and "know-what" (strategic understanding).

[12]Some basic difficulties in these processes are discussed in Sanchez (1996).

discussed and appraised in a firm, detection and correction of error at the strategic level may become undiscussible within an organization, and the organizational capacity to learn at the strategic level may become dysfunctional.[13]

An important objective of strategy researchers in the double-loop learning process of Figure 2.3 would be to develop integrative theories of competence-based competition in which, for example, strategy content would be defined in terms of competences that arise from building certain kinds of capabilities and coordination processes within the firm. In order for managers to apply competence theory in defining and developing firm competences in specific competitive contexts, the assumptions, norms, and practices of a firm's theories-in-use must come to the surface and become identifiable, discussible, testable, and changeable. In testing alternative conceptions of how a firm can develop an "ability to sustain the coordinated deployments of assets and capabilities in ways that help a firm achieve its goals" (Sanchez, Heene, and Thomas, 1996), both managers' and researchers' concepts of strategy theory must explicitly include recognizing and, where needed, creating processes for sustaining organizational learning at several levels. Double-loop learning requires that espoused theories and theories-in-use within a firm come into alignment by establishing organizational processes through which

> . . . mistaken assumptions can be reformulated, incongruities recon-
> ciled, incompatibilities resolved, vagueness specified, untestable
> notions made testable, scattered information brought together into
> meaningful patterns, and previously withheld information surfaced
> (Argyris and Schön, 1978: 131).

By developing competence-based strategy theories that address the systemic interdependency of resources and processes for coordinating and renewing resources in creating competitive advantage, strategy researchers may begin to provide managers with general principles for reconnecting strategy formulation with strategy implementation. Managers who understand those principles and apply them in creating new competences may improve their own understanding of what competence consists of and how it can be achieved in their competitive

---

[13]The authors know of a large organization with a strong "top-down" management system in which discussion of strategy issues was *prohibited* at the functional unit level, strategy being posited as the exclusive concern of top managers. To try to carry on discussions of needed changes in objectives within the firm, employees resorted to referring to the "S-word" as an acronym for "strategy", thereby paying the required deference to the reconstructed logic of top management, while carrying on with improving the logic-in-use which actually guided their activities.

context. Those insights, when shared with strategy researchers, can help those researchers further develop the elements of a generally applicable competence theory.

DOUBLE-LOOP LEARNING'S IMPACT ON THEORY BUILDING BY RESEARCHERS

While strategy researchers may have a natural tendency to talk primarily to each other, it is critical to building a theory of competence that dialogue be established between researchers and managers. Bowman (1990: 25, 27) sums up the argument for greater theoretical interaction between management researchers and managers:

> There is always the risk that the professor would rather interact intel-
> lectually with other professors and doctoral students than with execu-
> tives. While the first interaction is obviously worthwhile, to miss the
> second is folly. Most of us exist in professional business schools that,
> as with all professional schools, exist to help the professions—the
> worldly managers and managers-to-be.... The practitioner and the
> researcher are *doubly linked*: the researcher supplies insights, relation-
> ships, and theory for the practitioner. But the practitioner supplies
> puzzles, ideas, judgments, and priorities for the researcher [emphasis
> added].

Just as managers may be challenged to bring espoused theory and theory-in-use into alignment by the double-loop process for competence theory building, many researchers may be challenged by the double-loop model of research to establish new priorities for strategy inquiry.

The dialectic of the double-loop learning process suggests an alternative paradigm for the theory-building process in strategy in which continuous intellectual interactions between researchers and managers over substantial periods of time create a reciprocating process of inquiry from the outside and inquiry from the inside. How this process might be institutionalized and carried out is suggested by the example of the Impulse Centers established by De Vlerick School voor Management, Ghent, Belgium, as explained in Figure 2.4.

CONCLUSION

Both managers and researchers alike must construct simplified mental models of the real world in an attempt to make sense of overwhelming complexity. The processes of dissociative thinking are essential first

Founded in 1995, the Impulse Centers are collaborations between De Vlerick School and companies interested in the "... development and dissemination of knowledge in a specific domain" of competence considered important by both De Vlerick and the partner companies. De Vlerick School intends to establish six Impulse Centers focused on researching six "domains of competence" by 1996. The objective is "interdisciplinary and multifunctional" research in which "theory formulation and diffusion, conception and implementation happen in parallel and simultaneously" with partner companies. Participation in the research programs requires a commitment from partner companies to maintain an "honest and open dialogue" within the companies themselves and with researchers from the Impulse Center. Participating companies are also expected to provide "Inputs of experience, applications, experiments, and know-how" for research projects.

Academic researchers determine the research agenda of each Center and participate in and evaluate the research undertaken with partner companies. Researchers provide partner companies with periodic appraisals of "what is happening elsewhere in the world" in the domain of interest, based on research and information gathered from a worldwide network of researchers. Research in each competence domain also investigates the practicality of applying concepts developed in other areas to the domain of interest.

FIGURE 2.4   Impulse centers at De Vlerick School voor Management (summary and extracts from a statement of purpose by Professor Aimé Heene, De Vlerick School voor Management)

steps in the human process of sense-making, but to understand competence we need to go beyond dissociative patterns of thought. Researchers and managers both need to understand ways in which simplified schema derived from dissociative thinking can be interrelated and integrated in strategy theory. Perhaps the greatest opportunity for strategy research to contribute to improving the performance of organizations would result from recognizing and directly confronting the limits to human rationality, from going beyond narrow or overly simplistic strategy prescriptions based on dissociative thinking, and from developing implementable approaches to improving the management of complexity and uncertainty.

Much prior strategic management research has used either cognitive modeling (e.g. Huff, 1990) or economic modeling (e.g. Balakrishnan and Wernerfelt, 1986) to drive inquiry in strategy. As we have suggested several times in this chapter, much of Simon's research (e.g. Simon, 1982) has focused on overcoming dissociative thinking in economic and cognitive theories. There are signs that the current interest in competence is inducing new lines of inquiry by economics-oriented thinkers addressing the processes by which resources and competences are used and renewed (e.g. Amit and Schoemaker, 1993; Conner, 1991; Mahoney and Pandian, 1992; Peteraf, 1993). New attention is also being given to developing concepts of dynamic capabilities (Teece, Pisano, and Shuen, 1990), strategic flexibility (Sanchez, 1993, 1995), various forms of organizational learning, and the interrelationships of resources and organizational processes for deploying resources (Barney, 1992; Spender, 1992). In addition, some cognitive researchers have recently begun to investigate ways in which mental models of managers direct processes for acquiring resources and developing firm competences (Barr, Stimpert, and Huff, 1992; Fiol, 1991). These emerging lines of research suggest that many researchers have begun to recognize that cognitive and economic issues are closely—perhaps inseparably—intertwined in competence-based competition.

The objectives of competence theory building seem well suited to discovering and accommodating interactions between cognitive processes and economic goals in strategy. Competence theory suggests, for example, that differences in firm performance can result from not only heterogeneous resource endowments, but also from heterogeneous mental models (Mahoney and Pandian, 1992) and coordination capabilities of managers deploying resources (Sanchez, Heene, and Thomas, 1996). Thus, competence theory building may at last begin to explore the theoretical implications of Penrose's (1959: 54) early observation that a firm may achieve strategic advantage not just because it has better resources, but also because it makes better use of its resources. Thus, there are important, rich, and relatively unexplored connections among a firm's competences, its resources, and the cognitive models— both espoused theories and theories-in-use—operative within the firm.

We have suggested that the mission of competence theory building is integrating strategy content and process, which requires understanding their complex interrelationships. In the dynamic context of competence-based competition, a central challenge to strategy theory building is to relate a firm's knowledge and other resources and its organizational learning processes to a changing array of opportunities or threats. If firm strategy is viewed as a dynamic process that seeks a dynamic balance between processes of building and leveraging competences, a central task of strategy research in competence-based competition is to develop new ways of thinking about resources and resource uses that integrate the cognitive processes of managers and the economic content of specific decisions affecting resource use and development. Competence theory may therefore lead to a substantive shift in the focus of strategy to *flexible resources and capabilities*—especially human resources and capabilities—that may find a variety of changing end-uses (Sanchez, 1995).[14]

We have suggested that in strategy theory building by managers, learning at the strategic level may consist of effecting changes in both the espoused theory and the logic-in-use of the organization. We have also suggested that strategic learning may be assisted by joining the learning of researchers and managers in a process of double-loop learning intended to promote informed reflection on the fundamental processes of competence-based competition by both groups of strategists. The process of double-loop learning requires that both firms and communities of researchers keep themselves open to deep and challenging questions. As Schön (1983: 338) noted,

> Reflection-in-action is essential to the process by which individuals function as agents of significant organizational learning, and it is at the same time a threat to organizational stability. An organization capable of examining and restructuring its central principles and values demands a learning system capable of sustaining this tension and converting it to productive public inquiry. An organization conducive to reflective practice makes the same revolutionary demand.

Barney suggests that "in the analysis of competitive advantage, process issues must always be integrated with content issues" (1992: 56). This chapter suggests that the "strategic intent" of competence theory building should be to achieve an integration of process research on organizational learning and dynamic capabilities (Levitt and March, 1988; Teece, 1990) and the deductive resource-based approach (Conner, 1991; Rumelt, 1984; Wernerfelt, 1984). Process-oriented research dissociated from economic concerns may not be able to adequately distinguish management practices and organizational processes of greater strategic importance from those of lesser strategic importance (as judged by the criteria of substantive rationality). Resource-based economics dissociated from human cognitions and organizational processes, on the other hand, is silent as to the managerial cognitions and management practices that might enable firms to identify and deploy resources required to compete successfully.

How *are* firm resources and managers' mental models related? In what respect does the need for increasingly frequent or constant

---

[14]In essence, a potential conceptual resolution to the dilemma of integrating substantive and procedural rationalities that is approachable through competence theory is the realization that in the face of irreducible uncertainty and complexity, the substantively rational strategy may be the one that provides the greatest opportunity for procedural rationality to operate over a wider range of future possibilities (Sanchez, 1993).

strategic change demand new mental models for organizational adaptation? How does the accumulation of resources create a base for organizational learning, and how does it constrain organizational learning that would recognize the need for new kinds of resources? To what extent, and in what ways, can organizational learning processes allow firms to increase their rates of resource accumulation (Mahoney, 1995)?

In the context of competence theory building, as elsewhere, there is not really a choice to be made between content and process research, pragmatically speaking. We must choose both together and attempt to describe and manage their complex interrelationships. The agenda of integrating process and content in competence theory building opens up new questions for pragmatic inquiry. To begin to answer some of the more salient questions to be addressed, we have proposed a new model for conducting pragmatic inquiry as an essential addition to current approaches to strategy theory building.

REFERENCES

Amit, R.H. and Schoemaker, P.J.H. (1993). Strategic assets and organizational rents. *Strategic Management Journal*, **14**(1), 33–46.

Argyris, C. and Schön, D.A. (1978). *Organizational Learning: A Theory of Action Perspective*, Reading, MA: Addison-Wesley.

Balakrishnan, S. and Wernerfelt, B. (1986). Technical change, competition and vertical integration. *Strategic Management Journal*, **7**(4), 347–59.

Barney, J.B. (1992). Integrating organizational behavior and strategy formulation research: A resource based analysis. In Shrivastava, P., Huff, A.S. and Dutton, J. (eds), *Advances in Strategic Management*, Volume 8. Greenwich, CT: JAI Press, pp. 39–61.

Barr, P.S., Stimpert, J.L., and Huff, A.S. (1992). Cognitive change, strategic action, and organizational renewal. *Strategic Management Journal*, **13** (Summer), 15–36.

Boisot, M.H. (1995). *The Information Age*. London: Routledge.

Bowman, E.H. (1990). Strategy changes: Possible worlds and actual minds. In Frederickson, J. (ed.), *Perspectives on Strategic Management*. New York: Harper, pp. 9–37.

Conner, K.R. (1991). An historical comparison of resource-based theory and five schools of thought within industrial organization economics: Do we have a new theory of the firm? *Journal of Management*, **17**(1), 121–54.

Eisenhardt, K.M. (1989). Agency theory: An assessment and review. *Academy of Management Review*, **14**(1), 57–74.

Evered, R. and Louis, M.R. (1981). Alternative perspectives in the organizational sciences: "Inquiry from the inside" and "inquiry from the outside." *Academy of Management Review*, **6**(3), 385–95.

Fiol, C.M. (1991). Managing culture as a competitive resource: An identity-based view of sustainable competitive advantage. *Journal of Management*, **17**(1), 191–211.

Geneen, H. (1984). *Managing*. Garden City, New York: Doubleday.

Glaser, B.G. and Strauss, A.L. (1967). *The Discovery of Grounded Theory: Strategies for Qualitative Research*. New York: Aldine de Gruyter.

Hill, C.W.L. and Jones, G.R. (1995). *Strategic Management: An Integrated Approach*. Boston, MA: Houghton-Mifflin.

Hogarth, R. (1987). *Judgement and Choice* (2nd edition). Chichester: John Wiley.

Huff, A.S. (1981). Multilectic methods of inquiry. *Human Systems Management*, **2**, 83–94.

Huff, A.S. (1990). *Mapping Strategic Thought*. Chichester: John Wiley.

Jensen, M.C. and Meckling, W.H. (1976). Theory of the firm: Managerial behavior, agency costs, and ownership structure. *Journal of Financial Economics*, **3**(4), 305–60.

Kahneman, D., Slovic, P., and Tversky, A. (1982). *Judgment Under Uncertainty: Heuristics and Biases*. Cambridge: Cambridge University Press.

Kaplan, A. (1964). *The Conduct of Inquiry: Methodology for Behavioral Science*. San Francisco, CA: Chandler Publishing Company.

Levitt, B. and March, J.G. (1988). Organizational learning. *Annual Review of Sociology*, **14**(3), 319–40.

Mahoney, J.T. (1995). The management of resources and the resource of management. *Journal of Business Research*, **33**(2), 91–101.

Mahoney, J.T. and Pandian, J.R. (1992). The resource-based view within the conversation of strategic management. *Strategic Management Journal*, **13**(5), 363–80.

Mintzberg, H. (1994). *The Rise and Fall of Strategic Management*. New York: Free Press.

Nonaka, I. and Takeuchi, H. (1995). *The Knowledge-Creating Company*. New York: Oxford University Press.

Pearce, D.W. (ed.) (1992). *The Dictionary of Modern Economics*, 4th edition. Cambridge: MIT Press.

Penrose, E.T. (1959). *The Theory of the Growth of the Firm*. Oxford: Blackwell.

Peteraf, M.A. (1993). The cornerstones of competitive advantage: A resource-based view. *Strategic Management Journal*, **14**(3), 179–191.

Polanyi, M. (1962). *Personal Knowledge*. Chicago: University of Chicago Press.

Rumelt, R.P. (1984). Toward a strategic theory of the firm. In Lamb, R. (ed.), *Competitive Strategic Management*. Englewood Cliffs, NJ: Prentice Hall, pp. 556–670.

Sanchez, R. (1993). Strategic flexibility, firm organization, and managerial work in dynamic markets: A strategic options perspective. *Advances in Strategic Management*, **9**, 251–91.

Sanchez, R. (1994). Higher-order organization and commitment in strategic options theory. *Advances in Strategic Management*. **10B**, 299–307.

Sanchez, R. (1995). Strategic flexibility in product competition. *Strategic Management Journal*, **16** (summer special issue), 135–59.

Sanchez, R. (1996a). Strategic product creation: Managing new interactions of technology, markets and organizations. *European Management Journal*, **14**(2), 121–38.

Sanchez, R. (1996b). Managing articulated knowledge in competence-based competition. In Sanchez, R. and Heene, A. (eds), *Strategic Learning and Knowledge Management*. Chichester: John Wiley.

Sanchez, R. and Heene, A. (1996). A systems view of the firm in competence-based competition. In Sanchez, R., Heene, A. and Thomas, H. (eds), *Dynamics of Competence-Based Competition*. Oxford: Elsevier.

Sanchez, R. and Thomas, H. (1996). Strategic goals. In Sanchez, R., Heene, A. and Thomas, H. (eds), *Dynamics of Competence-Based Competition*. Oxford: Elsevier.

Sanchez, R., Heene, A. and Thomas, H. (1996). Towards the theory and practice of competence-based competition. In Sanchez, R., Heene, A. and Thomas, H. (eds), *Dynamics of Competence-Based Competition*. Oxford: Elsevier.

Schendel, D.E. and Hofer, C.W. (eds) (1979). *Strategic Management: A New View of Business Policy and Planning*, Boston, MA: Little, Brown and Company.

Schön, D.A. (1983). Organizational learning. In Morgan, G. (ed.), *Beyond Method*. Newbury Park, CA: Sage Publishers, pp. 114–28.

Simon, H.A. (1947). *Administrative Behavior*. New York: Free Press (3rd edition, 1976).

Simon, H.A. (1957). *Models of Man*. New York: John Wiley.

Simon, H.A. (1976). From substantive to procedural rationality. In Latsis, S.J. (ed.), *Method and Appraisal in Economics*. Cambridge: Cambridge University Press, pp. 129–48.

Simon, H.A. (1982). *Models of Bounded Rationality: Behavioral Economics and Business Organization*. Cambridge, MA: MIT Press.

Simon, H.A. (1989). *Models of Thought*. New Haven: Yale University Press.

Spender, J.C. (1992). Strategy theorizing: Expanding the agenda. *Advances in Strategic Management*, 8, 8–32.

Teece, D. (1990). Contributions and impediments of economic analysis in the study of strategic management. In Frederickson, J.W. (ed.), *Perspectives in Strategic Management*. New York: Harper Business, pp. 39–80.

Teece, D., Pisano. G., and Shuen, A. (1990). Firm capabilities, resources, and the concept of strategy. CCC Working Paper #90–8, University of California, Berkeley, CA.

Weick, K.E. (1989). Theory construction as disciplined imagination. *Academy of Management Review*, **14**(4), 516–31.

Wernerfelt, B. (1984). A resource-based theory of the firm. *Strategic Management Journal*, **5**(2), 171–80.

3

Predicting Rent Generation in Competence-based Competition

ELAINE MOSAKOWSKI, BILL MCKELVEY

In this chapter we focus on the question of whether we can predict *ex ante* which competences will lead to rent generation. We examine two aspects of this question: our ability to operationalize attributes of rent-generating competences independent of firm performance and our insight into where the critical focus of managerial attention may lie when seeking rents. In addressing the first aspect, we propose a theoretical basis for choosing *ex ante* predictors of rent generation that are tied to a firm's environment. Similarly, we address the second aspect with a solution to the trade-off between managerial attention directed inside the firm and managerial attention directed outside the firm that depends upon a firm's environmental characteristics.

INTRODUCTION

An essential problem in the resource-based view of strategy (Penrose, 1959; Rubin, 1973; Lippman and Rumelt, 1982; Rumelt, 1984, 1991;

Competence-based Strategic Management.
Edited by Aimé Heene and Ron Sanchez.
Copyright © 1997 John Wiley & Sons Ltd.

Wernerfelt, 1984, 1995; Barney, 1986, 1991; Dierickx and Cool, 1989; Conner, 1991; Mahoney and Pandian, 1992; Mosakowski, 1993; Peteraf, 1993) is that there is no clear or agreed basis for *selecting* which of the vast number of a firm's resources are in fact those that contribute to firm performance. Upon close examination, all firms become bundles of essentially idiosyncratic resources that could never be perfectly replicated at any cost. Even though the concept of *scarcity* is a cornerstone of the resource-based view's arguments for the conditions that lead to rent generation, in and of itself this concept does little to sift through the plethora of idiosyncratic resources of a firm. As Conner (1991: 145) notes, "at some level, everything in the firm becomes a resource and hence resources lose explanatory power".

To some extent, it is the difficulty of predicting which resources will generate rents *ex ante* that motivates such criticisms as Porter's (1991: 108):

> At its worst, the resource-based view is circular. Successful firms are successful because they have unique resources. They should nurture these resources to be successful. But what is a unique resource? What makes it valuable? Why was a firm able to create or acquire it? Why does the original owner or current holder of the resource not bid the value away? What allows a resource to retain its value in the future? There is once again a chain of causality that this literature is just beginning to unravel.

Resource-based view scholars should not disregard this criticism simply because Porter is working in a different research tradition.

We agree with Porter in that the current state of the strategic management work on the resource-based view often represents tautological reasoning of the sort that (1) rents are used to define a firm's critical resources in that these resources are identified by comparing successful versus unsuccessful firms; and then (2) the question is asked whether resources generate rents, to which a resounding YES is heard. Resolving the tautology presents a formidable challenge to future researchers, including those working in related perspectives such as competence-based strategic management, and in this chapter we propose a preliminary answer to the general question: How can we predict which resources and competences will underlie a firm's long-run performance?

Our proposed solution focuses on two questions: what is a unique (or scarce) resource or competence, and what makes it valuable?[1] We focus on the difficulties of operationalizing uniqueness and value

---

[1] In a separate paper (Mosakowski, 1995), we address the related question of what actions managers might take to create or acquire a rent-generating resource or competence.

independently of firm performance outcomes. To do so, we suggest that the competitive environment in which resources and competences are embedded will determine which are unique and valuable. Thus, we depend on independent environmental characteristics as an external referent for answers to the scarcity and value questions.

In addition, we examine the impact of a firm's competitive environment on the appropriateness of managers adopting an inward-looking focus instead of an external-looking focus. Research on the resource-based view of strategy—and, in particular, the finding that business-unit effects have a greater impact on firm performance than do industry effects (Rumelt, 1991)—is in danger of being misinterpreted as dismissing the importance of the traditional Porterian (1980) view of strategic thinking that focuses on topics external to the firm, such as the analyses of competitors, customers, suppliers, and so forth.[2] However, suggesting that firm resources and competences are important to firm performance does *not* negate the necessity for managers to study their competitive environment and develop a strategic logic (Sanchez and Heene, 1996). In this chapter we develop arguments about how environmental conditions may affect the balance between a manager's attention to internal versus external issues.

A caveat about firm performance is warranted at this point. Although we acknowledge the possibility of a holistic perspective in which firms are pursuing multiple strategic goals (Sanchez and Thomas, 1996), we maintain the traditional emphasis on economic rents as our performance variable. In the calculation of rents, one needs to adopt an *ex ante* perspective to evaluate whether a resource or competence will lead to rent generation such that the *ex ante* cost of acquiring or developing the resource or competence is less than its *ex post* value—resulting in an above-normal return (Barney, 1986; Rumelt, 1987). However, in this chapter we do not explicitly take into account factor market considerations (Barney, 1986) that affect the costs of acquiring or developing resources or competences. Instead, we focus on the static situation in which firms' resources and competences are in place and we want to predict which firm will generate future rents.

---

[2]The potential for an inward-looking myopia is reduced in the approach of competence-based strategic management, which stresses both an internal and external perspective (Sanchez, Heene, and Thomas, 1996b: 27). This work acknowledges that critical resources may reside in the environment—that is, resources that are not owned by firms but can be addressed by them may play a critical role in determining the competitive advantage of firms (Sanchez, Heene, and Thomas, 1996b). In addition, the product market and competitive arenas have been integrated into the notion of competence-based competition. Bogner and Thomas (1996) emphasize that competences likely to generate rents are those capable of generating product traits that are desirable in their targeted market.

In this situation, many competences represent largely sunk costs and therefore our attention to rents translates into a focus on which competences are likely to generate the greatest *ex post* returns. Obviously, a more complete model would incorporate factor market considerations and the dynamic problem of firms building new competences and leveraging existing competences (Gorman, Thomas, and Sanchez, 1996).

In the rest of the chapter we develop our arguments in the following way. In the next section we begin by elaborating on some of the underlying difficulties associated with studying scarcity and value of resources or competences. In the third section we propose two operational solutions to these difficulties, both based on an environmental referent. In the fourth section we discuss two types of environments—severe and non-severe—to propose how the balance between an inward-looking focus versus an outward-looking focus may vary between these environments. In the fifth section we conclude our discussion.

COMPETENCE-BASED STRATEGIC MANAGEMENT

Selznick's (1957) early use of the term "core competence" and Penrose's (1959) work on managerial competences and firm strategy suggest that looking within the firm to understand sources of competitive advantage is not a new idea. Nonetheless, renewed research attention by strategic management researchers has attempted to systematize the conditions under which resources and competences may serve as sustainable sources of rents. This research perspective has been associated with many labels that include the term "competence" (McKelvey, 1982)—such as "core competence" (Prahalad and Hamel, 1990; Hamel and Prahalad, 1993; Henderson and Cockburn, 1994), "competence-based competition" (Hamel and Heene, 1994; Sanchez, Heene, and Thomas, 1996a), and "competence-based strategic management" (Sanchez, Heene, and Thomas, 1996a; Heene and Sanchez, this volume)—as well as with the "resource-based view", "strategic assets" (Winter, 1987; Amit and Schoemaker, 1993), "dynamic capabilities" (Teece, Pisano, and Schuen, 1992), "core capabilities" (Leonard-Barton, 1992), or just "capabilities" (Ulrich and Lake, 1990; Stalk, Evans, and Shulman, 1992). In referring to the extant literature, we use the phrases, *competence-based competition, competence-based strategic management* and *competences* to encompass this work in its entirety.

A fundamental tenet of competence-based strategic management is that, to explain differences in firm performance, one needs to examine differences in firms' competences. But as Peteraf (1993: 180) notes, numerous authors working within this general perspective disagree over terminology and other points. Since the objective of the current chapter is not to resolve these disagreements, we gloss over any differences to characterize competence-based strategic management as a cohesive theory. We acknowledge that by glossing over differences we are to some extent ignoring efforts by many of the authors to differentiate their work from previous work in this tradition, and do not intend to mislead the reader into believing that such differences are insignificant. Since the tautology problem appears to plague many of these efforts, we instead concentrate our efforts in this direction.

In painting this general picture, we rely upon what is perhaps the most comprehensive set of definitions proposed thus far—in the volume on competence-based strategic management by Sanchez, Heene, and Thomas (1996b). In addition, we rely upon Barney's (1991) suggestion that the critical conditions that initiate rent generation are: (1) that the competence is *scarce*, and (2) that the competence is *valuable*. For rent generation to be sustained, Barney argues that the competence must *remain* scarce—because of its inimitability and its non-substitutability—and *remain* valuable.[3] To facilitate competence-based strategic management's advance to the state of falsifiable theory, we propose the necessity of identifying *ex ante* competences that meet these conditions. The ability to identify those competences that are scarce and valuable will allow for the prediction of, and explanation for, the generation of rents. Otherwise, competence-based strategic management would also simply be an *ex post* rationale for why some firms are successful and others are not.

THE SCARCITY DILEMMA

The emphasis on competence scarcity is intimately tied to the concept of Ricardian rents, such that "the key to the existence of Ricardian rents is the presence of a fixed scarce factor; the scarcity is such that the extra profit (rent) commanded by the factor is insufficient to attract new competences into use" (Rumelt, 1987: 142).[4] Rumelt (1984)

---

[3] A related point is that the tradability/mobility of the competence will dictate who will capture the rents in the long run (Barney, 1986, 1989; Dierickx and Cool, 1989; Peteraf, 1993), but we do not address this as a separate issue.

[4] We note that Amit and Schoemaker (1993) differentiate between unique with regard to other players in the industry versus unique in the sense of limited use in other states of nature. Conner (1991) and Peteraf (1993) also discuss the importance of uniqueness with regard to the cospecialization to a firm's other assets and competences. In this case, we focus only on the uniqueness of a competence held by firms competing in the industry.

suggests the necessity of isolating mechanisms to limit the mobility of competences among firms by increasing the cost for competitors to imitate or substitute a competence. Barney's (1986, 1991) conditions of inimitability and non-substitutability capture two avenues through which isolating mechanisms operate and rents are sustained: through the increased cost of direct imitation of the competence in question, and through the increased cost of indirect imitation by substituting for the competence. Thus, not only must the specific *form* of a competence be scarce and costly to imitate, but so must the *function* of the competence. In discussing scarcity in this chapter we refer to the scarcity of a competence's function to represent this general logic, even though the current work on competence-based strategic management tends not to differentiate form from function.

A dilemma arises with regard to falsifiable propositions concerning scarce competences. We refer to this as the *scarcity dilemma*. The apparent dilemma arises in that if "scarcity" is critical and almost every competence held by a firm is to some extent scarce, that is, idiosyncratic to a particular firm, how do we operationalize scarcity? In studying the scarcity of an idiosyncratic competence, is it how scarce a competence is (i.e. one firm versus two firms); the nature of the scarcity (i.e. all firms can do something only to different degrees versus only one firm can do something); or something else that matters?

In order to use scientific methods based on the principal of falsifiability, one must be able to generalize about scarcity to test its necessity for rent generation. To do so, one may face the problem of generalizing about uniqueness—which Conner (1991: 144) suggests must necessarily be an impossibility. Without resorting to the extreme position that there is no way to study uniqueness systematically, we suggest that the scarcity dilemma represents a dilemma of operationalization. This is represented by Porter's (1991: 108) question of "But what is a unique resource?" Without a resolution of this dilemma, competence-based strategic management faces the risk that Peters (1991: 273) describes as:

> Operational impossibilities spawn tautological discussions that replace predictive theories with historical explanations, testable hypotheses with the infinite regress of mechanistic analysis, and clear goals for prediction with vague models of reality.

In fact, Peter's prediction that operational impossibilities will lead to a reliance on historical explanation is borne out by the *value dilemma* in the next subsection.

THE VALUE DILEMMA

The core of the value dilemma is the problem of differentiating between competences that enhance a firm's performance, detract from it, or have little effect. Given the multitude of relatively minor differences among organizations, we expect that the majority will fall into the last category. In particular, many competences may prove to be unimportant to a firm's rent stream. To address this issue, Barney (1991) adds the dimension of "valuableness" to those of scarce, inimitable, and non-substitutable. The addition of this fourth dimension is an attempt to complete the list of necessary and sufficient conditions for the generation of rents.

We use the term *value dilemma* to refer to the seemingly impossible problem of trying to predict which idiosyncratic competences are sources of value.[5] As noted above, the current practice for studying value suffers from circularity in that valuable resources are often identified by examining successful firms, and the proposition that these valuable resources generate rents is then subsequently confirmed. This tautological trap is in good company, in that behaviorist research on reinforcement as well as ecological research on natural selection suffer from similar traps. As with scarcity, we suggest that value poses a dilemma of operationalization. In this case, the operational challenge is that of establishing an independent operationalization of value that is not tied to the *ex post* incidence of rent generation.

As with the scarcity dilemma, the issue of generalizing about uniqueness arises. As a first step, we would want to predict which types of competences will be likely to generate rents; as a next step, we need to consider *whether* we can predict which idiosyncratic variant of these operations is likely to generate rents—i.e. firm A's version versus firm B's version. Thus, we must consider the point beyond which our predictive abilities do not apply.

Without the resolution of the value dilemma, an inability to identify *ex ante* those competences that are of strategic value would relegate competence-based strategic management to the realm of *ex post* description, rather than predictive science. Peters (1991: 268) notes the false comfort of historical explanations as often used in case study analyses:

---

[5]In this chapter we focus on the problem of identifying which competences lead to rent generation. A companion problem exists of identifying which *in*competencies (Leonard-Barton, 1992) lead to losses.

The challenge of historical explanations is to blend all the elements of competition so skillfully and convincingly that the resultant composite explanation will leave the audience intellectually satisfied. Thus the audience can claim to understand a process they could never predict, because they have achieved a complex, empathetic, and intensely personal feeling of understanding about what went on.

In the next section we propose operational solutions to these two dilemmas.

PROPOSED SOLUTIONS TO THE DILEMMAS

THE SCARCITY DILEMMA

The problem of operationalizing scarcity refers to the problem of distinguishing meaningful differences in competences from meaningless ones, given that we are assuming a world in which idiosyncracy is commonplace. Take the example of four automobile companies responding to dramatically higher gasoline prices during the oil crisis in 1979. We might observe firms developing competences in engine redesign by US automakers A and B, competences in the redesign of the materials and aerodynamics of the automobile body by US automaker C, and competences in selling to the US market by a foreign manufacturer of subcompacts (automaker D). On the surface, the competences held by automakers C and D appear to be unique whereas the competences held by automakers A and B are shared. If one examines these competences in more detail, however, one might observe that the two firms investing in engine design expertise may have behaved in very different ways in their specific design strategies, managerial processes integrating design with manufacturing, and so forth. It is not unreasonable to assert that the specific managerial processes operating across these firms are unique and that these unique processes are primarily responsible for the resulting competences (Sanchez, Heene, and Thomas, 1996b). Would these now be considered idiosyncratic competences? This represents the core of the scarcity dilemma, that is, how to study idiosyncratic phenomena scientifically.

We suggest a relatively straightforward solution that revolves around an examination of firms' specific achievements—that is, their *intermediate outcomes*—which paint an outcome-based picture of their competences. Our solution is similar to Godfrey and Hill's (1995: 530) call to use observables to replace unobservables in strategic management theories:

What scholars need to do is to theoretically identify what the observable consequences of unobservable resources are likely to be, and then go out [sic] to see whether such predictions have a correspondence in the empirical world.

In the automobile example, suppose that, at some time point after these firms responded to rising fuel prices, firm A produced cars with maximum miles per gallon of 22, 25, 24, 27, and 30; firm B produced cars with maximum miles per gallon of 31, 28, 26, 31, and 34; firm C produced cars with miles per gallon of 20, 22, and 25; and firm D produced cars with miles per gallon of 32, 35, and 29. These data suggest the relative scarcity of cars with miles per gallon over 30. Three out of the four competitors produced them; furthermore, two out of the four competitors replicated this feat at least once.

This outcome-based view of scarcity relies upon *demonstrated competences* as reflected in a firm's intermediate outcomes, rather than upon intentions, abilities, or inputs.[6] Perhaps the most salient demonstration of a firm's competences might be in the characteristics of the products the firm produces, including the cost of the product[7]—especially as these product characteristics translate into the satisfaction of customer needs. For example, a semiconductor firm's manufacturing skills resulting from its cumulative experience in clean-room techniques will be reflected in the cost and reliability of the chips produced. We propose that it is the scarcity of these intermediate outcomes, not of specific competences, that is necessary for rent generation since intermediate outcomes encompass both the form and function of a competence.

This compression of form and function points to one of many advantages associated with an emphasis on intermediate outcomes. In addition, since intermediate outcomes form the basis of consumers' purchase decisions, we can observe a more direct link to rent generation. In so doing, however, we need to pay comparable attention to how a firm's managerial processes and assets lead to its intermediate outcomes. Figure 3.1 illustrates how one might divide the problem of managerial processes leading to rent generation into two separate problems.

---

[6]We caution the reader that the relationship between competences, intermediate outcomes, and rent generation becomes significantly more complex if one allows the link between competences and intermediate outcomes to include a stochastic element. In this case, scarcity of competences may not be a necessary condition for rent generation—scarcity of intermediate outcomes may be necessary instead. We develop related arguments in Mosakowski (1995).

[7]Cost may be a generically critical competitive dimension, such that cost is important to some degree in all types of competitive environments.

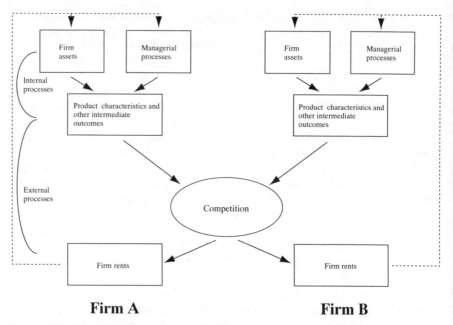

Firm A   **Firm B**

FIGURE 3.1   Dividing the problem of managerial processes leading to rent generation into two separate problems

Note that in Figure 3.1 we describe a causal chain that is similar to
the systems view of competence-based competition depicted in
Sanchez and Heene (1996). In the Figure we demonstrate how managerial processes may combine with a firm's asset base to produce firm
competences, which can then be observed in the form of a firm's intermediate outcomes in its product markets. Depending on other firms'
intermediate outcomes, rent profiles will emerge.

Another advantage of focusing on intermediate outcomes is that it
allows us to compare across firms in a scientifically meaningful way
because not only are intermediate outcomes *observable*, they are also
comparable as consumers do compare them as the basis for their
purchase decisions. Focusing on outcomes also makes possible the
study of competence bundles. This refers to the idea that certain
competences and/or incompetencies—for example, technological
creativity and managerial naiveté—may be inextricably linked. By
observing intermediate outcomes, we can observe the effects of this
bundling process in terms of actual product characteristics. In the
example, the combination of creativity and naiveté may lead to a
technologically superior product that is produced at a high cost; given

these characteristics and the nature of competition and consumer demand, the firm may or may not generate rents.

In focusing on intermediate outcomes we are not alone. What we refer to as intermediate outcomes is similar to what Penrose (1959: 25) refers to as *services*, in that "resources consist of a bundle of potential services and can, for the most part, be defined independently of their use, while services cannot be so defined, the very word 'service' implying a function, an activity". Similarly, Bogner and Thomas (1996) emphasize that competences likely to generate rents are those capable of generating product attributes that are desirable in their targeted market. Chatterjee (1995) proposes a similar product-market-based view of competences. Sanchez (1995) emphasizes how the uncertainty and dynamics of product markets affect the value of a firm's competences. Our contribution lies in recognizing that intermediate outcomes hold the key to overcoming the tautology problem.

This approach is not without its weaknesses. For example, Conner (1991: 145) also raises the possibility of looking at product market outcomes, but suggests caution when the "*outcomes* of application of firm resources [are] used as proxies for the underlying resources". Certainly, one can imagine situations in which competences are *not* made observable in product market outcomes such that some competences may lead to rent generation even when they are not put into use in the product market. For example, one might imagine that a technologically superior firm may suppress innovations because these innovations would only serve to cannibalize the firm's technologies currently in use in the product market. Still, this technological competence may contribute to a firm's rents (in this case, monopoly rents) even though it is not used in developing any of the firm's current products because it serves to pre-empt competitors from entering.

Nonetheless, even though our proposed solution moves the operationalization of a competence-based concept into the realm of what Wernerfelt (1984) refers to as "product strategies", it circumvents the impossibility of operationalizing scarcity in a world in which idiosyncracy dominates. This should not be taken to imply that operational difficulties magically disappear, however. In the fuel efficiency example, we acknowledge that each of the patterns of fuel efficiency produced by the automobile manufacturers is unique. The intermediate outcome of producing a car with at least 30 miles per gallon appears not to be scarce, while the ability to produce a car with 35 miles per gallon appears to be unique to firm D. Yet firm D has not replicated this outcome in other models. And what if the generation of intermediate outcome is stochastic? In this case, we must allow for the fact that not all outcomes can be readily repeated. In addition, firm B produced three cars with 31+ miles per gallon (one at 34 miles per gallon); whereas firm D produced two cars with more than 31 miles per gallon (32 and 35). The critical research design question is whether we can predict whether these differences matter.

Looking to this example, we can draw up a partial list of the critical operational questions that arise when one focuses on the scarcity of intermediate outcomes:

(1) How many instances of an intermediate outcome produced by competitors are sufficient for establishing the scarcity of the underlying competence? [8]
(2) How many observations of an intermediate outcome demonstrated by a firm are sufficient to deem that it is repeatable in the future?
(3) What magnitude of differences in outcomes is sufficient to affect the competitive outcome?

It is important to note that these questions can be resolved independently of firm performance. For example, these three operational concerns might be resolved with research on oligopoly, routinization of firm behavior, and marketing research, respectively—to name but a few of the research areas that address these issues. This is important since, by viewing the problem in these terms, we have moved away from a tautology toward a science that seeks to uncover how consumers detect and value small differences in product characteristics, for example. In addition, we acknowledge that one might need to raise other operational issues or look to other theoretical perspectives for guidance. We have only offered a first step toward untangling the specific questions whose answers allow us to operationalize uniqueness without resorting to tautological reasoning. Therefore, we resolve the scarcity dilemma by stating a general scarcity proposition as follows:

---

[8]For example, debate remains as to how scarce is scarce enough. In a strong statement that argues that the extreme case of uniqueness—not the less restrictive case of scarcity—is necessary for rent generation, Barney (1991) suggests that, for a competence to generate rents, it must necessarily be unique, inimitable, and nonsubstitutable. Others (Wernerfelt, 1984; Conner, 1991; Lippman and Rumelt, 1982) and earlier work by Barney (1986, 1989) suggest that a competence does not need to perform a singular function, but that its function only remain scarce. Thus, a competence may be rare, but not necessarily unique, for it to generate a competitive advantage (Barney, 1989). A nonunique competence may still generate a competitive advantage if the number of firms possessing the competence is less than the number of firms needed to generate perfect competition dynamics in an industry (Hirshliefer, 1980). Thus, scarcity may be a matter of degree, in which a unique competence eventually diffuses to a small number of firms, such that perfect competition does not result.

Proposed operationalization of scarcity: A competence is operationally defined to be scarce when the competence leads to an intermediate outcome that is rare among competing firms.

In this discussion we have implicitly looked to a firm's competitive environment to determine scarcity by comparing a firm's intermediate outcomes with the intermediate outcomes of competitors. However, we have not addressed which is perhaps the more salient question—which intermediate outcomes should one examine. In the next subsection we narrow our sights to a subset of intermediate outcomes that we predict will be closely tied to a firm's rent generation. In so doing, we address the value dilemma.

THE VALUE DILEMMA

In this subsection we set our sights on predicting that some types of firms or competences are more likely to generate rents than are others. Because Barney's (1991) use of the term "value" is separate and distinct from scarcity, it differs from the commonly accepted (i.e. Marshallian) use of the term "value", which combines supply-side concerns (as emphasized by Ricardo) and demand-side concerns (as emphasized by such economists as J.B. Say). "Value" in Barney's (1991) discussion[9] focuses solely on the latter's attention to the role of consumers' utility functions in price determination by suggesting that competences will yield rents only as long as the competences are suited to their environment—that is, the competences result in products that enhance consumers' utility. Naturally, since environments change, the value condition is also subject to temporal fluctuations—and concerns with sustainability—since changing environments may obsolete previously valuable competences.

The solution we offer here proposes an operationalization of competence value that is independent from the incidence of rent generation by looking to a firm's environment. Consider the following biological analogy. A wide variety of species of plants grow in the Mojave Desert, including such diverse plants as the Joshua tree, creosote bush, and opuntia cactus. An *ex post* explanation may be used to describe how each plant evolved in its own unique way under the same set of conditions, untangling which combination of characteristics facilitated a species's ability to store water, for example. It is unlikely, however,

---

[9]Also see Collis (1995) for a discussion of value in the context of the resource-based view of strategy.

that the science of desert plants will ever evolve to the point that it can predict *ex ante* how *specific* plant attributes emerged.

Thus, we do not expect that a deterministic model, applied to this problem, would succeed in generating accurate and specific predictions about plant attributes unique to each species. However, the nature of this environment suggests that plants that flourish will need to develop characteristics that perform critical functions, such as the ability to store moisture, protect against predators seeking to tap into their moisture reserve, or conserve on water use (Pianka, 1994: 109). Thus, in this environment, we can predict that desert plants will need to perform these functions in a much more efficient manner than will plants in a climate with more moisture (Box, 1981). This is the equivalent of stating that characteristics of the desert environment dictate that water storage, water conservation, and the protection of water reserves are three critical intermediate outcomes.

As the comparison to Marshall's theory of value points out as well as Barney's separation of the scarcity and value concepts illustrate, the three intermediate outcomes discussed in the Mojave desert example may be critical competitive dimensions for two reasons: water is scarce and water has a high utility associated with it because it is necessary for survival. Thus, our proposed solution to the value dilemma suggests that the value of a competence can be operationalized by the superiority of outcomes that the competence produces along the competitive dimensions having high levels of utility for consumers. Note that this operationalization of value is tied not to the rents produced but to independent dimensions of competition. Thus, techniques developed by marketing science for measuring consumer utilities (or calculating indifference curves) could be used to develop *ex ante* hypotheses about which competitive dimensions will be valuable.

> Proposed operationalization of value: A competence is operationally
> defined to be valuable when it leads to an intermediate outcome that
> is superior on a dimension that enhances consumers' utility.

This operationalization of the value of a firm's competences offers a more complete answer to the question of where rents come from. When both operationalizations of competence scarcity and value are adopted, we can develop *ex ante* predictions that rents will be generated by competences that produce scarce and valuable intermediate outcomes. Our general solution to the two questions raised in the Introduction does the following: it focuses on intermediate outcomes, rather than a firm's idiosyncratic competences, to operationalize both competence value and scarcity independently of firm performance. Like the tautological reasoning that depends upon the outcome of rent generation to identify key resources, we acknowledge that our solution is also outcome-based. By focusing on intermediate outcomes instead of rent outcomes, however, we can break the tautology by developing an independent understanding of competences that are likely to reduce a firm's costs, for example. In this way, we are one step closer to developing hypotheses about specific competences or specific types of managerial choices that will enhance a firm's chances of generating rents.

In the next section we extend this discussion of value to distinguish between different types of environments to suggest that the nature of the managerial problem may vary.

DIMENSIONS OF COMPETITION AND THE MANAGERIAL PROBLEM

In this section we suggest that the severity of a firm's environment affects the relationship between intermediate outcomes and rent generation. We define *severity* in a nontraditional way, however, to refer to the number of environmental dimensions on which organisms compete. This is supported by the biological argument advanced by Pianka (1994: 277–278) that "niche dimensionality strongly affects the *potential* [Pianka's emphasis] for 'diffuse' competition arising from the total competitive effect of all interspecific competitors (MacArthur, 1972)". Bruce Henderson (1983: 23) suggests that a similar phenomenon may apply to competition among firms.

In a severe environment, the critical competitive dimensions are relatively unambiguous; whereas the set of trade-offs among dimensions might be relatively uncertain in a nonsevere environment. In the desert example, organisms compete primarily for a single environmental resource, water. As such, we could characterize this environment as severe. A severe environment might be represented by the special case of commodity industries, in which competition is primarily along the dimension of cost. Alternatively, an environment with multiple dimensions of competition—such as a temperate-zone deciduous forest (in which plants compete for water, sunlight, and various nutrients) or the compact segment of the automobile market (in which automakers compete based on cost, safety, reliability, styling, interior space and trunk space, and fuel efficiency)—would be characterized as operating in a nonsevere environment, where no one factor drives the competition. In this case, multiple intermediate outcomes will be associated with rent generation.

Thus, in a severe environment, one might suggest that we can predict with a high level of certainty that firms performing best on one critical dimension of competition—i.e. cost—will generate rents. Some uncertainty is unavoidable since what defines superior performance will be uncertain since this depends upon the achievements of competitors, which may be unpredictable. In a nonsevere environment, there is clearly less certainty as to the best set of trade-offs among the different dimensions of competition. For example, one might argue that Mazda's Miata automobile excelled at styling, performed well on cost, reliability, and did not excel in interior and trunk space, safety, and fuel efficiency. In this case, the optimal trade-offs among the different product dimensions—which, one might argue, is a fundamental question for research on competitive strategy—are ambiguous. It is in this type of environment that a manager's cognition of his or her environmental context, as well as the construction of a strategic logic, will be critical (Sanchez and Heene, 1996).

Having said this, we note an important implication of our argument that varies between severe versus non-severe environments: where managerial attention will be most rewarded in the different environments. Consider how managerial processes affect firm performance. Intermediate outcomes may play an important role in that they mediate the relationship between a firm's assets and managerial processes and its performance. In fact, the relationship between assets and managerial processes and firm performance may be completely mediated by intermediate outcomes in that managerial processes will only affect rent generation when they are reflected in firm competences and, ultimately, product characteristics. Thus, managerial processes may describe what Itami (1987) refers to as "invisible assets"—and these assets cannot generate rents without becoming somehow "visible" in the form of lower-cost products, more reliable products, more desirable branding, etc. Therefore, we can decompose the effect that managerial processes have on firm performance into two component processes—the internal process that determines how managerial processes affect intermediate outcomes and the external process that determines which product strategy or strategies among competing firms generate(s) rents (see Figure 3.1).

In a severe environment, a larger share of managerial attention might be better directed internally toward managerial processes that attempt to improve a firm's performance on the single critical intermediate outcome, instead of toward defining on what dimension(s) the firm should compete. For example, in the case of a commodity industry, the low-cost firm will generate the most rents. In this environment, managerial attention might best be directed toward lowering costs internally instead of toward studying external environmental conditions to better understand what is the critical dimension. Thus, strategy may be economizing (Williamson, 1991) in a severe environment.

In a non-severe environment, managerial attention may need to be distributed across both sets of relationships—that is, the internal determinants of intermediate outcomes, as well as their external consequences. Managers in firms operating in non-severe environments cannot ignore environmental scanning activities and externally oriented strategic thinking to the extent that managers in firms operating in severe environments can. In particular, managing the trade-offs among critical competitive dimensions—for example, by allocating resources to pursuing one intermediate outcome instead of another—may emerge as a significant task for the strategic decision maker in nonsevere environments. Thus, an internal focus on developing competences for technological innovations, brand imaging, etc. should be combined with an external focus on the competitive dimensions on which firms are competing. This is consistent with Rotem and Kalish's study (1995), which found that managers that share their attention across both their external environment and their internal resources tend to perform the best.

Assuming a fixed level of managerial attention and two uses for this attention, a simple model would suggest that the optimal allocation of managerial attention would be at the point at which the marginal returns to allocating attention to internal issues would equal the marginal returns to allocating attention to external issues.[10] This suggests that:

> Proposition 1: At the point of optimal allocation of managerial attention, the portion of total attention allocated to external issues will be greater in a nonsevere environment than in a severe environment. *ceteris paribus.*

In the next section we conclude the chapter by discussing the broader issues associated with our attempt to increase the predictability of competence-based strategic management.

---

[10]Obviously, more complexities could be introduced into the calculus, such as differential probabilities of success between severe and non-severe environments. With multiple critical competitive dimensions, it is possible that there could be a greater chance of finding a sustainable combination of product attributes that generate rents than in a severe environment in which only the low-cost firm may be able to earn rents. However, as Lippman and Rumelt (1982) show, under certain conditions, even in an environment in which cost is the only important competitive dimension, many firms may be able to generate rents.

CONCLUSION

An essential problem for competence-based strategic management is that there is no agreed basis for selecting which of the vast number of organizational competences are in fact those that contribute to the generation and persistence of rents. To address this concern, past research has emphasized the scarcity and value. In this chapter we discuss operational issues regarding these two criteria by focusing on the scarcity and value of the intermediate outcomes produced by a firm's competences.

To understand where independent measures of intermediate outcomes might come from, we look to the environment. In addition, we distinguish between severe and non-severe environments. In severe environments such as a commodity industry, a single dimension such as cost may serve as the primary basis for determining which firms generate rents. In a nonsevere environment, in which firms compete on multiple dimensions, the trade-offs among the dimensions may be ambiguous. Thus, we have been relatively silent about the trade-offs among competitive dimensions in a nonsevere environment—such as whether achieving a 20% reduction in cost will produce an equivalent rent stream to achieving a 10% reduction in cost and a 10% improvement in quality. Resolving these ambiguities may represent one important aspect of the art of the strategic manager in non-severe environments. Thus, in non-severe environments, we expect more managerial attention to be directed toward external-looking activities, such as defining a firm's intended product strategy *vis-à-vis* its competitors and customers needs. However, we expect that such externally oriented attention will be complemented by internal attention to issues such as communicating this strategic vision within the organization and other managerial processes that reinforce this vision as well as monitor the appropriateness of this vision.

Thus, looking to the environment and intermediate outcomes provides a metric—in this case, a metric dictated by consumers' utility functions—that allows us to compare idiosyncratic firm competences. In arguing for the usefulness of this metric, we do not mean to suggest a deterministic model in which firms holding certain types of competences or firms employing certain types of managerial processes will always generate rents. Instead, we allow that in comparing firms we may only be able to predict the likelihood of generating rents associated with different categories of firms.

While incorporating some randomness in the processes that ultimately lead to rent generation, we recognize the need to develop further knowledge about how managerial processes influence firm competences, how firm competences influence intermediate outcomes, and how intermediate outcomes influence rent generation. In this chapter we have focused on the last link and not addressed the previous two. In effect, the recommendation to unravel the chain beginning with managerial processes and ending in rent generation suggests the need to develop more theoretical and empirical work along the line of Porter's (1985) value chain concept. To do so, one must take care to embed a firm's value chain squarely in the competitive environment. Thus, we need to understand how firms achieve different valuable intermediate outcomes as well as how they can do so uniquely or at least scarcely.

ACKNOWLEDGEMENTS

The authors would like to give special thanks to Steve Postrel and the editors of this volume for their valuable comments on this manuscript. We also thank Heather Elms, Esmeralda Garbi, Connie James, Peter Lane, Marvin Lieberman, Julia Liebeskind, Steve Lippman. Tammy Madsen, Danny Miller, Anne Marie Pulos, Hans Schollhammer, José de la Torre, George Yip, and participants in a seminar at UCLA for their comments. All errors remain the responsibility of the authors.

REFERENCES

Amit, R. and Schoemaker. P. (1993). Strategic assets and organizational rents. *Strategic Management Journal*, **14**, 33–46.

Barney, J. B., (1986). Strategic factor markets: Expectations, luck, and business strategy. *Management Science*, **32**, 1231–41.

Barney, J.B. (1989). Asset stock accumulation and sustained competitive advantage: a commentary. *Management Science*, **35**, 1511–13.

Barney, J. B., (1991). Firm resources and sustained competitive advantage. *Journal of Management* **17**, 99–120.

Bogner, W. and Thomas, H. (1996). From skills to competences: The playing-out of resource bundles across firms. In Sanchez, R., Heene, A. and Thomas, H. (eds), *Dynamics of Competence-Based Competition: Theory and Practice in the New Strategic Management*. Oxford: Elsevier.

Box, E.O. (1981). *Macroclimate and Plant Forms: An Introduction to Predictive Modeling in Phytogeography*. The Hague: Dr W. Junk.

Chatterjee, S. (1995). An outcome-based theory of firm strategy. Paper presented at the Academy of Management Meetings, Vancouver.

Collis, D.J. (1995). Understanding sustainable competitive advantage. The role of positioning, resources, and organizational capabilities. Paper presented at the Academy of Management Meetings, Vancouver.

Conner, K.R. (1991). A historical comparison of resource-based theory and five schools of thought within industrial organization economics. *Journal of Management*, **17**, 121–54.

Dierickx, I. and Cool, K. (1989). Asset stock accumulation and sustainability of competitive advantage. *Management Science*, **35**, 1504–11.

Godfrey, P.C. and Hill, C.W.L. (1995). The problem of unobservables in strategic management research. *Strategic Management Journal*, **16**, 519–33.

Gorman, P., Thomas. H. and Sanchez, R. (1996). Industry dynamics in competence-based competition. In Sanchez, R., Heene, A. and Thomas, H. (eds), *Dynamics of Competence-Based Competition: Theory and Practice in the New Strategic Management*. Oxford: Elsevier.

Hamel, G. and Heene, A. (1994). *Competence-Based Competition*. New York: John Wiley.

Hamel, G. and Prahalad, C.K. (1993). Strategy as stretch and leverage. *Harvard Business Review*, **71** (2), 75–84.

Henderson, B. (1983). The concept of strategy, in Albert, K. J. (ed.), *The Strategic Management Handbook*. New York: McGraw-Hill, pp. 3–26.

Henderson, R. and Cockburn, I. (1994). Measuring competence? Exploring firm-effects in pharmaceutical research. *Strategic Management Journal*, **15**.

Hirshliefer, J. (1980). *Price Theory and Applications*, 2nd edition. Englewood Cliffs, NJ: Prentice Hall.

Itami, H. (1987). *Mobilizing Invisible Assets*, Boston, MA: Harvard University Press.

Leonard-Barton, D. (1992). Core capabilities and core rigidities: A paradox in managing new product development. *Strategic Management Journal*, **13**, 111–26.

Lippman, S.A. and Rumelt, R.P. (1982). Uncertain imitability: An analysis of inter-firm differences in efficiency under competition. *Bell Journal of Economics*, **13**, 418–38.

MacArthur, R.H. (1972). *Geographical Ecology: Patterns in the Distribution of Species*. New York: Harper and Row.

Mahoney, J. T. and Pandian, J.R. (1992). The resource-based view within the con-versation of strategic management. *Strategic Management Journal*, **13**, 363–80.

McKelvey, W. (1982). *Organizational Systematics*. Berkeley, CA: University of California Press.

Mosakowski, E. (1993). A resource-based perspective on the dynamic strategy-performance relationship. *Journal of Management*, 819–39.

Mosakowski, E. (1995). Managerial prescriptions under the resource-based view of strategy. UCLA working paper.

Penrose, E. T. (1959). *The Theory of Growth of the Firm*. London: Blackwell.

Peteraf, M.A. (1993). The cornerstones of competitive advantage: A resource-based view. *Strategic Management Journal*, **14**, 179–91.

Peters, R. H. (1991). *A Critique for Ecology*, Cambridge: Cambridge University Press.

Pianka, E.R. (1994). *Evolutionary Ecology*, 5th edition. New York: HarperCollins.

Porter, M. E. (1980) *Competitive Strategy: Techniques for Analyzing Industries and Companies*. New York: Free Press.

Porter, M.E. (1985). *Competitive Advantage: Creating and Sustaining Superior Performance*. New York: Free Press.

Porter, M.E. (1991). Towards a dynamic theory of strategy. *Strategic Management Journal*, **12**, 95–117.

Prahalad, C.K. and Hamel, G. (1990). The core competence of the corporation. *Harvard Business Review*, **68** (3), 78–91.

Rotem, Z. and Kalish, S. (1995). What makes a better performer: Achieving closer 'fit' with the environment or having generic 'best resources' that suit any environment. Presentation at the Strategic Management Society, Mexico City, Mexico.

Rubin, P. H. (1973). The expansion of firms. *Journal of Political Economy*, **81**, 936–49.

Rumelt, R. P. (1984). Toward a strategic theory of the firm. In Lamb, R. (ed.), *Competitive Strategic Management*. Englewood Cliffs, NJ: Prentice Hall, pp. 556–70.

Rumelt, R. P. (1987). Theory, strategy, and entrepreneurship. In Teece, D.J. (ed.), *The Competitive Challenge*. Cambridge, MA: Ballinger.

Rumelt, R.P. (1991). How much does industry matter? *Strategic Management Journal*, **12**, 167–85.

Sanchez, R. (1995). Strategic flexibility in product competition. *Strategic Management Journal*, **16**, 135–59.

Sanchez, R. and Heene, A. (1996). A systems view of the firm in competence-based competition. In Sanchez, R., Heene, A. and Thomas, H. (eds), *Dynamics of Competence-Based Competition: Theory and Practice in the New Strategic Management*. Oxford: Elsevier.

Sanchez. R., Heene, A. and Thomas, H. (1996a). *Dynamics of Competence-Based Competition: Theory and Practice in the New Strategic Management* Oxford, Elsevier.

Sanchez, R., Heene, A. and Thomas, H. (1996b). Towards the theory and practice of competence-based competition. In Sanchez, R. Heene, A. and Thomas, H. (eds), *Dynamics of Competence-Based Competition: Theory and Practice in the New Strategic Management*. Oxford: Elsevier.

Sanchez, R. and Thomas, H. (1996). Strategic goals. In Sanchez R., Heene, A. and Thomas, H. (eds), *Dynamics of Competence-Based Competition: Theory and Practice in the New Strategic Management*. Oxford: Elsevier.

Selznick, P. (1957). *Leadership in Administration*. New York: Harper & Row.

Stalk, G., Evans, P. and Shulman, L.E. (1992). Competing on capabilities: The new rules of corporate strategy. *Harvard Business Review*, **70** (2), 57–69.

Teece, D., Pisano, G. and Schuen, A. (1992). Dynamic capabilities and strategic management. Working paper, Haas School of Business, Berkeley, CA.

Ulrich, D. and Lake, D. (1990). *Organizational Capability: Competing from the Inside Out*. New York: John Wiley.

Wernerfelt, B. (1984). A resource-based view of the firm. *Strategic Management Journal*, **5**, 171–80.

Wernerfelt, B. (1995). The resource-based view of the firm: Ten years after. *Strategic Management Journal*, **16**, 171–4.

Williamson, O. E. (1991). Strategizing, economizing, and economic organization. *Strategic Management Journal*, **12**, 75–94.

Winter, S. G. (1987). Knowledge and competence as strategic assets. In Teece, D.J. (ed.), *The Competitive Challenge*. Cambridge, MA: Ballinger.

Section II

Competence Dynamics

4

Strategic Renewal in Large Complex Organizations: A Competence-based View

CHARLES BADEN-FULLER, HENK W. VOLBERDA

How should organizations renew? By integrating the competence-based approach to the theory of the firm with the change mechanisms of organization theory, we develop four mechanisms of strategic renewal: venturing, restructuring, reanimation, and rejuvenation. We propose tentative propositions regarding their effectiveness in circumstances of urgency, risk reduction, and technological change.

INTRODUCTION

In the last decade many large organizations have felt strong pressures for change. The causes of these changes have been the pressures from new technology in its widest sense increasing globalization of markets, the deregulation of industries, the shift of firms from public to private sector, and the rise of new organizational forms such as the strategic network. In trying to respond, firms have adopted a wide variety of

Competence-based Strategic Management.
Edited by Aimé Heene and Ron Sanchez.
Copyright © 1997 John Wiley & Sons Ltd.

approaches including downsizing, outsourcing, re-engineering, corporate venturing, restructuring and rejuvenation. How can we explain the many differing kinds of responses of firms? Can we give guidance to researchers seeking to make sense out of the differing approaches? Can we even suggest logical choices to managers? To answer these questions, we suggest we need to return to first principles.

The theory of the firm addresses the question of why do firms exist and recent insights suggest that the answer is that they are mechanisms which exploit unique competences and knowledge (Nelson and Winter, 1982, Barney 1991, Nonaka, 1991). As explained by Conner and Prahalad (1996), this view stands in a contrast to other views such as those of minimizing transactions costs, or resolving principal–agent difficulties (Alchian and Demsetz, 1972; Williamson, 1975). However, the same literature does not deal with the question of how firms change and adjust to environmental shocks such as new technology. This has traditionally been the preserve of organizational theorists, and there is long tradition here stretching back to Barnard (1938), Chandler (1962), Pettigrew (1985), and Van de Ven (1986). As viewed from the perspective of the theory of the firm, these writers seem less concerned about the content of the change, and so there are obvious gaps between the two approaches.

In this chapter we seek to bridge some of these differences. Starting from the position of why firms exist and how they can change; we examine the inherent tensions in the change process, and in particular the tension that exists between change and stability. Next, we tie these ideas to those of competences (Sanchez, Heene, and Thomas, 1996), outlining the choices that firms have in terms of revitalizing or reordering competences, and the difficulties and risks they face in doing this. We trace the alternative mechanisms discussed in the literature and bring forward tentative propositions about their relative efficacy and risk profiles. Finally, we speculate on the possible appropriateness of some of our mechanisms to differing circumstances, as a simple contingency approach.

How do our concerns fit with the title of this issue? For many readers, technology may mean tangible items such as plant, processes, and manuals. However, the literature has long recognized that the technology of the firm extends into other areas, particularly questions of principles of organization (Levinthal, 1966; Loasby, 1996). Thus our attempts to join the literature and ideas on change management with those of competences can rightly be seen as an exploration in the subject "Technology and the theory of the firm" (Kogut and Zander, 1992).

THE PARADOX OF CHANGE AND STABILITY

We begin by pointing out that the problem of change in organizations is a relative one, for we do not wish to suggest that organizations are ever in a state of complete stasis. As many have pointed out (e.g. Bate, 1994), organizations are always changing, but the natural pace of change may be too slow, particularly in a hypercompetitive environment or one facing technological shifts (D'Aveni, 1994). Competition threatens survival. But adjustment to competition is also risky; change may fail or firms may over-react bringing consequences which are more severe.

Put another way, organizations' which wish to adjust need to find a way to reconcile the paradox of conflicting forces for change and stability. The pressure for stability is not just inertia, there are also short-term forces which require organizations to maximally exploit their existing competences and capabilities. The pressure to change comes not only from the threats to survival but also from the desire to grow and be more successful. These conflicting pressures have long been recognized (e.g. Burns and Stalker, 1961) and many scholars have explicitly discussed the dilemma (Poole and Van de Ven, 1989; Handy, 1989; Kanter, 1988; Hampden-Turner, 1990).

REJECTING THE PARADOX: INERTIA

In seeking to overcome the tension, the organization faces three generic choices. It can avoid the paradox rejecting attempts to change, it can accept the paradox and outsource the change problem to others, or it can seek to resolve the paradox by internal adaptation. Although the central thrust of this chapter is the exploration of resolution, it is necessary for completeness to explore the strategies of avoidance and acceptance because these represent viable alternatives and benchmarks to the difficult processes of internal change.

To some researchers, especially those from the population ecology school, it is futile for large organizations to attempt to change. Aldrich (1979) and Hannan and Freeman (1984: 152) see inertia as endemic inside large complex organizations, and, especially in the context of new technology, difficult to overcome. In the language of economics, the market selects out those firms which have the wrong competences (Barnett, Greve and Park, 1994; Barney and Zajac, 1994). The mechanism for renewal is the creation of new organizations which rise to displace the old. While it is clear that this may be one type of renewal process, it is not the only one. There is mounting evidence that some large complex organizations have managed change, and that this has been done in a wide variety of ways, through many different mechanisms. It is this issue which we now address.

ACCEPTING THE PARADOX: OUTSOURCING

According to the alliance or network view of organizations, the paradox of balancing capability exploitation and renewal can be *accepted* by the process of interaction with other organizations. According to network analysis the market is not abstract but concrete and exists everywhere as partners (Von Hippel, 1978; Hakansson, 1982; Matsson, 1987). Because they believe there is not clear distinction between competition outside the organization and cooperation inside, the process of competition as conceived by population ecologists or economists is too simplistic. Firms can and do use partners to overcome the tension.

The process of partnering has been seen as one which allows existing firms to capture new technology or new ideas in any one of its many forms (Contractor and Lorange, 1988). Sometimes these relationships can be *ad hoc*, and at other times they can be orchestrated and purposeful, and Miles and Snow (1986) have classified several of the differing possibilities for arranging networks. Although writers such as Bleeke and Ernst (1991) and Hamel (1991) give words of caution about the effectiveness of alliances in the process of transformation, the inherent attraction of spinning out from the vertically integrated firm is widely accepted. Many large, complex, vertically integrated firms commonly renew parts of their organizations by spinning out and spinning in. At the simplest level, there is a dynamic parent which, upon finding that one of its units is in crisis or maturity, spins it off. Under a new owner, or more often as a separate unit, it is freed from the direct controls of the old multi-unit organization. Separated from many of the forces of inertia, the innovation process can take hold. During the period of change, the spun-out division often continues to maintain links with its old parent, perhaps through trading. If the unit succeeds, it may be repurchased into the original firm, or bought by another complex organization. If it does not renew, it will fail but at no serious loss to the original organization.

That networks do provide an effective mechanism for renewal has been established through many different strands of research. Marshall (1920), writing at the turn of the century, documented industrial districts and noted that renewal was possible. Ouchi (1981) echoed the theme in his discussions of clans. More recently Thorelli (1986) and

Porter (1990) have noted the capacity of networks to effect change, and Lorenzoni and Baden-Fuller (1995) have highlighted the extraordinary capacity of innovation in strategic networks that have a strong central firm.

Notwithstanding the supposed advantages of networks, they are difficult to organize. In industries from machine tools to consumer electronics, many companies discovered that short-term flexibility resulting from transactions involving the externalization of supply for components, sub-assemblies, and other products had high costs in terms of loss of strategic interdependence and organizational learning capacity (Bartlett, 1993). We therefore turn to the third method of dealing with the paradox, namely that of *resolution* through change within the organization.

RESOLVING THE PARADOX: TWO INTERNAL MECHANISMS

Resolving the paradox of change and preservation means recognizing that continuous renewal inside a complex firm everywhere is misleading. Too much change will lead to chaos, loss of cultural glue, fatigue, and organizational breakdown (Volberda, 1996). While in the short term, organizations that are chaotic can survive, in the longer term they are likely to collapse (Stacey, 1995). The firm needs control mechanisms which prevent the fissuring (Sanchez and Heene, 1996). Our contribution is to emphasize that the two most important mechanisms are those which separate the change and stability either by *time* or by *place*.

In *spatial* separation, one part of the organization is responsible for undertaking the process of change and renewal while the other parts remain relatively stable. The classical view of the process of change is that it is undertaken by a specialist research and development group. More often, there is a self-appointed function such as marketing, or production which is seen as the spearhead of new ideas. In multi-divisional organizations the process of change may be undertaken by the upper tier (Chandler, 1962), the lower level (Bower, 1970) in one or two divisions, or a group of business units which are charged, or have appointed themselves as dynamic agents. In general, in spatial separation, the groups that are changing and the groups that are stable are clearly delineated with differential roles. Of course, those that are stable are not immune from change, for effective adjustment requires ideas generated by the dynamic sections to be carried over into the rest of the organization.

We suggest that the other method of resolving the dilemma is to have the whole organization alternating between periods of stability and periods of renewal. Such methods of orchestrating change have been discussed in the literature under many guises such as *punctuated change* by Tushman and Romanelli (1985), holistic change by Child and Smith (1987), and revolutions by Pettigrew (1985). Such changes are most apparent in organizations experiencing major change programmes, such as turnarounds. The detail of temporal change usually shows some spatial adjustment as well. For example, top management may be in a state of change while other parts are stable, and then the baton is handed down to the next level for it to change while top management regain some sense of stability. Looked at systemically, there are clear cycles. In Lewin's (1954) terminology, there is a cycle of *unfreeze, move, refreeze*, often repeated.

In making these opening remarks on the possibilities of resolving the dilemma of stability and renewal, we have purposefully been quite general, and focused on broad categories of processes. The literature relating to both these methods of managing change is enormous, and is dealt with at length in the next section. This categorization, even before a review, allows us to anticipate our later discussion on a potentially important difference between the two mechanisms: namely, the approach to time and risk. We suggest that the method of spatial separation of change and stability allows the organization to experiment in one place while keeping the other part constant. This method of managing change appears to be one of risk control, for some of the dangers of failure are contained simultaneously allowing variety (which spreads risk) to increase. Set against this containment is the factor that speed may be sacrificed. Temporal separation allows the whole organization to adjust to sharp and sudden shocks more holistically and quickly. Under temporal separation, the possibilities of failure may be greater if the change process loses control. Moreover, variety is not increased but the speed of execution may be faster. We advance our first hypothesis which will be explored and tied to prior literature more substantially later:

> The mechanism of spatial separation will be most effective where the organization needs to contain the risks of change and is not concerned with speedy reaction to outside events. In contrast, temporal separation will be more effective where there is a pressing urgency for the whole organization to respond collectively.

Before we explore this issue in greater detail, we turn the reader's attention to the content of the change, using the competence-based perspective.

THE CONTENT OF CHANGE PROCESSES, RE-ORDERING AND RENEWING COMPETENCES

The newly emerging competence-based theory of the firm (Sanchez, Heene, and Thomas, 1996) provides us with a framework for rethinking the content of renewal. There are important antecedents for this theory. For example, Nelson and Winter (1982) in their *Evolutionary Theory of Economic Change* present firms as repositories of routines which endow them with a focus to search, yet at the same time suppress their attention span and capacity to absorb new information. The routinization of activity, constitutes one of the most important aspects of a firm's potential competitive advantage. In a similar way, in the *resource-based view*, the firm is seen as a bundle of tangible and intangible resources and tacit know-how that must be identified, selected, developed, and deployed to generate superior performance (Penrose, 1959; Learned *et al.*, 1969; Wernerfelt, 1984). These scarce, firm-specific assets may form a basis for a competence. Like population ecologists, however, those posing the resource-based view of the firm have traditionally been pessimistic about change. In general, they assume (often implicitly) that firms are stuck with what they have, and have to live without what they lack.

This view that firms are stuck and find difficulty in changing has received echoes in later literature. Thus there is the idea that core competences can become core rigidities (Leonard-Barton, 1992; Burgelman, 1994; Barnett, Greve, and Park, 1994); or a competence trap (Levitt and March, 1988; Levinthal and March, 1993) and that high productivity can only be achieved at the cost of decreased flexibility (Utterback and Abernathy, 1975).

Speaking from a normative viewpoint, Teece, Pisano, and Shuen (1992) have suggested that firms can and should remain in a dynamic capability-building mode. New competences and capabilities should be built and incorporated into the firm. By implication, some old ones should be discarded. We examine quite simply two mechanism by which this may take place. The first mechanism is that of new rankings of competences at the "core" of the firm and the second is the process of altering a subset of these competences. To facilitate the discussion we elaborate a working distinction between competences and routines. Our definition echoes ideas set out by Prahalad and Hamel (1990), Grant (1991), Amit and Schoemaker (1993), and Sanchez, Heene, and Thomas (1996). Although we make this distinction between "routines" and "competences", the literature clearly has many similar terms to encompass our ideas, and uses our words for a variety of different meanings.

> We view *competence* as involving shared knowledge among a large
> group of units within the complex firm, whereas a *routine* is seen as
> the province of only one or, at most, a few units. A competence there-
> fore draws on several routines which have been refined, stored, and
> codified, or socialized.

Using this definition, let us think of the firm as having a set of
competences C1 ... Cn, and a set of routines and capabilities
R1 ... Rm. By our definition some or all of the set C1 ... Cn reside in
all (or nearly all) of the firm's units, whereas R1 ... Rm appear in-
frequently, perhaps only in a single unit.

The firm can significantly change its operations by altering what is in
the "core" and what is in the "periphery". For example, if it alters the
set of the competences by dropping one (C1, for example) and expands
one of the periphery routines into a new competence (R1, for example),
then the nature of the activities of its units will change. Those units
which had C1 as a key competence may disappear. In contrast, some
new units may appear which take on board R1. The process by which
this change takes place can be one of socialization, or codification, or
both (Nonaka, 1991).

Examples of firms undertaking such actions are numerous. Xerox, for
example, recently moved some new marketing skills from the
periphery to the core when it redefined the business from one of *photo-
copies* to that of *document processes*. In the privatized utilities in the UK,
firms which were once in the public domain and had little concept of
marketing or customer service have been obliged to add skills and
capabilities to their existing routines. Typically these have substituted
for highly honed skills relating to the political process of obtaining
money out of the UK Treasury. Prahalad and Hamel (1990) also give a
number of examples of this process where firms are extending their
core. Other writers have alluded to the reshaping of organizations
which have decided to reject businesses which once were around some
competence now no longer deemed to fit.

> We label the process which alters the role of some competences and
> upgrades peripheral routines as a *reordering mechanism*, reflecting the
> fact that it alters the hierarchy of routines and competences.

In the second possibility, the firm alters one or more of its competences, from something it has to something which did not previously
exist in the organization. This process means that a competence (C1,
for instance) is changed to C1', where C1' is unlike any other C or R.
Under this kind of change, all parts of the firm which participated in
C1 will also have to change.

An example of such a process of change occurs when large complex organizations shift from being, say, inflexible producers of service along a standardized line to a more flexible producer of service along flexible lines. The adjustment process of the major Western car assemblers from mass production to flexible production, so aptly documented by Womak, Jones, and Roos (1990), is one example. Kotter and Heskett (1992) document similar changes at British Airways, which moved from a production-oriented airline (passengers should alter their schedules and behaviours to fit our needs) to a more customer-oriented service firm (we are here to serve the customer).

> We label the process which alters a competence into something the organization did not previously possess as one of revitalization, to indicate the nature of the technical change.

In Table 4.1 we show the two processes of reordering and revitalization for a simple multiple-unit organization which has two competences C1 and C2 and two peripheral routines R1 and R2. C1 and C2 are present in each unit, whereas R1 and R2 appear only once. In the process of revitalization, C2 is transformed into C2', which alters both units. In the process of reordering, we assume that C1 is dropped from the core and R1 is upgraded. This means that a unit is lost and a new one is acquired.

Is the distinction between *reordering* and *revitalization* a meaningful one? We suggest that it probably is, because the content of the processes may differ. Moreover, we suggest that the difficulties of the two may also differ. The process of downsizing and reshaping of portfolios (reordering) appears to be different from the process of

TABLE 4.1 A simple example of reordering and revitalizing

	C1	C2	C2'	R1	R2
Initial position					
Unit X	*****	*****		******	
Unit Y	*****	*****			*****
Revitalize					
Unit X'	*****		******	*****	
Unit Y'	*****		******		*****
Reorder					
Unit X	*****	*****		******	
Unit Y					
Unit Z		*****		******	*****

substituting new competences for old ones in the core. Judging by the difficulties faced by complex companies, we suggest that in general, for a given firm, it is easier to engage in *reordering* than in *revitalization*.

> Reordering is less risky than revitalization in a large complex organization.

COMPARING FOUR RENEWAL PROCESSES

By superimposing two methods of managing change (spatial separation and temporal separation) on two differing change consequences (reordering and revitalizing competences) we identify four mechanisms for renewal (see Table 4.2). These which we will consider in turn are labelled as Venturing, Restructuring, Reanimation, and Rejuvenating. By examining their differing risk and time profiles we aim to suggest the different contextual factors which favour use of each of these different mechanisms.

VENTURING

In discussing the general problem of renewal, Van de Ven (1986) has drawn attention to "the structural problem of managing part–whole relationships" and noted the benefits of "venturing". Drucker (1985: 161–163) expressed the view that (new) flexible units should be organized separately, and should have substantial autonomy. Galbraith

TABLE 4.2 Four mechanisms for strategic renewal

	Spatial separation; risk control is vital	Temporal separation: speed is vital
Revitalizing some of the existing competences	*Reanimating* Bottom-up processes typically involving double-loop learning	*Rejuvenating* Holistic change programmes aimed at revitalization
Reordering "core" competences and peripheral routines	*Venturing* Top-level processes of moving competences around including creating new units and selling old	*Restructuring* Top-down process of restructuring divisions, setting of new priorities, defining new products

(1982) stressed the importance of "reservations" which are totally devoted to creating new ideas, while Peters and Waterman (1982) used the term "skunk works" for this phenomenon.

This kind of venturing clearly fits the category of *spatial separation*. However, in the general discourse, it is not always clear if these writers are talking of *reordering* or *renewal*. Among those who explore the subject further, there is the suggestion that it is reordering of existing competences and routines which is the issue and not revitalizing a competence. For example, Kanter (1983, 1988: 184–191) distinguishes between the "generation" of an innovation which, in her view, required frequent contact and closer integration with other parts of the organization, and the "completion" or implementation of the innovation in flexible modes, for which segregation or isolation from the rest of the organization would be helpful. It is clear that in Kanter's model the organization is required to lend its core ideas, stores of knowledge, and routines to help develop the new venturing unit.

Building on Burgelman (1983a,b), MacMillan (1985) and Block and MacMillan (1993) have taken up the research further, by examining the nature of corporate venturing. They find a wide variety of innovatory possibilities, all of which share the feature of some spatial separation. Such separation brings costs, such as the difficulty of integrating the new ideas back into the old organization. But it also brings some benefits, the new ideas are typically insulated from the inertia of the centre, and have the possibility to flourish without being suffocated.

Bearing in mind these findings, we tentatively suggest that the process of venturing has the lowest risk of any of the renewal processes, in the sense that failure can be contained and variety increased. However, as a mechanism for orchestrating change throughout the whole organization, many such as MacMillan (1985) note the obstacles. Of the four mechanisms it is potentially the slowest, because of the delays involved in first developing the ideas and then in transporting them more widely.

Venturing is the slowest but most controllable of all the processes of renewal.

RESTRUCTURING

Explaining the mechanisms by which change takes hold across the whole organization has long been the concern of the classical administrative theorists such as Barnard (1938) and Selznick (1957). They have typically described a multi-level approach to management, with top managers having a highly important role in the process. In the same vein, Chandler (1962) has explored how corporate management is the primary initiator of managerial action, while front-line managers were the implementers of top-down decisions. In summary, all these writers see very deliberate managerial processes, with spatial separation by level.

Because the idea of competences was not well developed at the time of many of the writers, we can only speculate as to whether their models favour ideas of *revitalization* or *renewal*. Doubtless many would not accept the idea of so limited a description, but nonetheless we suggest that the bias is towards *reordering*. The processes are manifestly top down and about *selection* of what is currently within the organization.

The notion of a very top-level process being one which emphasizes reordering is clearly taken by Hamel and Prahalad (1989). They see renewal of organizations as stemming from the strategic intent of the CEO dependent on superior industry foresight. Such a process of renewal is highly stylized, and is probably very exceptional. Evolutionary perspectives, such as Cyert and March (1963), suggest that strategy in large complex firms is rarely centralized at the top management, and it is usually multifaceted and less well integrated (Van Cauwenberg and Cool, 1982).

In thinking about the contexts and nature of *reordering* we suggest that the risks involved are essentially greater than those involved in venturing, if only because the change is taking place on a larger scale. The failure of top managers to execute such change is well documented, and so the risks are not trivial. However, there is an advantage, we suggest, in speed. Because of the top-down administrative process, with the parallel exercise of power, the possibilities of achieving a quicker transformation seem more likely.

> Restructuring is a quicker, but more risky way of managing a change process than that of venturing. It will be relatively more effective in achieving reordering of competences.

REANIMATING

Bower's work (1970) on the management of the resource-allocation process has suggested that an effective and powerful process of change is through originating, developing, and promoting strategic initiatives from the lower levels, often called bottom-up or middle-up (cf.

Sanchez and Heene, 1996). His ideas have been echoed in a stream of research including Kimberley (1979), Quinn (1985), and Bartlett and Ghoshal (1993) which suggests that renewal can emerge from autonomous behaviour of individuals or small groups at lower levels of the organization (Burgelman, 1983a). It is usually argued that front-line managers have the most current knowledge and expertise and are closer to sources of information critical to innovative outcomes. Within the *reactive bottom-up, emergent perspective* the role of top management is seen as retroactive legitimization (Burgelman, 1994) or judge and arbiter (Angle and Van de Ven, 1989).

While there is no clear suggestion from this literature, we suggest that it relates most directly to *revitalization*. Questioning existing processes by means of an emergent perspective suggests a process of new competence building from the lower levels through double-loop generative learning (Argyris and Schön, 1978; Senge, 1990). It is suggested that interaction with the market and demanding clients help front-line managers to alter the status quo. We compare this process with that of the reordering or exploiting already developed competences which is believed to take place at the upper levels by single-loop, adaptive learning. Upper level learning helps ensure the exploitation of existing competences and their transfer around the organization.

Because reanimation may be in part emergent, it is not fully controllable by top management, although clearly controllable by the organization. The emergent process may be slow and halting, giving rise to possibilities that top management may fail to provide the legitimization until a passage of time after the appearance of some outside triggers, as documented in Burgelman's (1994) study of Intel.

> Reanimation will be a process most suitable for the revitalization of competences, in which risk is controlled but at the cost of speed.

Rejuvenating

The possibilities of radical change have recently emerged in the literature, mainly based on a number of documented cases. In contrast to simple turnarounds (Slatter, 1984) where organizations go back to their roots and eliminate unprofitable activities and shed worthless routines, rejuvenation is the taking hold of wholly new processes to substitute for outdated routines and capabilities. These have been documented by Beer, Eisenstat, and Spector (1990), Grinyer, Hayes, and McKiernan (1988), and Baden-Fuller and Stopford (1994). The typical features of such change processes are that they are holistic, complete, and under-taken quickly. Guth and Ginsberg (1990) explain their close affinity with Schumpeter's (1934) notion of renewal.

Although there is no suggestion that these processes of change are exclusively focused on one kind of competence change, documented examples typically dwell on the effectiveness in *revitalizing* old outdated competences. The change processes are typically encom-passing of new thought processes (Spender, 1980) as well as routines. Tushman and Romanelli (1985) and Tushman and Anderson (1986) refer to such episodes as *punctuated changes*.

The dangers of such holistic change programmes are not so well documented, except insofar as they often fail to start. For example, in Stopford and Baden-Fuller (1994) it was noted that many firms which tried to engage in such holistic programmes failed to reach beyond the stage of ambition. The necessity of mobilizing the whole top team to achieve such revolution is well established, and represents a consider-able challenge. In addition, there are many other hurdles to cross.

> Rejuvenation represents one of the most difficult kinds of renewal pro-cesses. It requires the organization to revitalize existing core compe-tences at a speed and in a holistic manner which carries severe dangers. On the one hand, the risk is that the process may not start. On the other, there is a risk that when started the organization will disintegrate into chaos and so lose what it already has.

Table 4.3 provides an overview of the four propositions stated above.

TABLE 4.3   Contextual factors which favour different renewal mechanisms

	Spatial separation	Temporal separation
Revitalizing some of the existing competences	*Reanimating* A middle-up process which may be especially suited to revitalizing existing competences when speed is not vital but controlling risks is important	*Rejuvenation* A process which is most risky, because the scope of the change is large and the content of the change is most difficult
Reordering "core" competences and peripheral routines	*Venturing* A process of change which is best suited to occasions where speed is not important, and where the need to control risk is high	*Restructuring* A process of change most suited to attempts to re-order processes when speed is of importance

NEW AND EXISTING TECHNOLOGIES OF THE FIRM

When do firms have to apply which mechanism? Or are the mechanisms equal? We do believe that there are some contingencies under which certain mechanisms are more effective than others. One of these contingencies is technology (Van de Ven and Garud, 1988). In Table 4.4 we consider two kinds of technology evolution: those that are new to the firm and those whose roots lie in the firm. We briefly discuss four possibilities relating to the table.

TABLE 4.4   Technology and mechanisms of strategic renewal

	Competition is perceived benign by the firm; change is not urgent (spatial)	Competition is perceived to be intense and change is urgent (temporal)
Technologies new to firm (revitalizing)	Slow change of competence by local initiatives (peripheral change by reanimation)	Fast change of competences by holistic, multi-level initiatives (fundamental change by rejuvenating)
Technologies existing in the firm (reordering)	Risk reduction by corporate venturing (technology variation by venturing)	Quick response by combining competences across industries (managing technology convergence by restructuring)

TECHNOLOGY VARIATION

When competition is perceived to be benign to the firm, the firm can renew by creating variety and expanding by drawing on existing technologies. The mechanism of *corporate venturing* allows the firm to diffuse knowledge and technology throughout the firm. We argued that such an approach of intra-reordering of competences and routines is not speedy, but, more importantly, reduces the risks of the firm. By stimulating a variety of initiatives, the chance of survival of the firm is increased (Fast, 1979; Block, 1982; Block and MacMillan, 1993).

CONVERGING TECHNOLOGIES

In contrast, firms that operate in emerging industrial complexes in which many technologies converge have to respond quickly. In order to have a competitive advantage, these firms need superior "inter-reordering" capabilities in order to combine competences across multiple industries. One can expect to see incumbent firms becoming enveloped in a skein of inter-organizational relationships involving partial equity holdings and joint ventures (Teece, 1984). *Restructuring* their business, creating inter-industry joint ventures are adequate renewal mechanisms for such firms.

NEW PERIPHERAL TECHNOLOGIES

When faced with a resource-rich environment, firms can undertake competence renewal at low risk by organizing change in specialized subparts of the firm such as New Business Development Departments, R&D departments etc. Starting with a peripheral change in their technology, in the end such a *reanimation* may lead to a new competence throughout the firm. Smith's (1996) study of strategic renewal within Regional Bell Operating Companies is illustrative. She shows that resource-rich organizations can construct new capabilities in the telecommunications service industry through chaotic international expansion activities. Newly developed technologies in their unregulated businesses could only be deployed through top management support through a focus on certain types of telecom services, project types, and countries. Although the speed of renewal is slow, the process itself is reasonably controllable as firms reintegrate their mainstream activities with their newstream activities (Ansoff and Brandenburg, 1971).

NEW CORE TECHNOLOGIES

When firms face fierce competition involving radically new technologies, speed is most important. The crisis is one that may confront the entire organization, and requires a comprehensive response, not a partial one. Although the creation of separate change units accelerates progress in new areas of opportunity, it often leads to problems of morale, disruption, and reassimilation. A dramatic corporate-wide transformation may be necessary with holistic transformation of all managerial levels. Such renewal processes are explored extensively by Stopford and Baden-Fuller (1994) in their case studies of rejuvenating mature firms.

Of course, we realize that firms do not always have a free choice.

Some firms have become used to a particular mechanism of renewal and this mechanism becomes a part of their administrative heritage. Moreover, many firms use two or more of these mechanisms sequentially or simultaneously. Nonetheless, to remain effective, firms should continuously reflect on their mechanisms of renewal and be willing to change it when necessary. Table 4.4 summarizes our discussion.

DISCUSSION

The approach in this chapter has a number of obvious limitations. First, is it right to make a clear distinction between revitalization and reordering? While theoretically there appears to be a difference, in practice the boundaries are not so clear, and managers do not see it this way. However, we suggest that our partitioning may be justified and adds useful insights to those who research or practice. In a similar way, are we right to draw distinctions between differing kinds of change programmes? It is obvious that most mechanisms can take place at the same time in a firm, but with differing degrees of intensity, so our distinctions can only make sense in the context of emphasis. Researchers often suggest that one style dominates, but again we must be careful. The distinctions often exist only from a particular perspective. As Weick aptly points out, often strategy is present only after the event, not during or before.

We suggest that neither of these criticisms are unusually damaging. They are well known and understood in the literature, and we have learned to live with them. Probably more serious is the suggestion that firms cannot choose among change mechanisms. The historical perspective of research suggests that even when managers believe they have free choice, their latitude is very limited. History severely constrains the possibilities for action. For example, if a firm has recently undergone a holistic rejuvenation programme, it is probably impossible to undertake another successfully. Restructuring may also be resisted and the choice may be between venturing and reanimation.

The real test will be in the empirical work. Does our model help explain events in large complex organizations, and does it help managers? We suggest that to explore this issue we need data which cover both time series and cross-sections; only with pooled data can we get at both the process issues and those of competitive content. This is very demanding, and although we are engaged in the work we do not underestimate the difficulty.

CONCLUSIONS

In much of the literature on strategic management the discussion of the content of change is separated from the discussion of process. While this has facilitated a great deal of progress, it has also created an artificial dichotomy (Sanchez and Heene, this volume). Here, we explored the usefulness of putting the two sides together, and have shown how the subject of corporate renewal is capable of further insight by this process. Our chapter is an early exploration of ideas, which need refinement and testing. Even so, they suggest the value of this matching approach.

All organizations face a dilemma of encouraging renewal and assuring preservation. Stability is necessary for internal cohesion and to prevent self-destruction. Renewal is necessary because most organizations cannot routinely innovate as fast as the market requires, especially in periods of disequilibrium or hypercompetition. By posing somewhat artificial distinctions between competence reordering and competence revitalization, and by contrasting processes of change which resolve the paradox by spatial or temporal means, we have identified four mechanisms for renewal, and suggested a matching of processes to tasks in different contexts.

ACKNOWLEDGEMENTS

We gratefully acknowledge the helpful comments of members of the EMOT conference in Reading, the EGOS conference in Istanbul, and the SMS conference in Ghent where various versions of this chapter were presented. We particularly note the help of Aimé Heene, Oguz Baburoglu, John Cantwell, Yves Doz, Paul Evans, and Keith Pavitt. In addition, we have received encouraging comments from other colleagues.

REFERENCES

Alchian, A.A. and Demsetz, H. (1972). Production, information costs, and economic organization. *American Economic Review*, **62**, No. 5, 777–95.

Aldrich, H.E. (1979). *Organizations and Environments*. Englewood Cliffs, NJ: Prentice Hall.

Aldrich, H.E. and Pfeffer, J. (1976). Environments of organizations. *Annual Review of Sociology*, **2**, 121–40.

Amit, R. and Schoemaker, P.J.H. (1993). Strategic assets and organizational rent. *Strategic Management Journal*, **14**, No. 1, 33–46.

Angle, H.L. and Van de Ven, A.H. (1989). Suggestions for managing the innovation journey In *Research on the Management of Innovation*. New York: Harper & Row.

Ansoff, H.I. and Brandenburg, R.G. (1971). A language for organizational design: Parts I and II. *Management Science*, August, 350–93.

Argyris, C. and Schön, D. (1978). *Organizational Learning*. Reading, MA: Addison-Wesley.

Baden-Fuller, C. and Stopford, J.M. (1994). *Rejuvenating the Mature Business*. Cambridge, MA: Harvard Business School Press.

Barnard, C.I. (1938). *The Functions of the Executive*. Cambridge, MA: Harvard University Press.

Barnett, W.P., Greve, H.R. and Park, D.Y. (1994). An evolutionary model of organizational performance. *Strategic Management Journal*, Winter Special Issue, **15**, 11–28.

Barney, J. (1991). Firm resources and sustained competitive advantage. *Journal of Management*, **17**, No. 1, 99–120.

Barney, J.B. and Zajac, E.J. (1994). Competitive organizational behavior: toward an organizationally-based theory of competitive advantage. *Strategic Management Journal*, Winter Special Issue, **15**, 5–9.

Bartlett, C.A. (1993). Commentary: Strategic flexibility, firm organisation and managerial work in dynamic markets. *Advances in Strategic Management*, **9**, 293–8.

Bartlett, C.A. and Ghoshal, S. (1993). Beyond the M-Form: toward a managerial theory of the firm. *Strategic Management Journal*, Winter Special Issue, **14**, 23–46.

Bate, P. (1994). *Strategies for Cultural Change*. Oxford: Butterworth-Heinemann.

Beer, M.R., Eisenstat, R. and Spector, B. (1990). *The Critical Path to Corporate Renewal*. Cambridge, MA: Harvard Business School Press.

Bleeke, J. and Ernst, D. (1991). The way to win in cross border alliances. *Harvard Business Review*, March-April, 78–86.

Block, Z. (1982). Can corporate venturing succeed? *The Journal of Business Strategy*, **3**, No. 2, Fall, 21–33.

Block, Z. and MacMillan, I.C. (1993). *Corporate Venturing*. Boston, MA: Harvard Business School Press.

Bower, J.L. (1970). *Managing the Resource Allocation Process*. Boston, MA: Harvard Business School Press.

Burgelman, R.A. (1983a). A process model of internal corporate venturing in the diversified major firm. *Administrative Science Quarterly*, **28**, 223–44.

Burgelman, R.A. (1983b). Corporate entrepreneurship and strategic management. *Management Science*, **29**, No. 12, 1349–64.

Burgelman, R.A. (1994). Fading memories: a process theory of strategic business exit in dynamic environments. *Administrative Science Quarterly*, **39**, 24–56.

Burns, T. and Stalker, G.M. (1961). *The Management of Innovation*. London: Tavistock.

Chandler, A.D., Jr (1962). *Strategy and Structure*. Cambridge, MA: MIT Press.

Child, J. and Smith, C. (1987). The context and process of organisational transformation—Cadbury Limited. *Journal of Management Studies*, **24**, No. 6.

Conner, K. and Prahalad, C.K. (1996). A resource based theory of the firm: knowledge and opportunism. *Organizational Science*, forthcoming.

Contractor, F.J. and Lorange, P. (1988). Why should firms cooperate? The strategy and economic basis for cooperative ventures. In Contractor, F.J. and Lorange, P., *Cooperative Strategies in International Business*. Lexington, MA: Lexington Books.

Cyert, R. and March, J. (1963). *A Behavioral Theory of the Firm*. Englewood Cliffs, NJ: Prentice Hall.

D'Aveni R. (1994). *Hypercompetition*. New York: Free Press.
Drucker, P. (1985). *Innovation and Entrepreneurship*. New York: Harper & Row.
Fast, N.D. (1979). The future of industrial new venture departments. *Industrial Market Management*, **8**, 264–73.
Galbraith, J.R. (1982). Designing the innovating organization. *Organizational Dynamics*, Winter, 3–24.
Grant, R.M. (1991). The resource based theory of competitive advantage: implications for strategy formulation. *California Management Review*, **33**, No. 3, 114–35.
Grinyer, P.H., Hayes, D.G. and McKiernan, P. (1988). *Sharpbenders: The Secrets of Unleashing Corporate Potential*. Oxford: Blackwell.
Guth, W.D. and Ginsburg, A. (1990). Guest editors' introduction: Corporate entrepreneurship. *Strategic Management Journal*, Summer Special Issue, **11**, 5–15.
Hakansson, H. (1982). *International Marketing and Purchasing of Industrial Goods*. Chichester: John Wiley.
Hamel, G. (1991). Learning in international alliances. *Strategic Management Journal*, **12**, Special Summer Issue, 83–103.
Hamel, G. and Prahalad, C.K. (1989). Strategic intent. *Harvard Business Review*, May-June, 63–76.
Hampden-Turner, C. (1990). *Charting the Corporate Mind*. New York: Free Press.
Handy, C. (1989). *The Age of Unreason*. London: Hutchinson.
Hannan, M.T. and Freeman, J.H. (1984). Structural inertia and organizational change. *American Sociological Review*, **49**, 149–64.
Kanter, R.M. (1983). *The Change Masters: Innovation and Entrepreneurship in the American Corporation*. New York: Simon & Schuster.
Kanter, R.M. (1988). When a thousand flowers bloom: structural, collective, and social conditions for innovation in organization. In Staw, B.M. and Cummings, L.L. (eds), *Research in Organizational Behavior*, Vol. 10. Greenwich, CT: JAI Press, pp. 169–211.
Kimberly, J.R. (1979). Issues in the creation of organizations: initiation, innovation, and institutionalization. *Academy of Management Journal*, **22**, 437–57.
Kogut, B. and Zander, U. (1992). Knowledge of the firm, combinative capabilities and the replication of technology. *Organizational Science*, **3**, No. 3, 383–97.
Kotter, J.P. and Heskett, J.L. (1992). *Corporate Culture and Performance*. New York: Free Press.
Learned, E., Christensen, C., Andrews, K. and Guth, W. (1969). *Business Policy: Text and Cases*. Homewood, IL: Irwin.
Leonard-Barton, D. (1992). Core capabilities and core rigidities: a paradox in managing new product development. *Strategic Management Journal*, Summer Special Issue, **13**, 111–25.
Levinthal, D.A. (1996). Why organisation matters. *Journal of Economic Behavior and Organisation*, forthcoming.
Levinthal, D.A. and March, J.G. (1993). The myopia of learning. *Strategic Management Journal*, Winter Special Issue, **14**, 95–112.
Levitt, B. and March, J.G. (1988). Organisational learning. In Scott, W.R. (ed.), *Annual Review of Sociology*, Vol. 14 Palo Alto, CA: Annual Reviews, pp. 319–40.
Lewin, K. (1951). *Field Theory in Social Science.*. New York: Harper and Row.
Loasby, B. (1996), The organization of capabilities. *Journal of Economic Behavior and Organization*, forthcoming.
Lorenzoni, G. and Baden-Fuller, C. (1995). Creating a strategic centre to manage a web of partners. *California Management Review*, Spring.

MacMillan, I.G. (1985). Progress in research on corporate venturing: 1985, *Working Paper*, NY University, Center for Entrepreneurial Studies.

Marshall, A. (1920). *Industry and Trade*. 3rd edition. Macmillan, London.

Matsson, L.-G. (1987). Management of strategic change in a "markets as networks" perspective. In Pettigrew, A. (ed.), *The Management of Strategic Change*. Oxford: Blackwell.

Miles, R. and Snow, C. (1986), Network organizations: new concepts for new forms. *California Management Review*, Spring.

Nelson, R.R. and Winter, S.G. (1982). *An Evolutionary Theory of Economic Change*. Cambridge, MA: Harvard University Press.

Nonaka, I (1991). The knowledge-creating company. *Harvard Business Review*, November-December, 96–104.

Ouchi, W.G. (1981). *Theory Z: How American Business Can Meet the Japanese Challenge*. Reading, MA: Addison-Wesley.

Penrose, E. (1959). *The Theory of the Growth of the Firm*. London: Basil Blackwell.

Peters, T.J. and Waterman, R.H. Jr (1982). *In Search of Excellence*. New York: Warner Books.

Pettigrew, A.M. (1985). *The Awakening Giant*. Oxford: Blackwell.

Poole, M.S. and van de Ven, A.H. (1989). Using paradox to build management and organization theories. *Academy of Management Review*, **14**, No. 4, 562–78.

Porter, M.E. (1990). *The Competitive Advantage of Nations*. New York: Free Press.

Prahalad, C.K. and Hamel, G. (1990). The core competence of the corporation. *Harvard Business Review*, **68**, 79–91.

Quinn, J.B. (1985). Managing innovation: controlled chaos. *Harvard Business Review*, **63**, No. 3, 78–84.

Sanchez, R., Heene, A. and Thomas, H. (eds) (1996). *Dynamics of Competence-based Competition*. Oxford: Elsevier.

Sanchez, R. and Heene, A. (1996). A systems view of the firm in competence-based competition. In Sanchez, R., Heene, A. and Thomas, H. (eds), *Dynamics of Competence-based Competition*. Oxford: Elsevier.

Schumpeter, J.A. (1934). *The Theory of Economic Development*. Cambridge MA: Harvard University Press.

Selznick, P. (1957). *Leadership in Administration—A sociological interpretation*. New York: Harper & Row.

Senge, P. (1990). The leader's new work: building learning organizations. *Sloan Management Review*, Fall.

Slatter, S. (1984). *Corporate Recovery*. London: Penguin.

Smith, A. (1996). Baby Bells, garbage cans, and hypercompetition. *Organizational Science*, **7**, No. 4.

Spender, J.-C. (1980). *Strategy Making in Business*. University of Manchester, Doctoral Dissertation.

Stacey, R. (1995). The science of complexity: an alternative perspective for strategic change processes. *Strategic Management Journal*, **5**, 477–96.

Stopford, J.M. and Baden-Fuller, C.W.F. (1994). Creating corporate entrepreneurship. *Strategic Management Journal*, **15**, No. 7, 521–36.

Teece, D.J. (1984). Economic analysis and strategic management. *California Management Review*, Spring, 87–110.

Teece D.J., Pisano, G. and Shuen, A. (1992). Dynamic capabilities and strategic management. Working Paper, University of California at Berkeley, August.

Teece, D.J., Rumelt, R., Dosi, G. and Winter, S. (1994). Understanding corporate coherence: theory and evidence. *Journal of Economic Behavior and Organization,* **23,** 1–30.

Thorelli, H.B. (1986). Networks: between markets and hierarchies. *Strategic Management Journal,* **7.**

Tushman, M.L. and Anderson, P. (1986). Technological discontinuities and organizational environments. *Administrative Science Quarterly,* **31,** 439–65.

Tushman, M. and Romanelli, E. (1985). Organizational evolution: a metamorphosis model of convergence and reorientation. In Cummings, L.L. and Staw, B.M. (eds), *Research in Organizational Behavior,* Vol. 7 Greenwich, CT: JAI Press, pp. 171–222.

Utterback, J.M. and Abernathy, W.J. (1975). A dynamic model of process and product innovation. *Omega, The International Journal of Management Science,* **3,** No. 6, 639–56.

Van Cauwenberg, A. and Cool, K. (1982). Strategic management in a new framework. *Strategic Management Journal,* **3,** 245–64.

Van de Ven, A.H. (1986). Central problems in the management of innovation. *Management Science,* **32,** No. 5, May, 590–607.

Van de Ven, A.H. and Garud, R. (1988). A framework for understanding the emergence of new industries. In Rosenbloom, R.S. and Burgelman, R.A. (eds), *Research on Technological Innovation, Management and Policy,* Vol. 4.

Van de Ven, A.H. and Poole, M.S. (1988). Paradoxical requirements for a theory of organizational change. In Quinn, R.E. and Cameron, K.S. (eds), *Paradox and Transformation: Toward a theory of change in organization and management* Cambridge, MA: Ballinger.

Volberda, H.W. (1996). Towards the flexible form: how to remain vital in hypercompetitive environments. *Organizational Science,* **7,** No. 4.

Von Hippel, E. (1978). Successful industrial products from customer ideas. *Journal of Marketing,* **42,** 39–49.

Wernerfelt, B. (1984). A resource-based view of the firm. *Strategic Management Journal,* **5,** 171–80.

Williamson, O.E. (1975). *Markets and Hierarchies: Analysis and Antitrust Implications* New York: Free Press.

Womak, J.P., Jones, D. and Roos, D. (1990). *The Machine that Changed the World.* Englewood Cliffs, NJ: Prentice Hall.

5

Customers as the Originators of Change in Competence Building: A Case Study

JOHAN WALLIN

This chapter describes the change process of ABB Fläkt Oy, a subsidiary of the Finnish ABB Group. Over a period of four years (1991–5) ABB Fläkt, and especially its Industrial Division, has emerged from being a mainly domestic player to a significant exporter. The theory of competence-based competition can, in the light of the ABB Fläkt case, be further developed by introducing a new perspective on the individual customer and the idea of value creation. Seeing customers as co-producers has an impact on the way we understand strategic goals and the market test for competence. Grouping capabilities into four categories can improve decision making regarding competence building and competence leveraging. The ABB Fläkt case also gives some insights into the differentiation between firm-specific and firm-addressable resources from both a business unit and a corporate perspective.

Competence-based Strategic Management.
Edited by Aimé Heene and Ron Sanchez.
Copyright © 1997 John Wiley & Sons Ltd.

THE ISSUES ADDRESSED IN THE ABB FLÄKT CASE

For management, a very difficult task when setting goals is to define what the desired state of the firm's system elements (Sanchez and Heene, 1996) should be in the future. In 1985 AT&T projected that the number of US cellular users in 1995 would be 900 000. Based on this forecast, the company buried its cellular program. The number of cellular subscribers in the USA 1994 was 20 million. To correct this mistaken projection McCaw was acquired at a cost of $12 billion (Kupfer, 1994). The suggestion by Hamel and Prahalad (1994) to develop better industry foresight is one way to improve goal formulation.

The *managerial goal formulation* (Sanchez and Thomas, 1996) that leads to competence building and competence-leveraging activities is one of the elements described in the ABB Fläkt case. This chapter suggests that important customers can be co-producers in the goal-formulation process and improve industry foresight capabilities.

One element of the desired state of the system is the generation of future cash flows. Strategic decision making is about creating strategic options to develop, produce, and market products in the future (Sanchez and Thomas, 1996). Seeing products as bundles of product traits means that strategic decision making is about future products traits (Bogner and Thomas, 1996). This corresponds to the view of Normann and Ramírez (1994) saying that offerings, not firms, compete in the marketplace for customers. Normann and Ramírez (1993) expanded this idea by visualizing value creation as the ultimate goal of the firm. Therefore, a product, service or offering is not only an output of one value creation system (the "producer" or "supplier") but also an input to another value-creation system (the "customer"). The implication of seeing *products as inputs to value-creation systems of customers* brings more depth into the "market" notion applied in the suggested "market test for competence" (Sanchez, Heene, and Thomas, 1996). The way this issue was treated in ABB Fläkt also gives some insights into how the notion of "customer potential" can be practically addressed.

Resource building is, according to Normann and Ramírez (1994), connected to the customer base. Two basic strategic alternatives, are acquisition of competences to be offered to existing customer bases, and expanding by building on existing competences and applying them to new customer bases. In the case of ABB Fläkt, *competence building* was primarily seen as an activity which would enhance relationships with existing customers. *Competence leveraging* was seen as deploying existing competences to customers not yet served.

The concept of "business unit" versus "corporation" has in Sanchez,

Heene, and Thomas (1996) been touched upon when stating that the understanding of actual and potential coordination systems available to firms, at both business unit and corporate levels, is inadequate. When implementing "Customer Focus" at ABB Fläkt, *the role of the business unit within the context of the corporation* was relevant. This chapter examines why.

THE ABB FLÄKT PROCESS AND ITS CONTENT

THE INDUSTRIAL DIVISION PROCESS

In 1990 Percy Barnevik initiated a corporate-wide effort in ABB called "Customer Focus". The message he gave when introducing this program was as follows:

> We know the key to our long-term success and profitability: the unconditional and total satisfaction of our customers with every contact they experience and every product or service they receive from us. Whatever we do must be aimed at satisfying their needs, and expectations at an even higher level. We have to be aware that this is a moving target, because their needs and expectations change. We must welcome such changes as opportunities for adding more and new values for our customers.
>
> To install this uncompromising customer-driven attitude throughout our Group, we have started a process called "Customer Focus". To me, it is one of the most important processes that we have embarked on in our company. Quality and cycle time are vital elements of this process since improvement of both offers a huge potential for increasing customer satisfaction (Barnevik, 1990).

In 1991 the Finnish ABB Fläkt corporation had 1700 employees and its turnover was 920 million FIM. The Industrial Division of ABB Fläkt Oy, headed by Antero Hietaluoma, employed 75 people in 1991 and had a turnover of 223 million FIM. The Industrial Division's projects were air pollution control systems, pulp and paper dryers, industrial fans, and service contracts relating to these installations.

The Customer Focus process within the Finnish ABB Group was initiated in the industrial division of ABB Fläkt in October 1991 through a project called "Customer Base Management". Its first task was to conduct a customer base analysis, whereby the buying behavior of the 30 largest (by turnover) customers was analysed in detail for the period 1988–91. Based on this background material a seminar was held in November 1991 in order to define the goals of the project in greater detail.

The goal formulation of the project was addressed by asking the participants (the 15 most senior sales people of the division) to present their views on the business potential for three customer segments: domestic customers, East European customers, and other export customers. Each participant was placed in a matrix with a qualitative scale from 1 to 5 indicating their views on business volume development (decrease, status quo, or increase) within the coming 3–5 years. When aggregating the results, it became evident for the participants that the potential of the domestic market was perceived collectively as far poorer than existing budgets and plans indicated. On the other hand, the collective view of the potential of the East Europe segment was seen as much more promising than the existing corporate perception. Considerable Western export potential was also identified. The problem was that resources could not be deployed to develop these opportunities.

The results of this session created confusion within the top management of the ABB Fläkt Group. The following three months were, to some extent, a crisis stage in the process. The future outlook of business opportunities presented in the seminar did not coincide with top mangement's view. The Industrial Division was meanwhile conducting in-depth interviews with the most important customers. The results of these interviews further supported the earlier, fairly pessimistic, domestic industry outlook.

Based on these findings, it was decided in February 1992 that the Industrial Division should change its strategic goal formulation, and radically increase its deployment of resources to develop business opportunities in East Europe, as well as focus on more export projects abroad. Three categories of key resources were identified: the internal resources of ABB Fläkt, addressable resources within the ABB Group (including product development, marketing, and finance functions), and addressable external resources (primarily export alliances with Finnish companies such as Ahlström and Tampella).

Mr Hietaluoma gave the following credit to the "Customer Base Management" project in a presentation to ABB Fläkt management in autumn 1992:

- A substantially clearer view of business potential for the next 3-5 years
- Better possibilities to allocate resources efficiently
- A deeper understanding of customers and, in turn, of customers' businesses and of data-gathering possibilities
- Definition of key accounts (10 customers)
- Emphasis on export
- Increased cooperation between different business areas.

THE ABB FLÄKT GROUP PROCESS

In the first half of 1993, based on the success of the Industrial Division process, Harri Launonen, CEO of the ABB Fläkt Group, initiated a similar group-wide effort together with the author and other colleagues in SMG Finland. The project objectives were:

- To adapt key account management to ABB Fläkt Oy's current situation in order to support sales activities—in other words, to create a new mode of operation
- To gather information on important customers in order to be able to develop further customer-oriented strategies and to create customer-specific action plans
- To classify and analyse customer base management activities: what to do, how to do it, how to group customers.

When the ABB Fläkt Oy "Key Account Management" project was initiated early in 1993 the Industrial Division was already working towards its new strategic goal, i.e. increasing its export activities. Therefore the ABB Fläkt Oy process primarily involved the remaining divisions of the Group, with some participation from the Industrial Division.

The main objective of the "Key Account Management" project was to better understand the value-creation processes of customers in order to develop customer-specific strategies and action plans. The project was divided into three areas: definition of the account management organization, information gathering about important customers, and the development of a systematic approach to account management. Personal relationships were seen as major intangible assets, especially when dealing with the most important customers with whom ABB Fläkt had developed close cooperation over the years.

During a period of six months each participant (in total, 30 senior sales executives representing all divisions within ABB Fläkt Oy) gathered information about one particular customer. For customers who were defined as possible key accounts detailed action plans were prepared. These action plans included concrete proposals to the management team on how to handle the key account.

In June 1993, based on the proposals from the participants, the management of ABB Fläkt Oy nominated 21 customers as corporate key accounts. One person was appointed to be responsible for each key account. In most cases this person was the same individual who had been in charge of gathering information on that particular customer.

Implementation of the suggestions went rapidly and smoothly due to the "action learning" approach of the project. At the end of the project Mr Launonen stated that the "Key Account Management" mode of operation was well understood throughout the organization. Consensus prevailed regarding the selection of key accounts and the appointment of persons responsible for those accounts.

The "Key Account Management" project had also identified customer dissatisfaction with the way ABB was organized. ABB was very product-oriented from the customer's point of view. On a construction site, for example, there could be several different ABB units represented: the Ventilation Division of ABB Fläkt Oy providing air-conditioning installations, ABB SLM Oy taking care of electrical installations, and ABB Fläkt Service Oy providing service for existing equipment. Due partly to the results of the "Key Account Management" project a radical reorganization took place at the end of 1993. The Ventilation Division of ABB Fläkt Oy, ABB Fläkt Service Oy, and SLM Oy were combined into one company: ABB Installations Oy. At the same time, the Industrial Division was transferred to ABB Strömberg Power Oy and became a separate unit, ABB Environmental Systems Oy. The remainder, i.e. the genuine product divisions (Industrial Products, Ducts, Ventilation Products, and Air Terminal Units), formed the new ABB Fläkt Oy. From 1 January 1994 Harri Launonen became marketing director for the whole ABB Group in Finland.

Mr Launonen mentioned three reasons for the reorganization:

1. There was a higher-level (ABB corporate-wide) redefinition of ABB business areas and business segments; the changes in ABB Fläkt Oy conformed with this.
2. The structural changes in the Finnish construction market were forcing ABB to consolidate its activities and to reduce costs.
3. The new organization enabled a better grouping of competences focused on customer requirements.

THE ABB FLÄKT PROCESS IN PERSPECTIVE

The ABB "Customer Focus" initiative was communicated from corporate management to business areas and country organizations as an organizational imperative. At the same time, it was concluded that moving the organization from traditional product selling to strategic relationships with customers is a complex and slow process that requires cultural change, changes in organizational processes (e.g. performance measurement systems) and a concerted effort over many years. To move the organization to "strategic partnerships" involves multiple steps, each requiring continuous improvement, with measurable progress along the way. The ultimate goal, a truly customer-focused organization, bases its long-term direction on individual customer strategies and plans (Schulmeyer, 1992).

One ambition stressed by ABB management was to increase cross-business unit cooperation. This has been a real challenge within an organization that traditionally favored internal competition and a high degree of decentralization. Strong emphasis on products and technical skills are still very much the basic values at the business unit level.

When asked, in August 1995, what had changed between 1992 and 1995 Mr Hietaluoma answered: outsourcing. In 1995 the former Industrial Division employed fewer people than in 1992, but used much more subcontracting. Mr Hietaluoma felt that in 1995 ABB Environmental Systems Oy was fairly good at managing external firm-addressable resources.

IMPLICATIONS OF THE CASE FOR THE THEORY OF COMPETENCE-BASED COMPETITION

When the "Customer Focus" initiative was introduced in ABB Fläkt in September 1991 the goals of ABB Fläkt were driven by perceptions of product cash flow generating potential emanating from existing forecasts. In retrospect, as Figure 5.1 indicates, these perceptions were unreliable. Management faced an unprecedented discontinuity, and did not realize this or its implications in full.

The first to notice that the impending discontinuity within ABB Fläkt were the Industrial Division managers. They based their market view on in-depth interviews with the most important customers regarding their investment plans and business prospects. These interviews helped the Industrial Division to better estimate the buying potential of the existing customer base. As mentioned earlier, the insight derived was that cash flow projections would be unattainable if ABB Fläkt management continued to concentrate resources on providing present domestic customers with existing or new products, instead of redeploying resources to developing export business.

The close interaction between the Industrial Division and its most important customers helped the division to switch more quickly from competence building (for existing customers) to competence leveraging (for new export customers). Understanding the value-creation logic of their customers helped ABB Fläkt to redeploy resources and

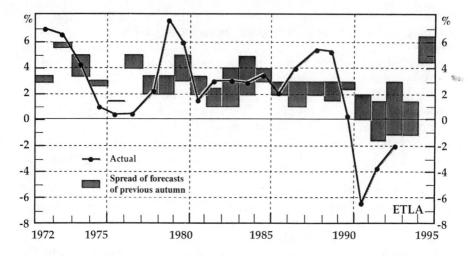

FIGURE 5.1   Dispersion of Finnish forecasts of economic development: forecast for
next year

redesign offerings to make the shift in strategic focus without adding
new resources. In February 1992 Mr Hietaluoma decided to deploy
more resources to exports. He applied for corporate support which
was granted to the Industrial Division in May 1992 in the form of
corporate funds to further develop the activities of the division in
Russia and the Ukraine. In the project export markets, alliances with
Ahlström and Tampella resulted in significant orders from the pulp
and paper industries of Indonesia, Thailand, and South Africa.

*The organizational restructuring of ABB Fläkt in 1993 suggests that the
appropriate boundary of a "business unit" is the organizational entity that
provides the same customer base with offerings that the customer perceives as
related.* As a result of this insight the electrical and ventilation installa-
tion units within the Finnish ABB Group were merged into one
business unit.

Based on ABB Fläkt's experience, the question of which resources
are firm-specific and which are firm-addressable may be addressed
from the point of view of the business unit. This means that there may
be firm-specific resources *internal* to the corporation which, from the
business unit point of view, are less addressable than *external* firm-
addressable resources. When the corporate culture favors internal
competition, the preferred addressable resource may prove to be
external. Whether this is "good" or "bad" has to be related to other
advantages/disadvantages within the existing mode of operation.

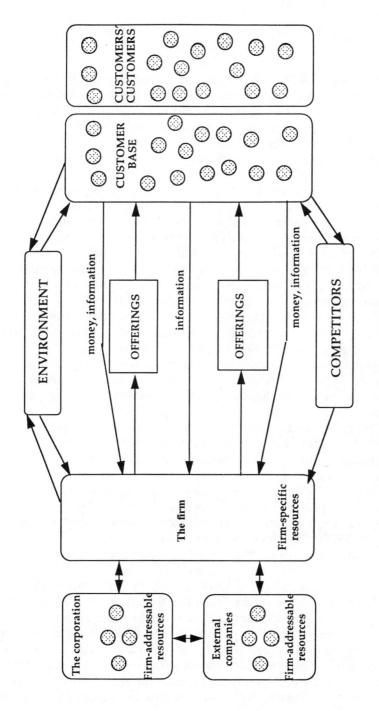

FIGURE 5.2   The framework of matching resources and customers

COMBINING COMPETENCE-BASED THEORY AND THE SMG FRAMEWORK

The experience of ABB Fläkt can be interpreted through the framework of Sanchez, Heene and Thomas (1996) with little difficulty. The complex and holistic nature of matching resources and customer bases can be described graphically, as in Figure 5.2 which divides the resource pool into three categories: business unit (firm-specific) resources, corporate (firm-addressable) resources, and external (firm-addressable) resources.

The framework used in the ABB Fläkt process also views the firm as an open system (see Sanchez and Heene, 1996). The Sanchez and Heene presentation facilitates a greater understanding of the firm's resources by presenting the firm as a system of stocks and flows of both tangible and intangible assets. The framework used in ABB Fläkt now puts more emphasis on individual customers as sources of intangible assets, like market knowledge. When looking at firm-addressable resources from the business unit point of view, it is relevant to separate corporate resources from external resources. As mentioned earlier, in a highly decentralized organization corporate resources can be less addressable than external resources.

The products and services or offerings are not only outputs, but also inputs. This interactive relationship between supplier and the customer is very significant. Seeing customers simply as product markets means that the individual requirements of each customer cannot be recognized. These requirements can best be understood by knowing how each customer is producing value for his customers. "A company's offerings have value to the degree that customers can use them as inputs to leverage their own value creation" (Normann and Ramírez, 1993). The offering can be described as a three-dimensional activity package, or as Bogner and Thomas (1996) suggest, as bundles of product traits. Similar conclusions are presented by Normann (1975). The dimensions of value creation include hardware, software, and peopleware (see Figure 5.3) of importance to customers and the next level of customers' customers.

The value-creating potential along each of the dimensions of offering depends on the value-creating system of the customer. Two customers from the same segment may have completely different value-creation systems, and thus view the elements of the "same" offering differently as, for example, General Motors and Toyota (see Treece, 1992, analysing the buying policy of these two companies). Toyota tries to develop long-term partnerships with its suppliers. General Motors is very transaction focused, and as such, a long-lasting relationship is not

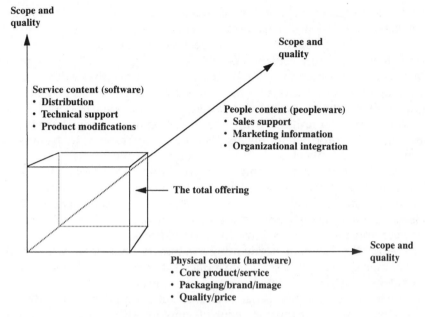

FIGURE 5.3   The three-dimensional offering

seen as a goal. For each dimension of the offering, the notion of threshold traits (traits that are obligatory to be competitive, but for which more than the minimum level will not elicit a better market response), central traits (traits for which a higher level of performance will elicit a better market response), and plus-only traits (traits that are not required to compete but which improve the market's response) apply. However, it is important to notice that what for Toyota might be considered as a threshold trait on the peopleware dimension (e.g. long-term personal relationships) might be considered as irrelevant by GM. Therefore the notion of market traits may be misleading, as traits exist for customers, not for markets. Developing a genuine customer orientation within a firm helps to understand customer-specific threshold traits, thereby avoiding the unnecessary costs attached to providing more than the minimum level of performance in any threshold trait for each specific customer. The logic for developing supplier–customer partnerships is to create a work- and risk-sharing formula that optimizes the total value creation of the two players, and thereby forms a genuine win–win situation; Normann and Ramírez (1994) call this co-production.

As established industry definitions become obsolete, strategic flexibility and learning are firm characteristics of growing importance (Sanchez, 1995, 1996). This means that, more than ever before, the market test for competence has to be seen as the customers' test for competence. Existing customers get increasing focus. (See e.g. Bill Gates' view in Schlender (1995) where he concludes that Microsoft has to obtain most of its revenues from existing customers rather than new ones.) When existing customer relations are developed in-depth, it is a radical shift in thinking from the traditional customer satisfaction paradigm. Co-production means that the supplier has to be able to deploy its available assets and capabilities simultaneously in a way that satisfies both Toyota and GM, providing the supplier has some distinctive competences (Selznick, 1957) which provide the foundation to create value for both Toyota and GM. Customer satisfaction takes a one-sided view of the customer; in co-production the goals of both the supplier and the customer have to be considered.

In ABB, the issue of segmenting customers was dealt with in the "Customer Focus" process. It was noticed that moving all customers to a strategic partnership level is not economically justifiable. Also, all customers may not want partnerships with suppliers for ABB-type products. However, from the point of view of ABB, the goal has to be that every customer should see ABB as a responsive and reliable supplier. For chosen customers ABB wants to be seen as a preferred supplier or strategic partner.

ABB sees building stronger relationships through customer-focused initiatives as an important way to achieve a competitive advantage. This requires an understanding of customers' businesses at a detailed level. It also requires focusing internal resources to create superior value for customers. Additionally, it asks for changes in internal processes (performance measurement systems, support systems, etc.) to support and reinforce customer-focused efforts. The ultimate goal is to achieve strategic partnerships with targeted customers. Using the terminology of Sanchez and Heene (1996), achieving the goal of becoming truly customer focused asks for learning, i.e. qualitative changes in the stocks of cognition-based higher system elements. As the comments from Mr Hietaluoma showed, the transition from a product-based culture towards a truly customer-oriented learning organization is still underway within ABB.

Developing closer supplier–customer relationships (as in the case of Toyota or as discussed in Magnet, 1994) asks management to monitor more closely their customer relations. In this chapter it is proposed that when defining resources, this customer relatedness should be explicitly recognized. Therefore this chapter next suggests a framework dividing firm capabilities into four different categories. (This classification has been developed in cooperation with Rafael Ramírez and Richard Normann.)

The case of ABB Fläkt suggests that the interaction between the firm and its customers is a useful starting point for analysis of the competence strategy process. The capability for this is termed here *relationship capability*, which refers to the interactive relationship, including the capability to listen to and understand the customer, as well as the ability to be able to communicate to the customer the value-creation possibilities of the firm (Figure 5.4).

Based on its understanding of customers, the firm should be able to design offerings that are optimal for the customer in a value-creating sense. This is called *transformative capability*. This capability refers to the ability to combine bundles of product traits whose hardware, software, and peopleware have the threshold traits required by each customer, as well as central traits and plus-only traits that increase the value creation of the customer, and can be offered at costs less than their value creating potential.

By *generative capability* we understand the ability to create genuinely new bundles of product traits that constitute firm-specific competences (see Lewis and Gregory, 1995).

Integrative capability refers to the capability to deploy firm-addressable assets and capabilities inside and outside the boundaries of the firm/business unit. It should be noted that these assets include both the customer base and the competitor base. The customer base is, for the firm, an increasingly valuable asset, not only as a tied-in market for its products, but also as a co-producer participating in goal formulation and providing strategic information. The network approach by Easton and Araujo (1996) (suggesting that person-to-person networks which link competing firms facilitate important forms of competence building and leveraging) also applies to supplier–customer relationships.

The four categories of capabilities suggested here all contribute to both competence building and competence leveraging.

By viewing the firm as an open system (Sanchez and Heene, 1995) the development of ABB Fläkt Oy was primarily taking place in the lower level system parts. Taking action to close the gap was primarily driven by data on the state of the market (lack of demand in Finland). In order to achieve the cash-flow goals, ABB Fläkt Oy had to respond to this change. Initially, in late 1991 there was a need to change some elements of the strategic logic and management processes, i.e. to accept that the existing world view had to be altered. Once this was done, most of the changes applied to lower-level resources. Thus the proposal by Sanchez and Heene that any strategic change includes

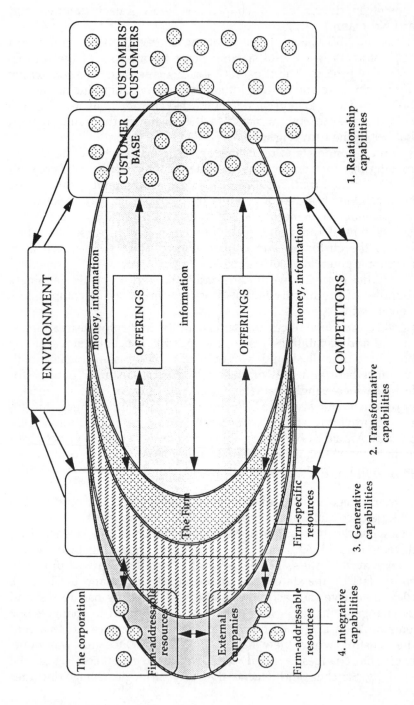

FIGURE 5.4 Resources, offerings, customers, and capabilities

elements of both competence building and competence leveraging applies also in the ABB Fläkt Oy case. Competence building included efforts to further strengthen those technical capabilities that offered opportunities for international projects. Competence leveraging was evident in the international ambitions shown by the Industrial Division.

There were two core competences in the Industrial Division which were used for leveraging: technological know-how for air pollution control for certain industrial applications and industrial know-how of pulp and paper processes. Both these competences had been developed in close cooperation with Finnish industrial companies engaged in these activities, domestically and abroad. The Industrial Division was, in competence terms, addressing external resources both from customers (such as Outokumpu and Kymmene) and from suppliers providing complementary products (like Ahlström and Tampella) when strengthening its core competences. In this way the Industrial Division was part of a strategic group where the focus of each member was on competence building. This supports the concept by Sanchez and Thomas (1996) that the firm, as a goal-seeking open system, creates strategic options through systemic interaction of many kinds of firm stakeholders.

On a Group level ABB Fläkt Oy had a mix of assets, including spearhead applications, e.g. innovative new state-of-the-art products in ventilation technology that were patented and developed into export successes. The bulk of the business, however, derived from standard applications supplied to regular domestic customers. In this area the concept of customer share, or the proportion that ABB was selling compared to sales by competing firms, became one of the key measurements within the company. Developing these relationships and related capabilities thus became the focus of ABB Fläkt Oy, leading to the complete reorganization of the company.

CONCLUSIONS

The ABB Fläkt case suggests that customer orientation can be a strong element in the meta-competence (Chiesa and Manzini, this volume) of deciding what competences to develop. Strategy or goal formulation in this case was "Competence Driven and Customer Oriented". By explicitly including customers as co-producers in the strategy-formulation process, the Industrial Division has improved both the speed and quality of its competence-based strategy process.

REFERENCES

Barnevik, P. (1990). "Customer focus". Internal ABB document.

Bogner, W.C., and Thomas, H. (1996). From skills to competencies: The "play-out" of resource bundles across firms. In Sanchez, R., Heene A. and Thomas, H. (eds), *Dynamics of Competence-Based Competition: Theory and Practice in the New Strategic Management*. Oxford: Elsevier.

Easton, G. and Araujo. L. (1996). Characterizing organizational competencies: An industrial networks approach. In Sanchez, R., Heene, A. and Thomas, H. (eds), *Dynamics of Competence-Based Competition: Theory and Practice in the New Strategic Management*. Oxford: Elsevier.

Hamel, G. and Prahalad, C.K. (1994). *Competing for the Future*. Boston, MA: Harvard. Business School Press.

Kupfer, A. (1994). AT&T's $12 billion cellular dream. *Fortune* 12 December, 22–34.

Lewis, M.A., and Gregory, M.J. (1995). Developing and applying a process approach to competence analysis. In Sanchez, R., Heene, A. and Thomas, H. (eds), *Dynamics of Competence-Based Competition: Theory and Practice in the New Strategic Management*. Oxford: Elsevier.

Magnet M. (1994). The new golden rule of business. *Fortune*, 21 February, 28–32.

Normann, R. (1975). *Skapande företagsledning*. Lund: Aldus.

Normann, R. and Ramírez, R. (1993). From value chain to value constellation. *Harvard Business Reveiw*, 65–77.

Normann, R. and Ramírez, R. (1994). *Designing Interactive strategy*. Chichester: John Wiley,

Sanchez, R. (1995). Strategic flexibility in product competition. *Strategic Management Journal*, **16** (Summer), 135–159.

Sanchez, R. (1996). Strategic product creation: managing new interactions of technology, markets and organizations. *European Management Journal*, **14** (2), 121–38.

Sanchez, R. and Heene, A. (1996). A systems view of the firm in competence based competition. In Sanchez, R., Heene, A. and Thomas, H. (eds). *Dynamics of Competence-Based Competition: Theory and Practice in the New Strategic Management*. Oxford: Elsevier.

Sanchez, R., Heene, A. and Thomas, H. (1996). Towards the theory and practice of competence-based competition. In Sanchez, R. Heene, A. and Thomas, H. (eds), *Dynamics of Competence-Based Competition: Theory and Practice in the New Strategic Management*. Oxford: Elsevier.

Sanchez, R. and Thomas, H. (1996). Strategic goals. In Sanchez, R., Heene, A. and Thomas, H. (eds), *Dynamics of Competence-Based Competition: Theory and Practice in the New Strategic Management*. Oxford: Elsevier.

Schlender, B. (1995). What Bill Gates really wants. *Fortune*, 16 January, 16–33.

Schulmeyer, G. (1992). Customer focus, an Organizational Imperative. Internal ABB document.

Selznick, P. (1957). *Leadership in Administration*. New York: Harper & Row.

Treece, J.B. (1992). The lessons GM could learn for its supplier shakeup. *Business Week*, 31 August, 69.

6

Strategizing for Innovation: Competence Analysis in Assessing Strategic Change

THOMAS DURAND

When facing an imminent innovation, a firm may be more vulnerable or, conversely, better positioned than existing or potential competitors. How, why, and to what extent? What strategic responses may be adopted in such situations? These are some of the questions this chapter intends to address by making use of the emerging theory of competence-based competition. More specifically, we shall refer here to the framework developed by Sanchez, Heene, and Thomas (1996). In so doing the chapter aims at both illustrating and testing the applicability of the competence perspective, thus potentially enriching and qualifying the framework.

INTRODUCTION

The strategic impact of innovation on the competitive dynamics of industry has been much documented in the management research literature (Abernathy and Utterback, 1978; Clark, 1985; Tushman and

Competence-based Strategic Management.
Edited by Aimé Heene and Ron Sanchez.
Copyright © 1997 John Wiley & Sons Ltd.

Anderson, 1986; Cooper and Schendell, 1976; McGee and Thomas, 1989; Foster, 1986; Durand and Gonard, 1986; Durand and Stymne, 1991). Classical distinctions have been suggested, e.g. technological (product/process) versus organizational innovations or incremental versus radical categories (Gomory, 1989; Dosi, 1982), thus characterizing the nature or the intensity of change (Abernathy and Clark, 1985; Nelson and Winter, 1977; Durand, 1992).

Here we address the issue of evaluating the intensity of change *ex ante*—i.e. before its impact may be analysed—by raising the following questions. What impact on the competence and strategic position of the firm should one expect from an imminent innovation? How can one assess the intensity of innovation to evaluate whether or not an organization is vulnerable to the anticipated change (or well prepared for it) and, compared, to competitors, to what extent?

This way of addressing the issue of change may seem to imply that a firm would be confronting innovation that apparently comes out of nowhere. Innovation, however, often results at least in part from the firm, its strategy, its behaviour on the market. The firm may help to shape innovation. Yet, to clarify our perspective, we will view innovation as exogenous to the firm: many forces, mostly external to the focal organization interact to generate and shape innovation. In most instances, firms are faced with innovation as change imposed by the environment.

Our objective here is twofold. On one hand, we aim at helping managers address the issue of the vulnerability of their firm facing innovation: for example, how should a TV magazine react to the imminent arrival of digital interactive TV? We also aim at helping firms benefit more when change actually creates an opportunity for them. How should a satellite manufacturing company prepare for the expected development of global mobile telephony services based on systematic satellite coverage?

On the other hand, we aim at contributing to the currently emerging competence-based theory of the firm. We attempt to show how the concept of competence may be specified in more detail and how it may be used to better deal with some unsolved questions, such as the one we address here, namely the operationalization of the concept of transilience (Abernathy and Clark, 1985).

We first present the issue of evaluating the intensity of innovation and its relation to the concept of competence, elaborating the concept of a "competence gap". We then turn to presenting a typology of competence based on the content of competence as well as on the various ways to hold or access the required competence. We finally discuss how the framework may be used in assessing the competence gap relative to competitors, thus making it possible to strategize innovation.

INNOVATION AND COMPETENCE

Raising the issue of the evaluation of the intensity of innovation leads to the question of the essence of innovation. What is it that is being changed, modified, transformed, or adapted through the process of innovation? What is being destroyed, outdated, rendered obsolete? In other words, what is the fundamental nature of innovation and change?

We suggest viewing innovation from the perspective of the competence of the organization. We use here the concept of competence in the emerging competence-based theory of the firm developed by Sanchez, Heene, and Thomas (1996). By competence, therefore, we mean not only all forms of available assets, capabilities, knowledge, know-how and skills, technologies and equipment in the organization, as most of the existing literature would suggest, but also the *coordinated deployment* of the above assets and capabilities.

A cook is competent because he or she can integrate ingredients into a dish to yield a tasty meal. In the terminology used by Sanchez, Heene, and Thomas, the cook's competence results from an *intention* (the cook knows what to look for), an *organization* or an effective process (the cook has a recipe which stands as a replicable protocol to combine or integrate the available ingredients or assets), as well as a *goal attainment* (if the dish is not tasty or eatable, the cook may not be regarded as competent).

This distinction between the assets and capabilities, on the one hand, and their integration through some coordination processes, on the other, is extremely valuable. One may, however, consider some aspects of the specification of the competence concept put forward by Sanchez, Heene and Thomas. Is there really a need for intention to be competent? The authors refer to luck (Barney, 1986) as not being a form of competence. Yet, one may argue that contingency may transform an incompetent firm into a very competent one on the market, and vice versa. When Bénéteau, the manufacturer of sailing boats, finds that its organization is very capable of designing, manufacturing, and selling mountain cabins, this may be regarded as an instance of luck while, at the same time, the competence was there, although not used. Indeed, not only were the main capabilities available, but so were the coordinating processes, as these are basically similar to those required for manufacturing sailing boats. Could not one say that, although not active in manufacturing mountain cabins, Bénéteau was competent for that business? Of course, it was not really by accident that they thought of using their existing competence to diversify into the mountain cabin business. They clearly searched for contracyclical activities, i.e. smoothing winter versus summer workloads. This search process required a significant strategic thinking capability of the "know what and know why" types, as Sanchez (1996) rightly calls them. However, we would argue that Bénéteau was "potentially" competent in that business even before being aware of it. In that sense, *potential* competence may not necessarily require intention. We recognize, however, that actually exploiting the full potential of a competence requires intention.

Along the same lines, one may also consider the "goal attainment" aspect. When is a goal significantly achieved? What is a tasty meal? A goal is reached only to a certain extent most of the time. The goal attainment concept covers in fact a wide continuum, ranging from failure to full success. Various competitors may fulfil their goals more or less than others. An ambitious firm may be more competent than competitors, but unable to achieve its too ambitious goals. Conversely, a firm with little ambition may be less competent than competitors but still achieve its limited goals. This in turn leads to the idea that competence is a concept which must be assessed relative both to competitors and to the goals set by the firm for itself, as discussed in Sanchez and Thomas (1996).

Strategy theory has thus far presumed that only an external referent for goals is valid, e.g. relative performance among competitors in an industry. Clearly, as they include intention and goal attainment of individual firms in their definition of competence, Sanchez, Heene, and Thomas (1996) challenge that presumption. The fundamental issue raised here thus relates to the choice of criteria for evaluating competence and performance: What kind of performance can essentially reflects the extent to which a firm is competent, or, conversely, have many resulting forms of competence performance including purely internal referents? If being competent means reaching the goals that the organization sets up for itself, then, we argue, limited ambition will make the firm competent in the sense of Sanchez, Heene, and Thomas. In any case, both the intention and the goal attainment criteria seem to figure more clearly, in our opinion, in the "strategic logic" of Sanchez and Heene (1996) than the competence definition itself (see left-hand side of Table 6.1).

Nevertheless, we would like to stress our support for the idea of the central importance of the firm's integrating/coordinating capability. As cuisine is more than the mechanistic addition of ingredients, and as a football team is more than the random grouping of individually skilled players, a competent firm is more than a collection of assets, skills, and know-how. Some cement is needed. As Sanchez, Heene, and Thomas put it, the ability to coordinate deployments of assets may be regarded as an asset of a different nature. In a way similar to the discussion of Chiesa and Manzini in this volume about different levels of competence in the organization, we advocate that, as Sanchez, Heene, and Thomas suggest, coordination capabilities are key elements of competence. Coordinated deployment stands as a meta-capability with an integrative role. We shall return to this.

With those preliminary definitions in mind, we turn our attention to these questions: What capabilities of the firm are going to be affected by the change? What competence will now be made useless by the requirements of the new technology or new organization brought about by the innovation? What piece of equipment, expertise of the human resources, linkage to suppliers, client relationship, or access to distribution channels will be reinforced or rendered obsolete by the change? To what extent will the individual and collective experience built within the organization through cumulative learning be made useless once the innovation has arrived? What new coordinated deployment processes will now be required?

We choose to follow Abernathy and Clark (1985) as they put forward the concept of *transilience*, a contraction of transition and resilience, i.e. what makes the organization bounce back through change. Measuring transilience means evaluating the "width" of the *competence gap* that the firm has to bridge in order to adapt itself to the requirements of the new technology/organization, once the change has taken place. Operationalizing the concept of transilience means developing a way to assess the extent to which the portfolio of competence of a firm is going to be rendered obsolete or, conversely, reinforced by the change. This means describing the content of the portfolio of competence of a firm and analyzing how it may be affected by an imminent change. This idea clearly relates to the complementary assets of Teece (1986), the core competences of Prahalad and Hamel (1990), and the currently emerging, broader theory of competence (Hamel and Heene, 1994; Sanchez, Heene, and Thomas 1996).

Change relates to both reinforcement and destruction of at least part of the progress made along a natural trajectory (Nelson and Winter, 1977). Dosi (1982) also adopts an evolutionary perspective to suggest that a trajectory presents some cumulative features, while a paradigmatic change means a shift in trajectory. Incremental innovation improves and thus reinforces the firm's routines, capabilities, and competence along what we chose to call a "seam" (Durand, 1992).

Radical innovation disrupts and breaks the routines and the organizational capabilities, requiring a more or less radically new set of competence. Schumpeter's (1941) "creative destruction" therefore needs to be complemented by some form of "improved continuation", what Tushman and Anderson (1986) identified as the "order breaking/order creating" duality.

Our focal issue thus evolves from a broad and unspecified "how to assess the intensity of an imminent change" into a set of more precise questions. "How do we measure the transiliency?" "What share of the competence of the organization will be disrupted by an expected change and to what extent? What other competence will turn out to be even more useful than before? How could some part of the existing competence even become counterproductive, operating as a burden when facing the requirements of the new competitive conditions?"

It should be stressed here that the competence perspective clearly implies that the intensity of an innovation is firm-dependent. What may be felt as a major change for one organization may be a simple adaptation to another. Clearly the firm-dependent variability in the intensity of an innovation comes both from the existing stock of capabilities in the organization and from its processual ability to build and deploy new capabilities.

This line of reasoning leads to the idea of assessing the potential impact of innovation on the competitive dynamics in the industry in terms of the relative difficulty for each competitor to address and access new competences (through competence building and/or competence leveraging), given its existing set of capabilities and coordinated deployment processes, i.e. its portfolio of competences. Note that this issue relates to Farjoun's (1994) analysis of resource related industry groups, as well as to the analyses of Durand (1988) and Kandel *et al.* (1991) of human expertise in organizations.

How far is the existing portfolio of competence from the newly required portfolio? How difficult will it be to bridge this "competence gap"? How much more difficult should this step be for some of the competitors? How might some other competitors be in a position to better leverage their own portfolio of competence and build new competences?

As we have mentioned above, our intent is to implement the concepts of transilience and competence as a first step to strategize innovation. Operationalizing the concept of transiliency means assessing the intensity of change for the firm, which requires measuring the "competence gap". In turn, however, this requires insights into the real nature of competence, as well as competence building and leveraging.

A DECOMPOSITION OF COMPETENCE

We first present our view of a decomposition of competence into five categories of "ingredients" before comparing the categories of Sanchez, Heene, and Thomas to ours (Table 6.1). Building upon classical categories of competence largely described in the management research literature (e.g. tangible versus intangible, tacit versus articulated, cognitive versus behavioural, individual versus collective), we suggest retaining five ingredients of competence which may serve our purpose:

- Stand-alone assets
- Cognitive capabilities
- Processes and routines
- The organizational structure
- Behaviour and culture—the identity

First, the *"stand-alone" assets* cover all artefacts, i.e. physical objects belonging to the firm (equipment, building, products, etc.) corresponding to tangible assets as well as not-so-tangible (but non-social) assets such as software and clearly intangible assets such as brand names. In a sense what we call the stand-alone assets category covers assets that may be sold or acquired without a need for transfer of human resources or major cognitive input. In that sense, the "stand-alone" assets may be viewed as "non-social" assets.

Second, the *cognitive capabilities* encompass individual and collective knowledge and know-how, individual skills, technologies and patents, etc. They tend to be partly explicit and partly tacit. Organizational processes might have been included in this second category, as they are indeed in some sense a form of cognitive capabilities, but we choose to consider them separately.

Third, *processes and routines* are the coordinating mechanisms which make the organization operate, combining the actions of individuals into collective functioning. Henderson and Clark (1990) suggest that these processes may become so dedicated to a specific product design that the corresponding organizations may become unable to perceive and cope with rather limited changes essentially affecting the architecture of the product design. They suggest that the firms that they studied lost their capacity to adapt to change and explore new architectural designs as their processes—including communication channels and interdepartmental problem-solving relations—generated in-depth but too-narrow cumulated learning.

Although from a different perspective, Iansiti (1992) points to a similar coordinating process. He suggests that integrating capabilities are needed to put together all the elements needed for an innovation. His empirical work shows that this strategic integration may be generated by senior technicians who gained a good understanding of customer needs through significant market exposure. This clearly relates to the coordinated deployment capabilities.

Fourth, the *organizational structure* may facilitate or hinder the ability of a firm to adapt to change. Wu *et al.* (1990) show how Telia, the Swedish telecom operator, was not structured properly to address the issue of high definition TV. Similarly, Doz (1986) shows how the decentralized structure of ITT turned out to be a handicap in the development of a time-division multiplexing switchboard, while Ericsson could benefit from the modular architecture of its first electronic product generation thanks to its more centralized R&D organization.

Finally, the *behavioural and cultural dimension* (i.e. the identity) should not be omitted. Shared values and beliefs, rites and taboos are all ingredients in the identity of an organization as a human construct.

If the culture of the firm may be seen as the cement holding individuals and sub-groups together, it may also largely affect the ability of the firm to accept or reject change. Many examples are known of organizations paralysed by their identity and incapable of addressing major innovations affecting their market, their technology, or the regulation of their industry. The difficult and painful transformation of regulated monopolistic utilities (e.g. in telecoms) into competitive firms stretching to satisfy their clients illustrates the point. This cultural dimension may also be included in the "strategic logic" element of the system view of the firm (Sanchez and Heene, 1996).

Our five categories are actually close to the Sanchez, Heene, and Thomas decomposition, as shown in Table 6.1. Two major amendments, however, to their systemic view are suggested. First, the "management processes" category covering the coordinated deployment capabilities in their model may be enriched and decomposed, as we suggest, into three subelements: the organizational structure, the processes and routines, as well as the identity. It seems that these categories are both comprehensive and workable in practice within the broad "management processes" category.

Second, and as discussed earlier, our reading of their framework suggests that we should relate the intention/goal attainment criteria directly to the strategic logic, where we feel they belong. Similarly, we view operations as part of the management processes, not a separate activity which would otherwise seem to combine the assets mechanistically. We feel that the integration/coordination dimensions, which Sanchez, Heene, and Thomas very rightly advocate when dealing with deployment of competence, are important at the level of the operations

TABLE 6.1 Compared definitions and categories

	Strategic logic			Our definitions and categories
Coordinated deployment	Management processes	Organization and processes for coordinated deployment of assets	Intention Goal attainment Efficient processes	• Strategy • Culture • Organizational processes • Structure — The organization
Resources	Assets — Intangible	Knowledge	Explicit / tacit Individual / collective	• Cognitive capabilities
		Capabilities	Skills …	
		…	Brand names Software	• Stand-alone assets
	Assets — Tangible	Products Equipment Buildings …		
Competence	Operations			

Our reading of the Sanchez, Heene, and Thomas definitions and categories concept as well. In other words, operations and strategy should perhaps not be split this way when dealing with competence.

However, the two amendments suggested here to the Sanchez, Heene, and Thomas model are relatively minor and do not contradict their framework, but rather refine it. We believe that the five categories discussed above may be easier to work with in practice when describing a real portfolio of competence in a firm. Note that some specific capabilities may fall into more than one category. For example, linkage to suppliers belongs to the cognitive capabilities (knowing the suppliers industry), the process/routine (e.g. operating just-in-time with them), and to the structure (having an organization of buyers in fit with both the needs of the firm and the specificities of the suppliers).

Based on this, we now turn to the issue of assessing the "competence gap" as a way to evaluate if and how a firm will find it more difficult than competitors to access the set of capabilities soon to be required by an anticipated wave of innovation.

HOLDING AND ADDRESSING COMPETENCE

When change appears on the horizon, be it hoped for or feared, it is usually not easy to describe in detail its future content and contours. What is anticipated is more a potential set of innovations with possible uncertainty about its components and its overall envelope. No precise specification of impending innovation is possible since latent market demand and uncertain upstream marketing on the supply side will take time before converging towards a well-defined market segmentation. However, we argue that it is usually possible to identify the *general* types of competence and capabilities which the new/renewed activity will likely require. The profile of human resources needed, the type of equipment to be used, the typical organizational processes to be adapted, the relevant coordinated deployment capabilities, and the type of structure and culture to be fitted to the anticipated future may be characterized.

This description of the types of competence which may be needed, should the innovation succeed, may not be precise or detailed. Some ambiguity and uncertainty may make it difficult to specify at length the competences soon to be required. Yet they may be qualified at least in broad terms.

In other words, we argue that even if it is not possible to describe exactly what an innovation will turn out to be, it is possible to identify the capabilities required to bring it about. As an example, one may consider the imminent innovation of a "device" (most probably a multimedia terminal) which may soon be offered to passengers seated in an aircraft or a train. Will that terminal be a simple TV screen, as is already the case in some aircraft? Will it be a PC, a gambling machine, a videophone, a fax, a video disk player, a combination of these? Will it be a terminal within the local area network (LAN) of the aircraft or will it be stand-alone equipment?

At this point no clear specifications of the market needs are available. We argue, however, that it is quite feasible to identify and characterize the types of capabilities which such an innovation may require, e.g. working relationships between aircraft manufacturers and equipment suppliers, marketing knowledge of the "jet set", access to software and entertainment facilities, etc. We argue that even the coordinated deployment meta-capabilities (i.e. in our model the relevant organizational structure, the desirable culture, as well as the appropriate management processes) may be anticipated, at least roughly.

Typically, in our example, a management-by-project type of organization with involvement of airline companies, cabin suppliers, and electronic systems designers would seem relevant. A strong experience in alliances and partnerships, a culture of joint projects, experimentation and testing, and quick feedback from client reactions to the development teams would also seem appropriate to cope with the requirements of this wave of innovation.

We thus suggest that it is feasible to evaluate analytically, namely capability by capability and competence by competence, the difficulty for a firm to stretch its existing portfolio of competence to access the newly required capabilities and coordinated deployments.

A preliminary but interesting way of analyzing this issue may be simply to distinguish whether the firm holds the capabilities for the two main categories of components of competence:

- Assets and cognitive capabilities
- Deployment capabilities (processes, structure, and culture)

As shown in Table 6.2, we suggest that it is difficult for a firm to face innovation when neither capability is held. More interestingly, we may hypothesize at this stage that it is probably more difficult for the firm to adapt to the change when the adequate deployment capability is lacking than when the assets and cognitive capabilities are lacking. We shall comment more on this later.

Going one step further, we must recognize that, if not already fully holding the competence, a firm may hold at least part of its ingredients or may be able to access these elements more or less rapidly,

TABLE 6.2   Preliminary typology of competence gaps

Assets and cognitive capabilities

		Held	Not held
Deployment capabilities	Held	Minor adjustment (leveraging) 1	Minor gap (building the assets base) 2
	Not held	3 Significant gap (rebuilding deployment capabilities)	4 Major gap (full building)

efficiently, and without high cost. The issue of identifying the competence gap is not just a matter of holding versus not holding competences, but relates to addressing competences.

We use the "addressing" term as a generic terminology covering all situations: the firm may already hold and essentially leverage competence, or it may not and thus needs to access competence through a building activity. Table 6.3 shows our choice and hierarchy of words.

Four modalities of competence addressing may be identified:

- *Reinforcement*: Already holding the competence within the business unit. The easiest way to face change corresponds to the situation when the competence soon to be required is identical to what it was: distributing human insulin instead of animal insulin uses the same distribution channels and basically requires the same client relationships. As Durand and Gonard (1986) show, this is very different for manufacturing competence, because genetics and fermentation have little to do with extraction and purification of animal insulin from the pancreas of pigs and cows. The distribution competence is here already held by the existing firms as the human insulin innovation did not affect that competence.
- *Synergetic fit*: holding the competence elsewhere in the firm. A second favourable situation for the firm arises when the newly required capabilities are held somewhere else in the organization. The profit center anticipating to be affected by the imminent change may thus leverage the larger portfolio of competence of the firm to access the corresponding competence. Synergies among business centers within the firm make it possible for the portfolio of competence to fit the new requirements. Gonard, Finkbeiner, and Rivalier (1993) discuss, for example, the case of Packinox, a fast-growing

TABLE 6.3   A continuum of competence leveraging and building

Addressing competence

	Holding		Accessing	
	Same competence required *"Reinforcement"*	Competence held elsewhere *"Synergetic Fit"*	Inter-organizational competence *"Networking access"*	Learning capability *"Adaptability"*
Leveraging	++++ Full leveraging	+++ Internal leveraging	++ External leveraging	+ Leveraging the learning capability
Building		and adaptation +	absorption and rebuilding ++	and competence building +++

start-up in heat exchangers, acquired by Framatome. Packinox could benefit from the very advanced soldering capabilities of the Framatome group which had developed world-class soldering expertise through its nuclear activities.

One may of course also argue the opposite. Following Prahalad and Hamel (1990), one may suggest that although available in another business unit of the same organization, competences needed elsewhere may not be easily transferred. "Competence may be locked in the business unit structure of the firm." This case would illustrate how organizational structure may alter the competence of a firm.

These first two modes may be regarded as static in that the organization does not need to build or access a new competence. It already holds it, one way or another. These "holding" modes correspond to the leveraging category of Sanchez, Heene, and Thomas, although the "synergic fit" mode may obviously require some adaptation and thus some rebuilding.

- *Networking access.* In contrast, a third mode relies on the ability of the organization to access external sources of competence in a timely and low-cost way. The firm could carefully build a network of partners and potential suppliers of specific capabilities. In so doing, the firm could develop an ability to address and access new competence in a dynamic mode. One may regard the "virtual firm" as an extreme case illustrating this situation. More often seen is the case of the R&D of a company working hard to maintain a wide variety of contacts with leading university laboratories (e.g. through contracted research) in order to remain in a position to call upon any of them, should the need arise. This corresponds to what Hedlund and Nonaka (1992) called the inter-organizational competence of the firm, as well as to the firm-addressable resources described by Sanchez, Heene, and Thomas. In a sense, when considering competence building through partnerships, Quélin (1996) is also dealing with this category.

- *Adaptability*: retaining a permanent ability to learn. There is a fourth mode for the firm to adapt its portfolio of competence. The firm may have developed a specific learning capability and a strong adaptability, making it possible to quickly imitate, learn, adapt, recreate, and master the newly needed competence. Some firms have built this ability to stay on the move, ready to unlearn and relearn, ready to destroy in order to reconstruct. This learning capability may in some instances be developed enough to enable the organization to adapt to significant competence gaps. Yet this situation is less commonly encountered as organizational inertia seems to be more widely seen in real-life situations of firms facing change. Rumelt (1995) deals with the same theme. This clearly refers to the unlearning issue. Indeed, we strongly believe that a significant part of the adaptability of a firm comes from its ability to unlearn while relearning.

These four modalities stand as generic ways to address competence. Other modalities may exist (e.g. learning and adaptability in networks). We argue, however, that they may in turn be described as a combination of the four generic modalities discussed above.

Both the "networking access" and the "adaptability" modes may be regarded as dynamic as they imply some form of competence accessing, absorbing, and learning. The absorptive capacity of Cohen and Levinthal (1990) is clearly at work here. In the Sanchez, Heene, and Thomas terminology, "networking access" would correspond to competence building through firm-addressable resources, while adaptability would be competence building through firm-specific resources.

However, we feel that the leveraging/building terminology, although useful, needs to be discussed. Indeed, "networking access" clearly involves some form of "external leveraging" plus some competence building. This point is summarized on Table 6.3. This table shows that there is a continuum between leveraging and building. This point is also addressed by Sanchez and Thomas (1996). Our four modes for competence addressing may stand as landmarks in this continuum. In turn, this also affects the quantitative versus qualitative nature of the competence leveraging versus building modes of Sanchez, Heene, and Thomas.

Typically, leveraging, both internal and external, needs some form of qualitative adaptation when it comes to "synergetic fit" or "networking access". Leveraging is thus not just quantitative. Similarly, one may argue that competence building needs a certain amount of learning capability. Again, our specific perspective of operationalizing the Sanchez, Heene, and Thomas framework leads to some hopefully useful qualification of their model.

Table 6.4 summarizes both the decomposition of competence discussed previously and the different modalities of competence addressing (holding/accessing). The table thus combines the "content" perspective of Table 6.1 (describing the elements of content of competence) to the "competence addressing" perspective of Table 6.3 (describing processes to access competence).

The static perspective corresponds to the well-known ecology theory of "the survival of the fittest" while the dynamic modes refer to what we may call interactionist and evolutionist theories, i.e. "the survival of

TABLE 6.4   Competence addressing to close the competence gap (an analytical sieve for competence)

	Static addressing of competence		Dynamic access to competence	
	Same competence required "Reinforcement"	Competence held elsewhere "Synergistic fit"	Inter-organizational competence "Networking access"	Learning capability "Adaptability"
Stand-alone assets				
Cognitive capabilities Know-how				
Structure				
Processes / routines Know-how to solve, coordinate, control				
Identity / culture Behaviour				

increasing difficulty to address the competence and thus cope with the change the connected/adaptable". Whenever unfit, unconnected and unadaptable, the firm should expect trouble. However, Table 6.4 refines this by suggesting that we identify the specific elements of competence that may be more troublesome, acting as a bottleneck to change for the firm. As an example, changing culture is believed to be significantly more problematic than changing the structure of the organization, adopting new coordinating processes and routines, or learning how to run a new piece of equipment. This again raises the issue of unlearning and inertia depending on the category of the capabilities.

Management is known to have more effect on some of the elements of competence identified than on others: stand-alone assets may be acquired; training sessions for a new piece of equipment may be set up to facilitate its operation. This may be costly and time consuming but it is clearly achievable. In contrast, changing the values and beliefs of an organization and destroying taboos and rituals may not be easy, and, above all, may not move the identity of the organization in the intended direction. Management control over the capabilities and thus the competence of the firm is far from being homogeneous. This leads back to the hypothesis formulated earlier together with the presentation of Table 6.2. We argue that, when facing change, the coordinated deployment of assets and capabilities is probably a subset of capabilities more difficult to address than other forms of capabilities.

We further argue that the difficulty to unlearn (a key step in the change process) is most probably higher for the identity—and, to a lesser extent, the processes and routines—than for other capabilities. This view thus supports Sanchez and Heene's (1996) discussion of dynamic response times in changing some elements of the firm's system. We suggest, however, a slightly different characterization of hierarchy in the system: if culture is difficult and takes a long time to transform, we believe that strategy may go much faster and probably even faster than changes in "processes and routines", due to organizational inertia. Thus we would suggest the following hierarchy in the difficulty and time responses when changing elements of the firm's system or addressing new capabilities. From the potentially longest/more difficult to the shortest/easiest, our hierarchy would be as follows:

- Culture/identity
- Routines and processes
- Strategy
- Structure
- Cognitive capabilities
- Stand-alone assets

This hierarchy is not empirically grounded at this stage and is presented essentially to illustrate our point. Empirical work would be needed on this specific topic.

STRATEGIZING FOR INNOVATION

Returning to our issue of innovation, clearly Table 6.4 acts as a sieve to compare the situations of the various competitors, existing or new entrants, facing an imminent change. The point is indeed not only to assess the "competence gap" of a particular firm but also to evaluate the "competence gap" relatively to existing or potential competitors, each leveraging, stretching, and building their own portfolio of competence.

More specifically, we suggest analyzing each of the main functions (R&D, purchasing, manufacturing, marketing, distribution, general management) as shown in Table 6.5. This procedure leads to raising systematically the questions of the changes potentially brought about by the imminent innovation: some of the items are shown in Table 6.5 for the sake of illustration. Also shown for each item presented are the corresponding categories of the competence decomposition (stand-alone assets, cognitive capabilities, structure, processes, identity).

For each item considered, for example for the "distribution channels", the following questions may be raised sequentially:

- *Reinforcement*? Are your existing distribution channels adapted to the new products/services to be offered?
- *Synergistic fit*? Would some other distribution channels used in the firm be better adapted?
- *Networking access* ? Could you access new and adequate distribution channels quickly and efficiently by calling upon your network of partners? How quickly? how efficiently?
- *Adaptability*? Could you build new distribution channels quickly and efficiently, e.g. by transforming and adapting existing channels to the new market conditions? How quickly? How efficiently?

These questions should obviously be answered for each relevant item, for each function, for the firm itself, as well as for existing and potential competitors. At the end of this analytical questioning an assessment should be obtained, qualifying the portfolio of competence of the firm with respect to its fit/vulnerability to the expected change. This assessment is clearly to be formulated relative to competitors— existing or potentially new entrants.

One should also identify the specific capabilities which may be fully or partially leveraged by the firm while not being available to competitors and, conversely, those lacking capabilities—especially those with anticipated long time responses—while being already or more easily available to some competitors.

Strategizing innovation may then start. The firm may anticipate and explore the new options opened up by the imminent wave of innovation through adapting its capabilities, entering new alliances, preparing its organization, its management processes or its culture to the new requirements, according to these elements of competence that may appear to constitute a potential bottleneck to the newly required portfolio of competence.

If it is unable to cope with the expected change, the firm may, conversely, work around its portfolio of competence in order to look for diversification, identifying new activities which may typically require the specific competence profile of the organization. This may be called pivoting around "core" competences or "valorization" of competences.

Even more interestingly, the firm may try to modify the content of the imminent change to make it fit better to its own competence profile and more unfit to those of competitors. Influencing the trajectory, i.e. the course of innovation, in order to better exploit the strengths of the firm's portfolio of competence as well as the weaknesses of competitors' thus becomes another form of "strategizing innovation through competence".

CONCLUSION

We have addressed the issue of developing a strategy for the firm when facing innovation. The firm's strategic goal in such instances is primarily to adapt to the new requirements of the change, addressing the relevant competence. Adopting a competence-based perspective, we have presented an analytical approach to assess to what extent the organization's portfolio of competence is better fitted or, conversely, more vulnerable to the expected innovation than that of competitors.

In so doing, we have discussed the Sanchez, Heene, and Thomas (1996) framework and suggested some potential amendments and refinements. These relate to (1) the content elements of competence, especially the specificity of the coordinated deployment metacapabilities, which, as we suggest, include organizational processes, structure, and identity, and (2) the competence-addressing continuum with four major modalities between two polar extremes (leveraging and building): reinforcement, strategic fit, networking access, and adaptability.

When strategizing innovation, we identify three major types of

TABLE 6.5 Measuring the competence gap. *Examples of capabilities: items for questioning*

Element of competence	Nature	Questioning (for each item)
R&D, design, Industrialization		• Does your firm already hold . . . ?
• R&D expertise	Cognitive	• Would some of . . . ?
• R&D linkages to other functions	Processes and structure	• Could you access . . . ?
• Technological scouting	Processes	• Could you efficiently build . . . ?
• Project management	Cognitive, processes	
Purchasing, supply		
• Linkages to suppliers	Processes, structure	
• New suppliers	Cognitive, processes	
• New components/materials	Cognitive	
• Subcontracting	Processes	
• Specifications, quality control	Cognitive, processes	
Manufacturing		
• Plants/lines operations	Assets, process, structure	
• Production management	Processes	
• Logistics	Cognitive, processes	
• Inventories	Assets, processes	
• Work design	Structure, processes	

- Process control — Processes, cognitive

Marketing, distribution, sales
- Distribution channels — Structure, processes
- After-sales services — Processes
- Client relationship — Processes
- Market knowledge — Cognitive
- Information on competitors — Cognitive
- Communication — Processes
- Firm's image, brand names — Assets

- **Reinforcement?**
  ⇒ Are your distribution channels adapted to the new products/services to be offered?
- **Synergistic fit?**
  ⇒ Would some other distribution channels used by firm be better adapted?
- **Networking access?**
  ⇒ How quickly and efficiently would it be to access new and adequate distribution channels by calling upon your network of partners
- **Adaptability?**
  ⇒ How quickly and efficiently could you build new distribution channels?

General
- Interfunctional linkages — Structure, processes
- Controlling — Processes
- Human resources management — Cognitive, processes
- Organization — Structure, processes
- Culture — Identity

response: stretching the firm's portfolio of competence for the change, pivoting around competence to diversify away from the change, and influencing the expected change to destabilize competitors against competence which the firm holds or can access but which they lack. This may be called strategizing innovation through competence analysis.

From a research and theory perspective, our development raises some further questions. From a broad, general perspective, the intent here is to build upon the emerging theory of competence in order to address a specific issue, namely the challenge of innovation. The clear line of research suggested by our framework concerns the need to relate the emerging theory to actual competitive contexts. What are the elements of competence in real innovations that we use conceptually? Some empirical work could help.

The key element is coordinated deployment. What is the real nature of this integrative capability? What is it that fulfils the coordinated deployment function? The Sanchez, Heene, and Thomas framework rightly identifies this type of capabilities. Yet along the line of reasoning adopted here, one would need to better grasp this concept in order to facilitate its subsequent operationalization. Is it a process, as argued here? Or does it also include some form of structural arrangement as well as elements of a vision?

It would also be useful to deal with the following questions from a theoretical perspective. What categories of competence are most difficult to address? Are they really the cultural dimension, the organizational processes? Where is the "core" of organizational inertia based? This would suggest what competences should be regarded as difficult to eliminate.

Incidentally, what do we mean by "difficult"? What are the different sorts of difficulties (time necessary, management implication required, amount of training, etc.)? In addition, when are the competence-addressing modalities most efficient? Why? Would some elements of the competences "soon to be" required by an expected innovation be more easily predicted than others? Why and when?

These are some of the typical questions which use of the competence-based theory of the firm raises when attempting to apply the theory to analyze change strategically.

REFERENCES

Abernathy, W.J. and Clark, K.B. (1985). Innovation: mapping the winds of creative destruction. *Research Policy*, No. 14, 3–22.

Abernathy, W.J. and Utterback, J.M. (1978). Patterns of industrial innovation. *Technology Review*, No. 50, June–July, 41–7.

Barney, J. (1986). Strategic factor markets: expectations, luck and business strategy. *Management Science*, No. 32, 1231–41.

Clark K.B. (1985). The interaction of design hierarchies and market concepts in technological evolution. *Research Policy*, No. 4, 235–51.

Cohen, W.M. and Levinthal, D.A. (1990). *Administrative Science Quarterly*, **35**, 128–52.

Cooper, A.C. and Schendell, D. (1976). Strategic responses to technological threats. *Business Horizons*.

Dosi, G. (1982). Technological paradigms and technological trajectories. *Research Policy*, No. 11, 147–62.

Doz, Y. (1986). *Strategic Management in Multinational Companies*. Oxford: Pergamon Press.

Durand, (1988). Programs competencies matrix: analyzing R&D expertise within the firm. *R&D Management*, **16**, No. 2, April.

Durand, P. (1992). Dual technological stress: assessing the intensity and strategic significance of technological change. *Research Policy*.

Durand, T. and Gonard, T. (1986). Stratégies technologiques: le cas de l'insuline. *Revue Française de Gestion*, No. 60, November–December.

Durand T. and Stymne, B. (1991). Lessons from the public switching past technological evolution in the telecoms. In Mattson, L.G. and Stymne, B. (eds.), *Corporate and Industry Strategies for Europe*. Oxford: Elsevier.

Farjoun, M. (1994). Beyond industry boundaries. *Organization Science*, **5**, No. 2.

Foster, R. (1986). *Innovation: the Attacker's Advantage*. New York: Summit Books.

Gomory (1989). From the ladder of science to the product development cycle. *Harvard Business Review*, November–December.

Gonard, T., Finkbeiner, F. and Rivalier, B. (1993). Heat exchangers—interests at stake, market, technological trends and innovation policy. *Editions Européennes Thermique et Industrie (EETI)*.

Hamel, G. and Heene, A. (1994). *Competence-based Competition*. New York: John Wiley.

Hedlund, G. and Nonaka, I. (1992). The dynamics of knowledge. In Lorange *et al.* (eds.), *Strategic Processes*. Chichester: John Wiley.

Henderson, R. and Clark K. (1990). Architectural innovation: the reconfiguration of existing product technologies and the failure of established firms. *Administrative Science Quarterly*, **35**.

Iansiti, M. (1992). Science-based product development: an empirical study of the mainframe computer industry. Working paper, Harvard Business School, Cambridge, Massachusetts.

Kandel, N., Remy, J.P., Stein, C. and Durand, T. (1991). Who's who in technology: identifying technological competence within the firm. *R&D Management*, July.

McGee, J. and Thomas, H. (1989). Technology and strategic management: progress and future directions. *R&D Management*, **19**, No. 3, 205–13.

Nelson, R.R. and Winter, S.G. (1977). In search of a useful theory of innovation. *Research Policy*, No. 6.

Prahalad, C.K. and Hamel, G. (1990). The core competence of the corporation. *Harvard Business Review*, May–June, 79–91.

Quélin, B. (1996). Competence of the firm and strategic alliances. In Sanchez, R. and Heene, A. (eds.), *Strategic Learning and Knowledge Management*. Chichester: John Wiley.

Rosenberg, N. (1976). *Perspectives on Technology*. Cambridge: Cambridge University Press.

Rumelt, R. (1995). Inertia and transformation. In Montgomery (ed.), *Resource Based and Evolutionary Theories of the Firm*. New York: Kluwer Academic.

Sanchez, R. (1996). Managing articulated knowledge in competence-based competition. In Sanchez, R. and Heene, A. (eds), *Strategic Learning and Knowledge Management*. Chichester: John Wiley.

Sanchez, R., Heene, A. and Thomas, H. (eds.) (1996). *Dynamics of Competence-Based Competition: Theory and Practice in the New Strategic Management*. Oxford: Elsevier.

Sanchez, R. and Heene, A. (1996). A system view of the firm in competence-based competition. In Sanchez, R., Heene, A. and Thomas, H. (eds), *Dynamics of Competence-Based Competition: Theory and Practice in the New Strategic Management*. Oxford: Elsevier.

Sanchez, R. and Thomas, H. (1996). Strategic goals. In Sanchez, R., Heene, A. and Thomas, H. (eds.) *Dynamics of Competence-Based Competition: Theory and Practice in the New Strategic Management*. Oxford: Elsevier.

Schumpeter, J.A. (1941). *Capitalism, Socialism and Democracy*. New York: Harper and Row.

Teece, D.J. (1986). Profiting from technological innovation: implications for integration, collaboration, licensing and public policy. *Research Policy*, No. 15.

Tushman, M.L. and Anderson, P. (1986). Technological discontinuities and organizational environments. *Administrative Science Quarterly*, **31**, 439–65.

Utterbak, J.M. and Abernathy, W.J. (1975). A dynamic model of process and product innovation. *Omega*, **3**, 639–56.

Wu, T.S., Ridderstale, J., Stein, J., Durand, T. and Stymne, B. (1990). HDTV at Televerket. Business case, Stockholm School of Economics and Ecole Centrale, Paris.

7

Assessing the Organizational Capacity to Change

JANICE A. BLACK, KIMBERLY B. BOAL

This research builds on Ghoshal and Bartlett's (1994) concepts of discipline, stretch, trust, and support and Black and Boal's (1994) emphasis on examining the configuration between firm resources and capabilities in creating higher-order competences which can lead to a sustainable competitive advantage. We address empirically how different configurations of stretch, trust, discipline, and support can result in differences in the capacity for change and/or performance. Using worksite data from two *Fortune 500* companies, operating in different industries, we find that there are some configurations that result in a capacity to change but not in high performance, and vice versa. However, we find that worksites that achieve strategic flexibility, i.e. both high performance and high capacity for change, all have similar configurations.

The resource-based view of the firm began a new orientation in the strategic literature in which practitioners and researchers became open to a view of corporate strategy that, as Rumelt (1994: iv) puts it, "place(s) technology, skill and synergy ahead of cash flow and control". It asserts that a bundle of resources that are valuable in attaining the firm's strategic goals, rare in the competitive arena, inimitable, for which there are few or no substitutes, and which the firm is organized to use (Barney, 1992), enables the pursuit of a sustainable

Competence-based Strategic Management.
Edited by Aimé Heene and Ron Sanchez.
Copyright © 1997 John Wiley & Sons Ltd.

competitive advantage (Wernerfelt, 1984). Work in this stream now highlights the importance of competence-based competition and of competence as a focal unit of strategy analysis (Sanchez, Heene, and Thomas, 1996).

Much of the empirical work utilizing the concepts of competence-based competition consists of descriptive case studies (Helfat, 1994; Klein and Hiscocks, 1994). These case studies are useful descriptions and illustrations, but their focuses have been weak in prescribing or even illustrating what to do to use, maintain, create, or change competences (Bettis, 1991). To move from generalities and description to specifics and prescription requires more studies, and, more specifically, studies that examine resources at the competency level. This chapter examines the "bundling" or "coordinated deployment" (Sanchez, Heene, and Thomas, 1996) that creates an important aspect of competence, the "capacity to change". We examine the coordinated deployment aspect of competence at three sites to determine if the bundling of resources is similar or different across the sites. This information will help in the movement towards illustrating what to do to use, maintain, create, or change competence by determining what patterns of bundling may be needed for the high attainment of the firm goals.

CONCEPTUAL FRAMEWORK

To examine resources at the competence level requires a clear definition of what a competence is. Sanchez, Heene, and Thomas (1996: 9) define competence as "the ability to sustain the coordinated deployment of assets in a way that helps a firm achieve its goal". Thus a competence is distinguishable by the presence of three conditions: organization, intention, and goal attainment. Black and Boal (1994) suggest that deployment is more than a bundle and is a configuration consisting of embedded resources, their cogency relationships (those enhancing, compensating, or suppressing relationships among them), and substituting relationships. They propose that a competence is composed of the network of the constituent resources and the cogency relationships. They suggest that it is the entire network that should be regarded as "rare" rather than the individual elements separately.

However, to examine how resources may be bundled or deployed as competences, a specific competence is required. While suggested current strategic competences range from communication competences to development competences to option management competences (Ghoshal and Bartlett, 1994; among others), the ability of a firm to change or to learn has been repeatedly presented as a central feature of competence (Brumagim, 1994; Hamel and Heene, 1994; Sanchez, Heene, and Thomas, 1996).

Ghoshal and Bartlett (1994) recently proposed that the context in which collective learning can occur consists of a set of four key attributes, which they termed discipline, stretch, trust, and support. Discipline is composed of clear performance standards, fast feedback, open communication, and management by commitment. The second attribute, stretch, is indicated by the presence of a shared ambition for the future across the organization, a collective identity which is epitomized by a mission statement accepted by all and understood by all, and finally by personal meaning where the link between the individual's work and the company priorities gives meaning to the individual's work and a motivation to "stretch". Trust is composed of elements of perceived equity or fair decision making, involvement in decision making, and individual competence which refers to the existence of specialized knowledge and skills at the individual level. The final attribute of support includes access to organizational resources involving inter-group cooperation and communication, autonomy as related to decentralized decision making, or, in other words, the freedom to make decisions, and finally, guidance and help which was evidenced by mutual help within groups and a climate of help, coaching, and support from management. In addition to the presence of these attributes and their embedded resources, Ghoshal and Bartlett (1994) suggest that it is the *gestalt* or the effect of all of these elements on each other as well as their presence that create the organizational context. This orientation of considering a *gestalt* of competence elements is very similar to Black and Boal's (1994) configuration perspective on firm resources in that both consider the entirety and that each element interacts to create that entirety.

Ghoshal and Bartlett (1994) assert that management is responsible for the creation of the organizational context in which collective learning can take place (cf. Baden-Fuller and Volberda, this volume). We agree, but believe there will be wide variability in terms of management's success in doing so, thus the creation of such an organizational context is itself an important aspect of a competence. We term this aspect of competence an *organizational capacity to change*. This meets the criteria of Sanchez, Heene, and Thomas (1996) for competence: it is about the coordinated deployment of firm resources and is intended to attain the goal of creating a necessary condition for collective learning, an orientation to change. Ghoshal and Bartlett have not indicated how the four resources might affect each other However, the work of Black and Boal (1994) suggests that enhancing, compensating, suppressing, or substituting relationships among the firm's resources are important ways that resources affect each other. This chapter addresses a key dimension of competence leveraging and building: examining the role of configurations in understanding competence building.

In addition, by investigating the organizational Capacity to Change and Performance, we seek to add insight into strategic flexibility which involves the simultaneous attainment of current performance while maintaining the capacity to change to enable the attainment of future performance. Sanchez and Heene (1996) suggest that strategic flexibility occurs through the use of flexible resources. If the configuration of the make-up of the competence is similar for both the attainment of high levels of an Orientation to Change and Performance, the organizational Capacity to Change appears to be a flexible resource that can be leveraged to facilitate the attaining of strategic flexibility without diminishing the attainment of current performance.

We thus examine three general hypotheses (see Table 7.1). The first hypothesis compares configuration maps associated with Performance levels, the second compares the configuration maps associated with Organizational Capacity to Change levels and the third compares maps across the two dependent variables. The focus is on the configuration among discipline, stretch, trust, and support at high and low levels of an Orientation to Change and Performance.

Given the definition of strategic flexibility as being able both to currently perform and to remain ready to take advantage of emergent opportunities, this set of hypotheses has the added advantage of also enabling a better understanding of strategic flexibility by comparing the Organizational Capacity to Change maps associated with Performance and Orientation to Change with each other. If similar configurations are present across high levels, the Organizational Capacity to Change can be useful for attaining strategic flexibility, as well as organizational learning.

TABLE 7.1   Hypothesis summary matrix

		Orientation to Change		Performance	
		High	Low	High	Low
Orientation to	High	Similar			
Change	Low	Not similar	Similar		
Performance	High	Similar	Not similar	Similar	
	Low	Not similar	Similar	Not similar	Similar

METHODOLOGY

SAMPLE

In 1992, the scales used to operationalize the above sets of embedded resources were administered as part of a larger research program via questionnaires to 455 workers at three sites from two different *Fortune 500* manufacturing organizations situated in the Midwestern part of the United States with an average 90% response rate of all employees at a site. The responses were delivered to the researchers administering the questionnaire and anonymity of respondents and their specific responses was maintained. The non-responses were across hierarchical levels and positions and no apparent non-response bias was detected.

Firm 1 is a consumer products firm and has operated since its founding in a small city with a population of about 100 000 in the mid-western region of the United States. The factory complex, with multiple distinct production sites on the same campus, is within sight of agricultural concerns. The firm takes care of its employees, for example downsizing occurs through normal attrition. The employees are not subjected to seasonal hiring and laying off, since part-time and temporary workers are used to satisfy seasonal demands. The factory site includes interconnected buildings. The offices are in the center of the complex with the factory floors on one side and cafeterias and mixing rooms on the other. Two sites, Sites 1 and 2, at this complex were surveyed. These two sites are physically separated although it was possible that employees from both sites simultaneously visited the corporate cafeteria.

The third site surveyed is one of many operated by the second firm which is in the chemical industry (plastics). Located in a small midwestern town on the outskirts of a large city, its operations included the manufacturing of products that were used by its customers to make their products. This supplier firm has a history of hiring and layoffs.

By choosing these firms, both firm and industry boundaries were spanned. This allowed for an initial examination for context-specific and context-free factors in the Orientation to Change. By thus using both a context-specific and cross-context examination, the usefulness of examining the configuration of a competence can be better evaluated.

VARIABLE OPERATIONALIZATION

The descriptions of the sub-dimensions of discipline, stretch, trust, and support on the part of Ghoshal and Bartlett enabled the matching of their descriptions to pre-existing scales obtained from the Texas Center for Productivity and Quality of Work Life which included scales originally developed for the Michigan Organizational Assessment Questionnaire and the Survey of Organizations. The dependent variables, Orientation to Change and Performance, are also operationalized with scales from these same questionnaires. To ensure that the constructs of discipline, stretch, trust, and support were adequately captured by the use of these pre-existing scales, each construct was subjected to confirmatory factor analysis using Lisrel 8 (Joreskog and Sorbom, 1993) following standard procedures (Anderson and Gerbing, 1988; Bagozzi and Yi, 1989; Byrne, 1989). Analysis of the data suggested that the scales adequately measured each construct using accepted criteria (Bentler and Bonett, 1980) (α's ranging from 0.70 to 0.87). These operationalizations were deemed of sufficient reliability to proceed with the analysis.

OPERATIONALIZATION OF CONFIGURATION MAPS

A configuration map for the Organizational Capacity to Change is the configuration of the resources, discipline, stretch, trust, and support, and the set of enhancing, compensatory, and suppressing relationships between them. Black and Boal's set of enhancing, compensatory, and suppressing relationships between the resources can be modeled using interaction terms (Baron and Kenny, 1986). The configuration map is operationalized by the expanded correlation matrix which includes the two-way interaction terms between the resources as well as the resources. The data obtained from each site were used to create the maps of the configurations present at high and low Performance levels and present at high and low Orientation to Change levels. This resulted in four matrices being created for each worksite.

These matrices were compared to each other using the quadratic assignment procedure from the UCINET program to determine the degree of similarity between the matrices. The assessment of the hypotheses involved both within- and between-site comparisons. Thus, the competency maps for high and low levels of Performance and Orientation to Change within each worksite were first compared to each other. Then the between-site comparisons were done sequentially by using each site's map as a separate base reference point. Three sets of decision rules were used. The first, the correlations between competency maps, had to meet traditional criteria of statistical significance (denoted in the results at "*" for 0.05 and "**" for 0.01) to ensure that the observed correlations were not due to chance.

The degree of similarity is assessed by examining both the magnitude and the relative values of the significant matrix correlations. These decision rules examine the absolute difference between significant correlations of two sets of map comparisons. If the difference is sampler for maps at the same level than the difference between levels, then the maps of the same level will be considered "more" similar than the between-level maps. Both the pattern of correlations and the magnitude of the correlations will be taken into account (including examining any overall patterns by level or site) to clarify mixed or very weak results.

RESULTS

The hypotheses were tested as described above. The results of the comparisons within Orientation to Change and Performance and across sites, the quadratic assignment procedure correlations, are found in Table 7.2. The comparisons across the configuration maps associated with the different Performance levels are on the top half of the matrix. The comparisons across the configuration maps associated with the different Orientation to Change levels are on the bottom half. The closer the value in a cell of the matrix is to one, the more similar were the two maps being compared. Table 7.3 reports the interpretations of these comparisons. The only clearly supported hypotheses are those

TABLE 7.2 Configuration map comparisons within dependent variable

	Site 1— high	Site 1— low	Site 2— high	Site 2— low	Site 3— high	Site 3— low
Site 1— high		0.31*	0.90**	0.84**	0.81**	0.93**
Site 1— low	0.61**		0.49*	0.55*	0.48*	0.54**
Site 2— high	0.76**	0.67**		0.83**	0.93**	0.92**
Site 2— low	0.16	0.18*	0.26**		0.75**	0.87**
Site 3— high	0.89**	0.74**	0.93**	0.21**		0.84**
Site 3— low	0.81**	0.71**	0.90**	0.21**	0.94**	

Key: Upper triangle of matrix reports correlations between the configuration maps for Performance and lower triangle reports correlation between configuration maps for Orientation to Change.

TABLE 7.3 Summary matrix of test results

		Orientation to Change		Performance	
		High	Low	High	Low
Orientation to Change	High	*Similar across sites* **Supported between sites**			
	Low	*Not similar* **Supported between sites**	*Similar* Not supported between sites		
Performance	High	*Similar* **Supported at all sites**	*Not similar* **Supported Site 2** Not supported Sites 2 and 3	*Similar* **Supported between sites**	
	Low	*Not similar* **Supported Site 1** Not supported Sites 2 and 3	*Similar* **Supported Site 3** Not supported Sites 1 and 2	*Not similar* **Supported between sites**	*Similar* **Supported between Sites 1 and 2 and other sites** Not supported between Site 3 and other sites

that involve the high-high level comparison of Orientation to Change maps, the high-high level comparison of Performance maps, the high–high level comparison across Orientation to Change and Performance, and the low–high comparisons of both Orientation to Change and Performance.

PERFORMANCE HIGH–HIGH COMPARISONS

We hypothesized that the competence configuration map associated with high Performance would be similar across sites. The three high–high comparisons made have significant correlation with magnitudes ranging from 0.81** to 0.93**. The correlations support a strong degree of similarity between the competence maps and provide strong support for the hypothesis.

PERFORMANCE LOW–LOW COMPARISONS

We hypothesized that the competency configuration maps associated with low Performance levels would be similar across sites. The three low–low comparisons have a set of correlations, which, while significant, are relatively low between Site 1 and the other sites (0.55*; 0.54*) but relatively strong correlation between Sites 2 and 3 (0.87*). There does not appear to be a consistent pattern across all sites. These mixed results indicate that no one configuration of discipline, stretch, trust, and support is associated with low Performance levels. To flesh out our understanding, we turn to the cross-level results, the high–low/low–high comparisons.

PERFORMANCE HIGH–LOW AND LOW–HIGH COMPARISONS

We hypothesized that the competence configuration map associated with a high Performance level would be *different* from the competency configuration map associated with a low performance level. To test this hypothesis, we examined configurations both within and between sites. The comparisons consisted of the high-level map at a specific site being compared with the low-level map from that same site and then compared to the low-level maps of the other two sites. The same pattern is followed with the low-level map at a site being compared to the high-level maps. Of the resulting eighteen correlations (see Table 7.2), six clearly supported the hypothesis that the high and low maps are different upon initial examination (i.e. had low or non-significant correlations). To flesh out this understanding and to examine "relative" dissimilarity, these between-level comparisons needed to be contrasted with the respective high–high and low–low comparisons. This same analysis also enabled further understanding of the low–low comparisons.

When Site 1 is the base of comparison, the four additional comparisons (high–high compared to high–low across sites and low–low compared to low–high across sites) result in three demonstrating a relative but weak difference. When Site 2 is the base of comparison, again three of the four additional comparisons support a relative difference between the maps. When Site 3 is the base of comparison, only the two comparisons from the high-level maps support there being a relative difference Site 3's low-level maps were more similar to other site's high-level maps than to other site's low-level maps.

In summary, of the twelve additional comparisons, eight support there being a relative difference. Of the four that do not support there being a relative difference, three are when the Site 3 low-level map is in the comparison. Since the high degree similarity behind the high and low maps at Site 3 appears responsible for the mixed results, we conclude that there may be weak relative difference between high and low configurations of relationships between discipline, stretch, trust, and support for high and low perceptions of Performance.

ORIENTATION TO CHANGE HIGH–HIGH COMPARISONS

We hypothesized that the competence configuration map associated with a high orientation to change level would be *similar* across sites. The three high–high comparisons made had significant correlations ranging in magnitude from 0.76** to 0.93**. Since the magnitudes support a moderate high to high degree of similarity, the configurations of discipline, stretch, trust, and support are deemed similar at high levels of Orientation to Change.

ORIENTATION TO CHANGE LOW–LOW COMPARISONS

We hypothesized that the competence configurations associated with a low Orientation to Change would be similar across sites. The three low–low comparisons made had resulting correlations of 0.18*, 0.21*, and 0.71**. The two very low magnitude correlations indicate that the map in use at Site 2 is very different from the maps at Sites 1 and 3. There was a moderate degree of similarity between Sites 1 and 3. Again the low-level maps do not appear to have a consistent pattern across sites. These mixed results indicate that no one configuration of discipline, stretch, trust, and support is associated with low Orientation to Change levels. We again turn to cross-level comparisons to flesh out our understanding of these results.

ORIENTATION TO CHANGE HIGH–LOW AND LOW–HIGH COMPARISONS

We hypothesized that the competence configuration map associated with a high Orientation to Change level will be *different* from the competence configuration map associated with a low Orientation to Change level. To test this hypothesis, we followed the same procedure used to examine high and low levels of performance. Again nine comparisons are done for the high–low comparisons and nine comparisons for the low–high comparisons. Of the 18 comparisons (see Table 7.2), seven correlations (across five of the six site comparisons) supported the hypotheses of different configuration maps for the different levels. Further analysis was needed to reveal relative differences. This required the between-level comparisons to be contrasted with the respective high–high and low–low comparisons.

Again starting with Site 1 as the base of comparison, only the high-level map comparisons support there being a relative, but weak, difference. Because Site 2's internal high–low and all low–high comparisons were of such low magnitudes, the hypothesis was supported in the earlier analysis, and no further analysis was needed. Even when the cross-site differences of the high-level maps are examined, weak relative differences are found. When Site 3 is the base comparison, again the high-level map comparisons support relative differences while the low-level map comparisons do not.

In summary, of the 10 additional comparisons examined, six comparisons support there being a relative difference. Of the four that do not support there being a relative difference, all occur when the comparison base point is a low level map. We conclude that there are relative differences in the configurations of discipline, stretch, trust, and support for high and low levels of Orientation to Change when the comparison point is a high level map. This reinforces our earlier conclusion that a wide range of low level Orientation to Change maps are possible.

ORIENTATION TO CHANGE AND PERFORMANCE: HIGH–HIGH COMPARISONS

Further illumination is provided when comparisons are made across Performance and Orientation to Change and across levels. These comparisons are shown in Table 7.4.

In keeping with ideas about strategic flexibility, we hypothesized that the competence configuration map associated with a high Performance level would be similar to that associated with a high Orientation to Change level. Support was found at all sites (0.84**, 0.94**, 0.91**). This leads to support for the concept that high Orientation to Change levels and high Performance levels have similar maps of configurations of the relationships between discipline, stretch, trust,

TABLE 7.4   Comparisons across orientation to change and performance

Site 1		Orientation to Change		Performance	
		High	Low	High	Low
Orientation	High				
to Change	Low	0.61**			
Performance	High	0.84**	0.89**		
	Low	0.52*	0.05	0.31**	
Site 2					
Orientation	High				
to Change	Low	0.26**			
Performance	High	0.94**	0.22*		
	Low	0.90**	0.17*	0.83*	
Site 3					
Orientation	High				
to Change	Low	0.94**			
Performance	High	0.91**	0.90**		
	Low	0.95**	0.94**	0.84**	

and support. This suggests that the high performers and the high orientation to change holders require similar configurations to attain those high levels. This implies that the variability found in the competence may be attributable to the miscoordination of discipline, stretch, trust, and support.

CROSS-ORIENTATION TO CHANGE AND PERFORMANCE: LOW-LOW COMPARISONS

Two of the three sites did not support the hypothesis that the maps between low levels within a site would be similar. Sites 1 and 2 had low level maps with correlations of 0.05 and 0.17 respectively. Site 3 did support similarity across dependent variables with the low-level maps (0.94*). In interpreting the above results, we note the differences in the patterns at each site. Site 1 has the lowest set of correlations, indicating that the maps are the most different among the high and low levels at that site. The range in magnitude of similarity evidenced by the wide correlation range (0.17* to 0.94**) at Site 2 really shows that the low Orientation to Change map is very different from the other maps at that site. Site 3's set of correlations shows the highest degree of similarity across all levels and types of maps.

CROSS-DEPENDENT VARIABLE: LOW–HIGH AND HIGH–LOW COMPARISONS

Except for the previously mentioned case of strategic flexibility, we hypothesized that the competence configuration maps for a low Orientation to Change level and high Performance level would be different and vice versa. This was supported at Site 2 (0.22*) but not at Sites 1 and 3 (0.89** and 0.90**) for the low Orientation to Change and high Performance comparisons. This indicates that those that have a low Orientation to Change have different configurations from the high performers at Site 2. However, at Sites 1 and 3, high performers have similar maps to those with low Orientation to Change.

With respect to high–low comparisons, support was found at Site 1 (0.52*) but not at Sites 2 and 3 (0.90** and 0.95**). This indicates that the low–level configurations between discipline, stretch, trust, and support were indeed different between having a high Orientation to Change and low Performance at Site 1. At Sites 2 and 3, the two maps were very similar.

The set of significant correlations between configurations that are in the 90s indicates that there is high similarity across all configurations. This provides some support for the arguments that performance and orientation to change are not necessary polar opposites. This shows that there is a very similar pattern across these levels. What it does not indicate is whether the overall firm is relatively oriented to change, relatively resistant to change, or just what change is being considered. If the firm is relatively oriented to change, then this pattern may be indicative of the presence of strategic flexibility.

DISCUSSION

SITE 1

This site had similar high-level Orientation to Change maps, high Performance maps, and low Performance maps with the other sites. It also supported the dissimilarity between the high and low maps within any dependent variable. There was mixed support from this site for the similarity of low-level Orientation to Change maps.

The correlation of 0.84** between the high-level maps of Orientation to Change and Performance indicates that those with a high perceived Orientation to Change had configurations for discipline, stretch, trust, and support more similar to those who perceived a high level of firm effectiveness on Performance measures than they were similar to those who had a low Orientation to Change or low Performance map. When the low–low cross-dependent variable (0.05) comparison is made, it is evident that there are very different configurations present in the low-level maps due to the low magnitude of the correlation.

Perplexing is the Orientation to Change/Performance low–high correlation of 0.89** which is greater than the high–high cross-comparison correlation of 0.84**. This says that those who perceived their organization to be effective have an Organizational Capacity to Change map that is slightly *more similar to a low* than a high Orientation to Change map!

There may be a number of reasons for this finding. An obvious one is that those who perceive high performance currently may not see any reason to change. This attitude may be due to the buffering from external market conditions that Firm 1 provides their employees. They might not have really internalized a reason to change and so are not as open to change. If so, this same pattern might show up for Site 2 as well.

Another reason might be that those with a high Orientation to Change map may be too willing to change and thus are always on the leading edge of the experience curve and hence are not the top performers. The top performers may be the ones that wait and see what happens with a new change and what glitches occur before stepping in on the backs of those who went before, a sort of early second-mover syndrome.

This pattern of similarity does not work in reverse. Although those with a low perception of Performance have maps more similar to those with a high Orientation to Change than those with a low Orientation to Change, it is still very different from the similarity between the two high maps. In other words, they do perceive a need to change that is closer to the high Orientation to Change map but still not as close as those with a high perceived Performance level.

SITE 2

Site 2, with the smallest number of employees, like its sister site had similar maps for high-level Orientation to Change, high-level Performance, and low-level performance with the other sites. There was also a difference between the high- and low-level Orientation to Change maps, the high- and low-level Performance maps, and across low-level Orientation to Change maps.

This site also has a great similarity between its Orientation to Change/Performance high–high maps (0.94**). However, it also has one low-level map that is more similar to the high maps than the other low map. In this case, it is the low perceived Performance map which is more similar to the high Orientation to Change map (0.90**) than it is to the high Performance map (0.83**). This is in contrast to Site 1 (Site 1 had a low Orientation to Change map more similar to a high Performance map than to the high Orientation to Change map). Buffering may not be a firm-wide reason for differences. The low Performance map is not as similar to the high Orientation to Change map as the high Performance map was. It is, however, very different from the map of those with a low Orientation to Change level (0.17*).

Even though Sites 1 and 2 are samples from the same organization, Site 2 has employees with a low Orientation to Change level whose *Capacity to Change* map is very different from any other map. This difference is even more than that between the low-level Performance map and the low-level Orientation to Change map at Site 1. Because both the levels of the Performance maps at Site 2 are very similar to the high-level Orientation to Change map, it may be that both Performance levels are motivated to consider change but for different reasons. Perhaps those with high Performance perceptions see a need for change to keep up the performance level (maintain performance in a changing world) while those with low perceived Performance see a reason to change now (to personally do better and get the rewards associated with high performance). This study did not include a contextual base for the orientation to change items in the survey, so motivation cannot be determined.

SITE 3

While Site 3 is only one site of many that Firm 2 has, it has a medium number of employees that falls between the numbers for Sites 1 and 2. This firm did not have a policy of protecting its employees from the fluctuations of the marketplace. This firm was further up the value change and is a supplier firm whose customers use their products as raw materials.

Support was provided by Site 3 for similarity of high-level Orientation to Change maps and high-level Performance maps across sites. Support was also provided for the relative dissimilarity of high and low maps across sites. Support was not provided for the dissimilarity of high and low maps within Site 3.

Site 3 had overall high levels of similarity between all maps. The lowest similarity was between those with high perceived performance and those with low perceived performance (0.84**). But that was just as high as the magnitude of the correlation at Site 1 for indicating similarity. The consistent similarity across the maps may indicate several scenarios:

1. All employees may be aware of reasons to change brought about by the awareness of how marketplace fluctuations directly affected them.
2. High and low levels of perceived Performance respondents may be open to change for different reasons (see discussion for Site 2).
3. Those who see the firm as needing to improve performance also are open to changing it and those who see the firm as currently being effective see continued need for change.
4. Something other than *Organizational Capacity to Change* is affecting both Performance perception and Orientation to Change perception.

Again, this study has not included the necessary information to tease out motivation and specific contextual issues. Despite this need for further analysis evident at all three sites, some trends are evident from this analysis.

IMPLICATIONS FOR STRATEGY THEORY, RESEARCH, AND PRACTICE

Our first implication is that the *Organizational Capacity to Change* from Ghoshal and Bartlett's model also appears in manufacturing firms in the midwestern United States. The patterns of similarity and the significant correlations lend support to the generalizability of Ghoshal and Bartlett's attributes of an organizational context. This is particularly so since their model was examined here at sites that were in different industries and countries from the site where they developed the model. The use of survey questions also facilitates the identification of deployment issues their linkages to performance (coordination/organization issues) by practitioners.

Second, the existence of similar maps (those that included the interaction terms operationalizing the cogency relationships suggested by Black and Boal, 1994) remained robust even when the data were standardized, thus implying that the similarity was attributable to something other than the mathematical relationships involved in the operationalization of the cogency relationships. This then lends support to Black and Boal's assertion that the relationships among the resources involved in the competence are also important to the creation and utilization of the competence. The existence of significant correlations between matrices lends support to the concept that it is not only the resources that are important in the determining of a competence but also the relationships between the resources.

We believe it is the management of the relationships between resources that is the key to creating competences on which to build a competitive advantage. This is clearly a mechanism through which hierarchy can aid in achieving the competitive advantage and strategic renewal (cf. Baden-Fuller and Volberda, this volume). In this vein, perhaps the most significant of the findings was the high degree of similarity of the configuration associated with high Orientation to Change and high Performance. This held true across sites and industries. This implies that managers can create contexts that support organizational learning without compromising their ability to attain high levels of current performance.

A final lesson to be learned from this study is that there are many ways to fall short of having a successful capacity to change. Some of those ways are very similar to those that work at other sites. This implies that competence is very sensitive to changes in the relations among the four underlying resources. Minor variations can spell the difference between success and failure.

In summary, in addressing firm resources at the level of analysis of the competence, we found that in some sites how the resources are "bundled" appears to make a difference by competence level and/or performance level. This analysis showed one way to untangle some of the elements so that competences can be consciously managed. This project utilizes what is best about previous empirical work—timeliness (quantitative cross-sectional surveys) and contextualization (firm-specific information)—thus providing a potentially powerful tool in the examination of firm resources and competences, as well as replication of this study in other industries and firms.

REFERENCES

Anderson, J.C., and Gerbing, D.W. (1988). Structural modeling in practice: A review and recommended two-step approach. *Psychological Bulletin*, **103**, No. 3, 411–23.

Bagozzi, R.P. and Yi, Y. (1989). On the use of structural equation models in experimental designs. *Journal of Marketing Research*, **26**, 271–84.

Barney, J.B. (1992). Integrating organizational behavior and strategy formulation research: A resource based analysis. In Shrivastava, P., Huff, A. and Dutton, J. (eds), *Advances in Strategic Management*, Vol. 10A. Greenwich, CT: JAI Press, pp. 39–61.

Baron. R.M. and Kenny, D.A. (1986). The moderator–mediator variable distinction in social psychological research: Conceptual, strategic, and statistical considerations. *Journal of Personality and Social Psychology,* **51** (6), 1173–82.
Bentler. P.M. and Bonett, D.G. (1980). Significance tests and goodness of fit in analysis of covariance structures. *Psychological Bulletin,* **88,** 588–606.
Bettis. R.A. (1991). Strategic management and the straightjacket: An editorial essay. *Organization Science,* **2**(3), 315–19.
Black, J. and Boal, K. (1994). Strategic resources: Traits, configurations and paths to sustainable competitive advantage. *Strategic Management Journal,* **15,** 131–48.
Brumagim, A.L. (1994). A hierarchy of corporate resources. In Shrivastava, P., Huff, A. and Dutton, J. (eds), *Advances in Strategic Management,* Vol. 10A. Greenwich, CT: JAI Press, pp. 81–112.
Byrne, B.M. (1989). *A Primer of LISREL.* New York: Springer-Verlag.
Ghoshal, S. and Bartlett, C.A (1994). Linking organizational context and managerial action: The dimension of quality of management. *Strategic Management Journal,* **15,** 91–112.
Hamel, G. and Heene, A. (1994). Conclusions: Which theory of strategic management do we need for tomorrow? In Hamel, G. and Heene, A. (eds), *Competence-Based Competition.* Chichester: John Wiley
Helfat, C. E. (1994). Firm specificity in corporate applied R & D. *Organization Science,* **5**(2), 173–84.
Jöreskog, K. and Sörbom, D. (1993). *LISREL VIII.* Chicago, IL: Scientific Software Inc.
Klein, J.A. and Hiscocks, P.G. (1994). Competence-based competition: A practical toolkit. In Hamel, G. and Heene, A. (eds), *Competence-Based Competition.* Chichester: John Wiley.
Rumelt, R.P. (1994). Foreword. In Hamel, G. and Heene, A. (eds), *Competence-Based Competition.* Chichester: John Wiley.
Sanchez, R. and Heene, A. (1996). A systems view of the firm in competence based competition. In Sanchez, R., Heene, A. and Thomas, H. (eds), *Dynamics of Competence-Based Competition: Theory and Practice in the New Strategic Management.* Oxford: Elsevier.
Sanchez, R., Heene, A. and Thomas, H. (1996). Towards the theory and practice of competence-based competition. In Sanchez, R., Heene, A. and Thomas, H. (eds), *Dynamics of competence-Based Competition: Theory and Practice in the New Strategic Management.* Oxford: Elsevier.
Wernerfelt, B. (1984). A resource-based view of the firm. *Strategic Management Journal,* **5,** 171–80.

8

Strategic Defense and Competence-based Competition

ZEEV ROTEM, RAPHAEL AMIT

We draw on the competence-based competition literature to develop the construct of Strategic Defense. This encompasses strategies used to defend the firm's bundle of competences against threats to its rent-producing capacities. These strategies include a narrow range of intelligence activities, along with a broad range of defensive actions within two generic defense strategies: Preservation and Alteration. Preservation is aimed at sustaining rents, whereas Alteration seeks to develop substitutes and make existing competences more flexible. We outline specific tactics associated with each generic strategy, and develop a model which incorporates the external and internal factors affecting the decision to invest in Strategic Defense. The empirical results suggest that intense competition is a catalyst to investment in strategic defenses, particularly the creation of alternative resources. Older and larger firms tend to rely on Preservation strategies, such as deterrence and deployment prevention. Also, firms' governance structures are shown to help in determining their approach to Strategic Defense. The results further indicate that low-performing firms tend to invest more in Preservation tactics, whereas high-performing firms mainly invest in intelligence activities and in attempts to deter competitors. High-performing firms also invest more in maintaining

Competence-based Strategic Management.
Edited by Aimé Heene and Ron Sanchez.
Copyright © 1997 John Wiley & Sons Ltd.

flexibility of their current resources than they do in creating alternative resources.

INTRODUCTION

The literatures on the resource-based view of the firm and competence-based competition focus on creating and leveraging valuable resources in ways that achieve superior profitability (Wernerfelt, 1984; Barney, 1991; Mahoney and Pandian, 1992; Amit and Schoemaker, 1993; Peteraf, 1993; Hamel and Heene, 1994; Collis and Montgomery, 1995; Sanchez, Heene and Thomas, 1995). The sustainability of the rent-producing potential of the firm's resources is ultimately threatened by the following four competitive forces: *imitation, substitution, mobilization* of the resources, and resource paralysis. A significant body of the literature contains analyses on the conditions that may lead to reducing the effect of these four threats on the rent-producing capacity of a firm's competences; factors that create the phenomena of imperfect imitability have received particular attention (Lipmann and Rumelt, 1982; Rumelt, 1984; Barney, 1986, 1991; Dierickx and Cool, 1989; Reed and DeFillippi, 1990).

In this study we draw on the work on competence-based competition (see Sanchez, Heene, and Thomas, 1996) and on the theoretical concepts cited above, to propose a typology of Strategic Defense, within which we outline strategies firms may use to defend themselves against threats to the rent-producing capacities of firm competences. We investigate the connections between firms' attributes and the Strategic Defense strategies they choose.

In developing the Strategic Defense construct, we draw on the industrial organization literature in competitive rivalry (Porter, 1980, 1985; MacMillan, 1988; Chen and Miller, 1994). This body of work suggests that firms constantly undertake offensive and defensive actions in their struggle for competitive advantage (Chen and MacMillan, 1992). Offensive actions are meant to improve the firm's position against its competitors (Porter, 1980); defensive actions are those taken in response to, or in anticipation of, competitors' actions. More recently, game-theoretic principles have been used to sharpen the discussion of strategy formulation as discussed by McMillan (1992) and, most recently, Brandenburger and Nalebuff (1995). These ideas are examined within the framework of competence-based competition; here, firm competences are the unit of analysis of competition.

There is a significant overlap between the product market-based theory of competitive rivalry and competence-based theory used in studying Strategic Defense in this chapter. However, significant differences exist between them, too—in their objectives, strategies, intensities, and potential outcomes; these differences result from the differences in the invoked loci of competition. The competitive rivalry literature uses the terminologies of either "action-response" or "offense-defense". However, the focus in competence-based competition may be taken simply as the latter, because both responsive actions as well as preventive actions are covered by the "defense" typology. The "offense-defense" terminology is also symbolic of the more aggressive and potentially more fundamental form of competition wherein firms' competences, rather than their products, are the objects of rivalry.

This chapter is restricted to Strategic Defense initiatives that involve irreversible investments meant to defend the firm's strategic assets. We focus on tactics that require irreversible investments of capital, time, and human resources. The purpose of tactics is presumed to be to prevent erosion of the rent-producing capacities of the firm's bundle of competences. Due to the uncertainty and complexity about the nature of strategic interactions, some of the investments in Strategic Defense may, *ex post*, turn out to be superfluous. We also consider investments in alternative capabilities as replacements for current competences, and investments that enhance the flexibility of current competences.

THEORY

THREATS TO RENT-GENERATING POTENTIAL OF FIRMS' RESOURCES

Competitive forces threaten the sustainability of the rent-producing potential of a firm's resources and capabilities. These threats include: *imitation; substitution; mobilization of resources;* and *resource paralysis*.

Imitation

A fundamental premise of the resource-based view is that resources and capabilities are heterogeneously distributed across firms in an industry. A resource must be rare among the competitors if it is to produce above-normal rents (Barney, 1991; Peteraf, 1993). To sustain the competitive advantage gained by using such a unique resource, its uniqueness must be preserved. In a dynamic environment, in which the loci of competition are firm competences, any unique and rare resource is exposed to competitors' attempts at imitating it. This situation, in fact, explains the phenomena of Schumpeterian rents, i.e. short-term rents eroded by imitation.

With the investment of time and money, almost every type of asset and capability eventually can be imitated: technology; brand management; design capability; innovative promotion; relationships with customers and suppliers, etc. The more difficult it is to imitate any of the firm's assets and capabilities, the more sustainable is the rent-producing capacity of the firm's competences. This phenomenon is referred to as "imperfect imitability" in resource-based theory (Rumelt, 1984; Dierickx and Cool, 1989; Barney, 1986, 1991).

The introduction of Windows 95 by Microsoft is a classic example of imitative behavior among firms. This software closely resembles Apple's Macintosh operating system introduced in 1989 and is thus referred to by critics as "Mac 89". Windows 95 eliminates much of the "ease-of-use" benefit that has been one of the main competitive advantages of Apple. Thus imitative behavior reduced the uniqueness of Apple's human-machine interface technology, and thereby reduced the economic rents it can generate in the post-Windows 95 era. It is noteworthy, however, that it took Microsoft six years to imitate Apple's asset.

Substitution

Substitutes for rent-producing resources reduce resource-owner's rents. Resources are said to be substitutes for each other when another resource enables a competitor to exploit the same strategy as the original resource owner (Barney, 1991). In the product-market domain, substitute products, which are one of Porter's (1980) "five forces", reduce the attractiveness of the industry to those who are already in it.

The introduction and wide adoption of VHS video technology, a substitute for Beta technology, reduced the rent-producing capacity of Sony's Betamax video technology. This example illustrates how a competitor's R&D investment, if it yields a new technology, can nullify the rent-producing capacity of another firm's technology. Here, substitution of technological resources has led to the introduction of substitute products which in turn reduced the rent-producing capacity of a firm's (Sony) competence in technological know-how. Another form of resource substitution is the development of an enabling resource that allows a firm to nullify some aspect of a competitor's competence advantage gained by technological superiority. Consider, for example, the development of a superior brand name or distribution capability that would allow a firm with an inferior technology to gain market share at the expense of the competitor with a superior technology. Lastly, the software technology that underlies Windows 95 can be viewed as a substitute for Apple's proprietary operating system technology.

Resource Mobilization

Mobilization of resources can result from an internal loss, e.g. an important employee leaves the firm. It can also result from external causes involving competitors, e.g. an important employee leaves the firm in order to join a competitor. Another example of an external attack is a competitor's acquisition of an important supplier. All these forms of resource mobilizations threaten the rent-producing capacity of the firm's competence.

Resource Paralysis

Direct attempts by competitors to reduce the value of the firm's resources represent another kind of threat to rent-producing potential. For example, a firm's reputation may sometimes be damaged through "negative advertisement", false complaints about the quality of its products, the dissemination of rumors about corruption, illegal acts, environmental pollution, abuse, and more. Competitors may also lobby officials to enforce laws that prevent or delay the use of a resource; import barriers, standards enforcement, and environmental regulations are some examples. In all these examples, the competitor tries to lower the demand for the firm's products. For example, a tariff imposed on luxury cars could decrease the demand for some of these vehicles by effectively increasing their price, and thus reducing the rent-generating potential of the quality and reputation owned by the car producers.

There are other examples of resource paralysis. Encouraging strikes among workers or to union leaders at a firm with superior labor relations would be one. Although we consider many of these tactics to be unethical, and perhaps illegal, we should ignore neither their existence nor the need for firms to defend against them.

STRATEGIC DEFENSE: THE TYPOLOGY

The essence of Strategic Defense is to shield the firm against threats to the rent-generating potential of its competences. Strategic Defense incorporates a narrow range of intelligence activities and a wide range of defensive actions.

Intelligence Activities

Competitors must, if they are to attack a firm's competences, obtain knowledge of the existence of firm competences and the attributes thereof. Their knowledge may result from systems for gathering business intelligence, specific surveillance efforts targeted at the firm, or even mere luck (e.g. unintended revealing of data during "small talk" with a colleague from another firm). It is in the firm's interest to make access to such knowledge more difficult, and accordingly the following three intelligence initiatives can be taken:

- *Creating causal ambiguity*—creating ambiguity regarding the cause-and-effect relationships in competence creation. This intelligence action is particularly relevant to organizational capabilities, e.g. *innovative capacity* or *short cycle time*. Organizational complexity, according to the resource-based literature, is a major source of causal ambiguity (Lipmann and Rumelt, 1982; Dierickx and Cool, 1989; Reed and DeFillippi, 1990; Barney, 1991; Sanchez and Heene, 1996). As part of Strategic Defense, *causal ambiguity* a deliberate creation pursuant to firm policy may be, not some unintended result of organizational processes. For example, many owners of private firms prefer not to raise money on public stock markets in order to prevent the publication of their financial reports. Many managers resist press interviews or even participation in academic research programs for fear of exposing inside information.
- *Counter-intelligence*—taking actions to prevent competitors from gathering business intelligence about the firm's resources. Many firms designate a unit (or at least a person) whose job is to prevent competitors from gathering intelligence on firm assets; they examine new employees and visitors, inspect existing employees, check outgoing mail, and attend meetings with customers and potential competitors. In some cases, they even eavesdrop on employees' telephone conversations.
- *Competitors' intentions intelligence*—gathering intelligence about competitors' intentions to attack the rent-producing capacity of the firm's strategic assets. Such intelligence efforts are intended to enable the firm to prepare, in advance, defenses against potential attacks. Intelligence on competitors' intentions can be gathered from public information (newspapers, magazines, TV) or by initiating activities to gather private information on rivals.

Defensive Actions: Preservation and Alteration

We can divide all defensive actions within the Strategic Defense typology into two generic strategies: *Preservation* and *Alteration*. Preservation actions attempt to preserve the firm's current competences and sustain the rents they produce. Alteration efforts, on the other hand, are about creating alternative competences or enhancing flexibility of current competences.

Preservation Actions

Preservation actions involve strengthening the firm's position and increasing its readiness against a potential attack. This preserves the rent-generating potential of the firm's competences. Eight specific tactics are as follows:

1. *Reducing mobility*—reducing a resource's mobility by preventing or delaying its ability and motivation to leave the firm. Many firms, for example, include a required "freezing period" in employees' contracts, and thus reduce their value outside the firm. Alternatively, firms may induce employees to stay at the firm, e.g. by granting stock options that vest over time, and thus increase the employee's opportunity cost of leaving the firm.
2. *Property rights*—enforcing the firm's property rights to the resource, thereby preventing imitation. Firms register patents to defend the proprietary nature of their innovations and take legal action to enforce them, particularly in industries where innovation requires heavy investments, e.g. pharmaceuticals. Trademark protection, copyrights, registered designs, and others are further ways of defending property rights (Hall, 1992) (e.g. Motorola has established itself as a company that fights vigorously to defend its property rights).
3. *External resource acquisition*—when a resource is required by a firm but is not under its ownership, the firm may choose to acquire it to prevent opportunistic behavior by the supplier/ owner of the resource. In the presence of some form of market failure, acquiring a supplier of important factors of production is one such example (Williamson, 1975; Klein, Crawford, and Alchian, 1978). Another example may be found in the retail industry: acquiring a department store building in an attractive location prevents the risk of exposure to competitors' attempts at renting the building and establishing head-on competition.

4. *Deterrence*—refers to a range of defensive actions aimed at impeding potential attackers from acting by signaling an uncompromising resolution to fight back. The IO literature has dealt with this type of strategy extensively, particularly in entry-deterrence situations (Tirole, 1988). The firm can deter attacks on its resource position by erecting or enhancing both mobility and entry barriers, and also by taking specific credible actions that would reduce rewards to competitors. Reward-reducing actions are common in numerous industries, including the specialty chemical industry, where firms invest in excess capacity to deter entry (Lieberman, 1987). Deterrence can take many other forms, including making public declarations, signaling and legal battles.

5. *Asset specificity*—sufficiently increasing the idiosyncrasy of assets and their patterns of uses such that they have limited or no use outside the firm. This reduces their potential value for competitors (Williamson, 1975). One example of this type of action is to divide up, among a number of co-workers, the "know-how" encompassed within a certain organizational capability, thus limiting each employee's knowledge to a very distinct part of that capability. An example is Michelin's segmentation of its tire production processes.

6. *Partial give-up*—firms may prefer to compromise and give up part of the rents produced by their resources, in order to reduce the incentive to attack and prevent an all-out confrontation. For example, the existence of credible threats of resource mobilization may force the firm to share rents with that resource owner, for example by increasing the compensation of key employees. Another example of partial give-up is a limit pricing tactic, whereby the firm gives up some of the rent from its resources through limit pricing so as to deter entry.

7. *Pressure on government*—Many firms use economic or political pressure on the government to help them prevent or delay an attack on their resources. In particular, monopolists or firms that have long-term contracts with the government may apply political pressure on the government to keep this asset. This pressure can take the form of lobbying, workers' strikes, demonstrations, etc. For example, firms like Intel have pressured the US government to enforce anti-dumping regulations in its fight with Japanese producers of Random Access Memory chips. Another example is the Japanese automobile industry's working closely with its government to protect its market share from competition by US car and truck manufacturers and suppliers of automobile spare parts.

8. *Preventing deployment*—preventing competitors from deploying a resource that has become mobilized or which they have imitated. This can be done by either using the market power of the firm or by taking legal action to prevent or delay deployment of the resource.

Alteration Actions

The generic strategy of *Alteration* is about creating alternative assets and enhancing the flexibility of a stock of strategic assets (Sanchez, 1995). The strategy aims to reduce the effect of an attack on the rent-generating capacity of the firm's resources. While *Preservation* strategy only preserves the rents of the existing resources, *Alteration* strategy has the important distinction of having potential to produce new rent for the firm. Two types of investment—*Alternative Resources* and *Flexible Resources*—are encompassed by *Alteration* strategy:

1. *Alternative Resources*—the firm prepares alternative assets and competences. For example, the firm might invest in next-generation technology which they can deploy once their current generation has been imitated. Many firms maintain a second source for important supplies in case their primary source mobilizes; this second source may be internal or external. The process of creating alternate competences requires investing current cash flows and new capital infusions into competences that create real options to generate new cash flows (see Sanchez and Thomas, 1996).
2. *Flexible Resources*—the firm enhances the flexibility of its competences. Many types of competences can be made more flexible, including activities in operations, engineering, and management. A flexible operational capability might be a production line that can adapt to different types of products with minimal retooling. A flexible engineering capability might be the assembling of engineering teams with wide knowledge of technologies, enabling them to switch from one technology to another (see Sanchez, 1995).

Although investment in alternative resources and investment in making the firm's resources more flexible are components of the same generic strategy, they are different from each other: while alternative resources may require developing new capabilities that are not part of the firm's set of strategic assets, flexible resources tries to make existing resources more adaptable to changing requirements and redeployable in new configurations.

TABLE 8.1   Available defensive strategies and threats they are defending against

Strategy	Threats			
	Imitation	Substitution	Mobilization	Value reduction
Intelligence				
1. Causal ambiguity	+	+	+	+
2. Counter-intelligence	+	+	+	+
3. Competitors' intentions intelligence	+	+	+	+
Preservation				
4. Reducing mobility			+	
5. Property rights	+		+	
6. External resource acquisition			+	
7. Deterrence	+	+	+	+
8. Asset specificity			+	
9. Partial give-up	+	+	+	+
10. Pressure on the government			+	+
11. Preventing deployment	+	+	+	
Alteration				
12. Alternative resources	+	+	+	+
13. Flexible resources	+	+		+

While intelligence activities usually defend against all four types of threats, defensive actions may not. Some of them, like deterrence, defend against all threats; others, like mobility reduction and asset specificity, defend only against the threat of mobilization. Table 8.1 lists the strategies and actions and the threats they defend against.

THE DECISION TO INVEST IN STRATEGIC DEFENSE

Which factors affect a firm's decision to invest in Strategic Defense? To predict the tendency of firms to invest in Strategic Defense initiatives we present in this section a model which examines internal and external factors that may affect a firm's decision to invest in Strategic Defense. The underlying assumptions of the model are tested empirically in the final sections of the paper.

We consider a dichotomous model of investment in Strategic Defense, in which the firm either invests in defense initiatives, or uses its capital for other purposes, such as making investments in the creation of new

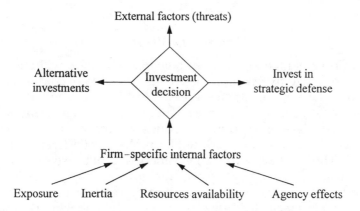

FIGURE 8.1   Strategic defense investment decision model

productive capital. There are two groups of factors affecting the decision to invest in strategic defense: (1) the extent of external threats to the rent-producing capacity of the firm's strategic assets and (2) internal firm-specific organizational and economic factors.

External Threats

Any Strategic Defense investment is motivated by the likelihood of an external attack on the rent-producing capacity of the firm's competences. Attacking the firm's resources is simply a mode of competition. Thus, the likelihood of attack increases as competition intensifies. Because of the differential positioning of firms in the industry and the complexity and uncertainty about factors such as the cost structure of rivals in the firm's environment, perceptions about the intensity of competition will vary among firms. Therefore, a firm's decision to invest in Strategic Defense is affected by the idiosyncratic perceptions of its managers about competition intensity. Thus, we suggest that investment in Strategic Defense is positively related to management's perception about the intensity of competition faced by the firm.

Internal Factors

Internal organizational and economic factors affect a firm's tendency toward Strategic Defense investment. Four of these factors are: *exposure to attacks; inertia; availability of resources;* and *agency effects.*

Exposure to Attacks

Where a firm has high exposure to potential attacks, it will increase its tendency to hedge by taking initiatives to prevent erosion of the rent-generating capacity of its resources. Market visibility affects firm exposure; this generally increases with firm size. High profile and public knowledge of a firm's productive resources increases the probability of an attack, as well as the probable effectiveness of such an attack. Threat of resource mobilization is another source of attack exposure (e.g. a key employee leaves the firm); such exposure increases as connectivity among the firm's entities decreases. Such low connectivity is usually associated with larger organizations where employees are generally less committed to the firm. Thus, we suggest that investment in Strategic Defense is positively related to the size of the firm.

Inertia

High organizational inertia increases a firm's tendency to invest in defending its current bundle of rent-producing assets. Rumelt (1994) classified the main sources of inertia into the following "five frictions": distorted perception; dulled motivation; failed creative response; political deadlocks; and action disconnects. Each of these drives the firm to focus on current resources, preserve status quo, and defend against rent erosion. The "acceleration effect" further increases the likelihood of organizational inertia to encourage Strategic Defense investment. Under the "acceleration effect" competitors are more likely to attack firms with high inertia, since they expect the inertia to decrease the likelihood of retaliation (Chen and Miller, 1994). These expectations of competitors raise the threat level perceived the firm, however, which in turn increases its tendency to defend its resources. Also, inertia is said to increase with organizational age (Hannan and Freeman, 1984; Singh, 1990). Thus, we suggest that investment in Strategic Defense is positively related to firm age.

Availability of Resources

A firm's tendency to invest in its defense is greater when it has a greater accumulated stock of productive resources, because competitors' attacks may result in a relatively larger loss to the rent-generation capacity of the firm's competences. We shall use sales as the proxy for the accumulated stock of productive resources, because it is the firm's productive resources which enable sales revenues. Availability of resources also has implications for the *type* of Strategic Defense investment. In smaller firms, where the stock of assets and capabilities may be incomplete, the marginal benefit of completing their stock and investing in their *preservation* exceeds the benefits of developing *alternative* competences. Consider, for example, an emerging technology firm with a unique technological know-how along with a precision manufacturing capability. This firm must first invest in developing a distribution capability in order to extract any rents from its technology and manufacturing. Second, it must engage in *preservation* initiatives to sustain the rent-producing capacity of the firm's technologies. With these investments in place, the search for alternative technologies to replace current technologies, as a mode of defending the rent-producing capacity of its competences, begins.

Thus, we argue that larger firms, which usually have a more complete bundle of assets and capabilities required to achieve competences, are more likely than smaller firms to invest in Strategic Defense and in the development of alternative resources.

Agency Effects

Agency theory (Jensen and Meckling, 1976) predicts that conflicting interests of different stakeholders will result in different attitudes towards Strategic Defense investment. In this study we consider three groups of stakeholders: owners, managers, and employees. We identify four different combinations of these groups and predict that the likelihood of Strategic Defense investment differs with each combination, and that the specific investment chosen differs as well:

1. *Full Separation*: This is the case in a widely held publicly traded firm. Owners and managers may have conflicting interests: stockholders want to maximize the NPV of future cash flows; managers, on the other hand, may have a large stock of non-tradable human capital invested in the firm, and are interested in reducing the risk of firm bankruptcy by, for example, Strategic Defense initiatives. The managers are more likely to invest in preserving and prolonging the rent-producing capacity of the firm's current bundle of resources rather than developing alternatives, given their vested interest in current firm competences. Among the possible Preservation initiatives, managers are more

likely to choose those with a minimal impact on current profits (i.e. requires minimal investment of current cash flows), because of the potential for adverse effects on their personal compensations.

2. *Unified ownership and management.* In this ownership structure, which applies to closely held private firms, the agency problem is eliminated. As owners and managers are the same group, the balance of power shifts away from employees and towards the owner–manager group. This in turn provides management with more freedom to take those defensive initiatives which may adversely affect employees, such as increasing asset specificity and. reducing factor mobility. The combination of imperfections in labor markets and the weak negotiating power of employees helps to explain this phenomenon's existence.

3. *Unified ownership, management and employment* is the governance structure which describes production cooperatives and firms owned by trade unions. In these situations there are no conflicts of interest that will favor a particular defensive initiative. The objectives of such organizations are more diverse than in other governance types, and their decision-making processes are more complex; thus, one would expect fewer irreversible investments in Strategic Defense. As some types of Preservation initiatives have an adverse effect on employees, cooperatives are unlikely to engage in such initiatives.

4. *Quasi-full separation* describes the governance structure of firms which are owned by government. In these cases there is a quasi-separation between employees, managers, and owners, because the employees, who are often unionized, have a disproportional amount of power *vis-à-vis* the owners, (i.e. the government). In a freely elected democracy employees can use their political power to bias owners' decision making in their favor. The owner in such cases is the government, which may have multiple and conflicting roles as firm owner, as a major buyer of its products and services (e.g. in the defense industry), and as the authority guaranteeing its monopoly position in the marketplace. Thus these firms will tend to exercise pressure on the government (their owner) to preserve the rent-producing capacity of their resources.

STRATEGIC DEFENSE AND FIRM PERFORMANCE

One of the fundamental premises of the resource-based view is that competitive forces ultimately threaten the rent-producing capacity of the firm's resources. Thus successful firms are those which succeed in amassing and utilizing valuable and unique resources, and which subsequently succeed in defending the sustainability of their rent-generating capacity. The defensive measures require irreversible investments that do not, in and of themselves, produce any new rents *per se*; at best, such initiatives delay the erosion of rent. In any industry, at any point in time, a firm's performance is determined by the rent-producing capacity of its competences relative to that of competitors. Disentangling the specific contribution of defensive strategies to firm performance is difficult both conceptually and empirically. Since that problem has such complexity, and in view of the current stage of theory build-up regarding the concept of Strategic Defense, we consider it more appropriate to make an exploratory attempt at identifying differences in Strategic Defense investment patterns between successful and unsuccessful firms. These exploratory results may later serve as nourishment for theory build-up.

OVERVIEW OF EMPIRICAL FINDINGS

In what follows we report on some of the results of an exploratory empirical analysis of a sample that consists of 69 Israeli manufacturing firms in 13 industries, encompassing a variety of technologies and market types. In each industry, the sample, which was created by conducting personal interviews with top management, covered at least 70% of total sales (to the local market) in that segment. The sampled firms varied in major factors such as age, sales volume, number of employees, and type of ownership. The managers were presented with a list of defensive strategies; these strategies are listed in Table 8.1. They were then asked to specify which of the strategies they had used in defending their firm's competences.

Table 8.2 depicts the means, standard deviations, and Pearson correlations among all the variables in the sample. The first 13 rows of the table present the results for the defensive strategies, whereas row 14 (total) displays the total number of defensive strategies used by the firm. Rows 15–17 present the results for the firm attributes; row 18 displays the perceived competition variable; and rows 19–22 present the results for the different types of firm ownership.

Among the 69 firms in the sample, only 4 (6%) claimed not to use defensive strategies. The average number of strategy types used by a firm is about 4, with a standard deviation of about 2 (see line 14 total). The maximum was 8.

The most frequently used strategic defense initiatives were: *reducing*

TABLE 8.2 Means, standard deviation and correlations

Variable	Mean	S.D.	15	16	17	18	19	20	21	22
Intelligence										
1. Ambiguity	0.30	0.46	0.05	-0.10	-0.12	0.03	0.14	-0.01	-0.19	-0.00
2. Counter-int.	0.42	0.50	-0.08	0.04	0.04	-0.08	0.01	0.01	-0.01	-0.02
3. Competition-int.	0.35	0.48	-0.4	0.04	0.02	0.03	-0.22[a]	0.13	0.03	0.05
Preservation										
4. Mobility	0.55	0.50	-0.10	-0.04	0.03	0.06	0.17	-0.12	0.03	-0.04
5. Property rights	0.55	0.50	0.14	0.02	0.11	-0.01	-0.05	0.06	0.03	-0.04
6. Acquisition	0.13	0.34	0.14	0.03	0.09	0.01	-0.09	0.16	0.06	-0.16
7. Deterrence	0.36	0.48	0.26[b]	0.02	0.11	0.10	-0.23[a]	0.21[a]	0.14	-0.14
8. Asset specificity	0.10	0.30	0.00	-0.07	-0.09	0.04	0.31[c]	-0.20[a]	-0.09	-0.00
9. Give-up	0.06	0.24	0.04	0.08	0.16	0.06	0.03	0.09	-0.07	-0.10
10. Press goverm.	0.07	0.26	0.11	0.14	0.13	0.15	-0.00	-0.22[a]	0.57[d]	-0.12
11. Prevent deploy.	0.07	0.26	0.24[b]	0.33[c]	0.26[b]	0.06	-0.00	0.01	0.14	-0.12
Alteration										
12. Alternative	0.46	0.50	0.08	0.32[c]	0.35[c]	0.35[c]	-0.00	-0.15	0.08	0.03
13. Flexible	0.35	0.48	0.05	-0.03	-0.01	0.17	0.11	0.01	0.08	-0.04
14. Total	3.78	1.95	0.16	0.14	0.21[a]	0.21[a]	0.01	0.01	0.12	-0.12
15. Firm age	29.30	19.00		0.28[b]	0.34[c]	0.19	-0.25[b]	0.06	0.08	0.14
16. Firm size	834.00	1,222.00			0.92[d]	0.23[c]	-0.27[b]	-0.00	0.45[c]	-0.02
17. Firm sales	77.00	115.20				0.28[c]	-0.25[b]	-0.04	0.41[c]	0.04
18. Competition	1.00	0.23					0.05	-0.2	0.18	0.19
19. Owner-private	0.20	0.41								
20. Owner-public	0.58	0.50								
21. Owner-goverm.	0.07	0.26								
22. Owner-cooper.	0.14	0.35								

$n = 69$, [a]$p < 0.1$, [b]$p < 0.05$, [c]$p < 0.01$, [d]$p < 0.001$

resource mobility and *defending property rights*—more than half of the firms declared they used these two types of tactics. The least-used initiative was *partial give-up* (less than 6%).

- *Intelligence activities:* All these initiatives that encompass the intelligence activities—*creating causal ambiguity; counter-intelligence;* and *competitors' intentions intelligence* are positively correlated. This suggests that those firms which are aware of the importance of business intelligence will use a range of intelligence activities, and not constrain themselves to a specific type.
- *Preservation actions:* The most frequently used preservation initiatives are: *reducing mobility* and *defending property rights*. The main ways in which firms implement *reducing mobility of employees*, as the interviews revealed, are through long-term contracts, "freezing periods" (usually one to three years), and through options and bonuses conditional on staying at the firm. Many managers suggested that they do not rely on negative measures (e.g. "freezing period") to reduce mobility. Instead, they prefer positive measures, such as increasing motivation and firm identity of the employees. *Reducing mobility* was also found to be used in long-term contracts with suppliers and distributors.

Firms implement property rights measures mainly by trademarks, writing patents, and securing copyrights. Many of the firms declared that they use legal measures to enforce property rights.

External resource acquisition is used mainly through vertical integration, i.e. acquisition of a supplier or distributor. This strategy is not used frequently (only 13% of the firms), which suggests that firms may either lack the capital or are aware of the negative effects of vertical integration (e.g. increased commitment, reduced flexibility). Thirty-six per cent of the firms use *deterrence*, especially by means of declarations and the signaling of resolutions to fight back. In cases where attacks have taken place, firms do not usually choose *preventing deployment of the resource* as their reaction. Managers tend to be of the opinion that such reactions will lead to counter-actions, and resultant "bleedings" of both parties (a "prisoner's dilemma" type), and they prefer not to engage in such wars.

- *Alteration actions:* Alteration initiatives were also quite popular among the firms (46% of the firms use alternative resources and 35% use flexibility). Alteration tactics were used heavily in relation to suppliers—many firms insist on having second sources for their necessary inputs. Many firms also train a "shadow employee", in key activities, in order to have "alternates" for key employees. *Flexibility of competence*, the second type of Alteration strategy, was manifested by flexible production (50%), engineering flexibility (24%), and organizational/managerial flexibility (26%).

Table 8.3 presents the results of the multiple linear regression analyses. The table presents only those equations that yield statistically significant results. Rows 1–5 present the models for 5 of the 13 available Strategic Defense initiatives. The dependent variable in rows 6–7 is the total number of initiatives taken by the firm in each of the two generic defensive strategy types: *Preservation* and *Alteration*. In row 8 the dependent variable is the total number of initiatives taken by the firm. In general, the results of the correlations and the linear regression analyses support the model presented in the theory section.

Table 8.4 presents the results of ANOVA between high- and low-performing firms. Generally the table reveals no significant differences between the two groups. However, some interesting observations can be made:

1. High-performing firms tend to invest more in intelligence activities in comparison to low-performing firms
2. Low-performing firms tend to invest more in Preservation tactics, whereas high-performing firms attempt more strongly to deter competitors, and are even willing, unlike low-performers, to give up a fraction of resource-generated rent in order to prevent retaliatory actions
3. While low-performing firms invest significantly more than high-performing firms in creating alternative resources, high-performing firms generally choose instead to maintain flexibility of their resources.

SUMMARY AND CONCLUSIONS

Strategic Defense strategies are meant to reduce the willingness of competitors to attack a firm's competences, and to make such an attack less effective if it does occur. We have presented a typology that centers on two generic Strategic Defense approaches: *Preservation*, which is aimed at preserving the firm's rents from its existing bundle of competences, and *Alteration*, which seeks to modify the firm's competences by developing substitutes and making existing competences more flexible so that they can be redeployed in different ways.

TABLE 8.3 Multiple linear regression

Dependent variable	Constant	Firm effects			Competition	Ownership effects				AdjR¹ (%)	F	P
		Age	Size	Sales		Private	Public	Government	Cooperative			
1. Deterrence	-0.144 -(0.51)	0.0058 (1.9)[a]			0.212 (0.82)		0.215 (1.84)			7.5	2.84	0.045
2. Asset	-0.018 -(0.11)			-0.0 -(0.25)	0.08 (0.49)	0.227 (2.49)[b]				5.7	2.36	0.079
3. Press government	-0.033 -(0.28)		-0.000034 -(1.41)		0.088 (0.75)		0.628	31.6 (5.57)[d]		11.47	0	
4. Prevent deployment	0.018 (0.13)		0.00007 (2.72)[c]		0.008 (0.06)				-0.813 -(0.93)	8.0	2.98	0.038
5. Alternative	-0.136 -(0.49)			0.000001 (2.36)[b]	0.56 (2.16)[b]		-0.09 -(0.79)			16.1	5.34	0.002
6. Preservation	1.2 (1.78)			0.000002 (1.53)	0.657 (0.95)				-0.81 -(1.89)[a]	5.8	2.4	0.076
7. Alteration	-0.21 -(0.5)			0.000001 (1.22)	0.98 (2.51)[b]		-0.5 -(0.29)			10.6	3.68	0.016
8. Total	2.18 (2.07)			0.000003 (1.35)	1.39 (1.31)					4.1	2.46	0.093

$n = 69$, [a] $p < 0.1$, [b] $p < 0.05$, [c] < 0.01, [d] $p < 0.001$.

TABLE 8.4   Analysis of variance: the frequency of use of defensive strategies and performance

Strategy	Low-perform.	High-perform.	F	p
Intelligence				
1. Ambiguity	0.31	0.29	0.03	0.858
2. Counter-intelligence	0.37	0.47	0.68	0.412
3. Competition-intentions	0.26	0.44	2.60	0.112
Preservation				
4. Mobility	0.60	0.50	0.68	0.411
5. Property rights	0.57	0.53	0.12	0.730
6. Acquisition	0.14	0.12	0.09	0.760
7. Deterrence	0.34	0.38	0.11	0.738
8. Asset specificity	0.11	0.09	0.12	0.725
9. Give-up	0.00	0.12	4.53	0.037[b]
10. Press government	0.11	0.03	1.84	0.179
11. Prevent deployment	0.09	0.06	0.18	0.672
Alteration				
12. Alternative	0.57	0.35	3.38	0.071[a]
13. Flexible	0.26	0.44	2.6	0.112
14. Total	3.74	3.82	0.03	0.865

F-ratio of analysis of variance.
$n = 35$ low performance, 35 high performance, [a]$p < 0.01$, [b]$p < 0.05$.

We drew on the resource-based view of the firm competence theory, and competitive rivalry literature in developing the underlying concept of Strategic Defense. We outlined specific tactics associated with each generic strategy, and delineated a model which incorporates the internal and external factors that affect the decision to invest in Strategic Defense.

The empirical findings provide broad support for the underlying hypotheses about Strategic Defense usage. We find that intense competition serves as a catalyst to irreversible investments in Strategic Defense, especially the creation of alternative resources. We find that older and larger firms tend to rely on Preservation strategies, such as deterrence and preventing deployment. Firm size (in terms of sales revenue) is positively correlated with the investment in alternative resources.

Agency effects, as emerged from the governance structure of the firm, affect Strategic Defense usage. Publicly traded firms tend to defend their assets by deterrence, in the form of declarations and signaling; this has a minimal impact on current profits. Privately held firms use more frequently, in comparison with other types of ownership, tactics that adversely affect the wealth of the employees in that firm. Cooperatives tend to make fewer investments in Preservation, and government-owned firms tend to pressure the government in order to sustain the rent-producing capacity of their assets.

Our exploratory research on the links between firm performance and the use of Strategic Defense and firm performance reveals that low-performing firms tend to invest more in Preservation tactics, whereas high-performing firms invest mainly in intelligence activities and in attempts to deter competitors. They will also more willingly give up a fraction of rent in order to prevent retaliatory actions that will "bleed" both parties. One might tentatively conclude that firms tend to have inferior performance if they are too heavily engaged in preserving their rent generation, at the cost of neglecting further resource development or the development of new competences.

The emphasis of low-performing firms on Preservation strategies reflects the internal inertial forces in these firms and their unadaptability to the changing environment. Their choice between the two Alteration strategies also reflects these inertial forces: high-performing firms tend to invest more in maintaining flexibility of their current resources than in creating alternative resources as future options. Making existing competences more flexible, as opposed to developing substitute competences, eliminates potential resistance of the resource owners (e.g. employees with specialty training, division managers, etc.) who wish to protect their interests, thus preventing the deployment of alternative resources.

IMPLICATIONS FOR STRATEGY THEORY, RESEARCH AND PRACTICE

The Strategic Defense typology which was outlined in this chapter extends the theoretical research in competence-based competition by suggesting tactics in which firms can proactively sustain the rent-generation capacity of the firm's competences.

We have presented the findings of an exploratory field research. There are numerous limitations to these empirical results; these limitations result primarily from constraints on the data set we compiled. The relatively small number of firms and the lack of specific quantitative investment data in each strategy are among the main limitations.

The defense–offense approach to competence-based competition opens up a wide range of research questions including issues in Strategic Offense, such as the desired balance between investments in offensive and defensive initiatives, as well as between such initiatives and competence-creation investment.

While having the limitations of the exploratory field research in mind, we believe that these results may suggest some practical implications to managers, especially in highly competitive and uncertain environments. The results point out to the importance of taking the appropriate initiatives to defend the rent-generation potential of the firm's competences. The type and level of initiatives should correlate with the level of external threats, on the one hand, and the size, age, resource availability, and governance structure of the firm, on the other. Managers are also advised to focus their efforts on intelligence activities and maintaining the flexibility of their current competences, more than preservation actions and creating alternative resources.

ACKNOWLEDGEMENTS

This is an abbreviated and practitioners-oriented version of a paper entitled 'Strategic Defense', submitted to the *Strategic Management Journal*. The first version of the abbreviated paper was presented at *The Third International Workshop on Competence-Based Competition*, Ghent, Belgium, November 1995. We thank Jay Barney, Aimé Heene, Bill McKelvey, Ron Sanchez, and other participants at the workshop for their helpful comments. The generous research support of the Peter Wall Foundation is gratefully acknowledged.

REFERENCES

Amit, R. and Schoemaker, P.J.H. (1993). Strategic assets and organizational rent. *Strategic Management Journal*, **14**(1), 33–46.

Barney, J. (1986). Strategic factor markets: Expectations, luck and business strategy. *Management Science*, **42**, 1231–41.

Barney, J. (1991). Firm resources and sustained competitive advantage. *Journal of Management*, **17**, 99–120.

Brandenburger, A.M. and Nalebuff, B.J. (1995). The right game: use game theory to shape strategy. *Harvard Business Review*, **73**(4), 57–71.

Chen, Ming-Jer and MacMillan, I.C. (1992). Non response and delayed response to competitive moves: the role of competitor dependence and action irreversibility. *Academy of Management Journal*, **35**(3), 539–70.

Chen, Ming-Jer and Miller, D. (1994). Competitive attack, retaliation and performance: an expectancy-valence framework. *Strategic Management Journal*, **15**, 85–102.

Collis, D.J. and Montgomery C.A. (1995). Competing on resources: strategy in the 1990s. *Harvard Business Review*, **73**(4), 118–28.

Dierickx, I. and Cool, K. (1989). Asset stock accumulation and sustainability of competitive advantage. *Management Science*, **35**, 1504–11.

Hall, R. (1992). The strategic analysis of intangible resources. *Strategic Management Journal*, **13**, 135–44.

Hamel, G. and Heene, A. (eds) (1994). *Competence-based Competition*. New York: John Wiley.

Hannan, M.T. and Freeman, J.H. (1984). Structural inertia and organizational change. *American Sociological Review*, **49**, 149–64.

Jensen, M. and Meckling, W. (1976). Theory of the firm: Managerial behavior, agency costs and ownership structure. *Journal of Financial Economics*, **3**, 305–60.

Klein, B., Crawford, R. and Alchian, A. (1978). Vertical integration, appropriable rents and the competitive contracting process. *Journal of Law and Economics*, **21**, 297–326.

Lieberman, M. (1987). Excess capacity as a barrier to entry: an empirical appraisal. *The Journal of Industrial Economics*, **19**(4), 607–627.

Lippman, R. and Rumelt, R. (1982). Uncertain imitability: An analysis of interfirm difference in efficiency under competition. *Bell Journal of Economics*, **13**, 418–38.

MacMillan, I.C. (1988). Controlling competitive dynamics by taking strategic initiative. *The Academy of Management Executive*, **11**(2), 111–18.

Mahoney, J.T. and Pandian, R. (1992). The resource-based view within the conversation of strategic management. *Strategic Management Journal*, **13**, 363–80.

McMillan, J. (1992). *Games, Strategies and Managers*. New York: Oxford University Press.

Peteraf, M. (1993). The cornerstones of competitive advantage: A resource-based view. *Strategic Management Journal*, **14**, 179–91.

Porter, M.E. (1980). *Competitive Strategy*. New York: Free Press.

Porter, M.E. (1985). *Competitive Advantage*. New York: Free Press.

Reed, R. and DeFillippi, R.J. (1990). Causal ambiguity, barriers to imitation and sustainable competitive advantage. *Academy of Management Review*, **15**, 88–102.

Rumelt, R.P. (1984). Toward a strategic theory of the firm. In Lamb, R., (ed.) *Competitive Strategic Management*. Englewood Cliffs, N.J: Prentice Hall, pp. 556–70.

Sanchez, R. and Heene, A. (1996). A systems view of the firm in competence-based competition. In Sanchez, R., Heene, A., and Thomas, H. (eds), *Dynamics of Competence-based Competition*. Oxford: Elsevier.

Sanchez, R. and Thomas, H. (1996). Strategic goals. In Sanchez, R., Heene, A., and Thomas, H. (eds), *Dynamics of Competence-based Competition*. Oxford: Elsesvier.

Sanchez, R. (1995). Strategic flexibility in product competition. *Strategic Management Journal*, **16** (Special Issue).

Sanchez, R., Heene, A. and Thomas, H. (1996). Towards the theory and practice of competence-based competition. In Sanchez, R., Heene, A., and Thomas, H. (eds), *Dynamics of Competence-based Competition: Theory and Practice in the New Strategic Management*. Oxford: Elsevier.

Singh, Y. (ed.) (1990). *Organizational Evolution:* Beverly Hills, CA: Sage.

Teece, D.J. (1986). Profiting from technological innovation. *Research Policy*, **15**, 285–305.

Tirole, J. (1988). *The Theory of Industrial Organization*. Cambridge, MA: The MIT Press.

Wernerfelt, B. (1984). A resource-based view of the firm. *Strategic Management Journal*, **5**, 171–180.

Williamson, O.E. (1975). *Markets and Hierarchies: Analysis and Antitrust Implications*. New York: Free Press.

Section III
Competence Systemics

9

Competence Levels within Firms: A Static and Dynamic Analysis

Vittorio Chiesa, Raffaella Manzini

Analysis of the various contributions on theory and practice of competence-based competition shows that the concept of competence has been related to different activity levels within the firm. Here we introduce a framework based on a multiple-level view of competence which attempts to integrate the different perspectives. At each of the three levels both the competences and their outputs are defined. This framework seems useful to make a distinction between static and dynamic analyses of a firm's competence. Static analysis means taking a view of a firm's competences at various levels at a given time; dynamic analysis means understanding how the three levels interact with each other in order to leverage and build competences. This framework also helps us to understand how the different competence levels affect a firm's competitive capability and performance. The framework was developed using three case studies, one of which is briefly outlined in the Appendix.

INTRODUCTION

The interest in competence-based competition presents an opportunity to rethink fundamental issues in strategic management. A growing

Competence-based Strategic Management.
Edited by Aimé Heene and Ron Sanchez.
Copyright © 1997 John Wiley & Sons Ltd.

body of literature is looking at the importance of firm-specific factors (including competences, capabilities, strategic assets) as an explanation for significant performance differences among firms (Hamela and Heene, 1994; Sanchez, Heene, and Thomas, 1996).

The seminal work of Prahalad and Hamel (1990) refers to the core competence of the corporation as "the collective learning in the organization, especially how to co-ordinate diverse production skills and integrate multiple streams of technologies". The authors emphasize that competences are the result of a cumulative process of learning within the whole organization, and essentially depend on superior technological leads. Dosi and Teece (1993) define a firm's distinctive competence as the set of activities in which it excels, and its "organizational competences" as the "capabilities of an enterprise to organize, manage, coordinate or govern specific sets of activities". They add that there are "higher level competences related to the ability to change existing competences". Schoemaker's (1992) examples of a firm's core capabilities include "high-quality manufacturing, good supplier relations, service excellence, innovation, short product development cycles, well-motivated employees, a marketing culture and a strong service reputation", thus locating a firm's competence at a more operational level. Leonard-Barton (1992), working from a knowledge-based view of the firm, defines a core capability as the knowledge set that distinguishes and provides competitive advantage. This set comprises four dimensions: employee skills, technical systems, managerial systems, and culture and norms. Recently, Sanchez, Heene, and Thomas (1996) have defined competence as "an ability to sustain the co-ordinated deployment of assets in a way that helps a firm achieve its goals".

A first observation emerging from the comparison of the different definitions and approaches is that different terminology has often been adopted for similar concepts. Second, it seems that these concepts of competence all refer to different levels of activities within the firm, while at the same time many authors adopt focused views of competences and link this concept to a firm's activities. Technologically focused analysis views competence as "a bundle of skills and technologies", while organizationally oriented analysis defines competence as the capability of an enterprise to "organize, manage, coordinate". In this chapter we propose a view of competence as a multiple-level concept, and attempt to integrate the different interpretations into a global perspective. In our view, this helps enrich the theoretical foundations of the competence-based theory of firms and competition.

Another aspect which has not yet been studied in depth is that of the dynamics associated with the concept of competence. Many studies have adopted a static view of competences identified within a firm.

Fewer studies have considered how competence can be changed and built. Sanchez, Heene, and Thomas (1996) introduce the distinction between competence-building processes (which qualitatively change a firm's existing stock of assets and capabilities) and competence-leveraging processes (which aim to apply existing competences to current or new market opportunities in ways that do not require quantitative changes). We believe that a multiple-level view of competence also helps to clarify the intrinsically dynamic aspect of the concept of competence itself.

To summarize, we will attempt to contribute to a more broadly valid definition of the competence concept by focusing on two critical aspects of the debate:

- The identification of different levels of competence within a firm
- The interactions between these different levels of competence.

These two aspects underlie two different approaches to the problem that may be usefully analysed separately. The first implies a *static* analysis and helps identify a firm's competences at a given time; the second involves a *dynamic* analysis of how a certain set of competences at a certain level is interrelated, and how this set interacts and affects the set of competences at other levels, contributing to the process of building and enhancing the latter.

The approach has been tested in three ongoing case studies. Subsequently, with reference to real cases, this chapter attempts to make a practical contribution to the transformation of the theoretical foundations of competence-based competition into management practice.

The chapter is divided into three sections: the first analyses the theoretical background of competence-based competition and in reviewing major interpretations of the competence concept provides the basis for the static analysis; the second looks at the dynamics of competences within firms; and the third attempts to extract managerial implications and normative principles from the analysis. A case study is briefly outlined in the Appendix.

STATIC ANALYSIS

As far as static analysis is concerned, a hierarchy of competences can be identified within a firm:

- The first level of competence refers to the *System View* capability of the firm, i.e. the capability to identify and understand the competitive context and the frame of reference of its actions.

- The second level is that of *Distinctive Capabilities*, i.e. "repeatable patterns of action" that allow "coordinated deployments" of the firm's knowledge and resources.
- The third level of competence is the capacity to embody the distinctive capabilities of the firm into *Core Outputs*.

The identification of different levels of competence is central in clarifying the link between the competence view of the firm and strategic decisions, operative management, end products, and services.

A complementary analysis to that presented in this chapter has been developed by Sanchez (1996), who investigates the *content* of knowledge, identifying three distinct levels—*know-what, know-why*, and *know-how*—and clarifying their specific strategic significance. That study describes the kind of knowledge that is related to each competence level of our framework.

THE FIRST LEVEL OF COMPETENCE: THE SYSTEM VIEW

A first level of competence can be seen as a firm's ability to envisage the evolution of the characteristics, boundaries, and actors of the competitive environment and to promote and develop management principles underpinning its actions and helping it to fulfil its expectations. In this sense, the system view consists of:

- The capability to foresee the evolution of the firm's context (industry foresight)
- The capability to view the firm as a coordinated and integrated set of resources and capabilities.

Industry Foresight

To foresee the shape of the context in which the firm will compete in the future is what Hamel and Prahalad (1993) call *"industry foresight"*. This does not mean a simple forecast; rather, it could include the expression of a personal, emotional, subjective, and non-rational "vision" of the future. Industry foresight relies upon a deep understanding of the current characteristics and the evolutionary trends of the environment in terms of technological and scientific knowledge, culture, social issues, tastes, habits, etc. It is also concerned with the role that the firm should have in future competition. Top management has to identify, obviously initially in a general way, how the firm will behave in relation to customer trends and their needs. This will help to create a framework for identifying the competences that will be critical in sustaining competition and supporting development.

The establishment of industry foresight requires an analysis and interpretation of the internal and external context of the firm. The internal analysis is focused on the resources available to and addressable by the firm that will be critical in sustaining competitive advantage over time. The external analysis not only concerns the industry in which the firm competes and its current competitors, because that industry and its competitive rules could rapidly change over time. Rather, it must consider a broader competitive space around the firm, i.e. different industrial and service sectors, and products/services/markets not traditionally served, thus defining the envisaged future environment as broadly as possible.

Internal and external analyses need to be integrated in a non-traditional way: the objective is not just to identify the present external threats and opportunities of the industry in which the firm competes and relate these to current internal strengths and weaknesses. On the contrary, the external analysis should allow the firm to recognize critical issues in *future* competition and the kind of resources and competences likely to become necessary, and provide the firm with information on the resources which can be found and acquired from other firms and actors. The internal analysis, then, should assess the gap between what the firm already possesses and what it should have.

The external analysis thus complements the internal assessment. In this way the firm should be seen as an *open system* (Sanchez and Heene, 1996), in which stocks and flows of assets, either internally among different units or between the firm and the external environment, dynamically interact and influence each other.

The integration of external and internal analyses gives the firm a base for its *managerial cognition*, i.e. a complete and long-term vision of the critical issues in the future (resources and competences to achieve) and ways to face these (where and how resources are available or can be generated, either inside or outside the firm). Managerial cognition determines the *strategic logic* that, at all levels within the firm, should guide employees when they have discretion in the use of resources or the management of activities, and thus ensures there is consistency among different and separate activities (Sanchez, Heene, and Thomas, 1996).

A Coordinated and Integrated View of Firm Resources

From the above it can also be argued that to create a true system view, the firm must be seen as a set of coordinated and integrated resources. Resources and competences should be seen as corporate assets and not as a property of business units or functions (Prahalad and Hamel, 1990). This is critical in identifying and exploiting all the opportunities provided by the internal capabilities of the firm, as a global and integrated view may suggest ideas for new uses of existing resources. In this sense, the system view of the firm depends on flexible coordination (Sanchez and Heene, 1996) that allows a firm to grasp market opportunities by alternative uses of tangible and intangible assets.

The system view of the firm has four key outputs. The first is the establishment of a firm's goals, i.e. "the set of desired states in a firm's system elements" (Sanchez, Heene, and Thomas, 1996). Indeed, the system view asks top management to identify the desired role of the firm in future competition and to pose a set of objectives that help accomplish specific firm goals. Second, the system view affects the shaping of critical procedures in strategic management, such as the decision-making process, as well as resource allocation and acquisition criteria. These procedures need to be defined in line with the desired evolution of the firm and its strategic goals. Third, the system view influences the design of a firm's organizational structure, as widely emphasized in the debate on the relationship between strategy and structure.[1] Fourth, it contributes to the definition of the culture and values to be diffused throughout the organization in support of strategy and actions.

THE SECOND LEVEL OF COMPETENCE:
DISTINCTIVE CAPABILITIES

The second level of competence is that of the repeatable patterns of action in the use of assets that allow coordinated deployments (Sanchez, Heene, and Thomas, 1996) of a specific *set of knowledge*. These define how to use certain technological and organizational skills and complementary assets that allow the firm to perform a certain set of activities better than competitors.

This concept of competence has three important aspects:

---

[1] The concept of "strategic intent" (Hamel and Prahalad, 1994), the output of which is the definition of the firm's strategic architecture, i.e. the firm's way to the future, is also relevant to this competence level. Its counterpart in terms of strategic management is the concept of "stretch and leverage" which defines strategies that stretch the organization and establish objectives which appear nearly impossible to achieve, so that, inevitably, an intentional "misfit" between what the firm is and what it wants to be in the future is created.

1. It is based on the set of knowledge a firm possesses, the set of technological and organizational skills and complementary assets which may be either internally available or externally accessible.
2. It requires a coordinated deployment of the firm's assets through the implementation of repeatable procedures (Sanchez, Heene, and Thomas, 1996). Coordination implies communication, interaction, and exchange of information among the firm's functions and divisions. The coordinated use of resources allows the firm to grasp more opportunities from the use of assets, so maximizing their deployment and the value they can create. Integration of these resources generates synergies through the joint and "collaborative" use of different knowledge, skills and capabilities. This can be seen as the result (at a lower level) of the coordinated and integrated view of resources described at the first level of competence;
3. It has to be able to create value for the customer, i.e. provide the functional characteristics of the product/service which satisfy customer needs and cannot be imitated by competitors.

Distinctive capabilities can be associated with a specific content which mirrors the nature of the set of knowledge, and distinguishes the firm from its competitors. They include "technology-based distinctive capabilities", i.e. knowledge (both tacit and explicit) about how to apply a certain set of scientific principles, technologies and skills in practice (production processes and products). NEC's in-depth knowledge of semiconductor production and application in electronics, information technology, and telecommunications, Honda's ability to exploit its expertise in engine design in various fields, Canon's capability to integrate and coordinate knowledge in optics, imaging and microprocessor control, and Kodak's experience across different technological fields such as materials, optomechatronics, and electronics for applications in the imaging business are typical examples of technology-based distinctive capabilities. There are also "service-based distinctive capabilities", that is, the ability to organize and manage activities that create value for the customer through services, such as quality, delivery time, cost,[2] etc., that distinctively

---

[2]Cost can be considered as a form of service in the sense that given the same technical performance, a product may be distinctive because it is sold at a lower price. Cost is then a product characteristic that is not conceptually different from quality (seen as conformity to product performance targets), time etc.

characterize the final product (Stalk, Evans, and Shulman, 1992). For example, Wal-Mart's logistics and store management to ensure "everyday low prices", and Honda's skills in dealer management (its ability to train and support dealers in operating procedures and policies for merchandising, selling, floor planning, service management) and product realization are service-based capabilities.

The distinction between technology- and service-based distinctive capabilities is critical in understanding the different ways in which firms can create competitive advantage. Whereas, for example, distinctive technological knowledge about the automobile production process and engineering is still a source of advantage in the luxury car segment, in other segments the source of advantage is related to ability in managing the product development process so that time-to-market and development costs are dramatically reduced. This is a service-based distinctive capability, because the customer can be offered new models very frequently, without increasing cost levels. The availability of the best price–performance labour ratio combined with strong central control and synergic exploitation of distribution channels has allowed South Korean *chaebol* to enter a number of unrelated businesses, in part by providing a form of service to the customer (lower cost).

A firm's distinctive capability may also be the result of a mix of service and technology-based capabilities. Asymmetries in one capability can probably explain why firms having comparable knowledge and skills in a certain activity have different profitability and success. Sony and Philips, for example, seem to have comparable technology-based capabilities distinguishing them from other consumer electronics firms, but Sony's products are undoubtedly more diffused and appreciated, have a strong brand image of quality and technological excellence, and are generally priced higher. The reason is a distinctive (service-based) capability on the part of Sony in managing and controlling distribution channels and promoting brand image.

Distinctive capabilities within firms enable the creation of organizational routines (Dosi and Teece, 1993) that allow a firm to exploit its distinctive resources and competences to bring activities in line with the goals a firm wants to achieve. Organizational routines can be defined as "patterns of interactions that represent successful solutions to particular problems" (Dosi and Teece, 1993) and may concern whatever 'distinctive' management process a firm develops to manage its activities (product development, distribution system, logistic system, brand image management, etc.).

THE THIRD LEVEL OF COMPETENCE: THE *CAPACITY TO EMBODY DISTINCTIVE CAPABILITIES*

The lowest level of analysis concerns the capacity of a firm to embody distinctive capabilities in tangible or intangible outputs. At this level, emphasis is on the firm's operating systems. Here "core outputs" (i.e. components, products, production processes, and services) are those which are unique and inimitable and differentiate the firm from its competitors, are a source of a potential extra profit, and can be used across different end products. These outputs ensure that a superior value is provided to customers and are therefore the real elements which give the firm a competitive advantage.

Various studies in the literature have focused on the characteristics of core products, identifying the categories of product traits (Huang, 1993; Bogner and Thomas, 1996) as follows: threshold traits which all products must possess to survive in competition, central traits that allow the firm to have a better response from the market if the performance of these traits is enhanced, and plus-only traits, that are not necessary to compete, but may give the firm a better market response. All traits need basic skills and knowledge, but only central traits and plus-only traits embody distinctive capabilities that may be firm-specific, unique, and inimitable. Indeed, it is these traits that make products/services superior with respect to competitors and provide higher customer benefits. Typical examples of core products or services are Honda's automobile engines, Canon's printer engines, and Wal-Mart's "cross-docking" logistics system. The three levels of competence and their outputs are shown in Figure 9.1.

THE DYNAMIC ANALYSIS

The dynamic analysis concerns the process by which a firm's competence changes and evolves, and is related to the links between the different levels of competence we have identified. In other words, at a dynamic level of analysis, we need to understand whether and how there is a cause–effect relationship between the different levels of competence, how the different levels of competence are interlinked, and, finally, how each level contributes to building a firm's competitive advantage. This would provide further insights into the intrinsic nature and roots of a firm's competitive advantage and could help to clarify the process of competence building and leveraging. To this end, it is necessary to focus on how each competence level relates to *learning* within a firm.

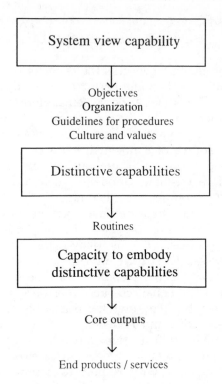

FIGURE 9.1   Three levels of competence

At the first level of competence, the System View establishes the "learning space", i.e. the boundaries of the "world view" within which the firm sees itself. With industry foresight and an integrated view of internal resources, top management defines the "region" of the context to be observed and with which the firm needs to interact, and the relevant signals for future activity. Given the local nature of enterprise learning, what firms can learn is constrained by what they have done in the past. Indeed, past behaviour determines the set of knowledge, resources, values and norms a firm possesses and, to a certain extent, its capacity to 'absorb' new knowledge (Cohen and Levinthal, 1990). The perception of what can be learnt depends on the perception of the "distance" between the current cognitive position of the firm (its knowledge domain) and the set of knowledge that characterizes the external context. A firm is most likely to focus its learning processes within the space that is perceived to be "near" its current knowledge domain. Therefore, the learning space depends on the firm's system view. In other words, different firms with the same cognitive position (i.e. the same set of knowledge) may learn differently because of a different perception of what knowledge is close to its own domain.

From a dynamic point of view, the system view of the firm establishes the domain within which to learn and gives the basic guidelines for the process of competence building. Through the definition of objectives, it stimulates and directs activities aimed at closing the gap between the actual and desired state of resources and capabilities within the firm, and these activities aim to create the new competences necessary for future competitive advantage. Second, the view defines the space that constrains the domain within which the firm can acquire the 'intellectual resources' underlying the process of competence building. Establishment of the learning space also helps define, to a certain extent, the path to be followed to achieve the desired state, or at least to limit the choice of possible paths. Finally, the system view provides fundamental criteria for the shaping of the organization and its procedures, especially with respect to the integration of current activities (which are aimed at exploiting current distinctive capabilities) with those which should create future capabilities. In other words, a system view reveals much about the processes of decision making, resource allocation, and resource acquisition which will allow the whole firm to act consistently in order to achieve its desired state—in other words, the firm's strategic logic.

A key issue in competence-based competition is that of competence leveraging, defined as the exploitation of competences already within the firm to perform activities and/or make products that differ from those available. We believe that the roots of the process of competence leveraging may also reside in the system view capability of the firm. The vision of potential further use of existing competences may come from the recognition, at corporate level, of market opportunities that can be exploited and/or created through the set of resources and capabilities already available within the firm.

As stated above, the result of the operation of a system view is the definition of long-term objectives, the guidelines for critical procedures, an organizational structure, and the culture and values diffused within the firm. These tangible results of the system view guide and develop the distinctive capabilities within a firm: they affect and influence the set of knowledge a firm can build, its ability to realize strategic objectives, and the integration and coordination of resources.

It is at the level of distinctive capabilities that a firm effectively realises processes of learning underlying competence building and leveraging. Through the definition of routines, the firm organizes and implements its activities to attain strategic objectives, create new competences, and leverage existing capabilities. Such routines, which by nature are cross-functional and cross-business, themselves stimulate learning at both individual and organizational level, as they are based on the integrated and coordinated use of resources and knowledge. They focus on the processes which are critical for the creation of distinctive capabilities and are the ultimate source of those capabilities which will differentiate a firm from its competitors. The knowledge generated within these organizational routines, which may include a strong tacit dimension, may be difficult to imitate and so provide the basis for differential performance *vis-à-vis* competitors. It can be argued that these routines represent the result and the source of distinctive capabilities, i.e. of the second level of competence. In other words, the organizational routines that a firm has developed to perform its activities better than its competitors will in themselves be the source of future advantage. It is through organizational routines that what has been outlined and defined in the system view is actually implemented.

The learning process realized at the second level of competence may influence both upper and lower levels of competence. At the system view level, the new knowledge learnt through organizational routines provides the basis for realizing and understanding the firm's knowledge domain and, consequently, its learning space. At the lower level of competence, this learning provides suggestions for reshaping operating systems in line with the new knowledge possessed by the firm.

Finally, the operating systems allow a firm to embody distinctive capabilities (i.e. what is learnt) into core outputs. In terms of learning, the firm's operating systems may be shaped to ensure that continuous improvement and learning take place in parallel with current activities. Therefore, on the one hand, the operating systems are themselves a source of continuous and minor improvements, while, on the other, they may identify areas for major changes or exploitation of capabilities, thus indicating scope for competence leveraging. Indeed, this process of learning specific and specialized activities sometimes provides new knowledge and/or ideas for further applications of existing competences, i.e. for competence leveraging.[3] Dynamic interac-

---

[3]The three levels of competence could seem similar to the system element view of the firm proposed by Sanchez, Heene, and Thomas (1996) who have introduced the levels of strategic logic, management processes and intangible assets, tangible assets, and operations. However, there are some differences which are worth highlighting. First, the aim of this work is to identify the nature of the competences which may allow a firm to develop distinctive capabilities and create unique advantages. Therefore, our three levels all refer to competences,

footnote continued overleaf

tions among the three levels of competence and their contribution to the process of learning are summarized in Figure 9.2.

CONCLUSIONS AND MANAGERIAL IMPLICATIONS

The identification of different levels of competence is useful for a deeper understanding of the theoretical foundations of competence-based competition and the fundamental reasons for performance differences between firms.

The approach suggests that firms may have competences at different levels which have different impacts on competitiveness. Third-level competences help sustain short-term competition allowing a series of products to be generated and commercialized. Second-level competences can sustain competition over the medium term. First-level competences are the basis for long-term competition and allow the frame within which the firm will act in the future to be defined. Firms cannot be divided into those firms which adopt a competence-based view and those firms which do not. Firms have different levels of competence which impact differently on competitive capabilities at different times. For example, the decline of IBM in the last few years may be partially related to a past lack of vision and understanding of the evolution of context (convergence of telecommunication, electronics, and information technologies; diffusion IT distributed systems) rather than to the absence of competences at lower levels.

This approach also suggests that success and rapid growth could be

---

i.e. to the capacities of a firm, whereas the outputs of the different levels of competences can be physical or intangible. The Sanchez, Heene, and Thomas model aims to identify the system elements of the firm and describe how these are used for competence building or leveraging. Therefore, their third level (tangible assets), for example, does not represent competences *per se*. Second, we introduce a distinction between level of competence and outputs at each level. The identification of the outputs at each level allows the results of a competence at a certain level to be identified, and specifies how competences at that level interact with the upper-level of competences and drive the level below. This helps to clarify differences between firms' competitive performance. It also distinguishes between a static and a dynamic analysis of a firm's competences. Whereas static analysis photographs a firm's competences at a given point in time, the dynamic view tests whether the appropriate mechanisms are in place to leverage existing competences and to build new expertise, i.e. it identifies at what levels appropriate learning processes are in place within the firm. The Sanchez, Heene, and Thomas model seems to be focused on how the system elements of the firm contribute to the dynamic aspects. Third, and in consequence, our definition of the first-level of competence appears to differ from the Sanchez, Heene, and Thomas model. What the authors define as strategic logic is more similar to the output of our first level, i.e. the system view, rather than to the first level itself. In our view, establishing strategic objectives and guidelines for procedures is the result of the capability to view the firm and the external context in a certain way. This system view is itself a level of competence.

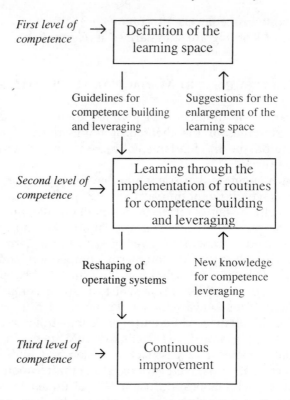

FIGURE 9.2   Dynamic interactions among different levels of competence

the result of a combination of different competences (at the three levels) and/or of different distinctive capabilities (at the second level). There is no simple division between highly successful firms and losers; many are located somewhere between the two extremes. The achievement of moderate success might be related to the fact that a firm has distinctive capabilities in some areas but competes with firms who excel also in others which are important.

Different levels of competence also have different impacts on a firm's growth potential. Understanding the future competitive frame of reference means grasping the opportunities which may allow high growth rates in the long term. This implies appreciating the effects of a change in context, such as the convergence of certain technologies, cross-business deployment of certain organizational processes, etc., in advance. Grasping these opportunities in advance, orienting the entire organization to learning in this direction and, subsequently, embodying the newly gained competences in products/services are the source of sustainable long-term competitive advantage. Beside the well-known examples (such as Canon, Honda etc. which are often technology-based), a good case in point is that of South Korean firms (one of our case studies concerns a South Korean group) which have been able to exploit their cost advantage together with strong market power and distribution capability across different, apparently unrelated industries. Competences at lower levels allow firms to generate less sustainable competitive advantages leading to lower growth rates in the long term.

Dynamics in competence building and leveraging tend to be industry-specific. Thus, in certain industries it may occur that a firm's growth is essentially linked to the learning process taking place at the third level as a result of continuous improvement and adoption of standards. A good example is the industrial machinery sector, in which the key success factors reside in customization and specialization. Nevertheless, things will not always go this way. Some German and Japanese producers have developed product platforms and components for a number of different industrial machines. Thus they are able to match a larger demand range and to produce higher volumes, giving in turn advantages in terms of costs. In this case, conceiving machines differently and building the required competences might provide these firms with the basis for reshaping the nature of competition in the sector. Recently, firms producing automobiles and household appliances have developed competences based on modular product design (Sanchez, 1995) allowing them to generate a variety of products of differing costs, quality and technical performance. This means that competitors will be forced to develop a system view and to rethink their competence basis in order to compete in the future. In other words, in our approach they will be forced to an upper level of competence and undertake changes at this level. In other competitive environments, however, where the change in contextual issues (actors, boundaries, technologies, organizations, etc.) is extremely rapid, continuous development of a system view and sustained competence building are the key for survival.

APPENDIX: THE APPLICATION OF THE APPROACH TO THE CASE OF PHILIPS

In this appendix we attempt to apply to a specific case the approach to the analysis of competence-based competition proposed in this chapter, i.e. the definition of different levels of competence and their interactions. The firm analysed is Philips, the Dutch group of which the principal activities are in the sectors of lighting, consumer electronics, components and semiconductors, communication systems, and industrial electronics. The analysis is conducted on the basis of industry reports, company publications, and literature contributions, which are available externally. A first interview has been done to check findings and results. In this brief report, we will make reference mostly to the three-level static analysis as defined in the chapter. At each level we will also mention what the firm is doing for the development of the multimedia business which will represent a key area in the future. The case of the development of the multimedia sector gives an example of dynamic analysis, i.e. how the three levels interact with each other.

The System View of the Firm

- *Industry foresight* The top management recognizes that there is a convergence of the "four C's": Components, Computers, Communication and Consumer Electronics; in particular, the firm realizes that the traditional boundaries among communication technologies and their industries and markets are rapidly disappearing. Integration and convergence of the technologies is leading to the birth of a new industry (now in the form of a pre-market): the multimedia industrial sector.
- *Coordinated and integrated view of resources* The firm recognizes that knowledge of "the four C's" is critical for competition and shows significant links and interactions. Resources which can contribute to improve this knowledge, both internally and externally available for the firm, must thus be maintained, developed and integrated for sustaining the future competition.

System view outputs

Objectives

- Exploit the convergence of the four C's
- Maintain and develop technological knowledge of the four C's
- Become a major player in the market for multimedia
- Improve product quality
- Maximize customer satisfaction
- Exploit "the environment opportunity"

Organization

- Reduce bureaucracy and hierarchy rigidities
- Emphasize communication and cooperation among different units

and functions: corporate suggestions for the creation of multi-level and cross-functional teams

Guidelines for procedures

- Centralize key procedures
- Strengthen relationships with suppliers
- Business control based on the integration of management control over operations, compliance with legal requirements and financial reporting
- Involve competitors through alliances in R&D

Culture and values

- Diffuse common values within the firm
- Delight customers
- Value people as greater resources
- Deliver quality and excellence in actions
- Achieve premium return on equity
- Encourage entrepreneurial behaviour at all levels

THE *DISTINCTIVE CAPABILITIES* OF THE *FIRM*

- *Integrated and coordinated use of assets and resources* Philips' distinctive capabilities are essentially technology-based. These capabilities concern the integration of core technologies, such as optics, magnetics, microelectronics, and mechanics. This is pursued through the implementation of routines in R&D and product development which involve people with different technological background (see below). Also the organizational structure mirrors this approach and recent structural changes have been made to this end. A deeper exploitation of the firm's existing resources and knowledge is also pursued through these changes. For example, Philips Corporate Design unit which designs products, systems and supportive communication for all Philips product divisions, has been created to favour and sustain the development of the multimedia sector. The creation of a joint design centre and process involving different skills has been considered crucial for the multimedia business development.

Distinctive capabilities outputs

Routines

- Centralization of the planning process
- Centralized R&D process (most R&D is at corporate level; two thirds

of corporate research work is geared to the activities of the product divisions with contractual agreements about programs and costs)
- Creation of a single corporate design unit (Philips Corporate Design) which design products for all Philips' product divisions
- Creation of a Centre for Manufacturing Technology (CFT), which provides support in the optimization of all manufacturing technologies and production resources

THE CAPACITY TO EMBODY DISTINCTIVE CAPABILITIES

Through its operating systems, the firm embodies its distinctive capabilities into outputs. Its core outputs (see below) are developed for and exploited in a variety of products, such as interactive media systems, cable·television systems, car stereo and car navigation systems, multimedia PC, televisions, audio and video equipment, video and game players, for many users, such as professional and home consumers, industry, schools.

Core outputs

- Flat panel displays
- ICs
- Optical modules
- Magnetic modules
- CD platform

As far as the media sector is concerned, recently a CD-i hardware platform has been developed to be used in CD-i players, in personal computers, as a CD-i insert, in CD-i players integrated into an audio system and a TV/CD-i combination. Alliances and joint ventures have been established to develop games for multiple platforms (so called Tribal Media joint-venture with Greenberg Associate Studios), for cable TV operations (with United International Holdings), for TV services in Europe (with Dutch PTT), for car navigation systems (with Navigation Technologies Corporation). Alliances in the multimedia sector are aimed at gaining knowledge in the technical and business areas which are not the core areas of Philips.

AUTHORS' NOTE

This paper is the result of the joint work of the authors. However, Vittorio Chiesa has written sections on "Dynamic Analysis" and

"Concluding Remarks", as well as the Appendix. Rafaella Manzini has written the "Introduction" and the section on "Statis Analysis".

REFERENCES

Bogner, W.C. and Thomas, H. (1996). From skills to competences: the "play-out" of resource bundles across firms. In Sanchez, R., Heene, A. and Thomas, H. (eds), *Dynamics of Competence-Based Competition: Theory and Practice in the New Strategic Management*. Oxford: Elsevier.

Cohen, W.M. and Levinthal D.A. (1990). Absorptive capacity: a new perspective on learning and innovation. *Administrative Science Quarterly*, **35**, 128–52.

Dosi, G, and Teece, D.J. (1993). Organizational competences and the boundaries of the firm, in market and organization: the competitive firm and its environment. Latapses, Nice, France and Iside, Rome.

Hamel, G. and Heene, A. (eds) (1994). *Competence-Based Competition*. New York: John Wiley.

Hamel, G. and Prahalad, C.K. (1993). Strategy as stretch and leverage. *Harvard Business Review*, March-April.

Hamel, G. and Prahalad, C.K. (1994). *Competing for the Future*. Boston, MA: Harvard Business School Press.

Huang, K.S.H. (1993). Integrating vertical and horizontal dimensions in a spatial framework of strategic product competition: an application to the U.S. photocopier industry. Harvard University doctoral thesis (Business Economics), Cambridge, MA.

Leonard-Barton, D. (1992). Core capabilities and core rigidities: a paradox in managing new product development. *Strategic Management Journal*, **13**, pp. 111–25.

Leonard-Barton, D., Bowen, H.K., Clark, K.B., Holloway, C.A. and Wheelwright, S.C. (1994). How to integrate work and deepen expertise. *Harvard Business Review*, September-October.

Prahalad, C.K. and Hamel, G. (1990). The core competence of the corporation. *Harvard Business Review*, May-June.

Sanchez, R. (1995). Strategic flexibility in product competition. *Strategic Management Journal*, **16**, 135–59.

Sanchez, R. (1996). A competence perspective on strategic learning and knowledge. In Sanchez, R. and Heene, A. (eds), *Strategic Learning and Knowledge Management*. Chichester: John Wiley.

Sanchez, R. and Heene, A., (1996). A systems view of the firm in competence-based competition. In Sanchez, R., Heene, A. and Thomas, H. (eds), *Dynamics of Competence-Based Competition: Theory and Practice in the New Strategic Management*. Oxford: Elsevier.

Sanchez, R., Heene, A. and Thomas, H. (1996). Towards the theory and practice of competence-based competition. In Sanchez, R., Heene, A., and Thomas, H. (eds), *Dynamics of Competence-Based Competition: Theory and Practice in the New Strategic Management*. Oxford: Elsevier.

Schoemaker, P.J. (1992). How to link strategic vision to core capabilities. (eds), *Sloan Management Review*, Fall.

Stalk, G., Evans, P. and Shulman, L.E. (1992). Competing on capabilities: the new rules of corporate strategy. *Harvard Business Review*, **70**, 2, 57–69.

10

Integrating Corporate Strategy and Competence-building Processes: A Case Study

ERIC CREMER, PIERRE-XAVIER MESCHI

In 1990, Merlin Gerin–Groupe Schneider embarked on a comprehensive reappraisal which led to the formulation of a "competence strategy" whose main objective was to improve and harmonize the collective competences and processes for building competences in the diverse functions of the company in order to achieve the objectives emerging from the process of corporate strategy. This "competence strategy" has been drawn up and implemented through a "network of functions" which is a complex organization involving all the divisions, departments, and other units in the company. The "network of functions" has been built according to a normative and reproduced process relying upon a chronology of reflections and actions which can be divided into three important phases: selection of differentiation criteria, corporate functional segmentation, and building and coordination of the "network of functions". The case presents, describes, and discusses

Competence-based Strategic Management.
Edited by Aimé Heene and Ron Sanchez.
Copyright © 1997 John Wiley & Sons Ltd.

these three phases, making the link with most of the themes dealt with in the literature on "competence building" and strategy.

> Merlin Gerin–Groupe Schneider has realized that, in the long term, competition is centered around competences rather than products, a fact which only a small number of companies are aware of when their financial profit is high (Cuvècle interview, organization director of Merlin Gerin–Groupe Schneider, 1994).

THE DIVERSITY OF THE COMPETENCE-BUILDING ANALYSIS

Most of the main themes of management literature deal in one way or another with the topic of competence building; each putting forward its relevant arguments, proper to its scope of investigation. Thus, certain studies take an interest in the acquisition of competences through internal mechanisms of individual and collective learning (Senge, 1990; Argyris, 1994). On the other hand, others lay emphasis on the importance of different strategic tools such as alliances, licensing, or company mergers and acquisitions (Teece, 1986; Hamel and Prahalad, 1989); these are often favored by companies because the acquisition of competences through external mechanisms provides flexibility that internal solutions cannot easily provide: "As market requirements change and new competence and resources are needed, new partnerships can be sought and old ones abandoned!" (Abell, 1993: 121). Although the flexibility argument is of primary importance for a company, the supporters of the prevalence of internal mechanisms stress the positive advantages of secrecy, exclusivity, and surprise associated with internally developed competences. Concerning the question of the organization and coordination of competences, one can highlight the same diversity of opinions. Certain studies recommend the centralization of the "core" competences (GEST, 1986; Zimmermann, 1989), while others suggest that the network organization enables a better spread of knowledge which constitutes the source of competences at an aggregated macro level.

These different approaches should not be considered as reflecting fundamental contradictions. Indeed, they demonstrate that the diversity of the competence-building analysis represents a real contingent process providing the strategist with the opportunity of benefiting from a wide range of actions through the existence of numerous alternative strategic "tools". According to its specific strategic objectives— i.e. the objectives emerging from the strategy process—each company will focus on a distinctive competence–building procedure. Thus, characteristics and direction of the competence building activity of a company are mainly contingent on its strategic objectives. Precisely defined by Sanchez, Heene, and Thomas (1996: 8) as "any process by which a firm qualitatively changes its existing stocks of assets and capabilities, or creates new abilities to coordinate and deploy new or existing assets and capabilities in ways that help the firm achieve its goals", competence building also involves the creation of new strategic options (Sanchez and Thomas, 1996). Competence building is the process by which a company develops a strategic configuration aiming to exercise and generate strategic objectives. Based on a recursive and self-nourishing process, this configuration works by, on the one hand, "receiving" input in the form of the present strategic objectives to achieve and, on the other, "producing" output, in the form of the future strategic objectives and also a perspective on the future.

From this contingent point of view, Hamel and Prahalad (1994: 10) proposed to set up a "strategic architecture" which represents "the medium-term capability-building program to support the goal—i.e., strategic intent for the authors". But one must bear in mind that "strategic architecture is not a detailed plan. It identifies the major capabilities to be built but doesn't specify exactly how they are built" (Hamel and Prahalad, 1994: 108). A strategic architecture or configuration emerges when a company reengineers qualitatively its different assets, tangible (e.g. machines, factories, etc.) as well as intangible (e.g. capabilities, knowledge, reputation, etc.) in order to use and combine them more effectively in pursuit of its strategic objectives. The emergence of a strategic architecture relies upon the implementation of certain strategic capabilities or assets (capabilities are included in the term assets in the terminology of our study) adopted and embedded in the competence-building process. This last statement is in keeping with those of Sanchez, Heene, and Thomas (1996: 8) for whom "often competence building involves creating or adopting new capabilities (new patterns of action) in the use of new or existing assets".

Nevertheless, some studies categorized within the "resource-based view" (Wernerfelt, 1984; Dierickx and Cool, 1989; Peteraf, 1993; Hall, 1993) postulate that an asset can only be defined as strategic—i.e., likely to procure a competitive advantage (sometimes defined in terms of "quasi-rent")—insofar as it is non-tradable, inimitable, and non-substitutable (Dierickx and Cool, 1989; Amit and Shoemaker, 1993). But if one considers these three factors in order to measure the strategic character of corporate capabilities, it appears that they apply mainly to internally developed capabilities. These internal capabilities emerge within the organization according to a slow and complex competence-building process which is reproduced with difficulty, if at all, by other firms.

The understanding of competence-building activity and resulting strategic architectures is very limited. The literature provides only a vague and sparse description of how such activity is implemented and how it affects the objectives emerging from the strategic process. In addition to the lack of theoretical and empirical studies on this theme, the development of a competence-building theory and practice has been impeded by the terminological inconsistency between studies. This chapter intends first to explore in-depth one aspect of the competence-based competition, competence building, in relation to emergence of strategic objectives of a large French company, Merlin Gerin–Groupe Schneider, and finally to contribute to furthering empirical application of the theory of competence-based competition.

METHODOLOGY

In this chapter it is important to remember that we aim to highlight empirically the relation between the competence-building process and the strategic objectives defined by top management. The implementation and the activation of what Merlin Gerin–Groupe Schneider calls a "Réseau de Fonctions" ("Network of Functions") or a "Réseau Fonctionnel" ("Functional Network") aim to set up a formal link between the process of competence building and the objectives defined by corporate top management. This relation was tested by using an in-depth methodology which, for 1 year, led us to analyze the competence-building phenomenon of a large French company (six different business units, 15 000 employees and 20 billion French francs in annual sales, 55% of which are earned from international export) by observing patterns of behavior, listening to organizational stories, and conducting in-depth and longitudinal interviews with several top managers (involved in the organization and the implementation of the "competence strategy") of the French company studied during a period of one year.

THE COMPETENCE-BUILDING EXPERIENCE OF MERLIN GERIN–GROUPE SCHNEIDER

DEVELOPMENT OF A "COMPETENCE STRATEGY"

In 1990 the company undertook a major strategic reappraisal in order to create an internal competence-building process with regard to the strategic objectives drawn up by the top management. The result of this reflection led to the development of a "competence strategy" whose main objective was to "improve and harmonize the collective competences embedded in the diverse functions of the company in order to achieve the objectives emerging from the process of strategy" (Merlin Gerin–Groupe Schneider, 1993). This "competence strategy" has been devised and implemented through a network of functions which is a complex organization involving all the divisions, departments, and other units of the company. This network is managed and controlled by a small task force related to the "Organization Department" of the company. Superimposed on the official organization chart, the network of functions associates directly 1500 employees, that is one employee in ten (one in four in the long term).

The network of functions has been built according to a normative and reproduced process relying upon a chronology of reflections and actions which can be divided into three important phases: selection of differentiation criteria, corporate functional segmentation, and building and coordination of the network of functions.

First Phase—The Selection of Differentiation Criteria

The dynamic role of Merlin Gerin–Groupe Schneider's top management has largely contributed to the success of the "competence strategy" and is characterized by three levels of involvement in the strategy building. First, the top managers set ambitious (and confidential) objectives for a term lasting from 5 to 7 years and notified the six business units of these corporate objectives. Second, they drew up a shortlist of a few differentiation criteria (e.g. ability to innovate, ability to guarantee production deadlines and delivery dates) expressing the main market expectations. Finally, the top management invited each business unit to select two or three criteria from this list. This choice is directly related to the nature of the corporate objectives. It involves each business unit having to develop the capability associated with each of the differentiation criteria that they have chosen. This capability must contribute to building and strengthening the competitive advantages sought by each business unit in the sense that the building and the strengthening of the business units' competitive advantages guarantee the complete success of the objectives emerging from the strategy process. Thus, the functioning of the network of functions depends entirely on the strategy process of the company. As such, the selection of differentiation criteria constitutes the first important step of the "competence strategy".

TABLE 10.1 The functional segmentation: description of the seven global functions and the 26 functions

Global functions	Functions
Industrial	• Purchasing • Industrial Management • Industrialization • Corporate Estate • Techno-Commercial
Commercial and Marketing	• Marketing • Sales
Technical	• Technologies Management • Methods and Tools • Application Techniques
Finance	• Financing • Accounting • Financial Management of Contracts • Legal
Human Resources	• Job-career Development • Social Planification and Development • Training • Social Relations • Global Remuneration
Steering	• Data Processing Applications • Communication • Cost Management • Organization • Quality • Security
Strategy	• Global Strategy

SECOND PHASE—THE CORPORATE FUNCTIONAL SEGMENTATION

The corporate functional segmentation represents the second important step of the "competence strategy". It corresponds to an exhaustive inventory and a classification of the capabilities necessary to the accomplishment of the operational tasks and to the corporate development, in the sense of the success of the objectives emerging from the strategy process. The functional segmentation aims to define the "competence matrix" of each function of the company. In order to understand what it represents, one must imagine the functional segmentation as a pyramid: at the top of the pyramid, one can find the global functions i.e. "a group of functions of similar nature regarding their contribution to the functioning of the company" (Merlin Gerin–

Groupe Schneider, 1993). The intermediate level is characterized by the presence of functions which are a "conventional regrouping of competences acting jointly in a same direction" (Merlin Gerin–Groupe Schneider, 1993). The functional segmentation defined by Merlin Gerin–Groupe Schneider includes seven global functions and 26 functions (see Table 10.1). This functional structure has a permanent character corresponding to a specific mission of the company.

A function is characterized both by specific capabilities and the application scope of these capabilities. The rule of segmentation is comparable to those applied for a range of products, each of whose segments corresponds to a particular type of customer.

At the base of the pyramid, one can find capabilities which are defined by Merlin Gerin–Groupe Schneider (1993) as "the sum of knowledge and experiences producing a value perceived by the customer, either directly (industrial, technical and commercial aspects of competences), or indirectly (of strategy, of steering, financial, social aspects of competences)" Merlin Gerin–Groupe Schneider expresses each capability in the form of a task associated with a goal. In other words, it is a collective mission, specified by its essential characteristics (e.g. "to elaborate adapted supplies so as to obtain the customer's order"). The mission of each function is ruled by a characterization called "Compétence Coeur de Fonction" ("Core Functional Competence"). The accomplishment of the mission also relies on secondary capabilities called "Compétences de Support" ("Support Competences"). For example, the capability "Marketing Achats et Choix des Fournisseurs" ("Purchasing Marketing and Choice of Suppliers") identified by Merlin Gerin–Groupe Schneider, constitutes the core functional capability of the "Purchasing" function. This capability is described by the following task: "To investigate and diagnose the potential suppliers, whose purpose is to select the suppliers". The task of "organizing the management of the suppliers' network in an international context" (Merlin Gerin–Groupe Schneider, 1993) corresponds to the support capability of the previous core functional competence.

Merlin Gerin–Groupe Schneider describes the scope of a function as "something on which or on what the competences specific to a function apply". A scope is thus specific to a sole and unique function. Each scope is subdivided into dimensions (between 3 and 12) according to its nature. Therefore the core functional capability "Purchasing Marketing and Choice of Suppliers" applies to four dimensions:

- Investments purchase
- Materials and components purchase

- Delivery services purchase
- Trade

The capabilities and dimensions of the scope of each function are presented on a competence matrix or grid (see Appendix). This matrix is useful for highlighting the poles of competences which are "entities aimed at developing and perpetuating a competence inside a particular function" (Merlin Gerin–Groupe Schneider, 1993) and which need to be created. Therefore the development of the core functional capability "Purchasing Marketing and Choice of Suppliers" rests on three distinct poles of this capability: the "Purchasing Marketing for Investments Purchase", the "Purchasing Marketing for Materials and Components Purchase", and the "Purchasing Marketing for Trade".

The creation of several poles of competence for the same function is justified by the fact that a competence does not apply the same way in each of the dimensions of its scope, even if its goal remains the same. Each pole aims to formalize and spread the right practices, routines, etc. in the context of one or several dimensions of its scope. The main difficulty of the functional segmentation is to identify scopes of functions and their dimensions. The competence matrix for each of the functions is the consequence of many iterations between the heads of different departments and units of the company. Though certain departments have been institutionalized as functions (e.g. accounting), the functional segmentation does not reflect the Merlin Gerin–Groupe Schneider organization chart.

THIRD PHASE—THE BUILDING AND COORDINATION OF THE FUNCTIONAL NETWORK

Building the functional network constitutes the last step of the "competence strategy". This network, superimposed on the official organization chart, represents "the equivalent for a function of what the organization chart is for an operational unit. Its objective is to improve the performance of the function, notably by coordinating the work of the poles of competences" (Merlin Gerin–Groupe Schneider, 1993).

Building the Functional Network (see Figure 10.1)

Each function relies on a "hard core" around which are some poles of competences and a few "Hommes Relais" ("Relay Individuals").

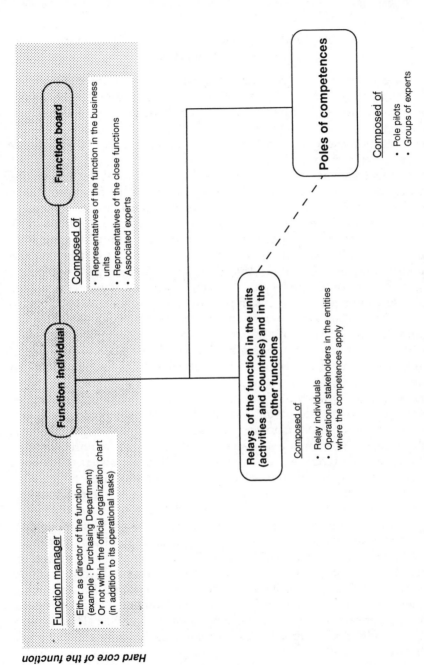

FIGURE 10.1   The stakeholders of a function: the functional network. (Source: Merlin Gerin–Groupe Schneider, 1993)

The "Hard Core" of the Function: Function Individual, Function Board, and Relay Individual

The hard core of the function consists of a "Homme Fonction" ("Function Individual") whose mission is to define and manage the function, assisted by a function board which has to help the function individual.

The function individual (one *per* function, 26 in total) is responsible for the performance of his or her function with regard to the top management and has to "organize the formalization of the knowledge and the know-how attached to the competences of his function, and to organize their spreading in the operational entities of the company" (Merlin Gerin–Groupe Schneider, 1993). The function individual is often the director of his or her function in the operational organization chart; e.g. in the case of the communication director who is also responsible for the "Communication" function. Sometimes, the director of the function can delegate the centralized management of the collective competences of his function to an assistant. It can also happen that certain functions have no operational responsibility in the organization chart; e.g. in the case of the "Industrial Management" function. In any case it is impossible for the director of a profit unit to be responsible for a function. The function individual is present in all business units.

Indeed, one must bear in mind that the function individual is present in all corporate operational entities' departments or units (see mission above). The ultimate objective of the functional organization is to drive each operational entity—i.e. profit unit—to a required level of performance, and this is valid for each of the competences of each function with regard to the selected differentiation criteria. Thus no operational entity must be in a privileged position to the detriment of others. If the director of a profit unit could become a function individual, then he could be tempted according to his objectives of personal success to favor his profit unit by granting it the core of his "functional efforts". For example, he could allocate a higher training budget or demand the transfer of the most competent professionals to his unit. In order to avoid these problems, Merlin Gerin–Groupe Schneider has decided that no "interference" between the functional and the operational responsibilities of a same individual is possible. That is why function individual status is not available to the directors of profit units (see Figure 10.1).

The function individual is assisted by a function board which works as an advisory entity made up of "the functional network's representatives whose role is to help the function individual to organize and manage his function. The function board approves notably the instructions and procedures" (Merlin Gerin–Groupe Schneider, 1993). The members of the function board are selected and appointed by the function individual: they are representatives of the function in the different business units, representatives of "close" functions (which are members of "brother" functions with which exchanges are frequent) and external associated experts. The function individual and the function board carry out two important missions which are closely related: identifying and enriching the capabilities of the function, and writing the official text of the function.

The achievement of the competence identifying and enriching mission requires first, the setting within the competences matrix of each function and the cartography of the poles of competences, i.e. the preferential competences in which Merlin Gerin–Groupe Schneider has decided to invest. This work has been implemented within the company for three years. The competences matrix and the poles of competences have been tested, improved, enriched, and even completely rebuilt many times, before being set in their present form. Then the function individual and the function board coordinate progress, i.e. they simultaneously supervise the transfer of competences to people concerned in the operational entities and improvement in the performance of these entities. Coordination of progress is mainly supported by a "relay individual" defined as "an active correspondent providing the interface between the function and either the operational units or the other functions" (Merlin Gerin–Groupe Schneider, 1993). The relay individual must reduce the actions of the pole towards the operational stakeholders by explaining the policy and the instructions of the function as well as inducing, assisting, and controlling their implementation. A relay individual is appointed for all the entities relevant to the function.

Second, the hard core of the function aims to write the official text of the function, i.e. to define the objectives and the rules of actions of the function. Three types of text shape the result of this work: the functional policies, defined as "the options representing the purposes and the orientations of the function at corporate level. They set the reference framework selected for a long time (5 to 7 years)", the functional instructions, defined as "the expression of a will to transform the political choice into rules of actions and of behavior organized and coordinated together. Of official and permanent character, the instructions are incontestable, and the procedures represent the expression of concrete terms of application of an instruction. A procedure is restricted to the minimum necessary to the consistency and the quality of the work" (Merlin Gerin–Groupe Schneider, 1993).

The Poles of Competences (see Figures 10.2 and 10.3)

Merlin Gerin–Groupe Schneider has developed the concept of "compe-tence investment" which means "the devoting of tertiary resources to the development of the transfer of know-how", through the creation of a pole of competence which is "an authority, driven by the function individual, in charge of the development and the continuity of a competence in a function". Each pole of competence is coordinated by a "pole pilot" selected by the function individual on the grounds of its expertise in a specific field (operational experience), his aptitude to communicate and to share his know-how (training experience), as well as for its involvement (objectives support). Attached to the function individual, the pole pilot organizes, enriches, and coordinates the implementation of a competence for all the business units of Merlin Gerin–Groupe Schneider through the world. He must manage its pole of competence according to compared performance criteria (e.g. bench-marking).

The setting up of the pole of competence involves first, the appoint-ment of the pole stakeholders: the pole pilot has to identify and appoint a committee of experts constituting strictly the pole of compe-tence. The committee of experts corresponds to the pole of competence

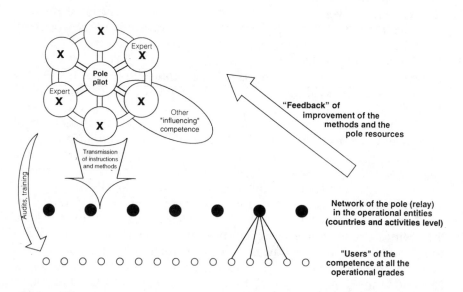

FIGURE 10.2 The structure of a pole of competence. (Source: Merlin Gerin–Schneider, 1993)

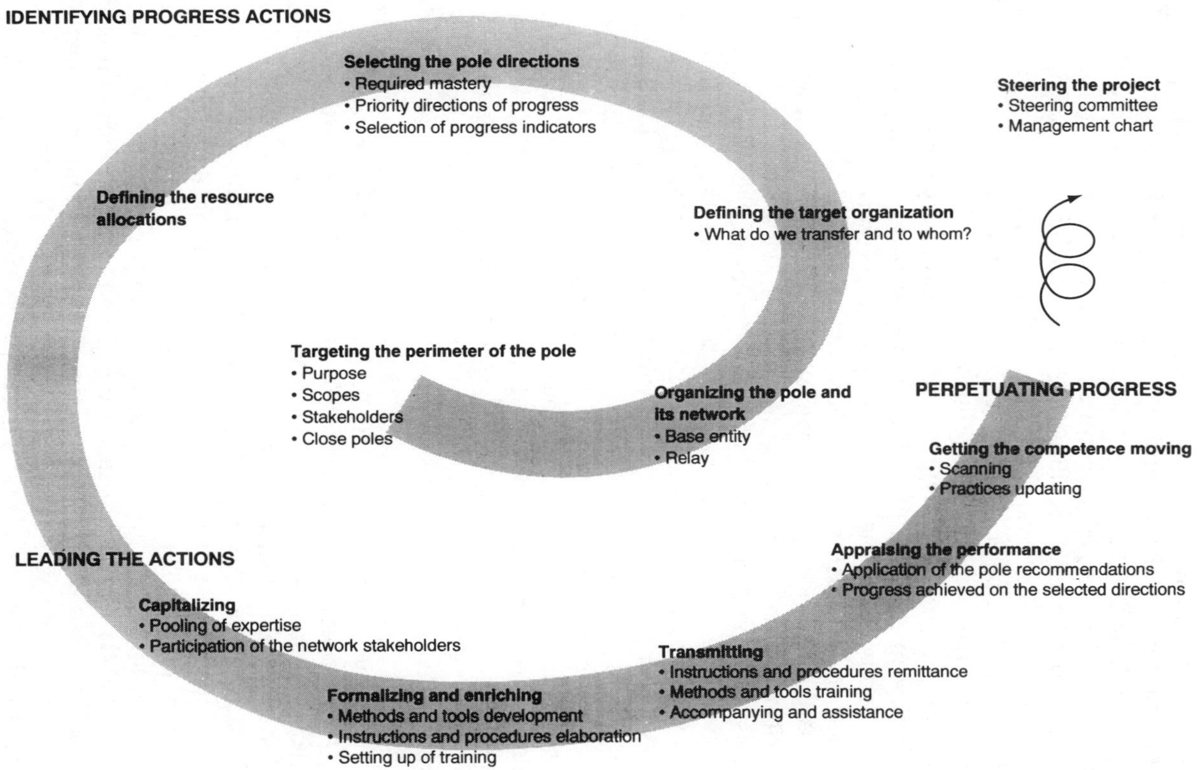

IDENTIFYING PROGRESS ACTIONS

Steering the project
• Steering committee
• Management chart

PERPETUATING PROGRESS

Getting the competence moving
• Scanning
• Practices updating

Selecting the pole directions
• Required mastery
• Priority directions of progress
• Selection of progress indicators

Defining the target organization
• What do we transfer and to whom?

Appraising the performance
• Application of the pole recommendations
• Progress achieved on the selected directions

Organizing the pole and its network
• Base entity
• Relay

Targeting the perimeter of the pole
• Purpose
• Scopes
• Stakeholders
• Close poles

Transmitting
• Instructions and procedures remittance
• Methods and tools training
• Accompanying and assistance

Defining the resource allocations

Formalizing and enriching
• Methods and tools development
• Instructions and procedures elaboration
• Setting up of training

LEADING THE ACTIONS

Capitalizing
• Pooling of expertise
• Participation of the network stakeholders

FIGURE 10.3   The coordination of a pole of competence.   (Source: Merlin Gerin–Groupe Schneider, 1993)

as the function board at the functional level. Then the pole pilot has to appoint relay individuals of the pole of competence in each of the operational entities where their presence is required. Finally, the pole pilot has to identify the priority beneficiaries of the pole actions. It is towards and through them that the spreading of the "correct practices" in the target's operational entities (user entities of the concerned competence) is directed. The achievement of this task requires making an inventory of all the people in the company mastering the competence concerned, i.e. those who carry out the mission associated with this competence.

A second step in the setting up of the pole of competence concerns the definition of a scope of action: a precise perimeter is given to the pole of competence therefore the pole of competence has to be positioned in a systemic way which means that it has to be located with regard to its close poles. For example, the "Financial Management of Contracts" function is related to "Legal", "Financing", and "Sales" functions; neither of the poles of competences of these four functions can act individually without knowing and integrating into its actions the priorities and the missions of the other poles of competences.

The mission of the pole of competence has to be defined: one can compare it to a four-stroke engine whose cycle is capitalization and enrichment, formalization, transfer, and perpetuating the competences. The first task of the pole of competence is to capitalize, i.e. "to put together the expert valuations and the know-how" (Merlin Gerin–Groupe Schneider, 1993). In order to attain this goal, the participation of as many stakeholders in the functional network as possible is imperative. They are invited to express their views of the jobs they perform and to describe the competences necessary to accomplish them. Past successes and failures are studied and their origins are discussed. A precise role according to its contribution to the effort of knowledge capitalization is assigned to each stakeholder. The second task, indissociable from the first, aims to formalize (i.e. to write) the knowledge and the expertise. This work of formalization is essential to guarantee the success of the next step and also to facilitate the replacement of the pole pilots (appointed for a minimum of four years). The third task is to transfer the language, the knowledge, and the "correct practices" to the stakeholders of the operational entities concerned. This transfer takes place in four ways: through an informal communication between the stakeholders of the network, an instruction book, training (for this purpose, the "Training Department" and the "competence strategy" steering committee place the list of training programs prepared by the functions and the poles of competences at the operational entities manager's disposal), and a direct advice and assistance for a project. The last task is to perpetuate the expertise. Indeed, a network, carrying a competence, is a "living system"; people enter and exit the system continuously. One must make sure that the competence does not depreciate through all these movements. The pole of competence performs two duties: environmental and internal scanning and performance appraisal. Scanning and performance appraisal help to develop the competence by the improvement of the methods, tools, training programs, or by the modification of the instructions and procedures. According to Merlin Gerin–Groupe Schneider, this resultant loop gives the pole of competence, and consequently the function, the role of a "learning organization" (Senge, 1990; Argyris, 1994).

Coordinating the Functional Network and Progress Appraisal
(see Figure 10.4)

The experiment embarked upon by Merlin Gerin–Groupe Schneider in 1990 involves a double challenge: on the one hand, if the company improves its mastery of each of its competences, its corporate performance will consequently be improved, and, on the other, the additional structural cost borne for the development of competences—i.e. the operating costs of the functional network—remains below the improvement of the corporate performance in any case.

The performance-appraisal tool implemented by Merlin Gerin–Groupe Schneider aims to analyze the progress made by the operational entities concerning mastery of the developed competences. The indicators used to appraise this progress are intermediate indicators of the economic performance of the company. The coordination of progress and the implementation of the performance-or progress-appraisal tool constitutes the ultimate mission of the poles of competences and of the functional network.

The selection of the performance indicators is a difficult operation because "conventional performance measures like profitability or market share . . . do not capture the full value of the strategic options being created by a firm's competence building" (Sanchez and Thomas, 1996: 74). The need to identify and parameterize new performance indicators directly focused on the value creation induced by the "competence strategy" has been pointed out many times by researchers. In order to "capture" the output of this strategy, Merlin Gerin–Groupe Schneider has developed conceptually adequate indicators embedded in a formalized performance appraisal methodology. A performance indicator is defined as "an appraisal tool of the performance of a function, of the mastery of a competence or a process"

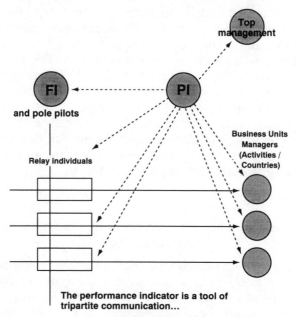

The performance indicator is a tool of tripartite communication...

(1) Between the top management, the managers of the functional network and the managers of the business units concerning:
  • The resource allocations
  • The relevance of the progress objectives (as a result of the benchmarking)
  • The priority actions (as a result of the mapping)

(2) It enables the functional steering of the operational units by the the function individuals and the pole pilots:
  • The implementation of progress solutions
  • The improvement of competences mastery

PI : Performance indicator
FI : Function individual

FIGURE 10.4 Selection of a performance indicator. Source: Merlin Gerin–Groupe Schneider, 1993)

(Merlin Gerin–Groupe Schneider, 1993). The performance indicators are related to the directions of progress—i.e. what the company wants to improve—described in the functional policies and instructions. The selection of a progress and performance indicator requires identifying the leverage acting on the performance. The performance indicators are selected by the function individuals and the pole pilots in keeping with the top management and managers of the business units. This collective discussion and agreement on the choice of the performance indicators aims to guarantee the consistency of the selected indicators with the corporate strategic objectives and the operational stakes.

The number of progress and performance indicators ranges from 1 to 5 according to function and competence (see Table 10.2). These indicators can assume diverse forms: activity indicators which enable us to follow up the application of the functional instructions, competence mastery indicators, and cost indicators of the functional network.

Merlin Gerin–Groupe Schneider expresses the imperative of distinguishing two levels of performance indicators: of the functions and of the competences. In fact, some directions of functional progress are not directly related to the competences. Indeed, one of the directions of progress for the "Purchasing" function could be to reduce or increase the "concentration ratio of purchasing" calculated from the total volume of purchasing, the number of suppliers, and the amount of purchasing per supplier. This ratio arises from the implementation of the competences specific to the "Purchasing" function. However, neither will identify it as a direction of progress. Thus, one should qualify it as a direction of progress and appraise it at a functional level.

In short, the performance indicators must perform three objectives: to

TABLE 10.2   The progress and performance indicators

Types of indicators	Directions of progress	Nature of indicators	Examples
Activity indicators	• Application of policies • Spreading of methods • Implementation of means and plans of actions	Qualitative and quantitative	• Percentage of communication actions • Percentage of people having received a specific training
Competence mastery	• Performance of a capability or a know-how: productivity, quality, delay	Qualitative and quantitative	• Percentage of orders delivered just in time • Defects rate • Speed of the production cycle • Quality of the commercial propositions.
Cost indicators	• Cost of a function or of a pole of competence	Quantitative	• Labor costs • Capital invested.

appraise the progress (with some indicators of solutions implemented), to organize a steering system of the functional network (with the performance appraisal of a function or of a competence), and to constitute an objective communication tool between the functions, the top management, and the operational managers. As a result of the progress appraisal and the organization of a steering system, the performance-appraisal methodology has provided Merlin Gerin–Groupe Schneider with the opportunity to remove some uncertainties related to the corporate positive impact of the "competence strategy". The third objective associated with the performance indicators—i.e. the constitution of an objective communication tool between key stakeholders (functions, top management, and operational managers)—is focused rather on the improvement of the corporate ability to create and seize new valuable strategic options than on the construction of quantifiable performance measures. Though the role of corporate intuition concerning the success of the "competence strategy" has been undeniable from the very beginning, because of the qualitative and systemic character of the experiment, the development of adequate performance indicators by Merlin Gerin–Groupe Schneider is in keeping with the theoretical perspectives on company performance which, on the one hand, postulate the need for precise measures reflecting the company's success in building competences and, on the other, "recognize the value of strategic options that can only be created through the systemic interactions of many kinds of firm stakeholders" (Sanchez and Thomas, 1996: 74).

The second operation is characterized by determination of the performance and progress objectives. This determination is the result of the comparison with the information held by the functional network and the operational managers. The action plans and the performance and progress objectives are set according to an annual periodicity.

The last operation aims to appraise the performance and progress. This task is the responsibility of pole pilots and function individuals. It is carried out in all the operational entities of the company where the competences concerned apply. The information comes from the operational entities towards the functional responsibles via the relay individuals. The periodicity of this information flow fluctuates and depends on the will of the pole or of the function. Two tools enable a comparative reading of the performance evolution of the functions and competences: the "mapping" or the internal positioning and the "benchmarking" or the external positioning. The mapping is defined as the "setting up of the performance map in the operational entities" (Merlin Gerin–Groupe Schneider, 1993). In practice, it is a synoptic table enabling a compared reading of the progress and performance of an identical competence or function in all the operational entities where it applies. This permanent database constitutes the management chart of the poles and functions. The benchmarking is viewed as "the positioning of Merlin Gerin–Groupe Schneider's degree of mastery of a competence or of a process in comparison with other companies" (Merlin Gerin–Groupe Schneider, 1993). It is also a synoptic table enabling Merlin Gerin–Groupe Schneider to compare its own mastery of a competence or of a function to those of a group of companies selected as a performance standard.

In conclusion, the steering committee of the "competence strategy" supervises the whole organization process of the functional network as a result of a sequential program of actions:

- Appointment of a function individual
- Appointment of a function board
- Implementation of the functional network (relay individuals, etc.)
- Writing the policy of the global function
- Writing the functional policy
- Setting the functional matrix of competences
- Setting poles of competences based on the priority competences
- Writing the functional instructions
- Selection of the performance indicators
- Mapping
- Benchmarking

In practice, this sequence is not always respected; the empiricism remains present and can be explained by the novelty of the process and by the adjustments required between the different parts of the network.

CONSEQUENCES AND IMPACTS OF THE MERLIN GERIN–GROUPE SCHNEIDER EXPERIENCE

1995/1996 PROGRESS REPORT OF THE "COMPETENCE STRATEGY"

Table 10.3 summarizes the extent of the work by Merlin Gerin–Groupe Schneider since the beginning of the "competence strategy" in 1990. At the end of 1994, 75% of the functional policies were written and the main poles were already set up in most of the functions, which means that the competences' matrices were built. On the other hand, writing the instructions is not yet completed; its progress level is irregular

TABLE 10.3   1995/6 Progress Report

- Steering committee of the "competence strategy": three employees attached to the "Organization Department" (12 employees)
- Seven global functions grouping 26 organized functions
- 80 active poles of competences out of 200 potential poles (from 1 to 10 poles per funtion)
- Between 600 and 700 employees directly involved in the development of a pole of competences
- Around 1500 users in direct relation with a pole of competences (employees having received training or relay individuals)

---

from one function to another. On the whole, 15 out of 26 functions have set up their performance indicators and plans of actions.

The success of the "competence strategy" by Merlin Gerin–Groupe Schneider depends on the existence of a tripartite communication between the function (represented by the function individual and the function board), the top management, and the managers of the business units. This tripartite communication is of primary importance because it allows the functional policy and instructions to be consistent with:

- The medium- and long-term objectives defined by the top management
- The differentiation criteria selected by each of the business units in order to achieve these objectives.

The top management develops the medium- and long-term global strategy, but the latter collects and integrates information from business units (i.e. market analysis) and functional organization (i.e. the state of the corporate competences). The business units select the differentiation criteria but these must naturally be approved by the top management and take into account the state of the corporate competences. Finally, the competences are exercised at the business unit level and directed towards the business units (except for the centralized functions and competences). Thus, it is compulsory for the operational staff to be involved in identifying (reflection) and enriching the competences (active spreading) of the company under the supervision of the functional organization; the functional organization being itself under the hierarchical supervision of the top management. Therefore the definition of the functional policy and instructions, the construction of the cartography of the poles of competences as well as the choice of the directions of progress (depending on the selected differentiation criteria) are not and should not be based on the unique competence of a functional network operating independently.

Effects of the "Competence Strategy" on the Global Strategy of Merlin Gerin–Groupe Schneider

According to Merlin Gerin–Groupe Schneider's top management, the "competence strategy" process is characterized by five main advantages (see Figure 10.5):

- Creating a formal link between the global strategy (strategic intent) and the supply strategy (products)
- Allowing them to provide an acceptable allocation of resources aiming to create solid competitive advantages, which implies choices and renunciations
- Allowing them to define a resources optimization policy: setting up of poles of competences, global/local choice, synergy development, . . . etc.
- Constituting an efficient method in order to determine realistic but ambitious objectives

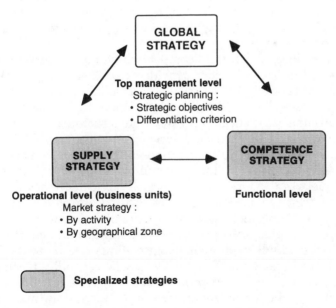

FIGURE 10.5 Global strategy, supply strategy, and "competence strategy" of Merlin Gerin–Groupe Schneider

- Coordinating the professionalism of the employees in relation to human resources management.

The supply strategy refers to the choice of Merlin Gerin–Groupe Schneider concerning its supply of products. It has been developed at the business unit level (activities and countries) by the "Marketing Department" and the managers of these entities; it is differentiated and adjusted with regard to the activities and the geographical area. Global strategy, supply strategy, and "competence strategy" are interactive: "the Merlin Gerin–Groupe Schneider strategy is the result of a permanent discussion between supply strategy and competence strategy, coordinated by the global strategy whose main orientations define the discussion mode between the first two strategies, the orientations of the global strategy being themselves both the expression of the top management will and of the customers' need analysis" (de Montfalcon interview, strategy director of Merlin Gerin–Groupe Schneider, 1994). Indeed, the process of strategic objectives definition, for which the final decision belongs to top management, calls for the intervention of top management, the managers of business units, as well as the managers of the functional network. The global strategy generates the supply strategy and the "competence strategy" but is supplied by the information from the market (activities and countries) and the functional network. The "competence strategy" is based on the objectives of the global strategy but is at the market's service, and thus at the supply strategy's service.

At the functional level, the "competence strategy" implemented by Merlin Gerin–Groupe Schneider provides a coherent framework which is clearly embedded in a competence-building perspective. The concrete processes and structures we describe in this case elaborates and extends the theoretical processes and structures for competence building suggested by Sanchez, Heene, and Thomas (1996). Many connections of our study to their proposed theoretical framework have been presented which provides a common frame of reference and a close link between theory and practice of competence-based strategy. Indeed, the "competence strategy" has focused on the development of an alternative "repeatable pattern of action" allowing the use and configuration of intangible assets in different but more effective ways. In essence, the adoption of a competence strategy leads to the integration of a new strategic capability. This specific capability is strategic in the sense that it is likely to procure a competitive advantage and it emerges within the organization according to a slow and complex competence-building process which "matures" by favoring the emergence of a more effective coordinated redeployment of intangible assets (Amit and Shoemaker, 1993). In addition, Sanchez, Heene, and Thomas (1996: 11) noted that "these coordinated deployments of assets constitute competences when they lead to positive market responses that help a firm to achieve its goals".

Concerning the supply strategy, it integrates the objectives of the global strategy and is stimulated by the information and ideas from the functional network: "The supply strategy of Merlin Gerin–Groupe Schneider has always been influenced by its competences (mainly technological), but the company had an intuitive knowledge of its effective capabilities. Today, Merlin Gerin–Groupe Schneider perceives its competences and those it must develop to grow more clearly" (Harmand and Hingant interview, steering committee of the "competence strategy", Merlin Gerin–Groupe Schneider, 1994). However, market analysis remains the starting point of the elaboration process of the strategic objectives. Therefore the operational level can be considered as the dominant pole of this strategic triptych.

LIMITS AND DIFFICULTIES OF THE IMPLEMENTATION OF THE "COMPETENCE STRATEGY"

From a general point of view, the implementation of the "competence strategy" takes place without any sizeable problems. But to appraise the performance of this strategy precisely, we are too close for a proper view: "At the present time, it is not sure that the competence strategy has led to any progress allowing Merlin Gerin–Groupe Schneider to distinguish itself from its competitors. It has not led to any negative effects, that is sure, but one must still wait to diagnose the positive effects" (de Montfalcon interview, strategy director of Merlin Gerin–Groupe Schneider, 1994).

However, the steering committee has had to face four difficulties which highlight the potential limits of this strategy. The first concerns the difficulty in learning the "competence strategy". In this pedagogical exercise, it seems easier to present the general philosophy and process than to explain the specific terms used. Indeed, it is essential to master the vocabulary used in order to access to the implementation step. It is also difficult to convince people of the usefulness of the "competence strategy". Some people were immediately convinced by the new process. However, they were not in the majority and, as always, "progressive" and "conservative" people have had differing views on the utility of the "competence strategy". The third obstacle is related to the stakeholders' behavior. In fact, the formalization of functional network disturbs the established powers. The departments (Marketing,

Purchasing, etc.) corresponding to a specific function did not face massive transformations concerning their functioning and their hierarchical link. However, the newly constituted functions have thrust forward new individuals with new missions (they are often subordinated to a double hierarchy, functional and operational). Thus, some stakeholders have perceived the "competence strategy" as an opportunity for personal development, while others have perceived it as a threat and a potential loss of power. The last difficulty concerns the formalism of the "competence strategy". Writing the policies and instructions, setting up the matrix of competences, etc. are often viewed as a constraint. Numerous employees consider that the process is too slow and bureaucratic to implement.

But the main obstacle to the implementation of the "competence strategy" lies elsewhere. Indeed, the steering committee of the "competence strategy" stresses that the success of such a strategy depends on a *sine qua non* condition, the presence of a stable business unit portfolio in the company. Depicting the "competence strategy" by Merlin Gerin–Groupe Schneider, Cuvècle observed that "it could only be performed in a relatively stable business unit portfolio" (Cuvècle interview, organization director of Merlin Gerin–Groupe Schneider, 1994). The successful implementation of certain characteristics specific to the experiment are guaranteed by stability in the business units' management. Indeed, the building and development of competences, mainly collective competences, is a slow process which requires a certain repetition of tasks. Moreover, as Sanchez, Heene, and Thomas (1996: 14) noted from a general point of view, "competence-based competition . . . may therefore be likened to a state of perpetual corporate entrepreneurialism in which continuous learning about how to build and leverage competences more effectively becomes a new dominant logic". The company's abilities in learning are the determinants of the success of a competence-building process. The building and development of competences require managers continually to develop new cognitive abilities and to try to imagine how to (re)organize new kinds of assets and capabilities in new ways. These learning and cognitive requirements have some human resource management consequences for the companies engaged in competence-based competition because they imply the emergence of a new kind of manager with intellectual and personality profiles distinct from the traditional ones (Hitt and Tyler, 1991).

The greater managerial insights into future resource requirements of the company, the gradualism of the process, the perpetuation of the corporate entrepreneurialism, and the continuation of the learning process are key conditions which can only be satisfied if the activities of the company remain the same in the long term. In the case of Merlin Gerin–Groupe Schneider it has not faced problems because its business activities portfolio has not been subject to significant modifications by a diversification strategy. From a general point of view, this analysis leads us to state that the success of corporate competence building is closely related to the strategic objectives defined by the company. However, although specialists of competence building agree to relate it to the objectives of corporate development or growth emerging from the process of strategy, they disagree on the most suitable type of strategy to implement: a growth strategy based on the internal stability of the business activities portfolio or one based on external development? Today, no-one can give a definitive answer to this question. Beyond the traditional aspects of the contingency theory, Doz (1994: 95-96) has shifted the debate onto a different plane with new questions and has expressed the idea that "the competence-based management process is intrinsically conservative, not only because of its cumulative and repetitive nature, but also because of its indirect effects ... Beyond the performance, a growing competence in a specific field generally involves a strong emotional commitment. The defense of the existing competences becomes then a real stake in the organization". This idea gives rise to a new debate. Does the success of a competence-building process, whether related to an external or an internal growth strategy, jeopardize the continuity of the company in the long run? In addition to the multiple choices (global *versus* local, short term versus long term) that the company must face, one can ask if the "competence strategy" constitutes another strategic uncertainty: "The culture of the competences is the key to competitive advantage, nevertheless the competences are such a deep source of inertia that it is less probable they can offer responses to new challenges" (Doz 1994: 98).

ACKNOWLEDGEMENTS

We are grateful to Guy-Alain Cuvècle and Dominique Harmand, organization directors (in charge of the "competences' strategy") of Merlin Gerin–Groupe Schneider, for their support. Guy-Alain Cuvècle, followed by Dominique Harmand and Marie-Hélène Hingant, conceived, implemented and consolidated the approach described in this case. Dominique Harmand and Marie-Hélène Hingant are henceforth responsible for extending the experiment to the whole of Groupe Schneider. They provided us with the means to make it possible to explore the "competences strategy" concretely and bring it into written form. We also thank Maurice Saias, professor at the Institut d'Administration des Entreprises in Aix-en-Provence. His deliberations on the "competences' strategy" and his great experience of the subject helped us to understand better the theoretical and practical implications of the method developed by Merlin Gerin–Groupe Schneider. Special thanks are due to Stephen Sutherland for his English expertise.

APPENDIX: MATRIX OF COMPETENCES OF THE "INDUSTRIAL MANAGEMENT" FUNCTION

Role: to manage the internal and external resources in order to satisfy the customers needs

Elements of the competence	Initials	Definition	I	II	III	IV
Production planification	IM1	To define the predictive and real production need, then to adjust the necessary resources, just-in-time		P1	P2	
Short-term needs/ resources	IM2	To maintain the needs/resources daily according to the planned capabilities and to analyze the deviance		P3	P4	
Information mastery	IM3	To provide quality, intelligibility, consistency and fluidity of the industrial information		P1 P6		
Industrial transfer	IM4	To coordinate the competences with a view to transfering the industrial capability without loss of performance		P5		
Physical flow management	IM5	To manage the inter-units or external physical flow (purchasing–selling) in the best time and cost conditions		P6		

Name of the scope: nature of the industrial activity
Dimensions of the scope
I.   Catalogued products
II.   Adapted products (with a small adaptation or a customization study)
III. Equipment (always with an engineering study)
IV.   Affairs (complex batches: barrages, electric power plant
IM. Industrial Management
P.   Pole of competence
Source: Merlin Gerin–Groupe Schneider (1993).

REFERENCES

Abell, D.F. (1993). *Managing with Dual Strategies.* New York: Free Press.

Amit, R. and Shoemaker, P. (1993). Strategic assets and organizational rent. *Strategic Management Journal,* **14,** 1, 33–46.

Argyris, C. (1994). Good communication that blocks learning. *Harvard Business Review,* **72,** 4, 77–85.

Dierickx, I. and Cool, K. (1989). Asset stock accumulation and sustainability of competitive advantage. *Management Science,* **35,** 12, 1504–14.

Doz, Y. (1994). Les dilemmes du management des compétences clés. *Revue Française de Gestion,* January-February, 92–104.

GEST (Groupe d'Etudes des Stratégies Technologiques) (1986). *Grappes Technologiques: Les Nouvelles Stratégies d'Entreprise,* Paris: McGraw-Hill.

Hall, R. (1993). A framework linking intangible resources and capabilities to sustainable competitive advantage. *Strategic Management Journal,* **14,** 2, 607–18.

Hamel, G. and Prahalad, C.K. (1989). Collaborate with your competitors and win. *Harvard Business Review,* **67,** 1, 133–9.

Hamel, G. and Prahalad, C.K. (1994). *Competing for the Future, Breakthrough Strategies for Seizing Control of Your Industry and Creating the Markets of Tomorrow.* Boston, MA: Harvard Business School Press.

Hitt, M.A. and Tyler, B.B. (1991). Strategic decision models: integrating different perspectives. *Strategic Management Journal,* **5,** 2, 327–51.

Merlin Gerin–Groupe Schneider (1993). *Glossaire des Stratégies de Compétences.* Paris.

Peteraf, M.A. (1993). The cornerstones of competitive advantage: a resource-based view. *Strategic Management Journal,* **14** (3), 179–91.

Prahalad, C.K. and Hamel, G. (1990). The core competence of the corporation. *Harvard Business Review,* **68,** 3, 79–91.

Sanchez, R., Heene, A. and Thomas, H. (1996). Towards the theory and practice of competence-based competition. In Sanchez, R., Heene, A. and Thomas, H. (eds), *Dynamics of Competence-Based Competition: Theory and Practice in the New Strategic Management* Oxford: Elsevier.

Sanchez, R. and Thomas, H. (1996). Strategic goals In Sanchez, R., Heene, A. and Thomas, H. (eds), *Dynamics of Competence-Based Competition: Theory and Practice in the New Strategic Management.* Oxford: Elsevier.

Senge, P. (1990). The leader's new work: Building learning organizations. *Sloan Management Review,* Fall, 7–23.

Teece, D. (1986). Profiting from technological information: Implications for integration, collaboration and licensing. *Research Policy,* **15,** 6, 285–305.

Wernerfelt, B. (1984). A resource-based view of the firm. *Strategic Management Journal,* **5,** 2, 171–80.

Zimmermann, J.-B. (1991). Groupes industriels et grappes technologiques. *Revue d'Economie Industrielle,* **47,** 89–102.

Section IV

Cognition in Managing Competences

11

The Blind Spots of Competence Identification: A System-Theoretic Perspective

ROLAND VAN DER VORST

Sanchez and Heene (1996) have indicated that the managerial identification of competences is an important dimension in the study of competence-based competition. Moreover, they have argued that this study should also be focused on how firms can pursue strategic flexibility. In this chapter we argue that the process of identifying competences produces blind spots that guide the leveraging and building of competences in particular directions. The blind spots underlying competence identification can be traced back to blind spots in corporate observation. The persistence of these observations can affect strategic flexibility: some potential future directions come into prominence while others are ignored. In order to enhance strategic flexibility firms should have the ability to identify and overcome these blind spots. We describe the blind spots of competence identification and draw a rough outline of a methodology that can be used to enhance cognitive variety in competence building and leveraging. This methodology is based on system-theoretic insights.

Competence-based Strategic Management.
Edited by Aimé Heene and Ron Sanchez.
Copyright © 1997 John Wiley & Sons Ltd.

INTRODUCTION

Sanchez and Heene (1996) have developed a systems view of the firm for studying competence-based competition. A benefit of this view is that it pays attention to "managerial cognition" as an important dimension. More specifically, the managerial dilemma of identifying which resources should be developed or accessed to build and leverage competences must be carefully considered. They identify the problem of causal ambiguity that affects a firm's decision processes for selecting, acquiring, and using resources (Sanchez and Heene, 1996). Moreover, their systems view incorporates the concept of adaptive behavior as a major issue that should be studied in this process.

In this chapter we will try to elaborate this framework and examine the managerial process of identifying competences more thoroughly. It will be argued that this process produces *blind spots* that guide the leveraging and building of competences in particular directions, thus neglecting other directions. Persistence in following these directions can block the adaptive behavior of managers in leveraging and building competences.

These blind spots result from the limitations that arise from corporate self-description and corporate observation. With the help of system-theoretic insights, we will analyze how corporate self-description and corporate observation guide the process of leveraging and building competences in particular directions. Various system-theoretic methods will be analyzed.

First, we will propose second-order cybernetics as a theory to study observation processes. Second, the role of reflection in competence building and leveraging will be considered to analyze which kinds of observation processes underlie the process of competence identification. By reflection, firms describe (and observe) themselves in relation to their environment. The way in which firms describe (and observe) themselves in relation to others is fundamental to the identification of competences. Orientation to these descriptions and observations produces blind spots in the process of leveraging and building competences. In consequence, the production of blind spots can be explained by elaborating the principles of reflection. Firms can enhance their adaptive behavior, and therefore their strategic flexibility (Sanchez, Heene, Thomas, 1996), by being able to overcome these blind spots. Third, we will argue that modern systems theory provides useful insights for developing a methodology that can help to overcome these blind spots and enhance cognitive variety.

In the next section we will analyze how second-order cybernetics can be helpful in studying observation processes, as opposed to first-order cybernetics. In the third section the concept of reflection will be introduced to analyze which kinds of observation processes underlie the identification of competences. The fourth section deals with the question of how corporate reflection directs the building of new competences and the leveraging of existing ones. We will argue that this causes three kinds of blind spots in the process of leveraging and building competences. In the fourth section we will examine a methodology that can be used to explore new directions for competence building and leveraging and escape the rigidity of existing observations. This methodology is based on second-order cybernetics and provides insights that can be transformed into a technique for improving the cognitive variety of managers, as described in the fifth section. The final section summarizes the implications of our research.

THE IDENTIFICATION OF COMPETENCES AND SECOND-ORDER CYBERNETICS

Some authors have stressed the importance of overcoming cognitive biases in competence building (Sanchez and Heene, 1996; Stein, 1996; Winterscheid, 1994). In this chapter we will present a general model to study the cognitive biases that result from observation processes. Moreover, the chapter will focus on the question of how corporate attention is directed. To study this, we introduce in this section the concept of second-order cybernetics. This stresses the role of the observer in analyzing systems. It can be helpful in analyzing observation processes underlying competence identification.

The focus of cybernetics and systems theory has shifted in the last two decades from first-order or traditional cybernetics to second-order cybernetics. Management science in particular has incorporated many ideas outlined in first-order cybernetics (Beer, 1979; Senge, 1992; Espejo, 1994). Adding to "the competence-based systems view" developed by Sanchez and Heene (1996), we can describe the process of competence building and leveraging in terms of traditional cybernetics.

Let us consider the firm as a system in its relevant environment. Ashby (1958, 1960) is considered a founding father of traditional or first-order cybernetics. In Ashby's description of the "ultrastable system" the focal system tries to keep its essential variables within certain limits; if not, the system will disintegrate. In the case of our focal system, the essential variables refer to the goals of the firm (for instance, "stay a market leader"). Let us say the system "disintegrates" if it does not achieve its goals. From a competence-based point of view the firm should coordinate the deployment of its assets in a proper way to achieve these goals.

When all the essential variables are within their limits the system is in a state of equilibrium. This means that the firm coordinates the deployment of assets in such way that it helps to achieve its goals. There are all kinds of disturbances from the environment that can threaten the system's state of equilibrium. The focal system can act and react in its environment and strive for maintaining its state of equilibrium after a disturbance or find a new state of equilibrium after a disturbance. *Regulation* is a process by which a system reacts in such a way that it either returns to the former state of equilibrium or attains a new one.

A state of equilibrium is maintained by maintaining competences or leveraging competences (Sanchez and Heene, 1996). In both cases the firm does not have to change existing assets and capabilities. At most, it applies its existing competences to current or new market opportunities (competence leveraging). However, it does so without making *qualitative* changes in the firm's assets or capabilities.

A new state of equilibrium must be found if the firm cannot achieve its goals without changing current assets or capabilities. For instance, a competitor may introduce a new product that threatens the firm's goal to stay market leader. Then our focal system should turn to a new state of equilibrium. It should build new competences to return to a new state of equilibrium, in which it can again correctly coordinate the deployment of assets and capabilities.

This is a description of competence management as a process of regulation in terms of traditional cybernetics. Although an analysis of competence-based management from such a cybernetic point of view can yield fruitful insights, it neglects processes that decide which assets and capabilities are actually considered as competences. In other words, processes of observation are not under consideration in traditional cybernetics. As Sanchez and Thomas (1996) have suggested, the fundamental differences in the strategic competence building and leveraging activities of firms can be traced back to the kinds of strategic gaps their managers *perceive* and to the kinds of actions managers undertake to close those gaps. Processes of perception and, more specifically, biases in perception can influence strategic competence building and leveraging activities negatively. Sanchez and Heene (1996), for instance, have indicated the negative effects resulting from cognitive biases of managers. Consequently, an analysis of competence-based strategy based on traditional cybernetics is not sufficient. We need a cybernetics that includes the cognitive processes of managers as well.

In the last two decades the focus of cybernetics has shifted from first-order, or traditional, cybernetics to second-order cybernetics. The important difference between first- and second-order cybernetics is that the latter emphasizes the role of the "observer" who in this case is the managers of the firm-as-a-system. In first-order cybernetics "the system in its environment" is considered as an entity ready to be modeled (Vriens, 1995). In our example, the firm was considered from an "outside perspective". It implies an outside observer studying the firm that tries to find modes of behavior (performing the proper competence-building strategies and leveraging activities) to (re)establish stability. In second-order cybernetics, the system in its environment is considered as a construction of an observer. The central question it tries to answer is: how does any observing system come to observe what it observes (von Foerster, 1985)? In second-order cybernetics, the focal systems under investigation are *observing systems*.

According to recent philosophical and biological concepts, the relation between that which is constructed by the observing system and what exists outside the system is not defined by *correspondence* (Maturana and Varela, 1980: von Glasersfeld, 1992). In other words, when we consider a part of the firm responsible for the identification of competences as an observing system, the knowledge produced by the firm is not a representation of what exists outside the firm. A firm identifying a market may think that it has defined something in its environment in perfect correspondence with reality, but in the end this market still remains a construction made by the firm itself! This does not mean that these constructions are completely arbitrary. As Vriens (1995) notices: "Although we cannot know anything 'outside' us, we hypothesize about what may be there and act accordingly. In our daily life these hypotheses seem to be the real thing, but this is beyond knowledge. Second-order cybernetics explains how we, in spite of the impossibility of any direct access, are able to survive" through this process of hypothesizing.

Instead of studying how "real things" can establish stability, second-order cybernetics focuses on how the constructions produced by observing systems are stabilized (Vriens, 1995). This process of stabilization takes place by hypothesizing a construction (for instance, defining a market) and acting accordingly (for instance, launching a product). When the actions based on the construction are not problematic, the observing system will adhere to these constructions. If the product that the firm has launched sells well, the defined market (the construct) will not be questioned. We could say that the constructions stay in a state of equilibrium. However, our actions may lead to problems that may result in changing our hypotheses and making other constructions. This reconstruction process can be thought of as a way of establishing stability and finding a new state of equilibrium.

Firms act according to their constructions because these have brought them where they are, but they can never be sure about their correspondence with reality. A metaphor used very often to illustrate this is that of a blind man moving through a forest. Each time he bumps into a tree the construction needs revision. Through this continuous process of (re)construction he finally manages to find his way through the forest. The blind man is able to know the forest only in some negative sense: it gives him clues where not to move (von Glasersfeld, 1992).

According to Vriens (1995) this example illustrates two interesting points. First, the constructions are always related to some goal. In this example the goal was to cross the forest. Second, there are many methods for constructing a reality. The man could cross the forest in many different ways. Every construction made by the blind man is contingent. Making a construction implies making a selection.

Except for a few cases (Ulrich and Probst, 1984; Bronn, von Krogh, and Vicari, 1993; Espejo, 1994) second-order cybernetics is relatively unknown in the field of organizational research. Applying the second-order perspective to the study of competence-based strategic management can be helpful in analyzing the observation processes that underlie the identification of competences. Moreover, it creates an opportunity to analyze their influence in the process of competence building and leveraging.

For this purpose we consider the part of the firm-as-a-system responsible for the identification and leveraging of competences as our focal system. This focal system could be one manager or more. In the latter case, constructions become *mutually stabilized* (Vriens, 1995). That means that two or more individuals have developed a stabilized construction. Second-order cybernetics thus provides a framework for analyzing perception processes in competence building from both an individual cognitive perspective (Winterscheid, 1994) and a social-cognitive one (Stein, 1996).

Whether the observation processes under consideration are individual or social, we will focus in this chapter on an observing system at a higher systems level, the level of management processes and strategic logic (Sanchez and Heene, 1996). At this level competences are identified. The identification of competences takes place by various observation processes. Based on these observations, competences are constructed (hypothesized).

We can consider identified competences as constructions that are highly influenced by observation processes. As we illustrated in the example of the blind man, constructions are always related to some goal. Similarly, competences are related to strategic goals (Sanchez and Thomas, 1996). *As a blind man making constructions to find his way through a forest, the firm as an observing system makes constructions of competences to achieve its strategic goals.* If some constructions (identified competences) "do not work" they will be adjusted or revised. Like the blind man, the part of the firm considered as an observing system can construct different possible competences to achieve the firm's goals. However, it makes a choice for *particular* constructions. Other constructions are neglected. That implies that firms construct competences by making selections, and thereby the process of constructing competences leaves *blind spots*. This endangers a firm's strategic flexibility, because the construction of competences becomes implicitly biased.

One way of overcoming these dangers is to increase one's awareness of the selective character of constructions. If the observing system is able to create some kind of overview of the selections influencing new constructions, it creates the possibility of enhancing its strategic flexibility. To analyze the selections and restrictions that follow from the identified competences as constructions, we should analyze the observation processes that underlie these constructions. In the next section we will analyze the observation processes underlying competence identification by considering competence identification as a process of reflection.

COMPETENCE IDENTIFICATION AS REFLECTION

In the previous section, we introduced the concept of an observing system as the part of the firm that is responsible for strategic competence identification and identifying leveraging activities. The competences the firm identifies can be considered as constructions that it creates itself. These constructions become stabilized by observation and action processes. The constructions imply selection. Some constructions are selected and others remain out of sight. The selections become the basis for guiding the process of leveraging and strategic competence building in particular directions. Increasing insight into the kind of selections made in the process of competence identification can therefore be helpful in enhancing strategic flexibility. To identify which selections result from observation processes, we will look at the process of competence building and leveraging as a process of *reflection*. The process of competence identification can be considered as a way of reflecting. Both competence identification and reflection are particular ways in which systems reduce possibilities and create options at the same time.

In identifying competences firms determine their own direction themselves:

> Competences are the glue that bind existing businesses. They are also the engine for new business development. Patterns of diversification and market entry may be guided by them, not just by the attractiveness of markets (Prahalad and Hamel, 1990: 82).

As this definition indicates, organizational performance is focused on particular directions as defined by competences.

Competences provide a focus and in that sense restrain the production of possibilities. At the same time, competences provide a way to create new options. Competences provide the opportunity for leveraging and building new competences: "Competence leveraging, in effect, is the exercising of one or more of a firm's existing *options* for action *created by* prior *competence building*. Competence building creates, in effect, *new options for future action* for the firm in pursuing its goals" (Sanchez and Thomas, 1996).

The options selected and created by building competences can be compared with the production of a particular kind of complexity: *operational complexity*. Some system theories emphasize the fact that systems must regulate their own production of complexity instead of studying the influence of environmental complexity on systems (Ashby, 1958; Willke, 1994). Systems produce various kinds of complexity to develop themselves into autonomous systems in their environment (Willke, 1994). Firms can be considered as social systems that produce and again regulate complexity.

The competence concept, as developed by Sanchez, Heene, and Thomas (1996), refers to the production and regulation of *operational* complexity. Firms are capable of producing operational complexity and are able therefore to reduce their dependence on the environment considerably (Willke, 1994). By producing operational complexity, they define their own *goals* by internal functional differentiation, internal models of the environment, and internal time manipulations (Willke, 1994: 103). With respect to firms, the production of complexity contains the creation, production, and marketing of products (goods or services) for a market.

However, firms as social systems cannot produce limitless complexity. By developing operational complexity to a large extent, they can produce options for themselves to such a degree that it becomes more difficult to handle these options. Individual firms cannot create, produce, and market limitless goods or services. The first reason firms cannot produce limitless complexity is that their operations would lack direction.

The second reason deals with the fact that systems do not stand alone. For isolated systems, almost anything is possible (Ashby, 1960: 115). However, firms are systems that are surrounded by and connected to other systems that produce operational complexity to some degree. The activities of a firm and its surrounding systems must be geared to one another. Firms are forced to take notice of activities of other systems as a source of restriction on and guidance for their production of operational complexity.

By reflecting, firms regulate the creation, production, and marketing of products (goods or services) for a market. Reflection makes "the system in its environment" an issue in the system itself (Luhmann, 1975: 74). It consists of two principles: "the systems becoming an issue for itself" and the fact that it "takes into account other systems" in doing this (Luhmann, 1975: 73; Willke, 1994: 110).

The notion of "core" competence also reflects these two principles and can be considered as a way of organizational reflection. As Hamel and Prahalad state (1994: 221): "A multitude of dangers await a company that can't *conceive of itself and its competitors* in core competence terms."

Reflection restricts and guides the production of operational complexity in particular directions. These restrictive and guiding effects of reflection are based on *two principles*. The first principle refers to the fact that competences can be considered as self-descriptions and these descriptions guide the operations of the firm. In firms, as in all social systems, self-observation and self-description are necessary because it reduces the range of all possible alternatives to certain actions (Luhmann, 1984: 234). It is reflexively determined which actions are selected. Therefore, orientation to self-description, like a competence description, reduces operational complexity by the fact that it selects particular actions.

Second, competence as reflection reduces one's options by taking into account other systems. Both the way other systems are perceived and the fact that firms open their "scope of reflection" to other systems are sources of restriction and guidance. Firms are engaged in all sorts of interactions. This implies that firms do not produce certain options because of the way in which they perceive other systems and let themselves become influenced by these perceptions.

Let us now return to our analysis of the focal system in the previous section. We identified the focal system as the observing system of the firm that is responsible for the identification of competences. According to our analysis in this section this observing system can be considered as responsible for the process of reflection. It reduces and then produces operational complexity by making constructions of competences based on corporate self-description and corporate observation of the environment.

This process of corporate self-description and corporate observation of the environment causes selections in competence constructions. In the next section, we will argue that the selections made by corporate self-description and corporate observation can cause blind spots in the process of building new competences and undertaking leveraging activities.

Blind Spots in Leveraging Existing Competencies and Building New Ones

In this section we will discuss the two principles of reflection in detail. They are both ways in which the leveraging of existing competences and the building of new ones are restricted and guided in certain directions. This means that other directions in markets or competences are neglected. In other words, considering the identification of competences as reflection, we can identify blind spots in both leveraging activities and strategic competence building.

The two kinds of blind spots relate to the two principles of reflection. First, reflection refers to a self-description (see below). These self-descriptions guide leveraging activities and new competence building. Previous research (Winterscheid, 1994) supplies empirical evidence especially for this kind of blind spot. Second, the concept of reflection shows that the environment is considered in describing competences. This implies that a firm's susceptibility to environmental developments also creates blind spots.

Blind Spots Resulting from Competence "as Self-description"

How the Leveraging of Existing Competences is Restrained by Self-description

In leveraging competences firms apply existing competences to current or new market opportunities. This implies that firms analyze their markets in terms of an existing competence description. This can result in a blind spot to other markets.

Competence descriptions guide a firm's observations of markets but these descriptions are always limited. Defining competences means that firms make choices. They choose from a vast amount of potential assets and capabilities. It is not the assets and capabilities that place restrictions on the leverage of competences in the first place, but the *definition* of assets and capabilities. The choice itself implies a restriction: firms consider some aspects of themselves as assets and capabilities, thus being blind to other potential assets and capabilities not seen as competences.

The self-simplification induced by self-description can restrain the leverage of existing competences. What is defined as "existing competence" reflects only a limited part of a firm's potential assets and capabilities. Because of this self-simplification, *firms neglect particular markets*. Moreover, because corporate observation is fixed on particular competences, firms become blind to the opportunities to leverage existing competences to other markets (Figure 11.1).

Therefore, the orientation to a competence description can cause blind spots in environmental observation. As a result, particular markets become more likely to be explored. Even so, the need to explore new markets can become less compelling because of a firm's persistence in orienting toward existing competences. In other words, new markets are the blind spots that can result from orientation to existing competence descriptions.

These blinds spots do not necessarily have to have a bad influence on a company's performance. Blind spots imply focus which is necessary to some extent. The question is how to stimulate new directions in exploring new markets. There are several possibilities to be considered here. A first solution is to encourage the building of new competences: produce new competences proactively. Another solution deals with describing competences that are broad enough to cover

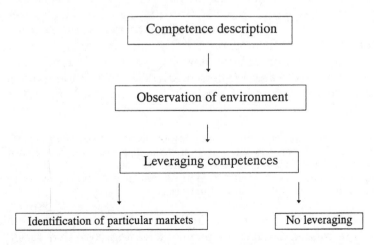

FIGURE 11.1   Existing competence description produces blind spots for leveraging activities

many different markets. The neglect of particular markets caused by a particular description can be prevented by describing competences in more abstract terms.

The Dutch Post and Telecommunications Company has recently begun to explore the market for security services. This is possible because the company has expertise in providing security to their large number of personnel and the goods they transport. If they had defined their competences in the area of "providing services in the area of post and telecommunications," the choice of exploring this new market would not be apparent.

The recognition of competences as a *choice* might lead to overcoming blind spots. Recognizing the fact that the description of assets and capabilities as competence always concerns a choice, might widen corporate attention to redefining or buildling new competences and thus enter new markets.

How "Building New Competences" is Restrained by Self-description

Blind spots in building new competences can arise because new competences are built from the perspective of existing competence descriptions. These descriptions influence corporate attention by focusing on the identification of *particular* new competences. Let us say a firm has identified "international transport" as its competence. New competences can be identified within the domain associated with "international transport", but the firm may not even recognize other possible uses of its assets and capabilities as new competences it can build on. Moreover, fixation on existing competence descriptions can take away the ambition to build new competences: (Figure 11.2).

In her "Newbox" case, Winterscheid (1994: 287) found evidence for the existence of such blind spots in the perception of individuals within the firm:

> Individuals who perceive the organization to be competent in a particular area will perceive the *new* competence required in terms of their existing core competence. Little attention will be devoted to discovering the required new capability in areas that they do not know, or [it will be] take for granted, in the first place.

These blind spots become a problem when competence-building chances are missed because of them. Increasing cognitive variety can therefore become necessary.

Firms can try to overcome the negative effects caused by the blind

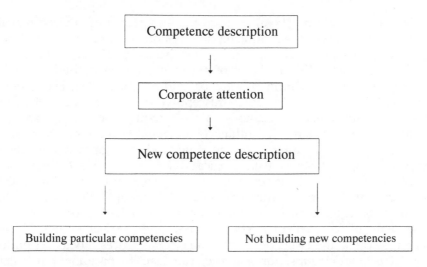

FIGURE 11.2   Existing competence descriptions produce blind spots for building new competences

spots of existing competence descriptions by increasing the level of abstraction of existing competence descriptions, making new directions more visible and corporate attention less narrow.

Another way of exploring new directions is trying to overcome the guiding force of existing competence descriptions by building new competences that are built independently of existing competence descriptions. Consider again the example of the transportation company that described its competence as "international transport". Ignoring this competence description could make it possible to see that the network of offices the company owns all over the world could be used for other purposes as well.

BLIND SPOTS RESULTING FROM SUSCEPTIBILITY TO OTHER SYSTEMS

In the previous section we discussed the blind spots that resulted from the fact that competences as a description guide both corporate attention and environmental observation (more specifically, the identification of markets). A second characteristic of reflection is that organizations consider other systems in describing their competences. In this section we will deal with the question of how this susceptibility to other systems influences the building of new competences.

Sanchez and Heene (1996) indicate the importance of environmental scanning as a driver for producing new options for firms in the future. However, managers' perceptions of the behavior of competitors are likely to influence the direction of a firm's competence building and leveraging activities (Gorman, Thomas, and Sanchez, 1996; Hamel and Prahalad, 1994). By being highly susceptible to the influences of other systems, firms make concessions to their own choice of options by allowing other systems to influence the identification of their own competences. These influences are perceived developments in their environment, for instance technological developments, market developments, or the behavior of competitors. The biases in observation of the environment that result from environmental susceptibility can lead to blind spots in building new competences that make it more likely the firm will build particular competences and neglect others. They therefore cause the selection of *particular* competences. Focus on particular customer groups, for instance, can lead to building particular competences and neglecting others.

Biases that result from environmental observation can also result in not building new competences at all. A good example is given by the way in which large Dutch newspaper proprietors deal with new media developments. They are not very anxious to develop activities in new media. They are quite susceptible to each others' behavior but are reluctant to change because of perceived stability in the behavior of other competitors. If the behavior of their competitors did change, it would become more likely that the behavior of other firms would also change. Because of susceptibility to the competitors' behavior, firms often do not build new competences (Figure 11.3).

In this section we have presented some intuitive ideas for exploring new directions to overcome the negative effects of blind spots. In the next section, we will introduce a technique that can be helpful to widen a manager's scope in leveraging activities and strategic competence building in more systematic ways.

HOW TO INCREASE COGNITIVE VARIETY IN THE IDENTIFICATION OF COMPETENCES

Sanchez and Heene (1996) have used systems theory in the study of competence-based competition. In doing this, they argue that adaptive behavior in the identification of competences is important to enhance strategic flexibility. In the previous section we saw that the way in which firms describe themselves and observe their environment induces blind spots in the process of leveraging and building com-

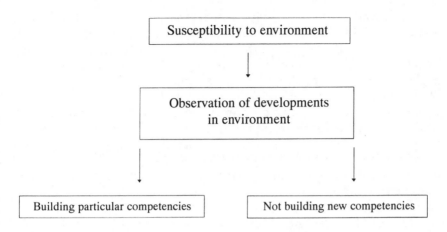

FIGURE 11.3 Environmental observation produces blind spots for building new competences

petences. The persistence of blind spots can block adaptive behavior and strategic flexibility. Therefore, it is important to overcome these blind spots and search proactively for new ways of leveraging and building competences. As Sanchez and Heene (1996: 56) suggest: "Managers may also try to expose their cognitive frameworks to alternative viewpoints and new conceptual frameworks that directly challenge the appropriateness of their strategic logic or management processes."

The question is how "alternative cognitive frameworks" can be produced and how "managerial imagination" can be stretched. To achieve this, firms need to identify existing blind spots underlying their corporate observations and proactively trigger new observations. In the previous section we discussed ways of widening the cognitive scope in leveraging activities and strategic competence building. In this section we will use second-order cybernetics for developing a technique in more systematic ways. This technique can be used to stimulate cognitive variety.

Earlier we identified several blind spots in the process of identifying competences and building new competences. These blind spots are induced by competence descriptions and environmental susceptibility. Both competence descriptions and environmental susceptibility, however, are constructed by the observations the firm makes of itself and of its environment. The blind spots that underlie competence descriptions can be traced back to the blind spots in self-observation and observation of the environment. These blind spots guide the identification of markets (leveraging competences) and the identification of assets and capabilities (building new competences) in particular directions. A methodology to explore new directions and solve these particular blind spots should be based on finding new ways of self-observation and observation of the environment.

In our discussion of second-order cybernetics above, we identified an observing system as our focal point. This observing system represents the part of the firm responsible for the identification of competences. It uses all kinds of constructions in observing itself and its environment. Observation takes place by making constructions that become stabilized. Firms act according to those constructions and keep to those constructions or, if they prove to be problematic, reconstruct. In due course every firm has stabilized a whole complex of constructions that guides their observations and actions. This complex provides the basis for the new constructions the firm makes. Also, these new constructions can adjust the complex of constructions a firm has lived with so far.

This analysis suggests that one complex of stabilized constructions serves as a basis for other constructions. Possible complexes of stabilized constructions that play a major role in the process of competence based management are represented by, for instance, strategic logic (Sanchez and Heene, 1996) or shared beliefs (Stein, 1996). Such a complex of stabilized constructions may refer to both the rationale(s) as to how things should be done or to the mutually stabilized world views of individuals (Stein, 1996). In both cases this network of stabilized constructions defines the boundaries between which the other set of constructions is made. Existing competence descriptions can also be considered as such stabilized constructions that guide the process of building new competences.

The question remains, however, of how to analyze more thoroughly the particular directions by which these constructions are guided and how this can help us to explore new directions. The answer may be found in the concept of distinctions. By analyzing the distinctions underlying observation, the particular directions of a construction become clear. Moreover, new directions can be explored by drawing new distinctions. Many contributions in systems theory and second-order cybernetics relate observation to the act of making a distinction (Spencer Brown. 1969; Baecker, 1993). A construction being made can be considered as a distinction that is drawn. The concept of distinctions provides a way to analyze the biases of observation more thoroughly, compared to the concept of construction. Furthermore, using the concept of distinctions becomes a way to enhance cognitive variety.

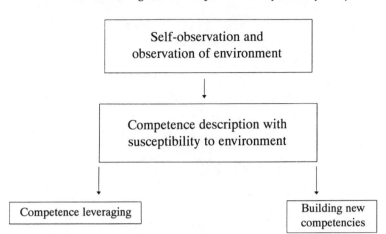

FIGURE 11.4   Self-observation and environmental observation produce blind spots for leveraging activities and building new competences

The act of making a distinction is basic to observation. As Maturana and Varela (1980) state: "the basic operation that an observer performs in the praxis of the living is the operation of a distinction. In this distinction an observer brings forth a unity as well as the medium in which it is distinguished". By drawing a distinction, an indication of something comes into prominence against a particular background. A distinction that is made draws the attention of the observing system toward an indication of particular "objects" and makes others fade away or seem less important. The particular distinctions that are drawn determine the way we look at the world. In other words, the distinctions prescribe the direction of the constructions made by an observing system.

Observing systems, like firms, have their own history of observations. They have developed a complex of constructions that serves as a basis for the future constructions it makes. In other words, every observing system has built up a whole complex of distinctions determining the direction of the constructions it makes. This stabilized complex of distinctions is constitutive for the distinctions to be made, which in turn have influence on the stabilized complex of distinctions. In Figure 11.6 we can now see that one complex of distinctions always guides the distinction to be drawn.

The figure tells us that every distinction drawn is drawn against the background of a whole set of other distinctions. Following Spencer, Brown, Vriens, and van der Vorst (1996) have suggested that this background can be considered as the *domain* in which a distinction is

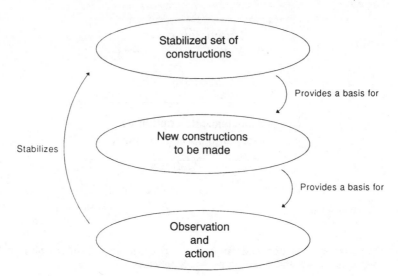

FIGURE 11.5   Stabilization of constructions

drawn. This domain defines the boundaries within which distinctions are drawn.

This principle can be used in looking for new constructions. According to this principle, the direction of a particular construction depends first, on the distinction underlying that construction. The distinction underlying a construction directs this construction towards the indication of particular objects (for instance, particular machines or customers). This entails that alternative objects are ignored. Therefore the distinction underlying a construction selects particular indications. Second, the distinctions underlying the constructions are guided by the set of stabilized distinctions the firm has built and which seem to have worked. This set of stabilized distinctions is the background against which the indications (particular machines or customers) take place. Therefore, the direction of a particular construction depends also on the background (domain) against which particular indications are made.

Where does this leave the firm that wants to overcome the rigidity of its constructions in the process of leveraging competences and building new ones? The principle discussed above can be used as the basis of a technique for increasing cognitive variety in leveraging activities and strategic competence building. The following are possible ways of "stretching a manager's imagination".

- Identify the distinction underlying a particular construction. Which indications are made? For example, a way in which the firm itself observes possible indications made by the observing system could be the retail outlets of a firm.
- Identify the domain in which the distinction is drawn. For instance, the retail outlets are considered in the domain of "distribution". This means that they are regarded as providing ways to distribute goods.
- Use the indications made as a domain in which new distinctions can be drawn. For instance, the indication "retail outlet" can be considered as domain. This means that new products can be developed that fit into the retail concept. By considering the retail outlet as a domain, particular products become important.
- Use the identified domain for drawing new distinctions. If the identified domain is "ways of distribution", all kinds of new distinctions can be drawn using this domain as a background. Looking at a firm's assets from the background of this domain can open up new ways of viewing potential uses for existing assets.
- Find new domains in which new distinctions can be drawn by attributing functions to the identified objects of a distinction. Use these domains again to draw new distinctions. Let us consider the retail outlets as the objects of a distinction that are identified by a firm. Various functions can be attributed to a retail outlet. It provides a way of distributing goods. Another possible function of a retail outlet can be "place to shop" or "place to communicate directly with customers". Again these domains can be used to draw new distinctions. Against the background of owning 500 places to communicate directly with customers these outlets are viewed as different kinds of assets compared to identifying 500 places to distribute goods as important assets!

IMPLICATIONS FOR STRATEGY THEORY, RESEARCH AND PRACTICE

Cognitive processes are an important subject for both research in and practice of competence-based strategic management. Bias in observation is one aspect of cognitive processes that needs investigation. Several kinds of blind spots influence leveraging activities and strategic competence building. To analyze these blind spots we should consider the part of the firm that is responsible for the identification of competences as an observing system. This observing system constructs competences by employing self-observation and environmental observation. In the process of stabilizing these constructions it produces

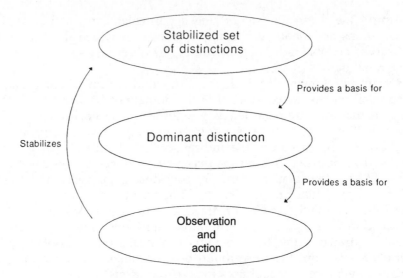

FIGURE 11.6   Stabilization of distinctions

blind spots in leveraging activities and competence building that endanger strategic flexibility.

The first possible blind spot is caused by the fact that existing competence descriptions influence the selection of markets that can be explored by firms. The second blind spot arises from the fact that existing competence descriptions guide the building of new competences in particular directions, thus neglecting other directions. The third blind spot results from biases in environmental observations. Because of the particular selection of environmental developments, particular new competences become more likely to be built than other competences.

System-theoretic insights can be helpful in both the study and practice of competence-based strategic management for several reasons. First, they provide a model for analyzing observation processes of the firm and for investigating how these processes influence strategic decision making. Second, with the help of systems theory various different kinds of perspectives of cognitive processes can be related to each other (for instance, the relation between individual perspectives and social perspectives). Third, second-order cybernetics in particular provides a methodology and a framework for studying managers' cognitions that can be used to create new directions in researching competence leveraging and building new competences. Using this methodology can help to overcome the negative effects of the blind spots we have identified.

ACKNOWLEDGEMENT

The author would like to thank Dirk Vriens and Wil Martens for their contributions to this chapter.

REFERENCES

Ashby, W.R. (1958). *An introduction to Cybernetics.* London: Chapman & Hall.

Ashby, W.R. (1960). *Design for a Brain: The Origin of Adaptive Behaviour.* London: Chapman and Hall Ltd.

Baecker, D. (ed.) (1993). *Kalkül der Form.* Frankfurt am Main: Suhrkamp Taschenbuch Wissenschaft.

Beer, S. (1979). *The Heart of the Enterprise.* Chichester: John Wiley.

Bogaert, I., Martens, R. and Van Cauwenbergh, A. (1994). Strategy as a situational puzzle: the fit of components. In Hamel, G. and Heene, A. (eds), *Competence-Based Competition.* New York: John Wiley, pp. 57–77.

Bronn, P.S., Von Krogh, G. and Vicari, S. (1993). Auto-What? A new perspective on corporate self-awareness. *European Management Journal*, 3 342–6.

Espejo, R. (1994). What is systemic thinking? *System Dynamics Review.* 10, Nos 2–3, 199–212.

Gorman, P., Thomas, H. and Sanchez, R. (1996). Industry dynamics in competence-based competition. In Sanchez, R., Heene, A. and Thomas, H. (eds) *Dynamics of Competence-Based Competition: Theory and Practice in the New Strategic Management.* Oxford: Elsevier, pp. 85–9.

Hamel, G. and Prahalad, C.K. (1994). *Competing for the Future.* Boston, MA: Harvard Business School Press.

Luhmann, N. (1975). *Soziologische Aufklärung 2, Aufsätze zur Theorie der Gesellschaft.* Opladen: Westdeutscher Verlag.

Luhmann, N. (1984). *Soziale Systeme, Grundriss einer algemeine Theorie.* Frankfurt am Main: Suhrkamp.

Maturana, H. and Varela, F. (1980). *Autopoiesis and Cognition. The realization of the living.* Dordrecht: Reidel.

Prahalad, C.K. and Hamel, G. (1990). The core competences of the corporation. *Harvard Business Review*, 82, May-June, 79–91.

Sanchez, R., Heene, A. and Thomas, H. (1996). Towards the theory and practice of competence-based competition. In Sanchez, R., Heene, A. and Thomas, H. (eds), *Dynamics of Competence-Based Competition: Theory and Practice in the New Strategic Management.* Oxford: Elsevier, pp 1–35.

Sanchez, R. and Heene, A. (1996). A systems view of the firm in competence based competition. In Sanchez, R., Heene, A. and Thomas, H. (eds) *Dynamics of Competence-Based Competition: Theory and Practice in the New Strategic Management.* Oxford: Elsevier, pp 39–62.

Sanchez, R. and Thomas, H. (1996). Strategic goals. In Sanchez, R., Heene, A. and Thomas, H. (eds), *Dynamics of Competence-Based Competition: Theory and Practice in the New Strategic Management.* Oxford: Elsevier, pp. 63–84.

Spencer Brown, G. (1969). *Laws of Form* London: Allen & Unwin.

Stein, J. (1996). On building and leveraging competences across organizational borders: A socio-cognitive framework. In Heene A. and Sanchez, R. (eds), *Competence-Based Strategic Management.* Chichester: John Wiley.

Ulrich, H. and Probst, G.B.J. (eds) (1984). *Self-organization and Management of Social Systems*. Berlin: Springer-Verlag.

Von Foerster, H. (1984). Principles of self-organization—in a socio-managerial context. In Ulrich, H. and Probst, G.B.J. (eds), *Self-organization and Management of Social Systems*. Berlin: Springer-Verlag.

Von Glasersfeld, E. (1992). Konstruktion von Wirklichkeit und des Begriffs der Objektivität. In Gumin, H. and Meier, H., (eds), *Einfuehrung in den Konstruktivismus*. München: Piper.

Vriens, D. (1995). Second-order cybernetics and organization: The case for continuous negotiation In Larrasquet, J.M. (ed.), *Proceedings of the Conference on Projectics*, pp. 284–98.

Vriens, D. and van der Vorst, R.R.R., (1996). Can the blind spot the blind spot? How to overcome our observing biases. Working Paper, Nymegen Business School, Nymegen.

Willke, H. (1994). *Systemtheorie: Einfürung in die Grundprobleme der Theorie sozialer Systeme*. Stuttgart: UTB.

Winterscheid, B.C. (1994). Building capability from within: the insider's view of core competence. In Hamel, G. and Heene, A. (eds), *Competence-Based Competition*. New York: John Wiley, pp. 265–93.

12

On Building and Leveraging Competences Across Organizational Borders: A Socio-cognitive Framework

JOHAN STEIN

This chapter synthesizes insights concerning coordination mechanisms which have an effect on the building and leveraging of competences through interorganizational networks. In order to capture the manifold nature and complexity of such mechanisms, a socio-cognitive framework is presented. A central thesis of this framework is that competence building and leveraging are consequences of both changes of shared beliefs and social representations, such as rules and routines, of these beliefs. The chapter contains a case on how research and development activities are organized in the networks of three firms: Ericsson Components, ABB Signal, and CelsiusTech Systems. Throughout the chapter, implications for theory and practice are presented.

FAILING MARKETS AND ORGANIZATIONS

Competitive advantage is increasingly equated with the capability of an organization to build and leverage competences to serve market

Competence-based Strategic Management.
Edited by Aimé Heene and Ron Sanchez.

needs more quickly and at a lower cost than competitors (Prahalad and Hamel, 1990; Teece, Pisano, and Shuen, 1992; Sanchez, Heene and Thomas, 1996). Adopting a Schumpeterian view of competition, dynamic capability theory has attempted to further the understanding of this issue beyond the endogenetic resource-based school. No longer is the "environment" seen as an empty uninhabited space outside the possible control of organizations. Nevertheless, the dynamic capability theory is still based on an inside-out perspective (cf. Teece, 1977; Barney, 1986; Diedrickx and Cool, 1989; Kogut and Zander, 1992). Much attention is focused on the dissemination of information through networks so that organizations can absorb the competences of others while keeping their own competences private. Thus, the creation of competence is believed to take place mainly within organizations.

This chapter will partly challenge this presumption of the dynamic capability theory by considering the building and leveraging of competences which may be either separable or inseparable among two or more organizations in a network—i.e. competences which can and cannot be replicated by individual organizations. Competence building is here seen as qualitative changes in assets and capabilities, whereas competence leveraging refers to the application of existing competences (Sanchez, Heene, and Thomas, 1996). The very existence of interorganizational alliances results from failures of markets and organizations to build and leverage competences. The chapter discusses such failures to shed light on why firms form strategic alliances, vertically and laterally, in order to innovate, produce, or market new products/services.

In relation to the theory of competence-based competition (Hamel and Heene, 1994; Sanchez, Heene, and Thomas, 1996), this chapter aims at furthering the understanding of how the deployment of assets may be coordinated. Given the definition of competence as "an ability to sustain the coordinated deployment of assets in a way that helps a firm achieve its goals" (Sanchez, Heene, and Thomas, 1996: 8), our interest in coordination appears to be important. Notably, it has been observed that coordination is an aspect of the theory of competence-based competition that needs to be developed (Sanchez, Heene, and Thomas, 1996).

BUILDING AND LEVERAGING COMPETENCES IN NETWORKS— A ZERO-SUM GAME?

Two different views on the driving forces underlying interorganizational relations can be found in the literature. One group of scholars accentuates the need for companies to gain bargaining power relative to suppliers and customers in order to bring home a larger portion of the rents created (cf. Porter, 1980; Caves, 1987). However, on the basis of their studies of how companies interact with their environment, another group of scholars stresses the learning effects which result from collaboration around joint interests (cf. Håkansson, 1987; Easton, 1992). As regards dissemination of competence, the demarcation line between these two views is obvious. In the former, there is a belief that firms should try to absorb as much competence as possible while giving away as little as possible. The latter view portrays more of a win–win situation if the collaborating parties can learn to trust one another. According to this view, trust can only be established if the parties exchange competence with the purpose of contributing to each other's competences. Trust is also seen as a way of solving the paradox of information—i.e. the value of information can only be revealed to another party by disclosing the information, but such disclosure destroys its value.

Collaboration may lead to the development of transaction-specific assets so that an asset cannot be redeployed without a substantial reduction in its value. In such cases, the transaction costs are likely to increase because the collaborating parties must try to protect themselves from unobservable actions—i.e. moral hazard—which can be taken after they have agreed on a certain transaction. Trust is therefore important so as to lower the costs of network transactions.

Based on a study of about 500 relationships between customers and sellers on the industrial markets in Britain, France, Germany and Sweden, Hallén (1986) shows that relationships between firms cannot generally be categorized as short-term market transactions. The average duration of the relationships studied was 11 years. Networks with firms from the same country appeared to be especially stable. The average duration of the relationships was 30 years in Britain, 21 years in France, 15 years in Germany, and 24 years in Sweden. Hallén's statistics also reveal substantial differences regarding the duration of international relationships. While the relationships among firms from Germany and Sweden lasted around 16 years, firms from Britain and France collaborated for about 4.5 years.

For several reasons, it becomes relevant to distinguish groups or networks of firms with complementary competences from *competence groups* of firms with substitutable competences as defined by Gorman, Thomas, and Sanchez (1996). Mapping groups with complementary competences can be important when trying to evaluate the value of a firm as ". . . the net present value of the cash flows expected from its current uses of assets, and the value of the firm's real options to generate new cash flows from new uses of new or existing assets in the future" (Sanchez and Thomas, 1996: 66). The risks involved in creating and exercising strategic options can probably be better portrayed with, rather than without, such mapping of groups with complementary competences.

Hallén (1986) also studied to what extent collaborations involved strict business relations, with no personal commitments, or close personal relations. In line with other studies (Håkansson, 1987; Laage-Hellman, 1987; Liljegren, 1988), he found that slightly more time was spent on personal relations than on strict business relations. It may seem irrational that so much time is devoted to personal relations. However, the result ought to be seen in the light of how important trust is. That is, if trust is established, transactions costs are likely to decrease and the exchange of information can be stimulated, thereby fostering competence building and leveraging.

Trust does not come without a cost. To establish and maintain trust require resources. The alternative cost of trust can also be high if there is emotional inertia in changing to better alternatives which are available. Trust may blind, so that alternatives are perhaps not even perceived.

ORGANIZING COMPETENCE BUILDING AND LEVERAGING IN NETWORKS

Organizing can be seen as a process which involves both the *division of competences* and the *coordination of competences* among interacting parties, such as firms or business units within firms. The division of competences among firms interacting in networks obviously differs. While some firms may have the competence to innovate certain products, others can have the competence to produce or market these products, and still others may have the competence to coordinate the competences of other firms. Mapping how competences are divided among collaborating firms can provide important information concerning which of the structural network constellations are the most efficient in building or leveraging competences.

As regards the coordination of competences, eight coordination mechanisms (cf. Cyert and March, 1963; Mintzberg, 1989; Douma and Schreuder, 1992) can be identified when considering the conceptual framework presented by Sanchez, Heene and Thomas (1996):

1. Mutual adjustment as the tacit or articulated exchange of information without the use of authority

2. Standardization of inputs in terms of assets (tangibles and intan-gibles), capabilities, and competences
3. Standardization of processes in terms of work routines and responsibilities
4. Standardization of outputs (or goals) in terms of quantity and quality
5. Standardization of strategic logics
6. Standardization of norms and values which define how things are and how things should be done
7. Use of authority—i.e. tacit or articulated exchange of information from a party who directly or indirectly tries to overcome the resistance of those receiving the information, and has the power to do so
8. Prices.

Hence, standardization of inputs, processes, outputs as well as normative principles of governance are important ways of coordinating competences. What, then, are the pros and cons of each coordination mechanism?

In-depth case studies were used to gain insight on how competence building and leveraging was organized and the effects that followed therefrom. Data were collected through taped interviews with 16 top-level managers at three firms; Ericsson Components, ABB Signal, and CelsiusTech Systems. Secondary sources, for example internal documents, provided further data. Following the procedures advocated by Van de Ven and Poole (1990) for studying innovation processes, a list of events in competence building and leveraging was established from the gathered data. The basic unit of analysis was the "coordina-tion mechanism" which was defined as a "major recurrent activity or a change in one of the core concepts in the research framework" (Van de Ven and Poole, 1990: 320). The core concepts were types of competence creation (building or leveraging), context (organizational, interorganiza-tional), and forms of influence (technical, political, economic, cognitive—see further below).

The head offices of all three companies are situated in Stockholm, Sweden. Ericsson Components with some 1600 employees is a supplier of advanced micro-electronic and power components. The largest single buyer is the Ericsson Group. ABB Signal AB, which is part of the ABB Group, has around 400 employees and supplies customized signalling solutions for railways. The third company studied, Celsius-Tech Systems, employs 900 people and specializes in advanced systems technology for a wide range of defence and civil applications.

On the basis of the case studies of Ericsson Components, ABB Signal and CelsiusTech Systems, the following aspects stand out regarding various coordination mechanisms. Due to the qualitative nature of the study, it was difficult to get a clear picture of transaction costs. Hence, conclusions regarding transactions costs are borrowed from transaction cost theory (Williamson, 1975, 1985):

Mutual adjustment
+   Can handle both competence building and leveraging
−   Limited ability to handle situations with many interacting parties since the transactions costs increase with the number of transactions.

Standardization (of inputs, processes, outputs, strategic logics, norms and values)
−   Can create a kind of interpretative inertia so that environmental changes are not observed
+   Low transaction costs under high-frequency transactions
+− Fosters competence leveraging rather than competence building.

Authority
−   Limited ability to handle complex situations with many interacting parties
−   Can lead to a less open atmosphere when exchanging information
−   Makes the many dependent on the judgements of the few, which may be a problem under conditions of a high degree of uncertainty and complexity
+   Low transaction costs under high-frequency transactions
+   Makes it possible to change things quickly.

Prices
−   May lead to short-sightedness
−   Can be difficult to set prices which reveal underlying efficiency
−   Reveal no information other than the price itself
−   High transaction costs under asset specificity and complexity
+   Prices can be used to disclose inefficiencies which may be a way of overcoming political and cultural inertia with regard to competence building and leveraging.

In the three firms studied, it is apparent that all kinds of coordination were applied, although to a varying extent. Managers at Ericsson Components sometimes tried to avoid standardization in order to promote the establishment of new competences. They did not want the technicians to be limited to known fields of competence since this could hamper the development of the next generation of microchips the company was to produce. Instead, these managers invested in trying to establish arenas where information could be exchanged on both a formal and an informal basis—i.e. mutual adjustment. The offices in Stockholm were rebuilt to house more meeting places, information technology was used to build networks of communication, and the large majority of technicians received mobile office phones. Several managers note that the advance of information technology in general allowed them to rely more on mutual adjustment as a coordination mechanism than used to be the case. They thereby tried to follow the strategic vision of the Ericsson Group: "It's about communication between people. The rest is technology." The trend toward mutual adjustment can also be found in the relationships with other firms. In the development of microchips, Ericsson Components worked closely (and still does) with Texas Instruments. In the early stages of this collaboration, managers of Ericsson Components recall the extensive use of contracts which defined the assets, capabilities, and competences the firms should contribute. However, if standardization was the dominant coordination mechanism during the first few years, the importance of mutual adjustment grew substantially thereafter, according to managers at Ericsson. They add that the contractual framework with Texas Instruments reduced their uncertainty about the relationship, thereby fostering the trend toward mutual adjustment. Trust is seen as a prerequisite for establishing mutual adjustment that works without much friction.

In the case of CelsiusTech Systems, standardization of outputs was observed among managers to be the primary coordination mechanism in the beginning of customer relationships. At ABB Signal, a similar departure from a customer relationship basis was usual. Standardization of inputs seems to have been less common in the cases of both CelsiusTech Systems and ABB Signal. Managers note that customers had complementary rather than substituting assets, capabilities, and competences, which implied that formal standardization of inputs was not particularly meaningful. Thus, coordination could be achieved by virtue of almost automatic response to each other's specialized areas of competence. Nevertheless, advanced customers, such as Swedish Rail Administration (a customer of ABB Signal), often had their own specialists in the fields of competence of ABB Signal and CelsiusTech Systems. It was not unusual for such specialists to take a larger and more active role in the realization of goals than was specified in contracts. Here, as in the relationship between Ericsson Components and Texas Instruments, mutual adjustment is revealed to have been a crucial coordination mechanism in the process of achieving goals and creating strategic options by building and leveraging competences (Sanchez and Thomas, 1996).

The issue of complementary or substituting inputs—i.e. assets, capabilities, and competences—needs some additional attention as it is important when discussing the organizing of competence building or leveraging in networks. The aim of the alliance between Ericsson Components and Texas Instruments was to exert an increased mutual business and, as observed, to achieve competence building. Notably, standardization of inputs was needed so that both firms could concentrate on the fields of competence they were best at; thus complementary roles were established. Despite this division of labor, managers at Ericsson reveal that it was helpful for the companies to have substituting competences since it would otherwise have been difficult to communicate with each other. According to the managers, dissemination of competence, particularly the tacit dimension, was substantially facilitated if the interacting parties, at least to some extent, had substituting fields of competence. Sometimes CelsiusTech Systems and ABB Signal entered into contracts which defined outputs, implying that they needed to build new competences in order to achieve the outputs. Such contracts were usually entered into when the customer was believed to be competent enough to be a contributing partner. For instance, when it was necessary for customers to specify their demands in technical terms.

Finally, it is worth mentioning that authority and prices were seldom used as dominant coordination mechanisms. Authority was obviously avoided since a majority of the managers interviewed feared that this could lead to a less open exchange of information. There was also a risk that complex situations could be too narrowly interpreted if only the managers with a large amount of authority were to make the judgements. The drawbacks with prices were mainly considered to be that they transferred too little information too slowly to propel quick and directed competence building or leveraging. Even so, price signals could help managers to legitimate change and thereby overcome barriers of resistance. Long-term price movements were also regarded as important indicators of how to coordinate the building and leveraging of competences.

A Socio-cognitive Perspective on Competence Building and Leveraging

In order to capture competence building and leveraging through networks, a socio-cognitive perspective can be applied. Here, the acquisition of skills is not assumed to follow from the utilitarian pursuit of self-interest by fully informed, rational, atomized, and maximizing individuals. The socio-cognitive perspective stresses social influences on human thought and action.

From a socio-cognitive perspective, competences of firms and networks are observed to be embedded in shared beliefs about both how things are and how things should be done, and in social representations which manifest these beliefs. Among such social representations, it is possible to find various kinds of routines, such as for searching for information, selecting information, and evaluating performance. Moreover, collective competences can also be stored in various "social representations" such as myths and symbols (Berger and Luckmann, 1966), narrations (Van Maanen, 1988), professions (Larson, 1977; Freidson, 1986), language (Weick, 1979), and formal and informal rules (Giddens, 1984). Accordingly, the ability to sustain the coordinated deployment of assets in ways that help a firm achieve its goals— i.e. competence—is stored both in the beliefs of individuals and in social representations of these beliefs. In relation to the concept of strategic logic defined by Sanchez, Heene, and Thomas (1996), the notion of shared beliefs is broader since it refers not only to the rationale(s) as to how things should be done when deploying assets, but also to the world views of individuals. For example, how individuals look upon resources, goals, and acceptable levels of goal attainment are included in the concept of shared beliefs.

In the light of the socio-cognitive perspective, changes of competences as collective abilities involve changes of shares beliefs and various social representations of these beliefs. Sometimes competence building and leveraging only involve changes of either beliefs or social representations (cf. Leonard-Barton, 1992). Managerial cognition, encompassed in managerial processes and strategic logics, is seen as an important aspect of competence building and leveraging (Hamel and Heene, 1994; Sanchez and Heene, 1996). A socio-cognitive perspective on learning, however, suggests that beliefs or interpretative systems, which include a consideration of norms and values, other than those of managers need to be incorporated into a model of the firm as an open system. Hence, the socio-cognitive view on the nature of competence implies that competences can affect the coordination mechanisms discussed. That is, changes in shared beliefs and/or social representations which encapsulate a competence may, in turn, alter the way individuals interpret system elements—i.e. operations, assets (including their perceptions of themselves), management practices, and strategic logics. qualitative changes of system elements may then stem from changes of belief systems.

From the socio-cognitive perspective, the interdependence between various processes of building and leveraging competences and established system elements of a structural nature, such as routines and resources, is seen as crucial. The structural character of system elements is likely to yield competence leveraging rather than competence building (David, 1975; North, 1990). Consequently, qualitative changes of a few system elements are sometimes not sufficient to promote competence building.

TENSION AS A VEHICLE OF COMPETENCE BUILDING AND LEVERAGING

The content of relationships among collaborating firms can be explained by considering technical, political, economic, as well as cognitive ties. Here, the technical ties relate to functional interdependencies among assets, capabilities and competences as defined by Sanchez, Heene, and Thomas (1996); the political ties refer to interdependencies needed to exert power on third parties; the economic ties relate to interdependencies which include economics of scale and scope; and, finally, the cognitive ties reveal socially shared beliefs, about the way things are and the way things should be done, which govern and legitimize actions and interpretations. These ties or interdependencies among parties interacting through networks are sources of tension (Rosenberg, 1977; Dahmén, 1988). Tension may arise when there is a need for adaptation in one or more of these four dimensions (Stein, 1993). For instance, such an adaptation may result from technological progress by one party or from shifts in power structures or when firms follow different strategic logics about how resources should be deployed. Tension may also spring from interrelationships between the various kinds of ties. For example, technological change can potentially be induced, stimulated, and constrained by shared beliefs. Hence, tension can obviously both facilitate and inhibit competence building and leveraging.

On the basis of the case studies of Ericsson Components, ABB Signal, and CelsiusTech Systems, a distinction can be made between networks in which the interacting parties try to avoid tension and networks in which tension is accepted as a way of triggering and directing the competence of the respective firms. The behavior of the involved firms can be categorized into three groups: *exit*—i.e. when firms leave the network; *voice*—i.e. when firms try to absorb and diffuse information so that others will adapt to them; and *loyalty*—i.e. when firms adapt to the demands of others without resistance (cf. Hirschman, 1970). In general, exit is chosen when neither voice nor loyalty works as a way of achieving defined goals.

A distinction can also be made on the basis of how proactive a firm's behavior is in relation to others. Hence, highly proactive behavior is demonstrated by a firm which tries to promote competence building by leading the way with qualitative changes of system elements which disturb the balance among established interdependencies. Such behavior can obviously create substantial tension if most of the coordination of competences with other firms is based on a standardization of inputs, processes, outputs, and/or normative principles of governance (Dahmén, 1988). Other coordination mechanisms must fill the place of standardization if the collaborating companies are to receive the benefits of the division of competences. Despite the potential problems of proactive behavior, managers of all the three firms studied note that this can be a necessary pursuit if competence building, in particular, is to take place. To increase the dynamic or Schumpeterian efficiency of entire networks by building and leveraging competences is then believed to be crucial in order to increase the dynamic efficiency of the single firms. An important task for managers is, in their own view, to position the firms into networks that could meet their goals on competence building and/or leveraging. The managers add that they have had problems with firms which were highly reluctant or unable to adapt to the goals or solutions of others.

TENSION AS A WAY OF OVERCOMING COGNITIVE INERTIA

Tension among firms can create an awareness of *strategic gaps* as unacceptable shortfalls between perceived and desired state of any of the firm's system elements (Sanchez and Heene, 1996). Further, tension may create an awareness of new opportunities for how to close a strategic gap, as regards quantitative as well as qualitative changes of system elements. Gap-closing activities within firms can be separated from those which are related to system elements of networks. For instance, managers of the firms studied recall that they promoted quantitative or qualitative changes of system elements of suppliers or customers so that these could help them close strategic gaps. Hence, managers have even tried, and obviously succeeded in, changing the higher-order elements of strategic logics and managerial processes of other firms. In some cases, managers have changed not only the system elements of existing collaboration partners but also the very constellation of networks. That is, they have established new relationships and terminated old ones.

Tension can obviously help a firm to overcome what can be

referred to as cognitive inertia. In order to economize on their bounded possibilities to process information, individuals have difficulties in developing competences which do not conform with their experiences (Anderson, 1990). As observed by Sanchez and Heene (1996), cognitive limitations is a problem in the detection of strategic gaps. On social levels, shared beliefs (like strategic logics) may lead to such inertia in perceiving environmental changes. Positive feedback from the network or the environment in general is likely to stimulate competence leveraging with quantitative changes of system elements, whereas negative feedback appears to stimulate competence building with qualitative changes of system elements (Stein, 1993). It is crucial to note that belief systems, including strategic logics, influence what is to be considered as positive or negative feedback. Since several belief systems can exist in firms and networks, the interpretation of feedback may vary. More specifically, competence building with qualitative changes of system elements seems to involve a kind of deinstitutionalization process in which anomalies of institutionalized strategic logics and other belief systems are observed. In this "falsification process", anomalies can stem from at least three sources: when an established logic cannot close *emergent* strategic gaps; when other logics apart from the established one(s) can close *existing* strategic gaps better; and when those other logics can close emergent strategic gaps better. Such underlying tension can create an awareness of the need to undertake qualitative changes of system elements, thus helping people to overcome their cognitive inertia.

Some of the managers who were interviewed observe that it is important that all employees are active in trying to absorb and analyze feedback or "control loops" (Sanchez and Heene, 1996). It also appears as if managers do not always try to reduce ambiguity since this could harm the detection of strategic gaps. That is, if everyone shares the same world view, there is a risk that nobody will perceive things that question that world view.

In sum, tension is important in the "creative destruction" of established competences since they bring both problems and opportunities. It is likely that tension is of particular importance for firms in which it is not legitimate to question management practices and strategic logics.

DILEMMAS OF ORGANIZING NETWORKS

The case studies of three electronics firms reveal dilemmas involved in competence building and leveraging through networks. The dilemmas, which can be portrayed as dichotomies, are as follows:

- *Differentiation versus integration.* There is a trade-off between the need to divide competences and the difficulty of coordinating competences. The more fine-tuned the division of competences, the higher is the need for coordination. Several managers note that they often have underestimated this need for coordination.
- *Loose versus tight structure.* There can be problems associated with tightly defined routines, responsibilities, goals, etc. among organizations. A high degree of tightness can result in a lack of creativity and failure in building competences, whereas a high degree of looseness can lead to a lack of clarity. As observed earlier, standardization was viewed by managers interviewed as unsuitable when competence building was needed. Morever, according to managers a tight structure can cause problems if situations arise which have not been considered when structuring how things should be done.
- *Complementary versus substituting assets, capabilities, and competences.* A focus on complementary assets, capabilities, and competences can lead to gaps in work processes so that things are not carried out in order to achieve goals. On the other hand, a focus on substituting inputs can lead to extensive overlaps so that several firms are simultaneously engaged in doing the same thing. However, communication problems may arise among individuals who specialize in different fields of competence, which then call for some overlap.
- *Autonomy versus interdependence.* Autonomy can result in sub-optimization if the economics of scale and scope resulting from cooperation are not considered. However, excessive interdependence, which can be caused by efforts to coordinate competences, can lead to inertia when trying to promote dynamic efficiency. Strong interdependence can also make it difficult to terminate a cooperation, and managers can be forced to accept compromises if for various reasons they cannot change partner.
- *Symmetrical versus asymmetrical balance of power.* A symmetrical balance of power among interacting parties can result in slow decision making about competence building and leveraging. On the other hand, an asymmetrical balance of power can result in a situation where only one actor dictates the development so that few ideas are exchanged and creativity is hindered.
- *Coherent versus incoherent cultures.* A coherent culture can facilitate coordination but it can also hinder creativity since there is a risk that things are interpreted similarly or that ideas contrasting the dominant culture are subverted. On the other hand, incoherent cultures may work in the opposite direction so that it becomes difficult to implement a strategic logic.
- *Goal-bound versus goal-less strategy.* A goal-bound strategy induces the

building of competence that can inhibit flexibility to changes in that strategy and in the strategy of other firms. That is, to specialize assets, capabilities, and competences along the lines of a certain strategic logic can cause problems when that logic needs to be changed. An important example of this is the dilemma of cost leadership versus product differentiation—i.e. a strategy of cost leadership induces the building of competences that can inhibit product differentiation, and vice versa. However, the extreme of goal-less strategy may cause even more severe problems since there is no operationalized logic of how to sustain a coordinated deployment of assets. In such a situation of "strategic vacuum", the deployment efficiency will suffer.

- *Closeness versus openness.* A very open atmosphere may involve the risk that competences are disseminated to competitors, whereas a closed atmosphere can impede the dissemination of important information and the building of trust.

In order to tackle the dilemmas, managers at the three case companies tried various alternatives. That is, since they did not really know what the best solutions were, they experimented. Several managers note that they sometimes made the mistake of believing that they had found the right solutions. They add that experimentation needs to be handled with care in order not to cause confusion. In addition, they often tried to avoid extreme solutions, such as establishing either a very tight or a very loose structure.

The results from the case studies of Ericsson Components, ABB Signal, and CelsiusTech indicate more than many other studies the complexity and uncertainty of managing competence building and leveraging. Few things appear to be given. Managers are ambiguous of whether they are doing right or wrong. The old recipe of establishing order is no longer seen as the given solution, especially not when promoting competence building.

PREMISES FOR INTERPRENEURSHIP

Interorganizational collaborations offer opportunities to build and leverage competences beyond the reach of one single party. In order to take advantage of this combinatory effect *inter*preneurship, managers at the firms studied identified certain factors of importance:

- *Being committed.* One of the managers interviewed concluded: "Either you collaborate, or you don't!" He and many others stressed that collaborations have to be taken seriously. Resources have to be committed and people have to be involved. To achieve this, the collaborating parties have to share a certain level of aspiration. If one party has high aspirations and the other does not, collaboration is likely to fail. What appears to be needed is an aspiration to support the achievement of one another's goals.

- *Trust.* Without trust, smooth collaboration appears difficult. Besides contract costs (including control and enforcement), a lack of trust may lead to important information never being disclosed. Hence, trust often means lower transaction costs and that information of a higher quality can be communicated. Some managers emphasize that trust can be an advantage when communicating negative feedback. The relationships should be so strong that it is possible for the parties involved to express all their opinions and interests, but in a constructive way.

- *Being patient.* It takes time to develop well-functioning collaboration. This calls for patience, not passivity. Even though resources are allocated to collaboration, it can take a long time to build the necessary trust. To invest in trust-building activities can be useful in order to shorten the time. For instance, trust is probably more likely to be established if people meet face to face rather than on the phone. Since there seem to be few collaborations without conflict, one should carefully consider if it is worth-while to terminate collaboration due to a conflict.

- *Voice.* A constructive dialogue is crucial for dynamic efficiency. Collaboration should tolerate the communication of ideas and demands. For instance, it might be necessary to inform a party of what an alternative party can offer. If the dialogue does not work adequately, there is a risk that too little important information will be communicated too late.

- *Defining responsibilities.* Trust is essential, but so is the definition of responsibilities. At times, especially in the early stages of a collaboration, trust is not always enough to reduce the uncertainty of the parties involved. By defining responsibilities, a platform for future collaboration can be set. Notably, the degree of specialization of responsibilities is another issue. That is, even if a definition of responsibilities is needed, the degree to which these responsibilities are to be defined needs to be carefully considered.

Obviously, several factors are important in establishing well-functioning collaboration. Those discussed above can be regarded as some of the fundamental ones. After all, one has to believe that interorganizational collaboration can lead to competence building and leveraging—i.e. interpreneurship.

CONCLUDING COMMENTS AND IMPLICATIONS FOR RESEARCH

This chapter has been devoted mainly to synthesizing insights concerning coordination mechanisms which have an effect on competence building and leveraging through interorganizational networks. The management of interdependencies within as well as across organizational borders appears to be a complex task with several dilemmas involved. However, this challenge can be worthwhile given the benefits of a collaboration. Among the coordination mechanisms discussed, mutual adjustment seems to be on the advance in comparison to standardization and authority. The progress of information technology is revealed to be a reason behind this development.

The chapter has not only observed various coordination mechanisms involved in competence building and leveraging in networks but has also looked at how ties or interdependencies among firms can hinder as well as facilitate the development of competences. Managers of the firms studied reveal that at times they have actively tried to create tension in networks in order to start domino effects of change. The purpose has been to make entire networks sustain their competitiveness since this has been crucial for the competitiveness of their firms. Naturally, there are dilemmas involved in trying to manage competence building and leveraging across organizational borders. Some of these dilemmas have been addressed in this chapter.

As regards future research, additional research needs to be conducted on the subject of coordination. An important task, which only has been touched upon in this chapter, would be to disclose under what circumstances various coordination mechanisms promote competence building and leveraging, respectively. The management of competence-based competition is another area that needs to addressed in more detail since an emphasis on competences may lead to new roles for managers.

REFERENCES

Anderson, J.R. (1990). *Cognitive Psychology and Its Implications*. New York: Freeman.
Axelsson, B. and Easton, G. (1991). *Industrial Networks: A New View of Reality*. London: Routledge.
Barney, J.B. (1986). Strategic factor markets: Expectations, luck, and business strategy. *Management Science*, **32**, 1231–41.
Berger, P. and Luckmann, T. (1966). *The Social Construction of Reality: A Treatise in the Sociology of Knowledge*. London: Penguin Books.

Caves, R. (1987). *American Industry: Structure, Conduct, Performance.* Englewood Cliffs, NJ: Prentice Hall.

Cyert, R.M. and March, J.G. (1963). *A Behavioral Theory of the Firm.* Englewood Cliffs, NJ: Prentice Hall.

Dahmén, E. (1988). Development blocks in industrial economics. *Scandinavian Economic History Review,* **1,** 3–14.

David, P. (1975). *Technical Choice, Innovation, and Economic Growth.* Cambridge: Cambridge University Press.

Dierickx, I. and Cool, K. (1989). Asset stock accumulation and sustainability of competitive advantage. *Management Science,* **35,** 1504–11.

Douma, S. and Schreuder, H. (1992). *Economic Approaches to Organizations.* Englewood Cliffs, NJ: Prentice Hall.

Easton, G. (1992). Industrial Networks: a review. In Axelsson, B. and Easton, G. (eds), *Industrial Networks: A New View of Reality.* London: Routledge, pp. 1–27.

Freidson, E. (1986). *Professional Powers: A Study of the Institutionalization of Formal Knowledge.* Chicago, IL: University of Chicago Press.

Giddens, A. (1984) *The Constitution of Society: Outline of the Theory of Structuration.* Berkeley, CA: University of California Press.

Gorman, P., Thomas, H. and Sanchez, R. (1996). Industry dynamics in competence-based competition. In Sanchez, R., Heene, A. and Thomas, H. (eds), *Dynamics of Competence-Based Competition: Theory and Practice in the New Strategic Management.* Oxford: Elsevier, pp. 85–98.

Håkansson, H. (1987). Product development in networks. In Håkansson, H. (ed.), *Industrial Technological Development: A Network Approach.* London: Croom Helm, pp. 84–125.

Hallén, L. (1986). A comparison of strategic marketing approaches. In Turnbull, P.W. and Valla, J.P. (eds), *Strategies for International Industrial Marketing.* London: Croom Helm.

Hamel, G. and Heene, A. (1994). Conclusions: Which theory of strategic management do we need tomorrow? In Hamel, G. and Heene, A. (eds), *Competence Based Competition.* New York: John Wiley, pp. 315–20.

Hirschman, A.O. (1970). *Exit, Voice and Loyalty.* Cambridge, MA: Harvard University Press.

Kogut, B. and Zander, U. (1992). Knowledge of the firm, combinative capabilities, and the replication of technology. *Organization Science,* **3,** 383–97.

Laage-Hellman, J. (1987). Process innovation through technical cooperation. In Håkansson, H. (ed.), *Industrial Technological Development: A Network Approach.* London: Croom Helm, pp. 26–83.

Larson, M.S. (1977). *The Rise of Professionalism: A Sociological Analysis.* Berkeley, CA: University of California Press.

Leonard-Barton, D. (1992). Core capabilities and core rigidities: A paradox in managing new product development. *Strategic Management Journal,* **13,** 111–25.

Liljegren, G. (1988). *Interdependens och Dynamik i Långsiktiga Kundrelationer.* Stockholm: EFI.

Mintzberg, H. (1989). *The Structuring of Organizations.* Englewood Cliffs, NJ: Prentice Hall.

Nelson, R.R. and Winter, S.G. (1982). *An Evolutionary Theory of Economic Change.* Cambridge, MA: Belknap Press.

North, D.C. (1990), *Institutions, Institutional Change and Economic Performance.* Cambridge: Cambridge University Press.

Porter, M. (1980). *Competitive Strategy.* New York: Free Press.

Prahalad, C.K. and Hamel, G. (1990). The core competences of the corporation. *Harvard Business Review*, **82**, May–June.

Rosenberg, N. (1976). *Perspectives on Technology*. Cambridge: Cambridge University Press.

Sanchez, R. and Heene, A. (1996). A systems view of the firm in competence-based competition. In Sanchez, R., Heene, A. and Thomas, H. (eds), *Dynamics of Competence-Based Competition: Theory and Practice in the New Strategic Management*. Oxford: Elsevier, pp. 39–62.

Sanchez, R. and Thomas, H. (1996). Strategic goals. In Sanchez, R., Heene, A. and Thomas, H. (eds), *Dynamics of Competence-Based Competition: Theory and Practice in the New Strategic Management*. Oxford: Elsevier, pp. 63–84.

Sanchez, R., Heene, A. and Thomas, H. (1996). Introduction. In Sanchez, R., Heene, A. and Thomas, H. (eds), *Dynamics of Competence-Based Competition: Theory and Practice in the New Strategic Management*. Oxford: Elsevier, pp. 1–36.

Stein, J. (1993). *Strategy Formation and Managerial Agency: A Socio-cognitive Perspective*. Stockholm: EFI.

Teece, D.J. (1977). Technology transfer by multinational firms: The resource cost of transferring technological know-how. *Economic Journal*, **87**, 242–61.

Teece, D.J., Pisano, G. and Shuen, A. (1992). Dynamic capabilities and strategic management. CCC Working Paper, University of California at Berkeley, Berkeley.

Van Maanen, J. (1988). *Tales of the Field*. Chicago, IL: Chicago University Press.

Van de Ven, A.H. and Poole, M.S. (1990). Methods for studying innovation development in the Minnesota innovation research program. *Organization Science*, **1**, 313–34.

Weick, K. (1979). *The Social Psychology of Organizing*. Belmont, CA: Addison-Wesley.

Williamson, O.E. (1975). *Markets and Hierarchies: Analysis and antitrust implications*. New York: The Free Press.

Williamson, O.E. (1985). *The Economic Institutions of Capitalism*. New York: The Free Press.

Section V

Holism in Managing Competences

13

Dynamic Corporate Coherence and Competence-based Competition: Theoretical Foundations and Strategic Implications

JENS F. CHRISTENSEN, NICOLAI J. FOSS

This explorative chapter addresses the notion of "corporate coherence", recently made prominent by Teece *et al.* (1994). We argue that the literature is confused on the meaning of the notion (and similar notions) in a number of dimensions. We put forward a dynamic understanding of corporate coherence as involving the corporate capacity to exploit, for example, complementarities between assets, rather than simply exploiting static economies of scope. Dynamic corporate coherence is seen as the corporate capacity to successfully exploit and explore synergies from a diversity of competences, capabilities, and other resources. Moreover, we suggest a number of theoretical building blocks for approaching this notion of corporate coherence drawn from evolutionary economics, organizational learning theory, and organizational economics.

Competence-based Strategic Management.
Edited by Aimé Heene and Ron Sanchez.
Copyright © 1997 John Wiley & Sons Ltd.

INTRODUCTION

Over the last decade a large literature has examined the relationship between the resources (including assets and capabilities) of firms and their strategies. This literature incorporates what is usually referred to as "the resource-based perspective" (Wernerfelt, 1984; Barney, 1991). More recent work on "competence-based competition" extends resource-base ideas in several ways (Prahalad and Hamel, 1990; Hamel and Heene, 1994; Sanchez, Heene, and Thomas, 1996b). In this chapter we link directly with the latter approach.

Two overall strands of research have animated the development of resource and competence-based approaches. There is, first, an overall inquiry into the conditions of (sustained) competitive advantage. Work here is concerned with clarifying how and on what terms firms may obtain access to superior inputs that allow them to articulate rent-yielding strategies, and also with understanding which mechanisms may sustain competitive advantage (as surveyed by Barney, 1991, or Peteraf, 1993).

The second main strand of research concerns diversification; it approaches such issues as the profitability of related versus unrelated diversification (Montgomery and Wernerfelt, 1988) and the resource-basis of diversification (Chatterjee and Wernerfelt, 1991), etc.[1] In connection with this strand of research, the concept of "*corporate coherence*" has recently been seen as a core issue in an influential article by David Teece, Richard Rumelt, Giovanni Dosi and Sidney Winter, "Understanding Corporate Coherence: Theory and Evidence" (1994). Widely circulated and much-cited working papers and earlier versions of the article by Teece and his colleagues seem to be primarily responsible for the present popularity of the concept.[2]

But what *is* corporate coherence? There have been few attempts to define and analyze the concept. Moreover, as we will demonstrate, there are no unambiguous and fully satisfactory *definitions*, nor consistent *theoretical framework*, or a clear *managerial and strategic perspective* to be found in the literature.

With respect to the *definition* issue, we may ask: Should corporate coherence be seen as referring to an aspect of the growth process of

---

[1]Although the close links between the diversification issue and the competitive advantage issue were evident from the inception of the resource-based perspective (Wernerfelt, 1984), only quite recently have the two research efforts been explicitly woven together (e.g. Markides and Williamsom, 1994).

[2]Various other concepts and catchwords—such as "the dominant logic" (Prahalad and Bettis, 1986), "core competence" (Prahalad and Hamel, 1990) and the "stick-to-your-knitting" metaphor (Peters and Waterman, 1982)—are representative of closely related ideas.

the firm, to a relation (such as "relatedness") between the constituent assets of the firm at a given point of time, or perhaps to both of these? Moreover, should corporate coherence refer to similarities or relatedness between a firm's products or business lines in terms of technologies and market characteristics, to similarities between underlying resources, to competences, or perhaps to both of these?

In any case, the way one defines "relatedness" is critical to how corporate coherence is defined. However, the term "relatedness" is not unambiguous either; it is also in need of analytical clarification and definition. Should it be defined as broad "similarities" between different (e.g. existing and new) assets in terms of industries, businesses, products, markets or technologies? Or does it relate to economies of scope (asset sharing and asset transfer), to the possibilities of transferring competence between business units in the corporation, or to the ability to develop various types of synergistic learning dynamics? With respect to defining both corporate coherence and relatedness the existing literature gives us little guidance.

However, we suggest that insight may be gained from addressing corporate coherence from the *competence-based competition perspective* (Prahalad and Hamel, 1990; Markides and Williamson, 1994; Sanchez, Heene, and Thomas, 1996a,b). We supplement our competence-based discussion of corporate coherence with insights from the *organizational learning literature* (March, 1991; Levinthal and March, 1993) and from *organisational economics* (Williamson, 1985; Milgrom and Roberts, 1995).

Based on these sources, we put forward a dynamic understanding of corporate coherence that (1) emphasizes the *resource and competence* side of firms, rather than the product-market side, and (2) focuses on *"synergistic dynamics"* (e.g. dynamic complementarities between activities) rather than on economies of scope (economies from input sharing). Thus, while static corporate coherence refers to competence leveraging based on economies of scope, dynamic corporate coherence refers to competence building based on broader types of relatedness other than economies of scope.[3]

---

[3]In an evolutionary economics context (Nelson and Winter, 1982), dynamic corporate coherence may be seen as the corporate-level capacity to generate and exploit "economies of diversity". With "economies of diversity", we associate the evolutionary argument that more variations increase the probability of finding an "optimum" type of variation (at least within a given range), and the Schumpeterian argument that more diversity in terms of resources, competences, technologies, etc. increases the probability of making new combinations. Clearly, such economies are constrained by the context of the firm, such as the dominant logic of its management team; for example, no firm can handle a number of new variations or combinations that approaches infinity.

Based on these premises, we define dynamic corporate coherence as *the corporate capacity to successfully exploit and explore synergies from a diversity of competences, capabilities, and resources.*

As a first approximation, dynamic corporate coherence may be thought of as a particular quality of competence, since competence more generally refers to an ability to sustain the coordinated deployment of resources (both tangible and intangible) in ways that help a firm achieve its goals (Sanchez, Heene, and Thomas, 1996a). It draws attention to the explorative aspects of competence—more specifically, to the process by which firms qualitatively change their asset-mix, that is, to *competence-building.* Thus, we see dynamic corporate coherence as *the successful management of competence-building from a corporate-level perspective.*[4]

We contrast our dynamic concept of corporate coherence with the static notion of coherence that focuses attention on the existing portfolio of product or business lines and their relatedness in terms of economies of scope. In other words, whereas dynamic corporate coherence is a matter of the management of competence building, static coherence is only concerned with competence leveraging. It is our general conjecture that the dynamic notion of coherence is highly relevant to a competence-based approach to corporate strategic management, while the static notion is useful primarily for short-term operational efficiency objectives.

We also argue that *theory* relating to corporate coherence is far from settled with Teece *et al.* (1994) (or other contributions, including the present one). They suggest a number of relevant theoretical building blocks for approaching corporate coherence, but do not consistently incorporate more "micro-theoretic' insights derived from the competence-based, organizational learning, or organizational economics literature in the discussion. In contrast, these are precisely the kind of insights that we plan to incorporate in our approach to corporate coherence, which takes its starting point in the work of Teece *et al.* (1994). We end by drawing a number of implications for corporate strategic management of our discussion.

CORPORATE COHERENCE: PREVIOUS CONTRIBUTIONS

In this section we briefly review existing literature that has a bearing on the issue of corporate coherence. On this basis we put forward

---

[4]In addition, one could interpret dynamic corporate coherence in terms of the option framework outlined in Sanchez and Thomas (1996). Since the terminological complexity is already considerable in this chapter, we shall refrain from doing so.

our own understanding of corporate coherence. We first discuss Penrose's contribution to the understanding of corporate coherence. Her work provided important inspiration for three streams of research and associated interpretations of coherence, which we discuss in turn:

1. The more empirically oriented literature on corporate diversification giving rise to an interpretation of coherence in terms of related diversification
2. The early "resource-based" literature on the growth process of firms (for example, Rubin, 1973; Wernerfelt, 1984) leading to an interpretation of coherence as a matter of balanced growth
3. The understanding of firm differentials in terms of asset or competence profiles resulting in a coherence perspective focusing on the interconnectedness of the constituent resources and competences of the firm.

PENROSE ON DIVERSIFICATION AND COHERENCE

Within the resource- and competence-based literature of recent years, Edith T. Penrose's seminal contribution, *The Theory of the Growth of the Firm* (1959), has become a standard reference, because of its role as a precursor of modern thinking on resources and competences of firms. Penrose (1959: 24) defines the firm as "a collection of productive resources the disposal of which between different uses and over time is determined by administrative decision". The coherence issue enters the agenda already in her opening discussions of the decisive features of the firm:

> One important aspect of the definition of the firm for our purposes, then, involves its role as an autonomous administrative planning unit, the activities of which are interrelated and are coordinated by policies which are framed in the light of their effect on the enterprise as a whole (1959: 15).

We should remember, however, that Penrose was explicitly concerned only with *successful* firms. Thus, such firms are by definition "coherent" in the broad sense that they efficiently coordinate interrelated resources and activities and assess the implications of those decisions for the firm as a whole; that is, they balance the need to specialize with the need for integration across functions and business units. This is clearly in conformity with a "holistic" perspective on the firm represented by, for example, Prahalad and Hamel (1990) and

points towards a notion of coherence as asset or competence interconnectedness (more about which later).

However, Penrose's primary theoretical contribution concerns the
growth process of the firm. As she argues, there are fundamentally
three significant obstacles precluding the firm from settling down in an
"equilibrium position" with no further internal incentive to expand:

> Those arising from the familiar difficulties posed by the indivisibility
> of resources; those arising from the fact that the same resources can be
> used differently under different circumstances, and in particular, in a
> "specialized" manner; and those arising because in the ordinary
> process of operation and expansion new productive services are con-
> tinually being created (1959: 68).

Thus, growth (including diversification) may result from an attempt
to exploit more fully idle resources (the opportunity cost of doing so
being zero), existing resources, and those continuously created "in the
ordinary process of operation and expansion". To dress Penrose's
reasoning in more modern garb, the growth of the firm is largely a
result of learning by doing (in operation and in management) and of
explorative learning (e.g. in R&D). This growth is articulated in
increasing and "coherent" diversification. What is "coherent" diversification, according to Penrose, is to a large extent a matter of the
knowledge and perceptions of the management team, since the firm's
productive opportunity set is itself a cognitive category (Penrose,
1959: 5).

As Penrose also points out, innovation is based on existing
resources—even when they lead to products that are radically new
both to the firm and to the consumer (e.g. Penrose, 1959: 84). This
introduces a seeming paradox. Even if growth is strongly path-
dependent with respect to the firm's resources and competences, the
manifestation in terms of new *product-markets* may be seen to be
almost wholly "unrelated" to existing product-markets. Nevertheless,
such a firm may exhibit coherence, because the coherence in question
is a matter of underlying competences and the cognition of the
management team rather than a matter of products.

In economics, specialization in the sense of the production of a single
product has normally been seen as incurring a premium in terms of
increasing productivity, while multi-product production has been
associated with decreasing productivity (or, so it was until the advent
of the concept of economies of scope). This should constitute an
argument for "coherent growth" through specialization and disintegra-
tion (e.g. Stigler, 1951). However, firm growth, beyond a certain size
level, nearly always involves diversification and some of the most

successful and efficient firms are highly diversified. From the competence perspective, the reason must be that the relevant dimension of specialization is not in terms of products but rather in terms of competence.

COHERENCE AS RELATED DIVERSIFICATION

Often from a perspective that views specialization in terms of resources and competences rather than products as critical, a burgeoning empirical literature has studied the relationship between corporate diversification and performance.[5] Yet no unanimous pattern of results has emerged. Richard Rumelt's 1974 study is one of the early important contributions, and the overall result of his research—that related diversifiers perform better than unrelated diversifiers on average has become almost conventional wisdom in much of the strategy literature.

However, subsequent studies have shown inconsistent results, some confirming Rumelt's results, others showing that firms involved in unrelated diversification are at least as profitable as those involved in related diversification (see e.g. Grant, Jammine, and Thomas, 1988). One fundamental problem in most of the empirical work on diversification and relatedness is that traditional measures of relatedness look only at the industry or market level—*not* at the level of competences, capabilities, or assets.[6]

In fact the standard measures of relatedness may sometimes indicate industry or market similarities that do not provide any potential to exploit these similarities for competitive advantage.[7] On the other hand, much of what is measured as unrelated diversification may actually provide dynamic synergies in terms of competences and strategic assets (we return to this issue later).

COHERENCE AS AN ASPECT OF THE GROWTH PROCESS OF THE FIRM

A conceptualization of corporate coherence as referring to the growth process of the firm has been suggested by resource-based scholars

---

[5]Ramanujam and Varadarajan (1989) provide an overview of the literature.
[6]However, there are a few papers that try to address relatedness in terms of underlying resources and competences; see, for example, Farjoun (1994).
[7]This is what Markides and Williamson (1994: 155) term "exaggerated relatedness".

inspired by Penrose (1959), such as Paul Rubin (1973) and Birger Wernerfelt (1984). Rubin (1973) constructed a dynamic programming model in which human resources are worth more to the firm than their market value because of specialized experience within the firm. Resources may be used either for production or for "training" new resources. This introduces a trade-off, and the problem may be solved in a dynamic programming framework, yielding the optimal time-path of investments and the optimal growth pattern.

In his 1984 article Birger Wernerfelt also addressed optimal growth and constructed a "resource–market matrix" in analogy to product portfolio theory to help him study optimal growth. One of Wernerfelt's main points was that in managing a resource portfolio, resources should not only be evaluated in terms of their present use, but also their immediate use in related diversification. They should also be evaluated in terms of their longer-term capacity to function as stepping stones to further expansion by the firm (Wernerfelt 1984: 179)—or, what is referred to in the modern competence-based competition literature, their ability to support "*competence-building*" (Sanchez, Heene, and Thomas, 1996a). Optimal growth becomes therefore a matter of finding the optimal trade-off between exploiting resources in present uses and using them for developing new resources.

Hence, in terms of the intertemporal framework introduced by Rubin and Wernerfelt, coherence may be seen as an aspect of the relation between the addition of new activities and the exploitation of existing ones. More precisely, in this framework corporate coherence becomes essentially the name for a particularly favorable trade-off between these two meta-activities (addition/exploitation). However, the nature of the trade-off is ill understood as are the determinants of the optimum trade-off.

COHERENCE AS ASSET INTERCONNECTEDNESS

A final understanding of coherence to be discussed here refers to the interconnectedness of the constituent resources or competences of the firm. Teece (1986) analyzes the role of complementary resources for the commercialization of technological innovation, and Christensen (1995) analyzes profiles of assets for technological innovation. Both the tradeability of the assets and the degree of interconnectedness between the assets involved (types of innovative assets involved in producing technological innovation, or between a product innovation and the complementary assets required to appropriate the rent from the innovation) are considered decisive parameters in determining make-or-buy decisions and creating a competitive advantage. Whereas there is a tendency in the resource-based approach to treat resources as singular distinct items (Peteraf, 1993), this approach highlights resource configurations and the ways in which resources and competences are nested within the firm or in inter-firm relations.

So far, this approach has primarily focused on configurations of resources and competences at *a given point of time*, and has not considered interconnectedness in a dynamic perspective—for example, how learning within a given activity may assist learning within other activities over time (e.g. marketing and R&D). Moreover, the nature of links between resources and the synergistic effects of such links are not fundamentally accounted for, except perhaps by pointing to the presence of economies of scope. Assuredly, economies of scope are important but they are only a small part of the meaning of corporate coherence.

For example, the concept of economies of scope does not capture the presence of dynamic (Edgeworth) complementarities (Milgrom and Roberts, 1995) between activities and resources, that is, the situations in which doing more of one activity (such as building an asset) increases the return from doing more of another (such as building another asset).[8] Economies of scope are a matter of a given production function and given cost functions; it refers only to costs and it does not allow for a changing asset mix. In contrast, the concept of complementarities is inherently more dynamic, for example, because it implies that processes of asset accumulation may feed on each other in an ongoing manner (Milgrom and Roberts, 1995). The exploitation of such complementarities is an important part of our understanding of dynamic corporate coherence.

TOWARDS A DYNAMIC UNDERSTANDING OF CORPORATE COHERENCE

Although the above contributions all have some bricks to add to the coherence building, none of them have erected the entire edifice. The insight that we associate with Penrose (1959)—that corporate coherence involves a *dynamic* dimension through growth-based learning, path

---

[8]A general example of such complementarities is network externalities. In the context of strategy research, Dierickx and Cool's (1989) notion of "asset-stock interconnectedness" is an example of a dynamic complementarity. In the conventional (economic) understanding, complementarities are present when the marginal returns for a variable is increasing in the levels of other variables. Utilizing lattice theory, Milgrom and Roberts (1990, 1995) demonstrate that the theoretical understanding of complementarities is not restricted, however, to situations in which the objective function is continuous.

dependence, and the accumulation of heterogenous knowledge resources—is not captured by associating coherence with the rather static concept of economies of scope, nor by associating it with relatedness (in terms of product markets) in diversification. Thus, our position is that we should in this sense go back to Penrose, and update her reasoning in terms of the competence-based literature.

In our view, this leads to an understanding of *dynamic corporate coherence* as, in a nutshell conceptualization, *the corporate capacity to exploit and explore synergies or new combinations from a diversity of competences, capabilities, and assets.*

The key words in the above definition are "corporate", "explore", and "synergies". As they indicate, achieving dynamic coherence necessitates some measure of strategic intent and centralized control ("corporate capacity"), involves discovering and acting on opportunities for combining existing competences and developing new ones ("exploring") (cf. Kirzner, 1973), so that new synergies—new complementarities—may be realized. In the following section we provide a number of theoretical building blocks that are necessary for approaching this understanding of corporate coherence. We argue that elements from both evolutionary economics and organizational economics are needed.

SOME ELEMENTS OF A THEORY OF DYNAMIC CORPORATE COHERENCE

INSIGHTS FROM EVOLUTIONARY ECONOMICS

A notable attempt explicitly to analyze the concept of corporate coherence is Teece *et al.* (1994). Their approach is based on evolutionary economics and they take as starting points three characteristic features of the modern corporation that are in need of an explanation: (1) its multi-product scope, (2) its non-random product portfolio, and (3) the relative stability in the composition of its product portfolio. Their concept of corporate coherence exclusively relates to multiproduct corporations:

> . . . a firm exhibits coherence when its lines of business are related, in the sense that there are certain technological and market characteristics common to each (Teece *et al.*, 1994: 4).

In the latter part of their paper they come somewhat closer to a "competence-based" conception of corporate coherence. The firm is there defined as an integrated cluster of competences and supporting complementary resources, and coherence is a quality of the relations between the constituent competences, corresponding to the notion of coherence as asset interconnectedness (see above).

The primary importance of the Teece *et al.* paper does not lie in the way in which they operationalize the notion of corporate coherence. Rather, its importance is in the fact that they have put the concept of coherence on the agenda of corporate strategy research, and, moreover, have taken the first steps in proposing some building blocks in a theory of corporate coherence.

Specifically, they argue that an understanding of corporate coherence requires the incorporation of essential elements of evolutionary economics—such as organizational *learning* dynamics within the firm, *path-dependency* characteristics, the dynamics of *complementary resources* (in, for example, restricting or providing new growth options and broadening the scope for "coherent diversification"), the depth and scope of *technological opportunities* in the neighborhood of the firm's present technological competences and R&D investments, the dynamic/static features of *firm competences* (both organizational and technological), and structural characteristics of *the selection environment*.

Organizational learning dynamics may be slow or rapid depending on the internally embedded routines and the technological opportunities available to the firm. Path-dependency may be high or low, tight or broad, depending on the nature of existing competences and supporting complementary resources and on the nature and richness of the technological opportunities that the firm faces. The selection environment may be tight or weak, depending on the strength of competitive forces, public policy and the nature of technological development (e.g. the frequency of technological discontinuity). Three fundamental propositions can be distilled from these insights:

- In the long run more coherent corporations tend to outperform less coherent corporations.
- The degree of corporate coherence is a function of the interaction between (a) learning dynamics in the firm, (b) path dependencies (as shaped by existing competences and complementary resources and technological opportunities), and (c) the selection environment.
- The tighter the selection environment, the more likely it is that the boundaries of the corporation are drawn "close in" to the competences (Teece *et al.*, 1994: 22) and that fewer coherent corporations will be outperformed.

We are in broad agreement with the above general propositions and theoretical reasoning. However, there are (at least) two issues which further research on corporate coherence should address in order to gain a more consistent theoretical framework. First, the evolutionary building blocks and their interdependencies should be better specified. We suggest that the recent studies on organizational learning and competence-based theory of strategic management could contribute to a better micro-theoretical foundation of the theory of corporate coherence. Second, the evolutionary building blocks do not provide any insights on internal organization and agency problems associated with corporate coherence. Thus, we find that organizational economics can contribute more significantly to a theory of corporate coherence than is recognized by Teece *et al.*

Insights From the Competence-based Competition Perspective

Because it explicitly focuses on the dynamic and managerial dimensions of competences and organizational learning, we submit that the competence-based competition perspective (Prahalad and Hamel, 1990; Doz 1995; Hedlund, 1994; Markides and Williamson, 1994; Teece and Pisano, 1994; Sanchez and Thomas, 1996; Sanchez, Heene, and Thomas, 1996a,b) is particularly likely to provide important micro-theoretical inputs to a more fine-grained theory of corporate coherence.

In fact, Prahalad and Hamel's (1990) notion of core competence as "the collective learning in the organization, especially how to coordinate diverse production skills and integrate multiple streams of technology" comes rather close to the notion of corporate coherence. Both concepts signify a corporate-level systemic capacity to create value and competitive advantage by exploiting resources and capabilities within the corporate framework. However, while Prahalad and Hamel tend to associate (in their examples, if perhaps not in their definition) the notion of core competence with a specific— although broad and more or less corporate-wide—technological competence (such as the miniaturization competence of Sony and the optical-media competence of Philips), our notion of corporate coherence is not confined to a specific functional and technological competence.

Rather, it signifies a corporate-level strategy *and* capacity to exploit and explore economies of diversity; it refers to the competence that allows the corporation to develop and recombine capabilities and assets) and exploit synergies between competences within a diverse portfolio of competences.[9]

The dynamics of competences and capabilities have been specified in different ways in recent contributions to the theory of competence-based competition. First, taxonomies of *competence dynamics* have been developed. For example, Sanchez, Heene, and Thomas (1996a) suggest a distinction between three categories of dynamics, as it were: "Maintaining competences" (which exist in order to avoid asset erosion), "leveraging competences" (i.e. applying existing competences to current or new market opportunities that require quantitative changes in stocks of resources that are similar to already existing resources), and "building competences" (i.e. creating new abilities to coordinate and deploy new or existing assets and capabilities, and thus, creating new options for the firm's future). Doz (1995) proposes three similar categories, but he also gives explicit attention to two other categories or dimensions of competences, namely "competence diffusion" (or competence transfer and sharing) and competence integration, which is the ability to integrate specific elements of know-how etc. into wider value-creating competences.

Markides and Williamson (1994) relate the issue of competence dynamics to the strategy of related diversification. They distinguish four types of potential advantages of related diversification that also account perfectly to the potential advantages and ways of pursuing corporate coherence, and reflect the dynamic interplay between what they term "strategic assets" and "core competences".[10]

- *"Asset amortization"*: The potential to reap economies of scope across SBUs that can share the same strategic asset

---

[9]Along similar lines, Teece and Pisano (1994) argue that "A hierarchy of competences/ capabilities ought to be recognized, as some competences may be on the factory floor, some in the R&D labs, some in the executive suites, *and some in the way everything is integrated*" (p. 541; our emphasis). Teece and Pisano (1994) term this higher-order competence "dynamic capability" and relate it to the role of strategic management ". . . in appropriately adapting, integrating, and re-configuring internal and external organizational skills, resources, and functional competences toward changing environment" (p. 538). In order to better grasp this distinction between lower and higher-order competences, Sanchez, Heene, and Thomas (1996b) propose a terminological distinction between capabilities ("repeatable patterns of action in the use of assets to create, produce, and/or offer products to a market" (p. 8)) and competence ("an ability to sustain the coordinated deployment of assets in a way that helps a firm achieve its goals" (p. 9)). Likewise, Doz (1995:3) defines organizational competences as "integrative task performance routines that combine resources (skills and knowledge, assets and processes, tangible and intangible) to result in superior competitive positions".

[10]Core competences in the sense of "the pool of experience, knowledge and systems, etc. in the corporation that can be deployed to reduce the cost or time required either to create a new strategic asset or expand the stock of an existing one" (Markides and Williamson, 1994: 150).

- *"Asset improvement"*: The potential to use a competence accumulated in the course of building/maintaining a strategic asset in one SBU to help improve an existing strategic asset in another SBU
- *"Asset creation"*: The potential to utilize a competence developed through the experience of building strategic assets in existing businesses, to create a new asset in a new business
- *"Asset fission"*: The potential for the process of related diversification to expand a corporation's existing pool of core competences because as it builds strategic assets in a new business it will learn new skills that in turn will allow it to improve the existing assets in existing businesses.

Markides and Williamson (1994) further argue that only the "asset dynamics" in which (core) competences play an active role (i.e. in the three latter categories) can provide the firm with a long-term competitive advantage. Thus, the first category ("asset amortization") that exclusively involves exploiting the existing stock of assets can only offer short-term advantages in the form of reduced costs and improved differentiation. The three other categories involve both "competence building" and "competence leveraging" as well as "competence diffusion" (or transfer) and "competence integration". In economic terms, these three categories refer to different kinds of dynamic complementarities rather than to economies of scope.

We suggest sharpening our view of dynamic corporate coherence not only to include the capacity to pursue these forms of competence and asset dynamics within the corporation *but also to balance the trade-off between the different categories* (or a combination of categories).

In recent work on organizational learning this issue has been analyzed in terms of the trade-off between *exploitation* of existing competences, capabilities, and assets, on the one hand, and *exploration* of new competences, etc., on the other. As James March (1991: 71) says, firms

> . . . that engage in exploration to exclusion of exploitation are likely to find that they suffer the costs of experimentation without gaining many of its benefits. They exhibit too many undeveloped new ideas and too little distinctive competence. Conversely, firms that engage in exploitation to the exclusion of exploration are likely to find themselves trapped in suboptimal stable equilibria.

Clearly, the categories of competence dynamics referred to above may be directly related to this trade-off. Thus, it is intuitively obvious that the "asset amortization" and "asset improvement" categories reflect different dimensions of the exploitation notion, while "asset creation" and "asset fission" reflect two dimensions of explorative efforts. Similarly, competence leveraging belongs to the exploitation dimension, while competence building belongs to the competence exploration dimension.

The critical aspect of dynamic corporate coherence relates to finding the appropriate balance between exploitation and exploration (and their respective sub-categories). Levinthal and March (1993) have shown that features inherent to the learning process may contribute to distort the exploitation/exploration balance: Either exploration drives out exploitation ("the failure trap") or—probably a more common problem—exploitation drives out exploration ("the success trap"). From the perspective of competence-based competition, a key managerial task is to avoid these traps—in effect, to achieve dynamic corporate coherence.

Another important aspect of dynamic corporate coherence relates to finding the appropriate balance between exploiting and exploring competences through unstructured emergent processes or through explicit rules, programmes, incentives, and control (Doz, 1995). A third, but related, aspect deals with the "tight–loose" dimension of the corporate organization of competences.

While the notion of corporate coherence involves the capacity to exploit relatedness and interdependencies between competences, capabilities and assets, this does not *necessarily* imply a general advocacy for "tight coupling" and strongly centralistic management. However, it *does* imply considerably less decentralization than in the traditional M-form organization with free-standing strategic business units, and much more intensive information flows. In the following section we draw on organizational economics in order to address this.

INSIGHTS FROM ORGANIZATIONAL ECONOMICS

As mentioned above, Teece *et al.* (1994) approached the coherence issue from an explicitly evolutionary position. This may have led to their playing down the potential analytical role of organizational economics (except for a few references to the importance of asset specificity and complementary assets). Moreover, they did not really have much to say about *internal organization.*[11]

We argue that the internal organization issues investigated in organi-

---

[11]It may be noted that recent work on competence-based competition also has not had much to say about internal organization in the context of contractual economics.

zational economics may have a bearing on the corporate coherence issue. As we state, the dynamic corporate coherence issue falls in a class of *organizational design problems with innovation attributes*, it raises the standard incentive issues connected with team-production, and it involves information and control costs of various sorts.

Design Problems and Innovation Attributes

In the context of organizational economics, coordination problems with design attributes ("design problems" in short) are problems with two specific features. First, there is some knowledge of the form of the optimal solution, that is, how relevant variables should be related (for example, the effort levels of workers in a team). Second, failing to achieve the right relation between the variables is more costly than other errors, including minor misspecifications of the overall pattern, as long as the individual activities fit (Milgrom and Roberts, 1992: 91). Mundane examples may be a team sport, the performance of a ballet company or a symphony orchestra. These are examples of synchronization problems; assignment problems may be other examples. Firms often solve design problems by routinization which makes possible a certain amount of decentralized decision making (Nelson and Winter, 1982).

But decentralization often performs poorly to the extent that the optimal resource allocation significantly depends on the use of knowledge that is not given to personnel at the operating level (Milgrom and Roberts, 1992: 92). Organizational restructuring, new product launches, the stimulation of inter-divisional knowledge flows, etc. are examples of design problems with an *innovation attribute*. These problems favor intensive knowledge flows and some extent of centralized control. Obtaining dynamic corporate coherence is also fundamentally a design problem with innovation attributes—it cannot be achieved without intensive communication and some measure of centralized control.

The Coordination of Complementary Activities

The reason for the need for intensive knowledge flows and centralized control is that divisional (and presumably also functional) activities in a dynamically coherent organization are complementary. As stressed by Markides and Williamson (1994), the relatedness that really matters is that between "strategic assets", such as the mechanical engineering competence in a specific division, the marketing competence in another division, etc. Although strategic assets may certainly not always be transferable across SBUs/divisions, a competence gained in the process of building or maintaining an existing strategic asset in one division/ SBU may be used as a catalyst to improve the quality of an existing strategic asset in another (Markides and Williamson, 1994: 156). Thus, important relatedness effects may arise because learning obtained in one SBU may be transferred to another SBU, and vice versa. Thus, the accumulation of asset stocks in different divisions/SBUs may feed on each other in a self-reinforcing way. Asset improvement, asset creation, and asset fission (Markides and Williamson, 1994) are all examples of such complementary activities, or, more technically, highly Edgeworth complementary activities (Milgrom and Roberts, 1990, 1995)—doing more of one of the activities increases the yield from doing more of the other activity.

Traditionally, it has been argued that such activities are best governed inside the firm (Malmgren, 1961), since internal governance eases the coordination of complementary activities and dampens opportunistic proclivities. Thus, the theme of relatedness in terms of complementary competence-building activities has important implications for the boundaries of the firm (see also Foss, 1993). Moreover, it has strong implications for the role of management. This is so because our understanding of corporate coherence implies—in line with the competence literature in general (e.g. Prahalad and Hamel, 1990)—a much less decentralized view of the corporation than has been standard fare, and accordingly necessitates more coordinative skill and effort on the part of top management. Since many of the tasks of top management directly turn on coordination issues, they directly involve information/coordination costs and incentive issues.

Information Costs

Information costs emerge in connection with design problems. For example, how should knowledge flows between divisions take place? who should be the key persons? Is there a need for cross-functional teams? For purposes of economizing on information costs, such design variables need to be determined by senior management, consulting with division and business unit managers—and the more so, the more divisions are involved, the stronger the knowledge flows, etc.

Even if we assume away any agency problems, and assume that

non-opportunistic agents in good faith assist in the achievement of *strategic goals* (cf. Sanchez and Thomas, 1996), there would still be a need for coordination, necessitating actions on the part of top management. Formally, this is so because the organizational pay-off to the actions of any one agent will still depend on the actions of other agents. Theoretically, if perhaps not in practice, such design decisions are logically and temporally primary relative to the incentive issues considered below.

Team Production and Incentive Issues

Since Alchian and Demsetz (1972), much of the work on optimal incentive configurations has been conducted within a team production framework. Technically, team production is production with non-separable production functions. A result of team production is that it is hard, perhaps even impossible, to tell the marginal product of each team member. All that can (easily) be observed is team output, and remuneration of agents have to be on the basis of the size of their joint output. This creates incentive problems, since the effects of reduced effort will be distributed throughout the team. The solution to this incentive problem is to appoint an employee to monitor team production. Moreover, in order to provide incentives for efficient monitoring, the monitor should be given title to residual profit streams.

Obtaining dynamic corporate coherence in our sense means that production will become more team-like (essentially because more complementarities and more complexity become involved). By implication, monitoring becomes less effective, since it becomes increasingly difficult to ascertain the contributions of individual team members, for example divisional managers. Thus, rather than engaging in monitoring, the role of top management is to provide the right incentive contracts (Holmström, 1982). However, because of the difficulties of ascertaining individual effort, team incentives may in fact be higher powered than individual incentives.

While one of the traditional advantages of the M-form is the relative ease of monitoring and providing incentives for the individual division, the coherent organization implies interdivisional cooperation. This may be supported from an incentive perspective by providing team incentives in the form of, for example, profit bonuses for divisional managers that are linked to *corporate* rather than to divisional profitability. On the other hand, basing payment schemes on team output reintroduces the original Alchian and Demsetz problem:

agents may still be subject to free-riding shirking by other members of the team. To the extent that agents want to be compensated for this risk, the coherent organization may incur agency costs that are not encountered in less coherent organizations.

Clearly, these agency costs may be substantially reduced by managerial action such as infusing employees with a corporate ethos. As Oliver Williamson (1985) explains in connection with what he calls "the relational team":

> The firm here will engage in considerable social conditioning to help assure that employees understand and are dedicated to the purposes of the firm, and employees will be provided with considerable job security, which gives them assurances against exploitation (p. 247).

Thus, a corporate ethos has at least two important roles in connection with dynamic corporate coherence. First, when agents differ in terms of their representations of the environment, there must exist a body of shared knowledge that can further the coherence of the various learning processes. This is the *cognitive* function (Prahalad and Bettis, 1986, refer to this as "the dominant logic"). Second, a corporate ethos helps keep agency problems at bay. This is the *incentive* function. The efficient working of both of these functions are crucial to dynamic corporate coherence.

However, providing "social conditioning" is certainly not a cost-less activity. On the whole, it seems reasonable to conclude that a firm that is coherent in our dynamic sense is likely to incur costs that are not confronted by a less coherent (more traditionally decentralized) organization. For example, Williamson (1975: 149) says that

> Optimum divisionalization involves: (1) the identification of separable economic activities within the firm; (2) according quasi-autonomous standing (usually of a profit centre nature) to each; (3) monitoring the efficiency performance of each division; (4) awarding incentives; (5) allocating cash flows to high yield uses; (6) performing strategic planning (diversification, acquisition, and related activities) in other respects.

Dynamic corporate coherence makes problematic virtually all these points. For example, it introduces costs of identification of separable activities, of monitoring, of awarding incentives, etc. that are not encountered by the traditional divisionalized, diversified firm. These costs should be balanced against the benefits of increasing dynamic coherence. Thus, we again encounter the observation that a key task of top management in the coherent organization is to balance the need for static efficiency, here in the form of low or moderate agency costs, with the need for dynamic efficiency in the form of developing competences, spawning new products, etc. (cf. Ghoshal and Mintzberg, 1994).

DYNAMIC CORPORATE COHERENCE: IMPLICATIONS FOR STRATEGIC MANAGEMENT

We suggest that a theory of corporate coherence based on insights from both evolutionary economics (including a competence-based view of the firm) and organizational economics will prove fruitful in providing practical guidelines for corporate management—particularly in large diversified corporations. At this stage, however, implications for management and strategy can only be tentatively indicated; something which we try to do in this section. We present the relevant implications in connection with three important issues relating to the strategy and structure of diversified corporations: (1) The strategy of related diversification, (2) the M-form organizational structure, and (3) the competence strategy.

FROM "RELATED DIVERSIFICATION" TO "EXPLOITATION AND EXPLORATION OF SYNERGIES"

Corporate coherence in our dynamic sense is not necessarily a matter of resources having to be "similar" or "close" in some technical or physical sense, or even in terms of skills. "Similarity" in these senses is (at best) a poor indicator of the dynamic concept of corporate coherence that we pursue. In our conception, similarity or closeness is rather an indicator of the comparative ease with which inter-asset synergies can be exploited (and later communicated and imitated within the organization). It is not a matter of objective similarity but essentially of subjective similarity. Since dynamic corporate coherence is the managerial or corporate capacity to exploit economies of diversity, the relevant relatedness resides inside the heads of the management team—not unlike the way in which Prahalad and Bettis (1986) described what they called "the dominant logic".[12]

---

[12]Analyzing the "Japanese way" of diversifying, Hedlund (1994) proposes an interpretation of relatedness close to our interpretation, and points out the inherent difficulties of operationalization: "Thus, Japanese diversification is "related" but "relation" is defined generously, and can only be understood in a company-specific, experimental framework, where the limits are set by the potential synergies given by intensive dialogue and combinatorial possibilities" (Hedlund, 1994: 82).

Thus, it is no coincidence that the quantitative literature on the impact on returns of different degrees of relatedness have produced ambiguous results (Grant, Jammine, and Thomas, 1998). If relatedness is firm-specific and has large cognitive components, this must be so. What is "related" to one firm will not be "related" to another—and this will be revealed in large-scale empirical investigations. Since relatedness is essentially a concept that is specific to the individual company, a first managerial implication is a negative one: objective measures of similarity or relatedness cannot be relied upon in general, since they may not measure the strategically relevant relatedness. They may therefore be poor guides to strategies of diversification.

There is some evidence (e.g. Campbell, Goold and Alexander, 1995) that often strategies of related diversification are based on what Markides and Williamson (1994) term "exaggerated relatedness" in which similarities are exploited with little potential for competitive advantage—for example, because the similar assets are non-strategic or easily imitable, or because the market-specificity of the related strategic assets is underestimated by the diversifier.

The positive implication is that management should stimulate the exploitation of "real" synergies, from the more static "asset amortization" and "asset improvement" mechanisms that exploit economies of scope or help to improve the quality of existing strategic assets and competence leverage, to the more dynamic types of synergies ("asset creation" and "asset fission") that involve asset and competence building (that is, dynamic complementarities). Moreover, it is also a critical task for corporate management to constantly monitor and influence the trade-off balance between the exploitation of existing versus the exploration of new competences, capabilities, and assets (and commercial territories), and especially to avoid the tendency to devote too much attention on exploitation—due to its mostly more urgent character and more certain returns—at the expense of exploration, the returns of which are both more uncertain and more distant in time (Levinthal and March, 1993).

FROM A "CORE" COMPETENCE STRATEGY TO A DYNAMIC CORPORATE COHERENCE STRATEGY

Corporations that want to exploit synergistic economies cannot base their corporate strategy on traditional portfolio management techniques, nor can they base their organizational structure on the conventional, decentralized M-form. Since the beginning of the 1980s many firms and corporations have pursued a "stick-to-your-knitting" strategy. This philosophy has led many firms to focus on their core businesses and shed the businesses they acquired when dominant management philosophies favored diversification. Although it may very well have refined excellency in existing areas, the "stick-to-your-knitting" philosophy may also have lead to lock-in positions due to too much exploitation and too little exploration.

In introducing the notion of core competence, Prahalad and Hamel (1990) proposed a somewhat clearer understanding of what were the positive implications of the "stick-to-your-knitting"metaphor, namely that firms should build portfolios of businesses around distinctive "core" competences. These are often illustrated in terms of specific (but broad and corporate-wide) *technological* competences, or aggregates of technological capabilities centered around complementary critical capabilities (e.g. Gallon, Stillman, and Coates, 1995).

Our notion of dynamic corporate coherence is not confined to such an interpretation. Rather, dynamic corporate coherence refers to a corporate-level capacity to exploit and explore "economies of diversity". That involves not only the nursing of existing competences but also sometimes the building of new competences and reconfiguring existing ones to match new technological opportunities and changing competitive environments.

Moreover, it involves a critical issue in corporate strategy that has not been adequately handled within the competence framework. This is the corporate parenting issue that has recently been addressed by Campbell, Goold, and Alexander (1995). In contrast to the core competence notion of Prahalad and Hamel (1990), the parenting notion focuses attention on the parent organization, and on its ability to create value for the businesses it owns

> that occurs when the parent's skills and the resources fit well with the needs and opportunities of the businesses. If there is a fit, the parent is likely to create value. If there is not a fit, the parent is likely to destroy value (Campbell, Goold, and Alexander, 1995: 122).

In a corporate parenting perspective, dynamic corporate coherence is a matter of exploiting synergies not only horizontally (i.e. across divisions and businesses) but also vertically, that is, between corporate headquarters and its staff functions and the individual businesses. This latter synergy (or "parenting advantage", as Campbell, Goold, and Alexander term it) may involve as diverse areas as R&D in product innovation (for example, a central research lab that has strong interactive relations to R&D units in the individual businesses), accounting techniques and financial control, manufacturing competences, human resource management, safety and regulation, or product branding.

FROM THE DECENTRALIZED M-FORM TO THE "SYNERGISTIC" M-FORM CORPORATION

Beginning with Prahalad and Hamel (1990), there has been a tendency in the competence-based literature to be highly critical of the more decentralized versions of the M-form corporation, which is thought to promote myopic static efficiency because of its divisionalized structure, focus on financial synergies, and profit-center orientation.

Although on the right track, this critique of the M-form and static efficiency has also tended to forget about the incentive advantages of the M-form as well as the incentive liabilities of a corporation organized on the principles outlined in, for example, Prahalad and Hamel (1990). Our discussion indicates that severe latent agency problems exist in an organization that is dynamically coherent. The old problem of finding the optimal trade-off between static and dynamic efficiency has been abandoned, in the emerging competence-based literature, in favor of dynamic efficiency. Managers cannot completely neglect static inefficiencies, simply because they carry their own cost penalties.

At the same time, it must be recognized that while diversified corporations exerting only static coherence (focusing on tight interdependencies and exploitation of existing competences) may very well be competitive at the shorter term, they do not possess the leverage capacities and incentives for long-term strategic change. As a result, they tend to become locked into trajectories that gradually diverge from those dominating the industry.

CONCLUSIONS

In this chapter we have surveyed the literature on corporate coherence and have put forward an explicitly dynamic conception of coherence. We conceptualized dynamic corporate coherence as the corporate capacity to exploit and explore synergies or new combinations from a diversity of competences, capabilities, and assets. Thus, we saw coherence as being "corporate" in the sense of spanning divisions and "dynamic" in the sense of emphasizing competence building. This understanding with its focus on dynamic complementarities should be contrasted with, for example, the static notion of coherence contained in the concept of economies of scope.

Addressing the concept of corporate coherence has also allowed us to put forward new implications of significance for the theory of competence-based competition and for corporate strategy. For example, corporate coherence in our dynamic sense is not necessarily a matter of resources having to be "similar" or "close" in some objective sense. "Similarity" is (at best) a poor indicator of the dynamic concept of corporate coherence that we are seeking. Moreover, based on reasoning from organizational economics, we pointed out that the benefits of increased corporate coherence should be balanced against the possible losses resulting from increased agency costs.

ACKNOWLEDGEMENTS

The comments of Esben Sloth Andersen, Max Boisot, Bo Eriksen, Kirsten Foss, Aimé Heene, Christian Knudsen, Peter Lotz, John McGee, Ron Sanchez and two anonymous referees are gratefully acknowledged. The usual disclaimer applies.

REFERENCES

Alchian, A.A. and Demsetz, H. (1972). Production, information costs, and economic organization, in Alchian, A.A. (ed.), *Economic Forces at Work*. Indianapolis: Liberty Press.

Barney, J.B. (1991). Firm resources and sustained competitive advantage. *Journal of Management*, **17**, 99–120.

Campbell, A. Goold, M. and Alexander, M. (1995). Corporate strategy: the quest for parenting advantage. *Harvard Business Review*, **73(2)**, 120–132.

Chatterjee, S. and Wernerfelt, B. (1991). The link between resources and type of diversification; theory and evidence. *Strategic Management Journal*, **13**, 33–48.

Christensen, J.F. (1995). Asset profiles for technological innovation. *Research Policy*, **24**, 727–745.

Dierickx, I. and Cool, K. (1989). Asset stock accumulation and sustainability of competitive advantage. *Management Science*, **35**, 1504–1511.

Doz, Y. (1995). Managing core competency for corporate renewal: towards a managerial theory of core competences. Working paper, INSEAD.

Farjoun, M. (1994). Beyond industry boundaries: human expertise, diversification, and resource-related industry groups. *Organization Science*, **5**, 185–199.

Foss, N.J. (1993). Theories of the firm: competence and contractual perspectives. *Journal of Evolutionary Economics*, **3** 127–144.

Gallon, M.A., Stillman, H.M. and Coates, D. (1995). Putting core competency thinking into practice. *Research Technology Management*, May-June, 20–28.

Ghoshal, S. and Mintzberg, H. (1994). Diversification and diversifact. *California Management Review*, **37** 8–27.

Grant, R.M., Jammine, A.P. and Thomas, H. (1988). Diversity, diversification, and profitability among British manufacturing companies, 1972–84 *Academy of Management Journal*, **31**, 771–801.

Hamel, G. and Heene, A. (1994). *Competence-Based Competition*. Chichester: John Wiley.

Hedlund, G. (1994). A model of knowledge management and the N-form corporation. *Strategic Management Journal*, 5 (Special Issue) 73–90.

Holmström, B. (1982). Moral hazard in teams. *Bell Journal of Economics*, 13, 324–340.

Kirzner, I.M. (1973). *Competition and Entrepreneurship*. Chicago, IL: University of Chicago Press

Levinthal, D. A. and March, J.G. (1993). The myopia of learning. *Strategic Management Journal*, 14, 95–112.

Malmgren, H.B. (1961). Information, expectations, and the theory of the firm. *Quarterly Journal of Economics*, 75, 399–421.

March, J.G. (1991). Exploration and exploitation in organizational learning. *Organization Science*, 2, 71–87.

Markides, C.C. and Williamson, P.J. (1994). Related diversification, core competences and corporate performance. *Strategic Management Journal*, 15, (Special Issue), 149–166.

Milgrom, P. and Roberts, J. (1990). The economics of modern manufacturing: technology, strategy and organization. *American Economic Review*, 80, 511–528.

Milgrom, P. and Roberts, J. (1992). *Economics, Organization, and Management*. Englewood Cliffs, NJ: Prentice Hall.

Milgrom, P. and Roberts, J. (1995). Complementarities and fit: strategy, structure, and organizational change in manufacturing. *Journal of Accounting and Economics*, 19, 178–208.

Montgomery, C.A. and Wernerfelt, B. (1988). Diversification, Richardian rents, and Tobin's q. *RAND Journal of Economics*, 19, 623–632.

Nelson, R.R. and Winter, S.G. (1982). *An Evolutionary Theory of Economic Change*. Cambridge, MA: The Belknap Press.

Penrose, E.T. (1959). *The Theory of the Growth of the Firm*. Oxford: Oxford University Press.

Peteraf, M.A. (1993). The cornerstones of competitive advantage. *Strategic Management Journal*, 14, 179–191.

Peters, T. and Waterman, R. (1982). *In Search of Excellence*. New York: Harper & Row

Prahalad, C.K. and Bettis, R. (1986). The dominant logic: a new linkage between diversity and performance. *Strategic Management Journal*, 6, 485–501.

Prahalad, C.K. and Hamel, G. (1990). The core competence of the corporation. *Harvard Business Review*, 68, 79–91.

Ramanujam, V. and Varadarajan, P. (1989). Research on corporate diversification: a synthesis. *Strategic Management Journal*, 10, 523–551.

Rubin, P.H. (1973). The expansion of firms. *Journal of Political Economy*, 936–949.

Rumelt, R.P. (1974). *Strategy, Structure, and Economic Performance*. Harvard University, Graduate School of Business Administration, Harvard.

Sanchez, R. and Thomas, H. (1996). Strategic goals. In Sanchez, R., Heene, A. and Thomas, H. (eds), *Dynamics of Competence-Based Competition: Theory and Practice in the New Strategic Management*. Oxford: Elsevier.

Sanchez, R., Heene, A. and Thomas, H. (1996a). Towards the theory and practice of competence-based competition. In Sanchez, R., Heene, A. and Thomas, H. (eds), *Dynamics of Competence-Based Competition: Theory and Practice in the New Strategic Management*. Oxford: Elsevier.

Sanchez, R. Heene. A. and Thomas, H. (eds) (1996b). *Dynamics of Competence-Based Competition: Theory and Practice in the New Strategic Management*. Oxford: Elsevier.

Stigler, G.J. (1951). The division of labour is limited by the extent of the market. *Journal of Political Economy*, **59**, 185–193.

Teece, D.J. (1982). Towards an economic theory of the multiproduct firm. *Journal of Economic Behavior and Organization*, **3**, 39–63.

Teece, D.J. (1986). Profiting from technological innovation: implications for integration, collaboration, licensing and public policy. *Research Policy*, **25**, 285–305.

Teece, D.J., Rumelt, R.P., Dosi, G. and Winter, S.G. (1994). Understanding corporate coherence: theory and evidence. *Journal of Economic Behavior and Organization*, **23**, 1–30.

Teece, D. and Pisano, G. (1994). The dynamic capabilities of firms: an introduction. *Industrial and Corporate Change*, **3**, 537–556.

Wernerfelt, B. (1984). A resource-based view of the firm. *Strategic Management Journal*, **5**, 171–180.

Williamson, O.E. (1975). *Markets and Hierarchies*. New York: Free Press.

Williamson, O.E. (1985). *The Economic Institutions of Capitalism*. New York: Free Press.

14

Reflection as a Building Block for Strategic Thinking and the Development of an Organizational Philosophy

Wanda D'Hanis, Luc Perneel

This chapter addresses the need for fundamental reflection as the basis for organizational structures and economic activities. We give a brief analysis of the alienating characteristics of the modern economic system. The gap between economic thinking and fundamental reflection is the origin of the failure to overcome the permanent crisis in which business life is involved. Therefore we trace briefly the bridge between managerial areas of attention and the fundamental questions in human reflection. This gives us the possibility to offer new building blocks for the concept of strategy and leadership.

Competence-based Strategic Management.
Edited by Aimé Heene and Ron Sanchez.
Copyright © 1997 John Wiley & Sons Ltd.

INTRODUCTION

Traditionally business strategy has been formulated as the answer to the rapidly changing *external* factors every business is facing. The primary purpose of this strategy is to sustain the continuity and stability of the organization.

Up to the beginning of the 1980s strategic activity was more or less the exclusive occupation of a special department within the company. But in the last ten years it has penetrated deeper into the organization. The working out of strategic *planning*, for example, now occurs in consultation with line management. From the mid-1980s onwards the conviction has grown that it is better to give managers insight into the determinative external factors than to confront them with correctly calculated but nevertheless unreliable forecasts.

This trend has continued to the present day. Within the organization short decision lines and fast reaction possibilities are regarded as the best means of survival. This has led, among other things, to the setting up of Business Units.

These changing strategies and their positioning within the organization also make new demands on Human Resources Management. Every modern personnel manager is now familiar with terms such as self-management, self-empowerment, internal leadership, and ownership. However, the success of this evolution in the concept and realization of strategic thinking has a number of important consequences. There is not only radical restructuring, systematic redundancies, and the moving of production centres to low-wage countries but, as a result of many European and other mergers, companies also are more frequently faced with problems caused by the multicultural content as well as by the intersubjective character of their new management.

SOCIAL RELEVANCE

Never before have the consequences of strategic decisions been felt so far outside the company. It seems as if industrial groups are, with increasing frequency, moving their activities outside the company under the claim of strategic necessity. As a result, business problems gradually become *social* problems.

The conclusion we reach is: managerial, i.e. economic and social responsibility, are no longer to be separated. This therefore requires that business strategy is rethought.

Within many companies the necessity of such renewal is already recognized by a great number of its employees. Examples of this are the renewed interest in business ethics and business codes and, in general, the interest in rethinking business processes (D'hanis, 1994).

THE GREAT FAILURE

In an embarrassing way, the latest crisis has demonstrated how strategic thinking has by and large failed to provide an adequate response purely to external business factors. The question is whether this is due to weaknesses in strategic thinking itself or whether it is the intractable nature of these external factors. Or perhaps there is still another reason for this failure?

Mintzberg (1994), for example, does not believe in the turbulence of the times as the reason for this failure: ". . . What we really face are not turbulent times but overinflated egos". As philosophers, we are more inclined to agree with Peter Senge's (1990) suggested explanation of the mental models managers use, as well as with the view that economic instability is not the result of external factors but of the way managers think, or do not think (Hamel and Prahalad, 1994). The success of a business indeed is not only ensured by exchange rates or relative wage costs, but overall by management's strength of vision. In other words, as a result of their lack of adequate thought and vision, many managers will never be successful in warding off crises. And their failure will result in an endless wandering in search of solutions that do not reach beyond the limits of their *safe* systems and their trusted paradigm.

GROWTH ECONOMY: ASYMPTOTIC INFINITY AND THE FEATURES OF A SURVIVAL STRATEGY

One of the basic features of our economic system is (preferably unlimited) *growth*. However, businesses increasingly are confronted by what is said to be diminishing marginal returns. Also, the tried and tested "solutions", such as exporting to new markets and the spiral of ever more expensive marketing campaigns, are likely to prove unable to escape this *asymptotic inevitability* of the limits to growth.

In contrast, the apparent impossibility of continued growth creates a feeling of unease and paralysis among an increasing number of managers. In fact, they lack the creativity to go beyond the system. By and large "profit" is still conceived and maintained in terms of reducing costs. In such a situation the asymptotic behaviour of the economy and the lack of creative solutions reduce the strategic activity to a series of survival tactics which often consist of no more than program planning for cost reductions. The employees—regarded in this as human capital—are reduced to a factor in the *calculus* of the reduction strategy. Let us summarize the features of such a survival strategy.

ORGANIZATIONAL LEVEL

Traditionally, the organizational level where strategic activity happens to be developed is strictly hierarchically determined. Even in the recent forms of business units, the strategic activity often remains limited to the *top managerial* level. The performing divisions in contrast are not, or are only minimally, involved in the development of the strategy itself.

LOGICAL DEDUCTION

In most businesses, strategy is mainly derived via the laws of *deductive* logic (the modus ponendo ponens), which therefore turns it into merely strategic planning. Strategic action is considered as being the unavoidable consequence of a given, specific situation. This means that strategy is mainly formulated within the framework of the common system of thinking. Dealing only with competence leverage is the consequence of an already established culture. On the other hand, competence building is conceived as a risky business since this involves dealing with an uncertain future (Sanchez and Heene, 1996).

REDUCTIONIST CHARACTER

The reductionist approach to strategy means reduction in the sense of restriction and decrease, turning into smaller amounts (e.g. cost reduction). A more fundamental meaning of reductionism is that of transforming a problem into a smaller (i.e. *manageable*) one that therefore can be solved. As they resolve such a manageable problem, managers assume that the fundamental problem has also been remedied. In so doing, general business problems—e.g. problems concerning management development—can be reduced and treated as if they only were related to cost reductions (e.g. external consultancy versus domestic) or technical problems (e.g. the development of technical skills).

QUANTITATIVE EFFECT

When formulating objectives the *measuring* culture prevails. Everything is supposed to be quantified and/or reduced to a quantitative standard. The idea of quality itself does not survive.

THE REALIZATION OF OBJECTIVES

Strategic planning remains dominated by management by *objectives*. As this is also encouraged by offering narrowly defined incentives, the danger of suboptimization and overindividualization is never far away.

REDUCTION TO LONG-TERM "PLANNING"

In recent decades strategic activity has been increasingly stripped of its *visionary* character. It has lost the *coherence* of thinking, feeling, and action. Traditional aspects of firms have became scarce, such as nurturing craftsmanship, the passing on of organizational knowledge, and the looking to the future from a position of respect for the past. When strategic planning is considered to be forward looking, it is hardly more than an exclusive focus on and calculation of future actions, whatever they may be (competence leverage).

CONCLUSION

These impoverishing elements are the main reason for the failure of the strategy as a business answer to external factors. The question immediately arises as to whether the crisis was created by economic factors or is it a structural crisis of human thinking and acting and therefore also a crisis of management?

THE CURRENT ECONOMIC PARADIGM IS AN ALIENATING ONE

The above mentioned asymptote of the growth economy also has an indirect effect on the world of meaning, ethics, reflection, and human values. It is as if a wedge has been driven between an economy and the rest of human life. The denial of the human factor in managerial activities irreversibly leads to alienation. Many people have this real and immediate sense of alienation. Never before has the frustration and stress level of managers been so high—not because of pressure of work but because of the personal experience of this alienation. Economic thinking has now overruled people and gone over the heads of individuals. As a result of the lack of fundamental vision and of the capacity to develop ideas, many of those economically powerful managers fail to define a really new way of working and of living—for themselves as well as for their employees.

CAPITAL VERSUS VALUES

This kind of *discrepancy* inevitably will lead to the essence of Human Resources Management. The employees of tomorrow will no longer wish to be validated according to their economic value but they will want to be respected for their human values as well, i.e. the idea of *human capital* becomes replaced by that of *human value*. Only such an approach will enable individual employees to re-establish the unity between their work and private life and between values and earnings. It is time for leaders in general and personnel managers in particular to take into account such serious developments. These problems can only be approached fundamentally and therefore not from within the existing system nor through merely leveraging present HRM capabilities. Therefore all this requires an essentially new strategic approach and the building of new HRM competences.

HISTORICAL BACKGROUND

One of the main reasons for the scarcity of genuinely renewing solutions in organizations is the lack of historical perspective as mentioned above. Most organizations give their employees no time or space for the development of a *constructive dialogue with the past*. Therefore they miss the *critical* awareness that is the basis of development of all visionary ability and dynamic thinking. In contrast, in many companies critical questions of individuals', uncontrolled creativity and their ability to transcend short-term problems are stifled.

Both the economic life and its action culture as well as philosophy and its highly abstract, *unworldly* reflections are the cause of the discrepancy between economic thinking and the world of fundamental reflection. While the economy upgraded its quantitative approach and made it the only measure for its actions, reflection was downgraded to an academic discourse whereby any reference to practical situations is preferably avoided. This is one of the many reasons why philosophy has lost contact with the world of business.

Today strategic thinking seems to be basically determined by a dominant orientation towards the future (the survival strategy). This can be seen from the terminology used, which is very similar to "planning" terminology: short, medium and long term. Yet Mintzberg (1989) was referring to Kierkegaard when he said that "life is lived forwards but understood backwards". Another philosophical theme tells us that in order to change reality, you first have to understand it. This quote is entirely applicable to business strategy: business strategy must focus on the future, but the strategy can only be understood from the point of view of the past. The creation of all true strategy therefore is the well-known synthesis of the past (competence), the present (competence leverage) and the future (competence building) (Sanchez, Heene, and Thomas, 1996a,b).

Today, however, some signals pointing to changes are to be perceived in the new trends in industrial thinking. Within the businesses the dominant way of thinking has started to evolve away from *product-oriented* towards *process-oriented*. And more recently automation has stimulated the change from information-oriented thinking to *quality awareness*.

However, even during this evolution, that which is quantifiable has again been preferred to values, in the sense that the objectivity of values and therefore their acceptance depends upon the extent to which they are measurable, i.e. definable in terms of quantitative entities and, as a result, universally communicable. Although values are communicable, they are never mentioned in the context of the proper character of "scientific" objects. With values it is not simply about "being"—as objects of positive science are used—but of "being in force", however this may be expressed. Quality "control" therefore risks reducing the essence of quality itself.

Nevertheless, it seems to come to a fundamental transition now that the trend to ecological thinking may be irreversible. Never before has any particular form of transition of the "profit-maximizing motive" towards "social awareness" had such a radical influence on business processes. A typical effect is, for example, the surprisingly fast change-over from end-of-the-pipe purification techniques to ecological business processes. The evolution of the eco-industry suggests the historical necessity of such a paradigmatic change.

CLEAN BUSINESS

Without any doubt, ecological thinking provides increasing opportunities for strategy renewal and innovation of organizational structures.

Indeed in its own way ecology itself initiates thinking concerning values within the business processes. Therefore, businesses which pursue a value pattern inspired by social responsibility with regard to nature and the environment in fact reintroduce the ecology of human thinking and acting.

During discussions on the implementation of ecological policy, the question of exorbitant costs is often raised. However, the effective implementation of this policy is increasingly regarded as being necessary, irrespective of cost. Moreover, the ecological revolution in turn appears to provide new economic opportunities. For the future we see the same scenario with regard to investments in *the ecology of human thinking and acting.*

REFLECTION AS A BASIS FOR A NEW ORGANIZATIONAL STRUCTURE

Every business has four main areas of organization: strategy, realization, function, and execution. The strategic area of the organization is represented by top management and the management team, the realizing area by the R&D, engineering, logistics and other departments, the functioning area by the staff and the executing area usually is said to be the "floor".

In recent decades these four areas each became specialized separately and gradually became one another's competitors. This has led to excessive suboptimalization and an increasing amount of hidden costs (Sanchez and Heene, 1996).

Four Points for Attention

Here we retain the division into these four areas. However, we do not regard them as building areas of an organization but rather as areas for special attention. We will therefore treat them as *points for attention*, i.e. as *shapes* of the total business and of its integral thinking. This integral thinking is not the sole property of the intellect but a dialectic interaction between the head, heart, and soul of the manager.

The four areas of attention are activated by four fundamental questions, and each of these questions requires its own dynamics. (Table 14.1 and Figure 14.1).

On the basis of this thinking model we can define the domains in Table 14.2. These domains are the results of mental activities. However, they are also the means of providing structure to our actions

TABLE 14.1

Areas of attention	Fundamental questions	Thinking dynamics
1. Strategy	What may I hope?	Inspiration
2. Operations	What can I do?	Practical plan
3. Policy	What should I do?	Reflection
4. Execution	Am I doing it correctly?	Reactive thinking

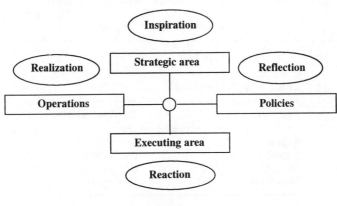

FIGURE 14.1

based upon the way we think. This structure will also form the basis for an organization in which reflection, i.e. the demand for meaning and values, will be included. Every area therefore asks for a special thinking profile (Table 14.3).

The relationship between these domains is determined in organizations by the specific economic objectives of the business, in the case of both profit and non-profit making businesses (Figure 14.2). The latter is, in turn, to be regarded as a fundamental part of the totality of social and human objectives.

In most organizations these domain structures are directly translated into departments which lead a life of their own and concentrate on achieving their specific objectives. In this sort of business there is little unity in reflection, thinking, and acting, in spite of their elegant new house styles.

TABLE 14.2

Domain	Formed by
1. Organization	The strategic and operational area (engineering) and thus the result of hope and practical ingenuity
2. Infrastructure	The planning and executing area and thus the result of realization and reaction
3. Culture	The strategic and policy area and thus the result of inspiration and evaluation
4. Standards	The policy and executing area and thus the result of moral reflection and practical feedback

TABLE 14.3

Domain	Thinking profile
Organization	Entreprising
Infrastructure	Producing
Culture	Integrating
Standards	Managing

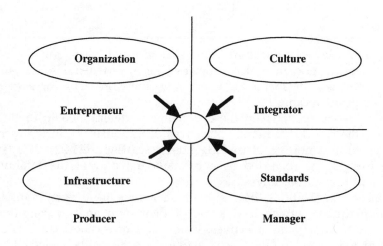

FIGURE 14.2

THE VARIOUS STAGES OF THE STRATEGIC PROCESS

The driving force for turning the objectives into a central source of power lies with the management. The "in-unison" thinking of the management then becomes concrete, being converted into the various stages which together form the strategic process.

The first step within the strategic process is the development of a *vision*. This is the explicit definition of the dream and the intuition top management has about the business. This first step is mainly based on a thorough education which should be as broad as possible. The second step is the working out of the *operational* and the *policy strategy*. In this stage we work at the level of the organization as a whole and we are in the "learning process". The last step in making the strategic process concrete is the *operational* and *policy execution* This is the area of planning. In this stage we are at the technical level, the translation into execution. However, in reality this often occurs the other way round. The plan is drawn up first, then extra training is given quickly to arrive finally at the conclusion that a general education is lacking.

These three steps towards concrete management thinking are usually found in the various departments within a business. In other words, each department (e.g. production, logistics, finance) has its own strategic team. But this often is only active at the planning level, which we suggested was the lowest level.

This is a fundamental mistake. If these teams were also to evaluate operational and policy execution and, not least, the development of a vision, then this could help form the basis for what we consider to be a *radical* change in strategic activity since we consider strategy as consisting of three components: as a *meaning*-giving issue, as an *organizational* issue and as a *planning* issue.

DOES RADICALITY ALSO MEAN RE-ENGINEERING?

The development of the strategy and the organization starting from a thinking model instead of a reductionist deductive one which is controlled by formulated objectives is, of course, a radically different approach. One of the most recent trends in management literature suggests the idea of *re-engineering* as a possible solution. In this radical questioning of the processes and the above mentioned reflective model, the term *radical* is the most important element, although these two approaches are fundamentally different.

The radicality of re-engineering is radicality within the system itself.

In the reflective model, on the other hand, radicality is the necessary condition for developing consistent and coherent thinking that creates the necessary space for working out a new dynamic system. This system must flexibly anticipate the economy as the momentum of a social total occurrence and this from the natural synthesis of the past, present and future, as mentioned above.

In this respect re-engineering only has a chance if it is an element of a total rethinking of the economic occurrence. Radical rethinking, as suggested in our reflective model, is divided into the following three stages.

BUSINESS RE-ANIMATION

The stage of business re-animation forms the basis for developing the vision. Working out the vision is usually nothing but *inspiring* the business operation, i.e. dealing with and reflecting explicitly on competence building and scoping its uncertainty. Giving shape to this attitude also provides inspiration for real leadership and ensures the authenticity of the business vision. An inspired vision—business re-animation—is created as a result of reflection on people and their world views in relation to the world of business which one wishes to develop. It takes economic activity back to its original sources, those of *successful life*. Working only makes sense if true human happiness is the aim, not just good fortune—i.e. wealth and power—but a good life for everyone involved in the process. It is at this level that there is an opportunity to call a halt to the alienation which has developed over the years and afflicts life in the West. This opportunity can be taken or ignored, and it is those at the top in business who must play a decisive role in this. As mentioned above, this presupposes a level of education, as broad as possible, not just limited to the culture of "doing things as much as possible".

BUSINESS REVALIDATION

In the second stage the vision takes on a more concrete form. This is the area of strategy as an organizational issue. The revalidation process gives back the full meaning to ethical terms, and to that of *responsibility* in particular. In this context business ethics are nothing but the explicit formulation of the reflection on the concrete business operation itself, the way in which the human relationships are developed *well* within a company, both in everyday practical matters and in important strategic decisions. Business ethics in that sense is not to be considered as another variation of the many trendy management tools.

This means that a number of characteristics and attitudes must be urgently revalidated, characteristics and attitudes which make human life *good*, characteristics which therefore can heal the discrepancy of modern business. Here we find the ultimate remedy for stress and the only authentic realization of quality management.

BUSINESS PROCESS RE-ENGINEERING

The last stage in the development of business is the stage in which the strategy manifests itself as *planning*. The special attention for the operational area takes shape as a result of the process of *communicative action*.[1] This is more than just a series of communicative skills to ensure that the message is transmitted free from interference. As the explicit realization of reflection, communicative action affects the very essence of intersubjectivity. It is the practice in which individuals basically rely on each other in their actions and in their thinking. Individuals literally ignore themselves. The culture of *individual* achievement, self-development and morality comes to an end.

This means that in a future-oriented business the interests of the business and of the individual no longer conflict. It is also because of the essential character of *communicative action* that we can speak of true business process re-engineering (BPR). We know that process-oriented thinking and working without constant interaction between thought and action remains an illusion.

The basic condition for an effective implementation of communicative action is working out, technically and strategically, the provision of an information strategy which, in addition to the bits and bytes, is also everyone's responsibility. Interference-free transmission of information then becomes much more than a psychological attitude, it becomes an objective, measurable fact, the profitability of which can rapidly be demonstrated.[2] The provision of information is then no longer the

---

[1] In our management development programs we apply the notion of communicative action following the theory of Habermas (1981, 1988). For further information contact Nikè Consult c.v.b.a., Brasschaat, Belgium.

[2] Through a well-developed and well-used information system only the first aspect of communicative action (interference-free transmission as the objectivity of a communicative psychological attitude) is realized. In addition, the capability of argumentation as well as the development of ethical awareness ensures the impartiality of the content (psychological attitude—logical argument—ethical awareness and the combination of those three aspects being the basis of communicative action). See footnote 1.

status symbol of a limited group within a business but the working instrument which, if properly maintained, demonstrates its worth daily.

Anyone wishing to remove the alienation between human action and thinking, on the one hand, and the world of economic thinking, on the other, cannot avoid a fundamental renewal of strategic thinking as described above. Going through the three above-mentioned stages may help to assure that the necessary *radicality* is obtained.

THE UPRIGHT MANAGER: AUTHENTIC LEADERSHIP

The integrity of the manager (i.e. *authentic leadership*) provides the necessary condition for solving the alienation between thinking and acting and therefore between economically and industrially oriented organizations and social intersubjective responsibility. Authentic leadership is characterized by a *three-part responsibility* which is sustained by charisma. The three areas of this responsibility are as follows:

1. The strategic ethical area: the care and responsibility for true human happiness in the long term, concerning the individual as well as society; in other words: the explicit awareness and conduct as following the notion of limitation of mere self-interest
2. The communicative and informative area: the care and responsibility for the realization of the immediate prerequisites of area 1
3. The area of total quality: the care and responsibility for the actual realization of area 1.

Charisma is based on the three features discussed below.

LOOKING FORWARD

A manager is only forward-looking when he or she is not influenced by the *compulsiveness of immediacy*. It is this compulsiveness that is the basis of the instability of many organizations. Within these organizations planning is no more than an illusion. Stability and flexibility are on the level of thinking and not on that of execution. Only on the basis of this mental stability can intersubjective trust develop. Real leaders succeed in passing this attitude on to employees. They do so in the first place by creating the necessary time and space to allow their employees to play a full part in the realization of the vision as a basis for further explicit formulation. This participation is, at the same time, the best guarantee for a correct decision-making process.

CONSISTENT APPLICATION OF A SYSTEM OF VALUES

Real authentic leadership is not accidental nor is it without *commitment*. It is also sustained by a consistently applied system of values. Within the business it is also the basis for *shared responsibility* and for the *freedom* of thinking and acting. This freedom is necessary in order to sustain responsibility. In turbulent times this system of values, experienced as being real, provides the mental stability and continuity mentioned above.

INTEGRAL THINKING AND ACTING

On the basis of an explicit vision and a system of values a stable *coherence* between thinking and acting can be achieved. Further suboptimization within departments becomes impossible because thinking and acting is always present as the continuously dynamic process within the business. It takes into account the qualities of the individuals present but always allows the whole to take precedence over individual interests.

Authentic leadership is also characterized by an *internal* factor. The theoretic and psychic maturity as well as the moral development of the leader are decisive for an individual's charisma. An individual's attitude to the business and employees as well as his concern for its position with regard to society all play a decisive role. Finally, authentic leadership is also visibly and tangibly present through the communication of the whole for which business leaders stand.

THE FIRST STEP IN THE REALIZATION IS THE REMOVAL OF FEAR: THE CREATION OF TRUST

In order to realize this radical renewal within the organization a business leader is primarily asked to earn the trust of the whole organization. To do this he or she must first overcome the employees' fears in an ethical way and then combine their renewed trust into a dynamic force. This task is often strewn with old problems: *collective uncertainty*, isolated group behaviour, and ineffective changes in behaviour, for example, will only disappear by removing individual fear patterns.

One of the most important but unexpressed fear factors which stands in the way of obtaining cooperation with radical changes is uncertainty with regard to the individual *job*. Radical changes as discussed here do not necessarily have to be job threatening.

It is different with regard to the fear for individual *status*. Status is not an aim in itself. The fear of losing status says much about the individual's capacity for bearing real responsibility. We are not arguing in favour of wage levelling but simply wish to point out that the status cult is repeatedly the basis of arguments for disputing the equality of people. In any case, it does not seem self-evident (any longer) that business status should be determined purely *hierarchically*. In the case of the radical renewal described above it is not about hierarchic power but about the responsibility of every employee as an individual.

This individual responsibility can only be assumed when individual capability can be called upon. This can, in itself, be a source of fear because this seldom occurs in practice. For example, the presupposition of having a particular knowledge—and therefore the proper authority—is often still linked to hierarchic position. Whatever the case, working out a vision within the organization will provide significantly more insight, particularly if this vision is also based on a system of values that are really *lived*.

Nevertheless, our experience shows that many employees fear such a system of values which provides insight. The reasons are varied: the unambiguity and strong link between one's thinking and acting makes it considerably more difficult to avoid responsibility. Greater involvement between customer and supplier can, for example, be a source of fear with regard to one's own shortcomings. But when the reflective model as described here leads to the development of true *communicative action*, mutual trust and interactive cooperation can be established. In this evolution the possibilities for the development of a renewing and inspiring role of the works council are to be considered.

REFERENCES

D'hanis, W. (1994). Reflections on business process re-engineering. In Coulson, T.C. (ed.), *Business Process Re-engineering: myth and reality*. London: Kogan Page.

Habermas, J. (1981). *Theorie des Kommunikativen Handelns*. Frankfurt/Main: Suhrkamp Verlag.

Habermas, J. (1988). *Nachmetaphysisches Denken*. Frankfurt/Main: Suhrkamp Verlag.

Hamel, G. and Prahalad, C.K. (1994). *Competing for the Future*. Boston, MA: Harvard Business School Press.

Mintzberg, H. (1989). *Mintzberg on Management: inside our strange world of organizations*. New York: Free Press.

Mintzberg, H. (1994). *The Rise and Fall of Strategic Planning*. Englewood Cliffs, NJ: Prentice Hall.

Sanchez, R. and Heene, A. (1996). A systems view of the firm in competence-based competition, In Sanchez, R., Heene, A., and Thomas, H. (eds), *Dynamics of*

Competence-based Competition: Theory and Practice in the New Strategic Management. Oxford: Elsevier.

Sanchez, R., Heene, A. and Thomas, H. (1996a). Towards the theory and practice of competence-based competition, In Sanchez, R., Heene, A. and Thomas, H. (eds), *Dynamics of Competence-based Competition: Theory and Practice in the New Strategic Management.* Oxford: Elsevier.

Sanchez, R., Heene, A. and Thomas, H. (eds) (1996b). *Dynamics of Competence-Based Competition: Theory and Practice in the New Strategic Management.* Oxford: Elsevier.

Senge, P.M. (1990). *The Fifth Discipline; The Art and Practice of The Learning Organization.* New York: Doubleday.

Index

Note: Page references in *italics* refer to Figures; those in **bold** refer to Tables

ABB Flakt Oy 14, 111–25
  combining SMG framework and
    competence-based theory 120–5
  Customer Base Management 113, 114
  Customer Focus 113, 116–17, 122,
    123
  group process 115–16
  implications of case on theory of
    competence-based competition
    117–19
  industrial division process 113–14
  issues addressed 112–13
  Key Account Management 115–16
  process in perspective 116–17
  reorganization 116
ABB Fläkt Service Oy 116
ABB Installations Oy 116
ABB Signal 271–2, 273, 274, 276
ABB SLM Oy 116
ABB Strömberg Power Oy 116
acceleration effect 180
action-response 171
Ahlström 114, 118
Alteration 169
Apple's Mackintosh operating system
    172, 173
asset amortization 299, 300, 307
asset creation 300, 301, 307
asset dynamics 300
asset fission 300, 301, 307
asset improvement 300, 307
asymptotic inevitability 315
authentic leadership 326–7
autonomy 279

balance of power 279
Barnevik, Parcy 113
benchmarking 232
Bénéteau 129–30
Betamax video 172
bounded rationality, principle of 48
British Airways 97
building and leveraging competences
  blind spots in 254–60
  continuum of 138, **139**, 141
  failing markets and organization
    267–70
  in networks 268–70, 278–80
  organizing in networks 270–5
  socio-cognitive perspective 274–6
  tension as 276–80
business process re-engineering 325–6
business re-animation 324
business revalidation 324–5

Canon 201, 203
causal ambiguity 174
CelsiusTech Systems 271–2, 273, 274,
    276
cognitive processes 44, 47
collaboration 281
collective learning 153
collective uncertainty 327
communicative action 325, 328
competence
  assets and capabilities 137, **138**
  behavioural and cultural dimension
    134

Competence (*cont.*)
  cognition in 19–21, 133
  compared definitions and categories
      134–6, *135*
  coordination 270
  decomposition of 133–6
  definition 7, 152
  division of 270
  holism in 21–2
  holding and addressing 136–44, **142**
    adaptability 140–1, 144
    networking access 140, 141, 144
    reinforcing 138, 144
    synergetic fit 138–40, 141, 144
  organizational structure 134
  processes and routines 133–4
competence alliances 8
competence-based competition 68
competence-based competition
    perspective 291
competence-based strategic
    management 68–72
  scarcity dilemma 69–70
  value dilemma 71–2
competence blind spots, identification
    of 20, 245–64
  competence identification as reflection
      251–4
  increasing cognitive variety in 258–63
  implications for strategy theory,
      research and practice 263–4
  in leveraging existing competences
      and building new ones 254–60
    resulting from competence "as self-
        description" 254–8
    restrained 254–6
    restrained by self-description
        256–8
    resulting from susceptibility to
        other systems 257–8
  second-order cybernetics in study of
      246–7, 247–51
competence building 8, 13, 112, 252, 294
  analysis 216–18
  see also building and leveraging
      competences
competence diffusion 299, 300
competence dynamics 12–16, 299
competence gap 128, 131, 133, 144
  assessing 136–44, **138, 142**
  measuring **146–7**

competence integration 299
competence levels 12–13, 198–212, *204,*
    299
  application to Philips 209–12
  dynamic analysis 197, 203–7
  dynamic interactions among 207, *208*
  managerial implications 207–9
  static analysis 197–203
    coordinated and integrated view of
        firm resources 199–200
    Core Outputs 198, 203
    Distinctive Capabilities 198, 200–2
    industry foresight 198–9
    System View 197, 198–200
competence leveraging 8, 13–14, 112,
    141, 248
  see also building and leveraging
      competences
competence strategy 215
competence systemics 16–19
competence theory and practice
  basic concepts 7–9
  cognition in managing competences
      19–21
  cognition in strategy theory 22–36
  competence dynamics 12–16
  competence systemics 16–19
  directions for 36–9
    coordination 37–8
    governance mechanisms in firms as
        open systems 38
    managerial and organizational
        cognition 38
    strategic learning and knowledge
        management 37
    vocabulary 38–9
  further issues 36
  holism in managing competences
      21–2
  objectives 9–12
    growing use of networks and
        alliances 11–12
    holistic nature of strategic goals
        and performance 12
    integrating competitive and
        cooperative processes 10
    integrating industry structure and
        change dynamics 10
    integrating "process" and
        "content" perspectives 9–10
    nature and critical rules of

cognition and coordination
10–11
role of learning as a critical
strategic variable 12
systemic interdependency of all a
firm's competences 11
competitive dimensions and managerial
problem 79–81
competitive dynamics 8
competitive rivalry 170, 171
compulsiveness of immediacy 326
control loops 16
coordinated deployment 7, 129
coordination flexibility 27
core competence 288, 299, 308
corporate coherence 287–310
as an aspect of the growth process of
the firm 293–4
as asset interconnectedness 294–5
existing literature 290–6
Penrose on diversification and
coherence 291–3
Rumelt on coherence as related
diversification 293
towards a dynamic understanding of
295–6
corporate venturing 90, 103

deductive logic 316
demonstrated competences 73
dialogue 281
discipline 153
dissociation, concept of 44
dissociative patterns of thought 46–50,
50
dissociative theories 43, 44
dominant logic 288
double-loop learning 46, 54, 55, 57
impact on theory building by
managers 55–8
impact on theory building by
researchers 58
downsizing 90
Dutch Post and Telecommunications
Company 256
Dutch PTT 212
dynamic corporate coherence 287–310
definition 296
implications for strategic
management 306–9

from a core competence strategy to
a strategy of 307–8
from the decentralized M-form to
the "synergistic" M-form
corporation 309
from "related diversification" to
"exploitation and exploration
of synergies" 306–7
insights from evolutionary economics
296–298
insights from organizational
economics
coordination of complementary
activities 302–3
design problems and innovation
attributes 302
information costs 303–4
team production and incentive
issues 304–6
insights from the competence-based
competition perspective 299–301
dynamic response times 15, 17

economy, growth, effect of 317–20
capital versus values 318
clean business 320
historical background 318–19
Environmental Systems Oy 116, 117
Ericsson Components 271–2, 273–4,
276
espoused theories 46, 53–4
exaggerated relatedness 307

firm-addressable resources 7
firm-specific resources 7
firm value 21
flexible coordination abilities 18
flexible resources 18, 27
Framatome 140

General Electric 52
General Motors 122, 177
value-creation system 120
generative capability 123
goal attainment 130
Greenberg Associate Studios 212
grounded theory building 46
growth economy 315–17

Hietaluoma, Antero 113, 114, 117, 118,
    122
holism in managing competences 21–2
Honda 201, 202, 203

IBM 207
imperfect imitability 172
Impulse Centers 58, *59*
inertia 91–2, 180
    tension as a way of overcoming
    277–8
innovation attributes 302
innovation, strategy for 144–5
    competence and 129–32
innovative capacity 174
integrative capability 123
Intel 176
interdependence 279
internal organization 301–2
interpreneurship, premises for 280–1

Kodak 201, 210

Launonen, Harri 115, 116
logic-in-use 53
Lopez 177

managerial goal formulation 112
mapping 232
Mazda 80
Merlin Gerin–Groupe Schneider
    competence strategy 19,
    215–40
    building and coordination of the
        functional network 222–33
    building the functional network
        222–5
        function board 224
        function individual 224–5
        relay individual 224
    coordinating the functional
        network and progress
        appraisal 229–33, *230*
    pole of competences 226–9, *226*,
        227
    progress and performance
        indicators 231, **231**
    consequences and impacts of
        experiences 233–9
    effects of competence strategy on
        global strategy 235–7
    limits and difficulties of
        implementation 237–9
    progress report of competence
        strategy (1995/1996) 233–5,
        234
    Core Functional Competence
        (Compétence Coeur de Function)
        221
    corporate functional segmentation
        220–1
    development of competence strategy
        215, 218–19
    Functional Network (Réseau
        Fonctionnel) 218
    matrix of competences of "industrial
        management" function **240**
    network of functions (Réseau de
        Fonctions) 215, 218
    Purchasing Marketing and Choice of
        Suppliers (Marketing Achats et
        Choix des Fournisseurs) 221–2
    selection of differentiation criteria 219
    Support Competences (Compétences
        de Support) 221
Michelin 176
Michigan Organizational Assessment
    Questionnaire 156
Microsoft 122, 172
model of firm as an open system 16, *17*

Navigation Technologies Corporation
    212
NEC 201
network of functions (*reseau des
    fonctions*) 19
New Business Development
    Departments 103

observing systems 249
offense–defense 171
operational complexity 252
organizational capacity to change 151
    conceptual framework 152–4
    implications for strategy theory,
        research, and practice 166–7
    methodology 155–7

operationalization of configuration
maps 156–7
results 157–63
cross-dependent variable: low–high
and high–low comparisons
163
cross-orientation to change and
performance: low–low
comparisons
orientation to change and
performance: high–high
comparisons 161–2
orientation to change high–high
comparisons 160
orientation to change high–low
and low–high comparisons
160–1
orientation to change low–low
comparisons 160
performance high–high
comparisons 158–9
performance high–low and low–
high comparisons 159–60
performance low–low comparisons
159
variable operationalization 155–6
organizational coherence 35
organizational level 316
organizing networks, dilemmas of
278–80
Orientation to Change 154, 156
outsourcing 90, 92–3

Packinox 140
path-dependency 297
patience 281
Penrose, Edith T., on diversification and
coherence 291–3
Performance 154, 156
Philips 202, 298
competence levels in 209–12
capacity to embody distinctive
capabilities 212
distinctive capabilities 211–12
system view 210–11
Philips Corporate Design 211, 212
planning, long-term 317
positivist inquiry 23, 24
pragmatist 23, 24
Preservation 169

procedural rationality 49
product-markets 292
punctuated change 94, 102

quantitative effect 317
quasi-rent 217

re-engineering 90
radicality of 323–4
reactive bottom-up, emergent
perspective 101
real options 21
realization of objectives 317
reamination 104
reductionist approach 316
reflection 251
as basis for new organizational
structure 320–1, **320**, **321**
as basis for strategic thinking and
development of organizational
philosophy 313–28
Regional Bell Operating Companies 104
rejuvenation 90
relationship capability 123
renewal 99, 100
rent generation, predicting 26, 65–83
reordering 97–8, **97**, 99, 100
resource-based perspective 288
resource-based theory 95, 217
resource-market matrix 294
resources matching *119*, 120
responsibilities, defining 281–2
restructuring 90, 104
revitalization 97–8, **97**, 100, 101

scarcity dilemma 69–70
solution to 72–7
service-based distinctive capabilities 201
short cycle time 174
social relevance of strategic decisions
314–15
Sony 172, 202, 298
spatial separation 99
stand-alone assets 15, 133
stick-to-your-knitting 288, 307–8
strategic architecture 217
strategic assets 299
strategic decisions, failure of 315

strategic defense 15, 169–90
　agency effects 181–2, 188
　　full separation 181–2
　　quasi-full separation 182
　　unified ownership and
　　　management 182
　　unified ownership, management
　　　and employment 182
　availability of resources 180–1
　decision to invest 178–9
　exposure to attacks 180
　external threats 179
　implications for theory, research and
　　practice 189–90
　inertia 180
　internal factors 179–82
　overview of empirical findings 183–6
　strategic defense and firm
　　performance 182–3
　threats to rent-generating potential of
　　firms' resources 171–3
　　imitation 170, 171–2
　　resource mobilization 170, 173
　　substitution 170, 172–3
　　value reduction 170, 173
　typology 173–8
　　alteration actions 177–8, 185–9
　　　alteration resources 177
　　　flexible resources 177, 186
　　intelligence activities 174
　　　competitors' intentions
　　　　intelligence 174, 185
　　　counter-intelligence 174, 185
　　　creating causal ambiguity 174,
　　　　185
　　preservation actions 175–7, 186–9
　　　asset specificity 176
　　　deterrence 176
　　　external resource acquisition 175,
　　　　185
　　　partial give-up 176, 185
　　　pressure on government 176
　　　preventing deployment 177, 185
　　　property rights 175, 185
　　　reducing mobility 175, 183–5
strategic flexibility 9, 18
strategic gaps 16, 277
strategic goals 304
strategic integration, managers' need
　　for 33, 50–2, 51
strategic intent 200

strategic network 89
strategic options 21
strategic planning 314
strategic process, various stages 323
strategic renewal 89–106
　content of change processes, re-
　　ordering and renewing
　　competences 95–8
　converging technologies 103–4
　mechanisms 98–102, **98**, **102**, **106**
　　reanimating 100–1, 103
　　rejuvenating 101–2
　　restructuring 99–100, 103
　　venturing 98–9, 103
　new core technologies 104–5
　new peripheral techniques 104
　paradox of change and stability 91
　　inertia 91–2
　　internal mechanisms 93–4
　　outsourcing 92–3
　technology 103–4, **106**
　technology variation 103
strategy as stretch and leverage 8, 19
strategy theory 22–36
　cognitive perspective 32–3
　　distinguishing performance from
　　　"luck" 32–3
　dynamic perspective 23–8
　　choice of research methodology
　　　23–5
　　role of uncertainty in strategy
　　　theory 25–8
　holistic perspective 33–5
　　intermingling of "means" and
　　　"ends" 35
　　specificity of firm goals 34–5
　inquiry from the inside and inquiry
　　from the outside 52–4
　systems perspective 28–32
　　boundary setting 30–1
　　influence of inappropriate
　　　metaphors on strategic
　　　thinking 31–2
　　necessary but not sufficient
　　　conditions 31
　　strategic value of resources and
　　　coordination capabilities 29–30
　　unidirectional versus
　　　multidirectional causality 28–9,
　　　29
stretch 153

see also strategy as stretch and leverage
substantive rationality 49
support 153
survival strategy 315–17
  logical deduction 316
  organizational level 316
  quantitative effect 317
  realization of objectives 317
  reduction to long-term planning 317
  reductionist character 316–17
Swedish Rail Administration 273
synergistic dynamics 289

Tampella 114, 118
technology-based distinctive capabilities 201
tension as vehicle competence building and leveraging 276–80
Texas Instruments 273, 274
theories in use 46, 53–4

Toyota 122
  value-creation system 120–1
transformative capability 123
Tribal Media i/v 212
trust 153, 281, 327–8

unfreeze, move, refreeze cycle 94
United International Holdings 212

value dilemma 71–2
  solution to 77–9
value-creation systems 18, 121
VHS video 172
VW 177

Wal-Mart 202, 203

Xerox 96

Index compiled by Annette Musker

Task.

Intro

The foundation o fmi.

Past analysis.

7
& J.

R C C